Lecture Notes in Computer Science 15918

Founding Editors

Gerhard Goos
Juris Hartmanis

AF166664

The series Lecture Notes in Computer Science (LNCS), including its subseries Lecture Notes in Artificial Intelligence (LNAI) and Lecture Notes in Bioinformatics (LNBI), has established itself as a medium for the publication of new developments in computer science and information technology research, teaching, and education.

LNCS enjoys close cooperation with the computer science R & D community, the series counts many renowned academics among its volume editors and paper authors, and collaborates with prestigious societies. Its mission is to serve this international community by providing an invaluable service, mainly focused on the publication of conference and workshop proceedings and postproceedings. LNCS commenced publication in 1973.

Sharib Ali · David C. Hogg · Michelle Peckham
Editors

Medical Image Understanding and Analysis

29th Annual Conference, MIUA 2025
Leeds, UK, July 15–17, 2025
Proceedings, Part III

 Springer

Editors
Sharib Ali (iD)
University of Leeds
Leeds, UK

David C. Hogg (iD)
University of Leeds
Leeds, UK

Michelle Peckham (iD)
University of Leeds
Leeds, UK

ISSN 0302-9743   ISSN 1611-3349 (electronic)
Lecture Notes in Computer Science
ISBN 978-3-031-98693-2   ISBN 978-3-031-98694-9 (eBook)
https://doi.org/10.1007/978-3-031-98694-9

Preface

The 29th Conference on Medical Image Understanding and Analysis (MIUA 2025) was held at the University of Leeds, UK, during July 15–17, 2025. The MIUA 2025 proceedings feature presentations from the authors of all accepted papers. MIUA is a UK-based international conference for the communication of image processing and analysis research and its application to medical and biomedical imaging and analysis. This year's edition was co-chaired by Sharib Ali (Lecturer/researcher in Medical and Biomedical Image Analysis, University of Leeds), David Hogg (Professor of Artificial Intelligence, University of Leeds), and Michelle Peckham (Professor of Cell Biology, University of Leeds). The conference was organized with sponsorship received from Frontiers in Medical Technology (Gold), AI-Medical (Silver) and Springer (Best Paper Award). The conference proceedings were published in partnership with Springer. The diverse range of topics covered in these proceedings reflects the growth in the development and application of medical and biomedical imaging including surgical data science. The conference proceedings feature the most recent work in the fields of (1) Image synthesis and generative AI; (2) Image-guided diagnosis; (3) Image-guided intervention; (4) Medical image segmentation; (5) Retinal and vascular image analysis; and (6) Frontiers in Computational Pathology.

The number of submissions to MIUA 2025 continued the growth trend that begun with MIUA 2024. In total, 99 submissions were submitted to the Conference Management Toolkit (CMT), and after an initial quality check, the papers were sent out for the peer-review process completed by the Program Committee and 134 volunteer reviewers. To keep the quality of the reviews consistent with the previous editions of MIUA, the majority of the reviewers were invited from (i) a pool of previous MIUA conference reviewers, (ii) a call for reviewers form, and (iii) authors and co-authors of papers presented at the past and current MIUA conferences. All submissions were subject to double-blind review by at least two reviewers and meta-reviewed by at least one of the Program Committee members. Based on their recommendations, 54 papers were among early accept papers, 25 papers were among early rejected and 20 papers proceeded into the rebuttal stage. The final outcome of the review decisions results in a total of 67 full paper accepted (68%). Out of these, 45 papers had an oral presentation (67%) and 22 papers were presented as posters (33%). These papers comprise three volumes of Lecture Notes in Computer Science (LNCS) proceedings.

Submissions were received from authors at different institutes from 23 countries, including Australia (6), Austria (3), Denmark (3), Finland (1), Germany (5), India (10), Republic of Ireland (2), Mexico (4), Nepal (2), Netherlands (1), Norway (2), Pakistan (2), Poland (1), Portugal (1), Russia (1), Singapore (1), Spain (4), Switzerland (1), T·urkiye (2), the UK (36), the UAE (2), and the USA (5). We thank all members of the MIUA 2025 Organizing, Steering, Program, Publicity, Social Media, Special Session, Sponsorship, and Doctoral Community Committees. In particular, we sincerely thank all who contributed greatly to the success of MIUA 2025: the authors for submitting their work, the reviewers for insightful comments improving the quality of the proceedings, the sponsors for financial support, and all participants in this year's in-person MIUA conference.

We thank our keynote speakers Andrew King (School of Biomedical Engineering and Imaging Sciences, King's College London) and Susan Astley Theodossiadis (University of Manchester) for sharing their success, knowledge, and experiences. The conference also hosted a panel discussion on "Transforming Medical Imaging with AI: Challenges, Data & Infrastructure, Advancing Research, and Translating Innovations", chaired by Susan Astley Theodossiadis and Bogdan Matuszewski. Our thanks to the session chairs and all the other people who made this event possible.

July 2025

Sharib Ali
David C. Hogg
Michelle Peckham

Organization

General Chairs

Sharib Ali   University of Leeds, UK
David C. Hogg   University of Leeds, UK
Michelle Peckham   University of Leeds, UK

Program Chairs

Nashid Alam   Aberystwyth University, UK
Binod Bhattarai   University of Aberdeen, UK
Luisa Cutillo   University of Leeds, UK
Ping Lu   University of Leeds, UK
Bartlomiej Papiez   University of Oxford, UK
Arash Rabbani   University of Leeds, UK
Nishant Ravikumar   University of Leeds, UK
Duygu Sarikaya   University of Leeds, UK

Special Session Chairs

Derek Magee   University of Leeds, UK
Anh Nguyen   University of Liverpool, UK
Pietro Valdastri   University of Leeds, UK

Sponsor and Publicity Chairs

Owen A. Johnson   University of Leeds, UK
Gilberto Ochoa-Ruiz   Monterrey Institute of Technology and Higher
                              Education, Mexico
Mohammad Yaqub   Mohamed bin Zayed University of Artificial
                              Intelligence, UAE

Doctoral Community

Pedro Chavarrias	University of Leeds, UK
Edward Ellis	University of Leeds, UK
Francisco Lopez-Tiro	Monterrey Institute of Technology and Higher Education, Mexico
Raneem Toman	University of Leeds, UK

Proceeding Chairs

Toni Lassila	University of Leeds, UK
Christian Mata	Polytechnic University of Catalonia, Spain

Local Organising Committee

Pedro Chavarrias	University of Leeds, UK
Alison Whiteley	University of Leeds, UK

Reviewers

Abdul Karim Abbas
Bashayer Abdallah
Asfak Ali
Mansoor Ali
Mohsin Ali
Omar Al-Kadi
Anissa Alloula
Ahmed Alshenoudy
Mohammed Yusuf Ansari
Connor Atkins
Akoramurthy Balasubramaniam
Shashvat Bargale
Subrata Bhattacharjee
Binod Bhattarai
Zhiyan Bo
James Borgars

William Cancino
Jacob Carse
Volodymyr Chapman
Nilanjan Chattopadhyay
Veronika Cheplygina
Wing Keung Cheung
Omar Choudhry
Allison Clement
Rhys Compton
Timothy Cootes
Fredrik Dahl
Theo Dapamede
Noémie Debroux
Rocio del Amor
Nanyu Dong
Daniel Dorda

Ant Duru
Mohamed Elawady
Di Fan
Xinqi Fan
Umar Farooq
Jamil Fayyad
Jiling Feng
Mona Furukawa
Carles Garcia Cabrera
Guillaume Garret
Elham Ghelichkhan
Sushobhan Ghosh
Deep Gupta
Gourav Gupta
Gousia Habib
Palak Handa
Mohammad Mehedi Hassain
Mansoor Hayat
Angie Hernandez
Rahmat Heroza
Mohammad Mithun Hossain
Raza Imam
Mostafa Jahanifar
Bushra Jalil
Syed Javed
Muhammad Jawaid
Xi Jia
Benjamin Jin
Robert John
Dmitrii Kaplun
Tushar Kataria
Benjamin Keel
Ayse Keles
Charan Kodi
Adrian Krenzer
Lalit Kumar
Marie-Ange Lebre
Duway Lesmes Leon
Zhibin Liao
Derek Magee
Anish Mahishi
Stephen J. McKenna
Oliver Mills
Nandini Modi
Carmel Moran

Souradeep Mukhopadhyay
Muhammad Amin Nadim
Sabrina Nefoussi
Fnu Neha
Mark Nixon
Varun Ojha
Pedro Osorio
Alessandro Perelli
Michalis Pistos
Sandesh Pokhrel
Nakul Poudel
Pranav Poudel
Payel Pramanik
Muhammad Qadir
Mohammad Areeb Qazi
Lavdie Rada
Aimon Rahman
Mohammad Masudur Rahman
Kashif Rajpoot
Shan Raza
Zia Rehman
Samuel D. Relton
Dewinda Rumala
Bertram Sabrowsky-Hirsch
Shaheer Ullah Saeed
Nematollah Saeidi
Johannes Schuiki
Mehwish Shaikh
Mohd Faraz Shaikh
Fahad Shamshad
Bheeshm Sharma
Tahira Shehzadi
MohammadJavad Shokri
Zuzanna Skórniewska
Ikboljon Sobirov
Yang Sun
Arvapalli Susmitha
Maciej Szymkowski
Aashay Tinaikar
Raneem Toman
Emanuele Trucco
María del C. Valdés Hernández
Maria Vasconcelos
Irina Voiculescu
Juan Wachs

Muhammad Wahab
Patryk Wasniewski
Fuping Wu
Hao Wu
Ye Wu
Varduhi Yeghiazaryan

Pak Hei Yeung
Louai Zaiter
Zeyu Zhang
Yalin Zheng
Yuhan Zheng
Reyer Zwiggelaar

Contents – Part III

Retinal and Vascular Image Analysis

Medical Image Segmentation

TransE²UNet: Edge Guided TransEfficientUNET for Generalized Colon Polyp Segmentation from Endoscopy Images

Subhashis Kar[1] , Souradeep Mukhopadhyay[2] , Shreyan Kundu[3] ,
Debesh Jha[4] , and Rammohan Mallipeddi[5](✉)

[1] Swami Vivekananda Institute of Science and Technology, Kolkata, India
[2] Indian Institute of Science, Bangalore, India
[3] Institute of Engineering and Management, Kolkata, India
[4] University of South Dakota, Vermillion, USA
[5] Kyungpook National University, Daegu, South Korea
mallipeddi.ram@gmail.com

Abstract. Colorectal cancer is one of the most prevalent cancers globally, and early detection of precancerous polyps is critical for preventing progression to malignant stages. To address the challenges in polyp segmentation, we propose TransE²UNet, a novel deep learning-based architecture that integrates EfficientNet-B7 as the backbone encoder, Transformer, and Dilated Convolutions in the bottleneck, and Edge-Aware Attention Modules in the decoder. This combination enhances contextual learning, multi-scale feature extraction, boundary delineation, and computational efficiency. We evaluate TransE²UNet on the Kvasir-SEG dataset, achieving a superior mean Intersection over Union of 0.9021 and mean Dice Similarity Coefficient of 0.9422, outperforming state-of-the-art methods. Additionally, we demonstrate the deployment potential of our approach by comparing it with several cross-domain datasets like BKAI-IGH and CVC-clinicDB. The superior performance in terms of standard metrics mIoU, mDSC, Precision, Recall, and F2 proves the efficiency of our method.

Keywords: Colonoscopy · Polyp segmentation · TransUNet · EfficientNet · Out-of-distribution

1 Introduction

For the diagnosis of colon cancer, colonoscopy is generally regarded as the gold standard. Since even a slight improvement in the adenoma detection rate can dramatically lower the incidence of interval colorectal cancer, early polyp detection is crucial [1]. The polyp miss rate is reported between 22% to 28% [2]. Polyp miss-rates in colonoscopies can be caused by several factors, including

---

S. Kar and S. Mukhopadhyay — Equal contribution.

ⓒ The Author(s), under exclusive license to Springer Nature Switzerland AG 2026
S. Ali et al. (Eds.): MIUA 2025, LNCS 15918, pp. 3–16, 2026.
https://doi.org/10.1007/978-3-031-98694-9_1

endoscopist expertise, the quality of intestinal preparation, quick withdrawal time, visibility, and variations in polyp features [25].

By emphasizing the existence of precancerous tissue in the colon and lowering the clinical burden, deep learning-based algorithms have become a viable method to enhance diagnostic performance. For the development of computer-aided diagnostic support systems in colonoscopy, OOD detection and generalization are crucial. Deep learning models' dependability and security are crucial. By considering the test dataset to be from the same distribution as the training data, traditional deep learning models are trained under the closed-world assumption. As a result, on OOD samples, even the best-performing model may not work.

We broaden our research by using a single center's dataset for training and evaluating datasets from other nations, which can have different distributions from the data used to train the models. To meet the urgent requirement for clinical integration of a real-time and extremely accurate polyp segmentation procedure, we provide the TransE^{2}UNet architecture in this work. The following are this work's primary contributions:

- TransE^{2}UNet integrates EfficientNet-B7 as the encoder, Transformer-based self-attention and Dilated Convolutions in the bottleneck, and Edge-Aware Attention Modules in the decoder. This combination improves contextual feature extraction, enhances multi-scale learning, and refines boundary delineation, leading to superior segmentation performance.
- The model achieves state-of-the-art results on the Kvasir-SEG dataset, with an mIoU of 0.9021 and mDSC of 0.9422, surpassing existing methods. Furthermore, its effectiveness is validated on cross-domain datasets like BKAI-IGH and CVC-ClinicDB, demonstrating strong generalization capabilities in real-world clinical scenarios.
- The proposed Edge-Aware Attention Mechanism (EAM) in the decoder refines segmentation maps by explicitly focusing on polyp boundaries. By incorporating an edge map into the final segmentation output, the model enhances the precision of polyp localization, reducing segmentation errors and improving clinical applicability.

2   Related Works

Colon polyp segmentation is a critical task in computer-aided diagnosis, particularly in colorectal cancer screening. Deep learning-based segmentation methods have demonstrated remarkable progress in improving accuracy, robustness, and real-time inference. The seminal U-Net architecture [7] introduced an encoder-decoder framework with skip connections, laying the foundation for many medical image segmentation models. Enhancing this, UNet++ [8] incorporated nested skip pathways to improve feature fusion. Further, ResUNet++ [9] integrated residual blocks and attention mechanisms for more robust feature extraction. Recent advancements include transformer-based architectures. TransResU-Net [15] and TransNetR [16] leverage transformers to capture global dependencies, outperforming CNN-based models. Similarly, DUAT [23] and SSFormer [24] introduce efficient transformer-based designs tailored for medical segmentation.

Polyp segmentation has also benefited from attention-based mechanisms. DDANet [18] and FANet [20] utilize feedback attention and dual decoder attention to refine segmentation boundaries. PraNet [13] integrates reverse attention to emphasize polyp regions, significantly improving segmentation performance. CarANet [19] enhances segmentation of small medical objects using axial attention. Lightweight models for real-time segmentation are also emerging. HarDNet-MSEG [10] achieves over 0.9 mean Dice score while maintaining 86 FPS. TransRUPNet [17] optimizes transformer-based segmentation for real-time applications, while DilatedSegNet [21] employs dilated convolutions for enhanced receptive fields. Cascaded attention decoding [22] further refines multi-scale segmentation.

Hybrid approaches incorporating multiple feature aggregation techniques, such as TGANet [14], which employs text-guided attention, and DANet [12], which leverages atrous convolutions, have also demonstrated strong performance. ResUNet++ [9] and FANet [20] integrate various attention-based enhancements for improved segmentation. Despite significant advancements, existing colon polyp segmentation methods face several drawbacks. U-Net-based models [7–9, 25, 26] struggle with small polyp detection and boundary refinement. Transformer-based models [15, 16, 23] require high computational resources. Attention-based approaches [13, 18, 20] improve accuracy but often introduce complexity. Real-time models [10, 17] trade off accuracy for speed, limiting clinical applicability.

3   Our Proposed Method

Here, we describe an overview of the architecture, architectural design, bottleneck, decoder, edge-aware attention mechanism, and loss function.

3.1   Overview of TransE²UNet

The proposed TransE²UNet is a novel hybrid deep learning architecture designed for precise polyp segmentation in colonoscopy images. The model integrates three key components: EfficientNet-B7 as the backbone encoder, Transformer and Dilated Convolutions in the bottleneck, and Edge-Aware Attention Modules in the decoder. This combination ensures a robust feature extraction process, global receptive field enhancement, and refined boundary-aware segmentation. The overall architecture is shown in Fig. 1.

3.2   Architectural Design

The encoder of our proposed method utilizes the EfficientNet-B7 Feature Extractor by leveraging the EfficientNet-B7 architecture, which provides a computationally efficient yet highly expressive feature extraction mechanism. The feature maps are extracted from predefined layers:

$$\mathcal{F} = \{f_0, f_1, f_2, f_3, f_4\} \tag{1}$$

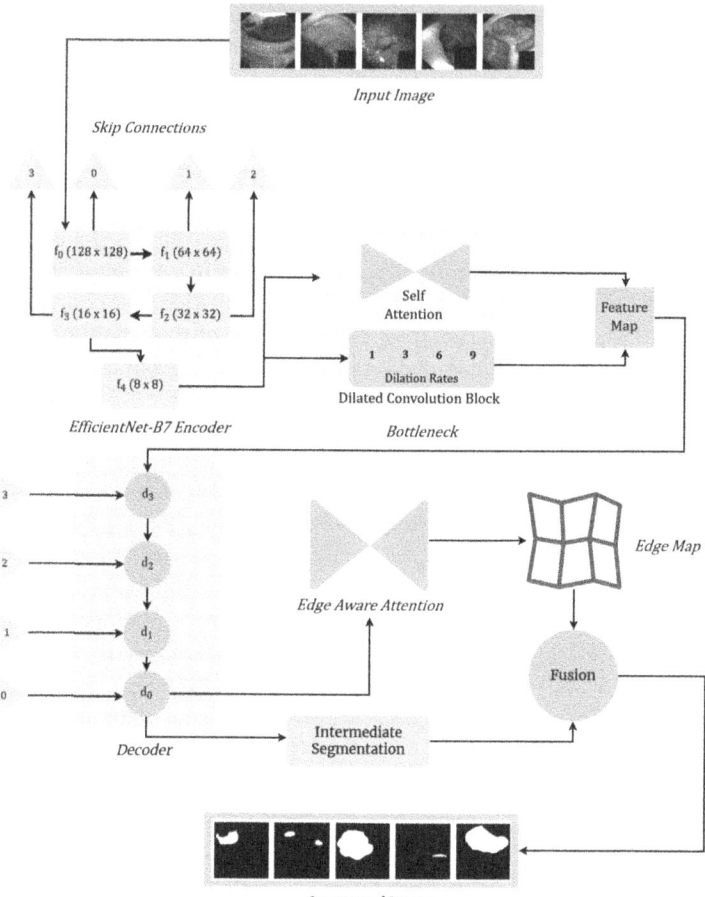

Fig. 1. Architecture overview of the proposed TransE^{2}UNet model for colon polyp segmentation. The network combines a powerful EfficientNet-B7 backbone encoder for multi-scale feature extraction with a novel bottleneck module that integrates transformer-based self-attention and dilated convolutions to capture both global and local contextual information. The decoder employs multi-scale feature fusion enhanced by Convolutional Block Attention Modules (CBAM) to progressively recover spatial resolution and semantic richness. A dedicated Edge-Aware Attention Module (EAM) refines polyp boundary delineation by explicitly incorporating edge information into the final segmentation output, improving boundary precision and reducing misclassification errors. This hybrid design effectively balances computational efficiency and segmentation accuracy, enabling robust and precise polyp detection across diverse endoscopy datasets.

where:

- f_0 represents the lowest-level feature map (spatial resolution: 128×128),
- f_4 represents the deepest feature map (spatial resolution: 8×8),
- Intermediate feature maps $\{f_1, f_2, f_3\}$ are used in skip connections for multi-scale fusion.

3.3   Bottleneck: Transformer-Based Contextual Refinement

The bottleneck module combines Transformer-based self-attention with dilated convolutions to enhance global receptive field perception. The Transformer block consists of a multi-head self-attention (MHSA) module:

$$Z = \text{softmax}\left(\frac{QK^T}{\sqrt{d_k}}\right) V \tag{2}$$

where, Q, K, V are query, key, and value matrices derived from the input feature map.

Simultaneously, a Dilated Convolutional Block (DCB) operates in parallel, employing four parallel dilated convolutions with dilation rates $\{1, 3, 6, 9\}$. The outputs are concatenated and transformed via a 1 x 1 convolution, ensuring a balanced mix of local and global feature representations:

$$X_{\text{DCB}} = \text{Conv}_{1\times1}\left([\text{DilConv}_1, \text{DilConv}_3, \text{DilConv}_6, \text{DilConv}_9]\right) \tag{3}$$

3.4   Decoder: Multi-scale Feature Fusion with Attention

Each decoder block is designed to fuse high-level semantics from the encoder with spatially rich features using skip connections. The decoder follows a progressive feature upsampling strategy:

$$d_i = \text{CBAM}(\text{ResBlock}([\text{Upsample}(d_{i+1}), f_i])) \tag{4}$$

where:

- d_i is the feature map at decoder level i,
- f_i is the corresponding encoder feature from EfficientNet-B7,
- CBAM (Convolutional Block Attention Module) refines channel and spatial attention.

3.5   Edge-Aware Attention Mechanism

To ensure sharper polyp boundaries, we integrate an Edge Attention Module (EAM) at the lowest level of the decoder:

$$E = \sigma(\text{Conv}_{1\times1}(\text{ResBlock}(f_0))) \tag{5}$$

where, E represents the edge map refined via a sigmoid activation function. This edge map is fused with the final segmentation output:

$$S_{\text{final}} = S + \text{Upsample}(E) \tag{6}$$

where, S is the raw segmentation map before edge refinement.

Table 1. Segmentation Performance on in-distribution datasets.

Dataset	mIoU ↑	mDSC ↑	Precision ↑	Recall ↑	F2 ↑
Kvasir-SEG [3]	0.9021	0.9422	0.9467	0.9505	0.9496
BKAI-IGH [5]	0.9023	0.9356	0.9418	0.9481	0.9449
PolypDB (BLI) [4]	0.7899	0.8591	0.8605	0.8824	0.8749

4   Loss Function and Optimization

The loss function combines Binary Cross Entropy (BCE) and Dice Loss, ensuring both pixel-wise accuracy and structural coherence:

$$\mathcal{L} = \alpha \cdot \mathcal{L}_{BCE} + (1 - \alpha) \cdot \mathcal{L}_{Dice} \tag{7}$$

where $\alpha = 0.5$ for a balanced optimization.

5   Results

5.1   Datasets Used

We make use of four publicly accessible colonoscopy polyp segmentation datasets: CVC-ClinicDB [6], BKAI-IGH [5], PolypDB [4], and Kvasir-SEG [3]. The source of Kvasir-SEG was Norway. Likewise, PolypDB was gathered from Sweden, Norway, and Vietnam. CVC-ClinicDB was gathered in Spain, and BKAI-IGH was gathered in Vietnam. For in-distribution testing, we employ Kvasir-SEG and PolypDB (BLI); for cross-domain evaluation, we use BKAI-IGH and CVC-ClinicDB.

5.2   Experimental Setup

To expand the quantity of training samples, we carry out comprehensive data augmentation. The PyTorch framework is used to implement all of the experiments. We use an NVIDIA RTX 3090 GPU setup for all of our tests. With a batch size of eight and a learning rate of 1×10^{-4}, we employ the Adam optimizer. Furthermore, we train our models using a combination of Dice loss and binary cross-entropy.

5.3   Result of Our Method

Tables 1 and 2 assess segmentation performance across datasets using metrics like mIoU, mDSC, precision, recall, and F2. In the first table (in distribution), Kvasir-SEG and BKAI-IGH record mIoU values of 0.9021 and 0.9023, respectively, with F2 scores around 0.95, while PolypDB (BLI) lags with an mIoU of 0.7899 and F2 of 0.8749. In the second table (out-of-distribution, training on Kvasir-SEG), BKAI-IGH achieves an mIoU of 0.6633 and CVC-ClinicDB 0.7482, with corresponding declines in mDSC, precision, recall, and F2, indicating reduced segmentation performance on unseen datasets.

Table 2. Segmentation Performance on Out-of-distribution when trained on Kvasir-SEG).

Test Dataset	mIoU ↑	mDSC ↑	Precision ↑	Recall ↑	F2 ↑
BKAI-IGH	0.6633	0.7299	0.8406	0.8056	0.8124
CVC-ClinicDB	0.7482	0.8102	0.9086	0.8119	0.8295

Table 3. Backbone ablation study: Comparison of EfficientNet and Other CNN Models (Train Dataset: Kvasir-SEG, Test Dataset: Kvasir-SEG).

Backbone	mIoU ↑	mDSC ↑	Precision ↑	Recall ↑
ResNet50	0.8814	0.9273	0.9490	0.9268
ResNet101	0.8861	0.9351	0.9481	0.9305
DenseNet121	0.8936	0.9415	**0.9491**	0.9397
MobileNetV2	0.8992	**0.9442**	0.9478	0.9467
EfficientNet-B4	0.9006	0.9414	0.9469	0.9455
EfficientNet-B7	**0.9021**	0.9422	0.9467	**0.9505**

Table 4. Ablation study comparing different loss functions such as Binary Cross Entropy (BCE), Dice Loss, and their combination on Kvasir-SEG dataset.

Loss Function	mIoU ↑	mDSC ↑	Precision ↑	Recall ↑
Only $\mathcal{L}_{BCE}$	0.9005	0.9402	0.9495	**0.9570**
Only $\mathcal{L}_{Dice}$	0.8964	0.9375	0.9381	0.9333
$\mathcal{L}$	**0.9021**	**0.9422**	**0.9467**	0.9505

5.4   Ablation Study

Table 3 compares various CNN backbones on polyp segmentation performance using IoU, DSC, Precision, and Recall. EfficientNet-B7 achieves top performance (mIoU=0.9021, Recall=0.9505) via compound scaling, balancing depth, width, and resolution for improved feature extraction and superior segmentation. MobileNetV2 excels in DSC, DenseNet121 in Precision, and ResNet101 is also competitive overall.

Table 4 compares performance with BCE loss, Dice loss, and their combination, measuring mIoU, DSC, Precision, and Recall. Combining BCE and Dice yields top mIoU (0.9021) and DSC (0.9422). BCE excels at pixel-level differences, while Dice counters class imbalance, producing superior segmentation accuracy overall. Precision and Recall also remain high.

EAM is used because accurate polyp boundary delineation is crucial for segmentation quality. By explicitly focusing on edge features, EAM refines boundary representations and reduces misclassification along lesion margins. As shown in Table 5, incorporating EAM improves all metrics (mIoU, DSC, Precision, and Recall), demonstrating its effectiveness for more precise segmentation.

Table 5. Impact of Edge-Aware Attention Mechanism (EAM) on Performance (Train Dataset: Kvasir-SEG, Test Dataset: Kvasir-SEG).

Method	mIoU ↑	mDSC ↑	Precision ↑	Recall ↑
Without EAM	0.8973	0.9324	0.9409	0.9416
With EAM	**0.9021**	**0.9422**	**0.9467**	**0.9505**

Table 6. Comparison of our method with the existing SOTA methods on the Kvasir-SEG dataset.

Method	mIoU	mDSC	Recall	Precision	F2
U-Net [7]	0.7472	0.8264	0.8504	0.8703	0.8353
U-Net++ [8]	0.7420	0.8228	0.8437	0.8607	0.8295
ResU-Net++ [9]	0.5341	0.6453	0.6964	0.7080	0.6576
HarDNet-MSEG [10]	0.7459	0.8260	0.8485	0.8652	0.8358
ColonSegNet [11]	0.6980	0.7920	0.8193	0.8432	0.7999
DeepLabV3+ [12]	0.8172	0.8837	0.9014	0.9028	0.8904
PraNet [13]	0.8296	0.8942	0.9060	0.9126	0.8976
TGANet [14]	0.8330	0.8982	0.9132	0.9123	0.9029
TransResU-Net [15]	0.8214	0.8884	0.9106	0.9022	0.8971
TransNetR [16]	0.8016	0.8706	0.8843	0.9073	0.8744
TransRUPNet [17]	0.8445	0.9005	0.9195	0.9170	0.9048
Our Method	**0.9021**	**0.9422**	**0.9505**	**0.9467**	**0.9496**

5.5   Comparison with SOTA

Across the three in-distribution polyp segmentation datasets (Kvasir-SEG, BKAI-IGH, and PolypDB), the proposed method consistently delivers superior results compared to established baselines. Table 6 presents segmentation performance on the **Kvasir-SEG** dataset for various methods. **Our Method** outperforms all others, achieving the highest **mIoU (0.9021)**, **mDSC (0.9422)**, **Recall (0.9505)**, **Precision (0.9467)**, and **F2-score (0.9496)**. Compared to **TransRUPNet (previous best)**, our model shows a significant **5.8% mIoU and 4.2% mDSC improvement**, demonstrating superior segmentation accuracy, robustness, and generalization on the **same dataset used for training**.

Table 7 compares segmentation performance on the **BKAI-IGH** dataset. **Our Method** achieves the highest scores across all metrics: **mDSC (0.9356)**, **mIoU (0.9023)**, **Recall (0.9481)**, **Precision (0.9418)**, and **F2-score (0.9449)**. Compared to **DilatedSegNet**, the previous best model with **mDSC (0.8950) and mIoU (0.8315)**, our method improves by **4.0% mDSC and 7.1% mIoU**. It also surpasses **DeepLabV3+** with **mIoU (0.8314)** by **7.1%**. These results highlight the superior segmentation accuracy and generalization of our method on the same dataset used for training.

Table 7. Comparison of segmentation performance on BKAI-IGH using various models. All methods are trained and tested on BKAI-IGH.

Method	mDSC	mIoU	Recall	Precision	F2
U-Net [7]	0.8286	0.7599	0.8295	0.8999	0.8264
U-Net++ [8]	0.8275	0.7563	0.8388	0.8942	0.8308
DeepLabV3+ [12]	0.8937	0.8314	0.8870	0.9333	0.8882
ResU-Net++ [9]	0.7130	0.6280	0.7240	0.8578	0.7132
DDANet [18]	0.7269	0.6507	0.7454	0.7575	0.7335
PraNet [13]	0.8904	0.8264	0.8901	0.9247	0.8885
ColonSegNet [11]	0.7748	0.6881	0.7852	0.8711	0.7746
HarDNet-MSEG [10]	0.7627	0.6734	0.7532	0.8344	0.7528
FANet [20]	0.8305	0.7578	0.8285	0.9169	0.8243
CaraNet [19]	0.8948	0.8309	0.8907	0.9280	0.8911
DilatedSegNet [21]	0.8950	0.8315	0.9082	0.9111	0.8991
Our Method	**0.9356**	**0.9023**	**0.9481**	**0.9418**	**0.9449**

Table 8. Segmentation performance of all the methods on the PolypDB (BLI) dataset.

Method	mIoU	mDSC	Recall	Precision	F2
U-Net [7]	0.1822	0.2855	0.6862	0.2180	0.3962
DeepLabV3+ [12]	0.6055	0.7293	0.8462	0.7146	0.7751
PraNet [13]	0.6581	0.7831	0.8876	0.7390	0.8348
CaraNet [19]	0.5853	0.7237	0.6895	0.8052	0.6978
TGANet [14]	0.5217	0.6520	0.8108	0.6344	0.7076
PVT-CASCADE [22]	0.6737	0.7873	0.8750	0.7748	0.8205
DuAT [23]	0.6979	0.8048	**0.9082**	0.7647	0.8501
SSFormer-L [24]	0.6750	0.7848	0.8436	0.7708	0.8091
Our Method	**0.7899**	**0.8591**	0.8824	**0.8605**	**0.8749**

Table 8 evaluates segmentation performance on the **PolypDB (BLI)** dataset. **Our Method** outperforms all models, achieving the highest **mIoU (0.7899)**, mDSC **(0.8591)**, **Precision (0.8605)**, and **F2-score (0.8749)**. Compared to **DuAT**, the previous best method with **mIoU (0.6979) and mDSC (0.8048)**, our method improves by **9.2% mIoU** and **5.4% mDSC**. It also surpasses **PVT-CASCADE** with **mIoU (0.6737)** by **11.6%**. While DuAT achieves the highest **Recall (0.9082)**, our model balances high recall and precision, leading to a superior overall segmentation performance.

Table 9. Quantitative comparison of our and SOTA methods on BKAI-IGH and CVC-ClinicDB using Kvasir-SEG as the training dataset.

Method	Test Dataset: BKAI-IGH					Test Dataset: CVC-ClinicDB				
	mIoU	mDSC	Recall	Precision	F2	mIoU	mDSC	Recall	Precision	F2
U-Net [7]	0.5686	0.6347	0.6986	0.7882	0.6591	0.5433	0.6336	0.6982	0.7891	0.6563
U-Net++ [8]	0.5592	0.6269	0.6900	0.7968	0.6493	0.5475	0.6350	0.6933	0.7967	0.6556
ResU-Net++ [9]	0.3204	0.4166	0.6979	0.3922	0.5019	0.3585	0.4642	0.5880	0.5770	0.5084
HarDNet-MSEG [10]	0.5711	0.6502	0.7420	0.7469	0.6830	0.6058	0.6960	0.7173	0.8528	0.7010
ColonSegNet [11]	0.4910	0.5765	0.7191	0.6644	0.6225	0.5090	0.6126	0.6564	0.7521	0.6246
DeepLabV3+ [12]	0.6589	0.7286	0.7919	0.8123	0.7493	0.7388	0.8142	**0.8331**	0.8735	0.8198
PraNet [13]	0.6609	0.7298	0.8007	0.8240	0.7484	0.7286	0.8046	0.8188	0.8968	0.8077
TGANet [14]	0.6612	0.7289	0.7740	0.8184	0.7412	0.7444	**0.8196**	0.8290	0.8879	0.8207
TransResU-Net [15]	0.6457	0.7067	0.7363	0.8635	0.7148	0.7342	0.8082	**0.8331**	0.8861	0.8173
TransNetR [16]	0.5998	0.6601	0.6660	**0.9072**	0.6583	0.6912	0.7655	0.7570	**0.9201**	0.7565
Our Method	**0.6633**	**0.7299**	**0.8056**	0.8406	**0.8124**	**0.7482**	0.8102	0.8119	0.9086	**0.8295**

Tables 9 report results from training on Kvasir-SEG but testing on two different datasets (BKAI-IGH and CVC-ClinicDB) to assess out-of-distribution performance. Despite the domain shift, our method consistently outperforms or rivals existing approaches across key metrics like mIoU, DSC, Recall, Precision, and F2. For BKAI-IGH, it achieves a mIoU of 0.6633 and DSC of 0.7299, and for CVC-ClinicDB, it attains a mIoU of 0.7482 and F2 of 0.8295. This robustness indicates strong generalizability and boundary delineation across diverse polyp datasets, underscoring the proposed method's efficacy in handling unseen data with consistent segmentation accuracy.

6 Discussion

The proposed TransE^{2}UNet architecture demonstrates outstanding performance on in-distribution colon polyp segmentation benchmarks. On the Kvasir-SEG dataset, it achieves an mIoU of 0.9021 and an mDSC of 0.9422, representing improvements of 5.8% and 4.2% over prior state-of-the-art (TransRUPNet). The integration of an EfficientNet-B7 backbone for multi-scale feature extraction, Transformer-augmented dilated convolutions in the bottleneck, and an Edge-Aware Attention Module in the decoder collectively enhance contextual understanding and precise boundary delineation.

Cross-dataset evaluation further confirms the model's robustness: TransE^{2}UNet attains mIoUs of 0.6633 on BKAI-IGH and 0.7482 on CVC-ClinicDB despite significant domain shifts. This performance gap relative to in-distribution results underscores sensitivity to imaging variability and motivates future domain adaptation or self-supervised pretraining strategies(Fig. 2).

Original	Ground Truth	U-Net	PraNet	TransResU-Net	Trans RUPNet	**Our Method**

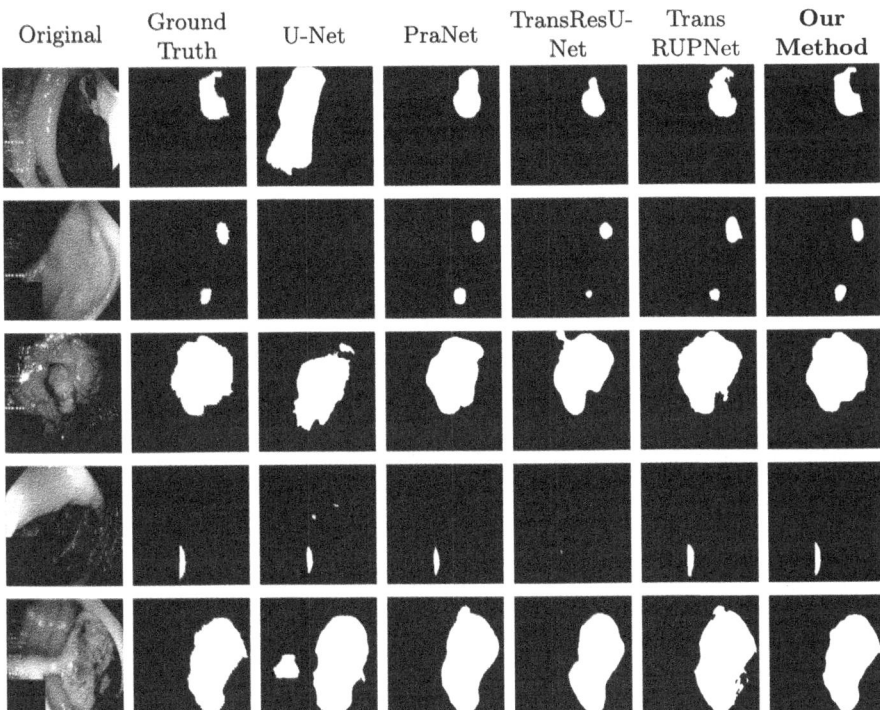

Fig. 2. Figure presents the comparison of segmentation results using different SOTA methods. Our method consistently produces segmentation maps that closely resemble the ground truth, with sharper polyp boundaries, better preservation of small polyp structures, and fewer false positives in background regions. Compared to U-Net and PraNet, which often show coarse or over-smoothed edges, TransE2UNet provides fine-grained boundary delineation due to the inclusion of the Edge-Aware Attention Module (EAM).

Ablation experiments indicate that combining Dice and binary cross-entropy losses yields the best balance of pixel-level accuracy and structural coherence, outperforming single-loss variants (combined mIoU 0.9021 vs. 0.8964âĂŞ0.9005). We also observe that hyperparameters such as batch size, optimizer choice, and input resolution substantially influence convergence behavior.

Despite high accuracy, the Transformer-based modules introduce computational overhead, and image resizing may discard fine-grained details. Future work will explore lightweight attention mechanisms, real-time quantization, and multimodal data fusion to enable efficient, clinically deployable segmentation models.

Algorithm 1. TransE^{2}UNet Pseudocode

Require: Input endoscopy image I
Ensure: Segmented polyp mask S_{final}
1: **Step 1: Feature Extraction (Encoder)**
2: Extract multi-scale features using EfficientNet-B7:

$$F = \{f_0, f_1, f_2, f_3, f_4\}$$

where f_0 is the lowest-level feature map and f_4 is the deepest feature map.
3: **Step 2: Bottleneck - Transformer-Based Contextual Refinement**
4: Compute self-attention in Transformer block:

$$Z = \text{softmax}\left(\frac{QK^T}{\sqrt{d_k}}\right)V$$

where Q, K, V are the query, key, and value matrices.
5: Apply Dilated Convolution Block (DCB) with dilation rates $\{1, 3, 6, 9\}$:

$$X_{\text{DCB}} = \text{Conv}_{1 \times 1}([\text{DilConv}_1, \text{DilConv}_3, \text{DilConv}_6, \text{DilConv}_9])$$

6: **Step 3: Decoder - Multi-scale Feature Fusion with Attention**
7: **for** each decoder level i **do**
8:    Upsample feature map d_{i+1} and fuse with encoder feature f_i:

$$d_i = \text{CBAM}(\text{ResBlock}([\text{Upsample}(d_{i+1}), f_i]))$$

9: **end for**
10: **Step 4: Edge-Aware Attention Mechanism**
11: Generate edge attention map:

$$E = \sigma(\text{Conv}_{1 \times 1}(\text{ResBlock}(f_0)))$$

12: Fuse edge map with segmentation output:

$$S_{\text{final}} = S + \text{Upsample}(E)$$

13: **Step 5: Loss Function and Optimization**
14: Compute combined Binary Cross Entropy (BCE) and Dice Loss:

$$L = \alpha L_{\text{BCE}} + (1 - \alpha)L_{\text{Dice}}$$

where $\alpha = 0.5$ for balanced optimization.
15: **Output:** Segmented polyp mask S_{final}

---

7   Conclusion

In this work, we introduced TransE^{2}UNet, a novel deep learning-based architecture that integrates EfficientNet-B7 as an encoder, Transformer-based self-attention, dilated convolutions in the bottleneck, and Edge-Aware Attention Modules in the decoder for accurate colon polyp segmentation. Our approach effectively enhances contextual learning, multi-scale feature extraction, and boundary refinement, achieving superior performance on the Kvasir-SEG dataset with an mIoU of 0.9021 and an mDSC of 0.9422. Comparative evaluations across cross-domain datasets further validate the generalization capability of our model. For future work, we aim to extend the robustness of TransE^{2}UNet by exploring self-supervised pretraining strategies and domain adaptation techniques to improve out-of-distribution generalization. Additionally, integrating real-time deployment strategies, such as model quantization and lightweight architectures, will facilitate its clinical applicability in colonoscopy procedures. Further research into multi-modal fusion with complementary imaging modalities can also enhance segmentation accuracy in challenging cases.

Acknowledgment. The research was supported by the Core Research Institute Basic Science Research Program through the National Research Foundation of Korea(NRF), funded by the Ministry of Education (RS-2021-NR060127).

References

1. Urban, G., et al.: Deep learning localizes and identifies polyps in real time with 96% accuracy in screening colonoscopy. Gastroenterology **155**(4), 1069–1078 (2018)
2. Leufkens, A.M., Van Oijen, M., Vleggaar, F.P., Siersema, P.D.: Factors influencing the miss rate of polyps in a back-to-back colonoscopy study. Endoscopy **44**(05), 470–475 (2012)
3. Jha, D., et al.: Kvasir-SEG: a segmented polyp dataset. In: Proceedings of the International Conference on Multimedia Modeling (MMM), pp. 451–462 (2020)
4. Debesh, J., et al.:(2024). PolypDB: a curated multi-center dataset for development of AI algorithms in colonoscopy. 10.48550/arXiv.2409.00045
5. Lan, P.N., et al.: NeoUNet: towards accurate colon polyp segmentation and neoplasm detection. arXiv preprint arXiv:2107.05023 (2021)
6. Bernal, J., Sánchez, F. J., Fernández-Esparrach, G., Gil, D., Rodríguez, C., Vilariño, F.: WM-DOVA maps for accurate polyp highlighting in colonoscopy: validation vs. saliency maps from physicians. Comput. Med. Imaging Graph. **43**, 99–111 (2015)
7. Ronneberger, O., Fischer, P., Brox, T.: U-net: convolutional networks for biomedical image segmentation. In: Navab, N., Hornegger, J., Wells, W.M., Frangi, A.F. (eds.) MICCAI 2015. LNCS, vol. 9351, pp. 234–241. Springer, Cham (2015). https://doi.org/10.1007/978-3-319-24574-4_28
8. Zhou, Z., Rahman Siddiquee, M.M., Tajbakhsh, N., Liang, J.: UNet++: A nested u-net architecture for medical image segmentation. In: Deep Learning in Medical Image Analysis and Multimodal Learning for Clinical Decision Support, pp. 3–11 (2018)
9. Jha, D., Smedsrud, P.H., Riegler, M.A., Halvorsen, P., De Lange, T., Johansen, D., Johansen, H.D.: ResUNet++: An advanced architecture for medical image segmentation. In: Proceedings of the International Symposium on Multimedia (ISM), pp. 225–2255 (2019)
10. Huang, C.H., Wu, H.Y., Lin, Y.L.: HarDNet-MSEG a simple encoder-decoder polyp segmentation neural network that achieves over 0.9 mean dice and 86 FPS. arXiv preprint arXiv:2101.07172 (2021)

11. Jha, D., et al.: Real-time polyp detection, localization and segmentation in colonoscopy using deep learning. IEEE Access **9**, 40496–40510 (2021)
12. Chen, L.C., Zhu, Y., Papandreou, G., Schroff, F., Adam, H.: Encoder-decoder with atrous separable convolution for semantic image segmentation. In: Proceedings of the European Conference on Computer Vision (ECCV), pp. 801–818 (2018)
13. Fan, D.P., et al.: Pranet: parallel reverse attention network for polyp segmentation. In: Proceedings of the International Conference on Medical Image Computing and Computer-Assisted Intervention (MICCAI), pp. 263–273 (2020)
14. Tomar, N.K., Jha, D., Bagci, U., Ali, S.: TGANet: Text-guided attention for improved polyp segmentation. In: Proceedings of the 25th International Conference on MICCAI, pp. 151–160 (2022)
15. Tomar, N.K., Shergill, A., Rieders, B., Bagci, U., Jha, D.: TransResU-Net: a transformer based resu-net for real-time colon polyp segmentation. In: Proceedings of the 45th Annual International Conference of the IEEE Engineering in Medicine & Biology Society (EMBC), pp. 1–4 (2023)
16. Jha, D., Tomar, N.K., Sharma, V., Bagci, U.: TransNetR: transformer-based residual network for polyp segmentation with multi-center out-of-distribution testing. Proceedings of Medical Imaging and Deep Learning (2023)
17. Jha, D., Tomar, N.K., Bagci, U.: TransRUPNet for improved polyp segmentation. In: 2024 46th Annual International Conference of the IEEE Engineering in Medicine and Biology Society (EMBC), pp. 1–4 (2023)
18. Tomar, N.K., et al.: DDANet: dual decoder attention network for automatic polyp segmentation. In: Del Bimbo, A., et al., (eds.) ICPR 2021. LNCS, vol. 12668, pp. 307–314. Springer, Cham (2021). https://doi.org/10.1007/978-3-030-68793-9_23
19. Lou, A., Guan, S., Ko, H., Loew, M.H.: Caranet: context axial reverse attention network for segmentation of small medical objects. In: Medical Imaging 2022: Image Processing. vol. 12032, pp. 81–92. SPIE (2022)
20. Tomar, N.K., et al.: Fanet: a feedback attention network for improved biomedical image segmentation. IEEE Trans. Neural Netw. Learn. Syst. (2022)
21. Tomar, N.K., Bagci, U., Jha, D.: DilatedSegNet: a deep dilated segmentation network for polyp segmentation. In: Conference on Multimedia Modeling (2022)
22. Rahman, M.M., Marculescu, R.: Medical image segmentation via cascaded attention decoding. In: Proceedings of the IEEE/CVF Winter Conference on Applications of Computer Vision, pp. 6222–6231 (2023)
23. Tang, F., et al.: Duat: Dual-aggregation transformer network for medical image segmentation. In: Proceedings of the Chinese Conference on Pattern Recognition and Computer Vision (PRCV), pp. 343–356 (2023)
24. Shi, W., Xu, J., Gao, P.: Ssformer: a lightweight transformer for semantic segmentation. In: Proceedings of the IEEE 24th International Workshop on Multimedia Signal Processing (MMSP), pp. 1–5 (2022)
25. Leufkens, A.M., Van Oijen, M.G., Vleggaar, F.P., Siersema, P.D.: 1178 Factors affecting miss rate of polyps during colonoscopy: results from a prospective, multi-center back-to-back colonoscopy study. Gastrointestinal Endoscopy **73**(4), AB165 (2011)
26. Jha, D., Riegler, M.A., Johansen, D., Halvorsen, P., Johansen, H.D.: Doubleu-net: a deep convolutional neural network for medical image segmentation. In: 2020 IEEE 33rd International Symposium on Computer-Based Medical Systems (CBMS), pp. 558–564 (2020)
27. Jha, D., et al.: Nanonet: real-time polyp segmentation in video capsule endoscopy and colonoscopy. In: 2021 IEEE 34th International Symposium on Computer-Based Medical Systems (CBMS), pp. 37–43 (2021)

CA-Seg: An Attribute-Based Medical Image Segmentation Framework for Unified Out-of-Distribution Medical Image Segmentation

Yunxiang Liu[1,2], Johan Verjans[1,2], Vu Minh Hieu Phan[1,2], and Zhibin Liao[1,2(✉)]

[1] University of Adelaide, Adelaide, South Australia 5005, Australia
{yunxiang.liu,johan.verjans,vuminhhieu.phan,zhibin.liao}@adelaide.edu.au
[2] Australia Institute for Machine Learning, University of Adelaide, Adelaide, Australia
https://www.adelaide.edu.au

Abstract. Accurate medical image segmentation is challenging due to the high variance of out-of-distribution (OOD) data, which is costly for acquisition and annotation. However, existing methods often focus on the sub-scenarios of the OOD problem (e.g., Domain generalization) and approach this via a pretraining and fine-tuning domain adaptation paradigm, which does not explicitly utilize the intrinsic semantic relationship among those OOD tasks. To address this problem, we introduce a novel Attribute-Based Segmentation (CA-Seg) method to unify the OOD problems, where only the OOD object class semantic information is required to bridge the domain gap. CA-Seg contains two stages of learning: high-level semantic abstraction learning and low-level visual pattern learning. In the first stage of the training phase, we extract morphological knowledge of the tissue/organ of interest using an off-the-shelf Vision-Language Model (VLM), leveraging its rich language and image pattern association ability to describe class semantics into a set of human-understandable text attributes. Subsequently, the concepts serve as a condition to guide the low-level visual pattern learning by using the flow-matching or dice loss. During the adaptation phase, CA-Seg only requires the OOD class labels to rebind the attributes and the target object class to achieve good segmentation performance. CA-Seg addresses the limitations of data scarcity in the broad OOD problems and is computationally efficient in adapting to the OOD data, making it ideal in resource-constrained settings. We evaluated CA-Seg on 3 common OOD tasks in medical image segmentation, demonstrating a high cross-domain segmentation performance with limited data availability. Our code is available at https://github.com/iClaude1998/CA-seg.

Supplementary Information The online version contains supplementary material available at https://doi.org/10.1007/978-3-031-98694-9_2.

Keywords: Out-of-distribution Segmentation · Medical Image
Segmentation · Knowledge Scoring and Ensembling

1   Introduction

Existing medical image segmentation algorithms assume the examples in the
training and test sets are independent and identically distributed (IID). However,
such a condition is hard to satisfy due to the high variety of medical images from
different sites, sequences, modalities, etc. [32]. To address this, lots of domain
generalization methods [2,6] generalize the medical images from multiple source
domains to the unseen target domain for solving this problem. However, due to
the data-sacrificing issue, it is hard to access the data from multiple sources.
Moreover, the problem those methods aim to solve is a single aspect of the
OOD problem, and the problem for which most methods tackle is relatively
simple (multi-site, multi-sequence). Therefore, there is a lack of a framework
to tackle multiple OOD problems simultaneously while extending the current
domain generalization problem to more OOD scenarios.

The core challenge is identifying a unified representation that is invariant to
the image domain. Since the segmentation targets can be effectively characterized
by low-level morphological attributes such as shape, texture, and spatial location,
our goal is to equip the model with the capacity to generalize to OOD examples
by explicitly incorporating morphological priors. Recent approaches [17,36] have
attempted to mitigate domain discrepancies by leveraging shape priors. Despite
achieving promising performance, these approaches depend heavily on manually crafted knowledge, either through dictionary learning or explicit annotation
of shape priors, thus limiting their general applicability in OOD segmentation
scenarios.

Recent advancements in Vision Language Models (VLMs) have spurred
efforts to enhance computer vision segmentation tasks by leveraging the extensive semantic knowledge of large pre-trained models in areas such as weakly
supervised learning [14], open-vocabulary segmentation [33], and fine-tuning [18]
strategies. Despite these advances, the application of pre-trained VLMs within
the medical domain, particularly for medical image segmentation, remains under-
explored. Existing approaches [1,10,16,20] leverage the image-text association
ability from CLIP and the off-the-shelf segmentation ability from the Segment
Anything Model (SAM), However, these methods still struggle in addressing
OOD medical segmentation tasks. The primary reason behind their suboptimal
performance is that they fail to sufficiently leverage the potential capability of the
VLMs to extract low-level morphological features through effective text-image
interaction.

In this paper, we introduce a unified framework that uses the semantic knowledge from vision-language models (VLMs) to enable effective and generalizable
out-of-distribution (OOD) medical image segmentation. We start by leveraging

a large language model to generate multiple textual descriptions of an organ's low-level characteristics and compute the GradCAM [22] (a visualization of the relevant image regions associated with the texts), which we simply refer to as CAMs. However, the initial CAMs are primitive and can highlight irrelevant image regions instead of the focused object. To align those CAMs to the target segmentation class, we learn to recombine the CAMs to a singular high-level concretization of the object class (a visualizable low-resolution segmentation prediction) We call the Semantic Shape Prior (SSP), guided by either pixel-wise ground truth annotations or high-level text descriptions. In the second stage of our framework, we refine the SSP into a fully depicted segmentation prediction by dice or flow-matching. We test CA-Seg on three common OOD scenarios in medical image segmentation: (1) cross-domain generalization, where target modality images were not seen during training; (2) cross-object segmentation in the same modality (e.g., segment an organ that was not labeled in the training images); and (3) cross-view segmentation, which aims to generalize segmentation of the same organ in a new imaging view (e.g., segment the same heart chamber imaged in a different echo ultrasound view).

In summary, our methodology decouples the segmentation process into two interrelated phases, materializing CLIP's semantic knowledge into Tangible semantics in segmentation outcomes. Our contributions are:

1. We introduce a two-stage OOD semantic segmentation framework where the first stage enables high-level semantic concretization, leveraging the morphological tissue/organ knowledge from PMCCLIP [15] to generate a coarse, low-resolution segmentation we call Semantic Shape Prior (SSP).
2. In the second stage, we show that low-level visual pattern learning is the key to achieving generalizability in medical OOD problems and demonstrate how the flow-matching algorithm can be used to generate a meticulous depiction of the target object from the SSP.
3. We identify three commonly encountered OOD scenarios in medical image analysis and establish benchmarks to validate CA-Seg in terms of generalization capability.

2   Relate Works

2.1   Domain Generalization for Medical Image Segmentation

Domain generalization aims to enhance model performance on unseen target domains by training with multiple source domains [25,32,40]. This problem is often divided into multi-source and single-source domain generalization. The key distinction lies in the number of source domains: multi-source involves more than one, whereas single-source does not [32]. Single-source domain generalization is more challenging, as it cannot learn inter-domain relationships due to having only one source. However, it offers higher research potential because it requires fewer datasets. Currently, single-source domain generalization methods are designed for specific, simpler scenarios like cross-site [2,5,9,24,26,27], cross-sequence [30,35,41], and cross-modality [23,30,41] tasks. There is, however, an opportunity to explore a unified framework capable of addressing multiple OOD scenarios, as customizing solutions for the diverse range of medical images can be cumbersome. Furthermore, there is potential to extend domain generalization to more complex OOD cases, such as when the target domain involves different organs or views, eliminating the need to train a model for each specific OOD example.

To unify and extend multiple OOD cases into a single domain generalization framework, it's essential to identify a representation that is easily shareable and extensible across domains. One such representation is shape. Currently, [17] addresses the cross-site domain generalization problem by developing a sparse shape dictionary shared among different sites. However, their method struggles when the shapes of the source and target domains differ. On the other hand, [36] tackles the cross-site domain generalization issue by learning shape priors through the optimization of aspect ratio, size, and location derived from manually designed templates. Despite achieving promising results, their approach requires handcrafted templates from experienced experts, thus increasing the method's cost. Additionally, since both methods focus on simpler problems, their effectiveness in more challenging OOD scenarios remains uncertain.

2.2   Leveraging the VLM for Medical Image Segmentation

The application of pre-trained VLMs within the medical domain, particularly for medical image segmentation, remains under-explored [15]. Notably, Anand et al. [1] employed CLIP for one-shot medical image segmentation by aligning similar pixels from the output feature maps of CLIP between query and reference image-label pairs, subsequently using these as prompts for SAM [10]. Similarly, [12] proposed MedCLIP-SAMv2, where they finetuned the BioMedCLIP [37] to prompt SAM for segmentation on three public datasets. Although this approach demonstrated promising segmentation performance, our experiment indicates that its reliance on SAM revealed limitations when confronting out-of-distribution (OOD) scenarios that were absent from SAM's pre-training data. Furthermore, Poudel et al. [20] adopted a CLIPSeg-like [18] structure to fine-tune BioMedCLIP [37], training a text prompt decoder aligned with the CLIP image encoder across eleven 2D image datasets. This method demonstrates the transferability of the image encoder, exhibiting overfitting to known domains and underperforming on unseen data. Similarly, Liu et al. [16] leverages semantic concepts derived from CLIP's text branch for universal organ segmentation, partially addressing annotation challenges through CLIP's word embedding, but they encountered difficulties generalizing to unknown domains owing to its fully supervised learning paradigm from image to mask.

3   Method

An overall of the CA-Seg pipeline is shown in Fig. 1, consisting of two stages: (I) the morphological knowledge concretization, and (II) the full resolution segmentation dictation stage realized by using the Flow-matching algorithm.

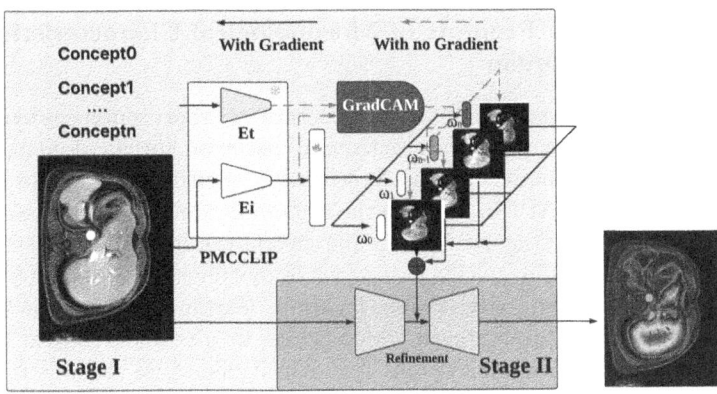

Fig. 1. Overview of the CA-Seg pipeline: Stage I utilizes a multimodal framework integrating PMCCLIP encoders to create attention-based features via GradCAM [22], combined with attribute scores (ω) derived from the attribute matrix ($\mathcal{W}_{\dashv}$) and image features. These features are then adjusted with morphological priors. In Stage II, a flow-matching model refines these priors using noise perturbation ($\epsilon \sim \mathcal{N}(0,1)$) and concatenated contextual information (CAT) to generate high-fidelity medical images.

Table 1. The prompt-instruction pair used in GPT-4o to generate morphological descriptions of healthy organs from radiography images is shown. The system message guides the model's behavior, while the user message defines the desired output structure.

System Message	User Message
You are a radiologist capable of identifying and describing the morphological characteristics of {organ} through {any modality} images.	Make 128 sentences for describing the morphological characteristics of healthy {organs} in axial-view abdominal images. Please follow these instructions while generating the sentences: 1. Each sentence should contain 8-10 words. 2. Present the list in numeric order with dots. 3. Do not include the organ class name in the sentence. 4. Describe from the aspects of size, shape, location, margin, signal characteristics, homogeneity, structural integrity, etc.

3.1 Generating the Prompts of Morphological Characteristics of the Target Organ

As Table 1 shows, we leverage GPT-4o to generate 128 short sentences to describe the morphological features of the target organ/tissue on specific domains, leveraging prompt engineering techniques. Specifically, we utilize the system message feature in the OpenAI API to indicate the organ and domain background information. For the user message, we first define several words of generated sentences (8-10 in our case) and the specific categories of morphological characteristics of the organ of interest, e.g., size, shape, location, margin, signal characteristics, homogeneity, and structural integrity. Meanwhile, we give an in-context example from [4] for generating a robust result. As a consequence, we are able to get the responses from GPT-4o, which is well organized for later GradCAM generalization. Here, we provide the answer in the cross-modality task as an example in the supplementary material.

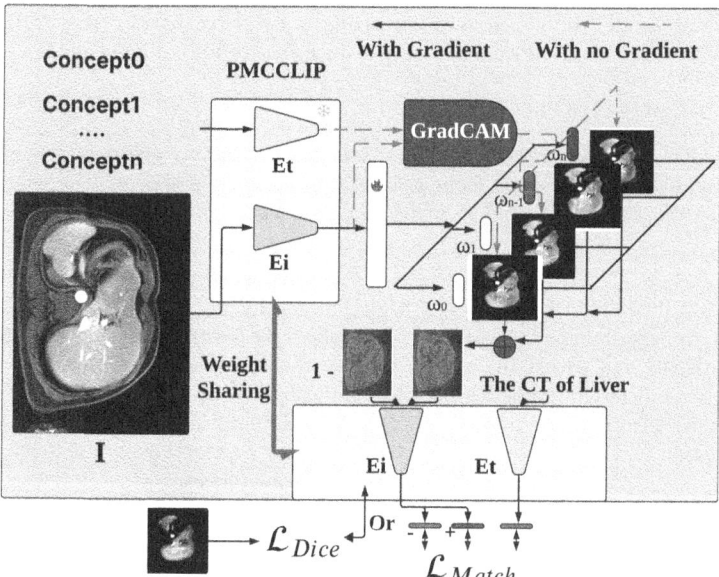

Fig. 2. The morphological knowledge concretization process in the stage-I training, we finetune the PMCCLIP by a linear layer to learn how to combine the GradCAMs into the SSP. Here, we provide two learning objectives in the fully supervised/weakly supervised scenarios. In the fully supervised case, the combined GradCAM $\mathbf{L}_n$ is optimized by the Dice Loss with the ground truth masks. In the weakly supervised scenario, we get the background count part of SSP by subtracting 1 from it 1, then we pass two maps through the image encoder of the PMCCLIP to get foreground and background features. Simultaneously, we extract the generalized text representation and compute the match loss among them. Here, + and − means $\mathbf{f}_{fg}$ and $\mathbf{f}_{bg}$

3.2 Stage I: Morphological Knowledge Concretization

As Fig. 2 shows, let $\mathbf{I} \in \mathbb{R}^{H \times W}$ be an image depicting an organ (or tissue) of interest and $\mathcal{C} = \{c_n\}_{n=1}^N$ a set of N text sentences describing morphological characters such as size, shape, and location of the organ, and c represents a single description. Following the terminologies of Concept Bottleneck Models [4, 11, 19], we call the text descriptions concepts. CA-Seg first computes their respective features $\mathbf{f_I} \in \mathbb{R}^M$, $\mathbf{f}_c \in \mathbb{R}^M$, and $\mathbf{F}_{\mathcal{C}} = [\mathbf{f}_{c_1}, \ldots, \mathbf{f}_{c_n}] \in \mathbb{R}^{M \times N}$ by feeding through PMC-CLIP [15]. Then we compute a softmax score $\mathbf{s} = \mathrm{softmax}(\mathbf{F}_{\mathcal{C}}^\top \mathbf{f_I}) \in \mathbb{R}^N$ of the image for all text descriptions, treating it temporarily as a concept classification model for computing GradCAM [22]. Next, we compute the GradCAM heatmaps $\mathbf{L}_n \in R^{h \times w}$ of the image for every concept c at the last convolutional layer of PMC-CLI's vision encoder, which has a spatial size of $h \times w$. Using the score of the n-th sentence $\mathbf{s}_n$, and the k-th feature map of the last convolution layer $\mathbf{A}_k \in \mathbb{R}^{h \times w}$, we compute $\mathbf{L}_n$ as a weighted linear combination of the convolution feature maps:

$$\alpha_k^n = \frac{1}{h \times w} \sum_{i,j} \frac{\partial \mathbf{s}_n}{\partial \mathbf{A}_k^{(i,j)}}, \text{ and } \mathbf{L}_n = \sum_k \alpha_k^n A_k, \tag{1}$$

where i, j represent the spatial indices. In simple words, GradCAM serves as a concretization procedure that visually describes various textural attributes of the target object.

After obtaining the GradCAM, we change the last linear projection layer at the end of BioMedCLIP's vision encoder to learn a new concept weight matrix $\mathbf{W} \in \mathbb{R}^{M \times N}$ to compute the concept score $\omega = \mathbf{W}^\top \mathbf{f_I} \in \mathbb{R}^N$ of input image features $\mathbf{f_I} \in \mathbb{R}^M$ computed by the frozen vision encoder of BioMedCLIP. The learning of the concept weight matrix is divided into two scenarios.

(1) Same organ different domains. In the cross-modality and cross-view task where the two domains both contain the same organ, we assume the organ's segmentation mask is available from the source domain and $\mathbf{G} \in \mathbb{R}^{h \times w}$ is a *downsampled* ground truth segmentation mask. Let us note the prediction of stage 1 as $\mathbf{P} = \sum_n \omega_n^\top \mathbf{L}_n \in \mathbb{R}^{h \times w}$, we choose Dice coefficient loss as the learning objective to combine the GradCAM to concretize of the morphology of the organ class:

$$\mathcal{L}_{\mathrm{Dice}} = 1 - \frac{2 \sum_{i,j} \mathbf{P}_{(i,j)} \mathbf{G}_{(i,j)}}{\sum_{i,j} \mathbf{P}_{(i,j)} + \sum_{i,j} \mathbf{G}_{(i,j)}}. \tag{2}$$

(2) Unseen organ in the same domain. In an unseen organ segmentation task where there is a lack of target organ annotations, inspired by [14], we adopt a weakly supervised learning process that aims to teach $\mathbf{W}$ how to merge the low-level GradCAMs so that the SSP would align with a highly abstracted description of the organ $c' \notin \mathcal{C}$, e.g., "liver in MRI image", and its featurized counterpart $\mathbf{f}'$. First, we compute a foreground-focused image feature $\mathbf{f}_{\mathrm{fg}}$ and its background counterpart $\mathbf{f}_{\mathrm{bg}}$ by:

$$\mathbf{f}_{\mathrm{fg}} = \mathrm{Ei}(\mathbf{I} \cdot \sigma(\mathbf{P})), \text{ and, } \mathbf{f}_{\mathrm{bg}} = \mathrm{Ei}(\mathbf{I} \cdot \sigma(1 - \mathbf{P})), \tag{3}$$

where $\sigma(.)$ denotes the sigmoid function that normalizes the pixels of $\mathbf{P}$ between 0 and 1, Ei$(.)$ is the image encoder of the PMCCLIP, creating a mask to highlight foreground/background regions in the image. We then set the learning objective to make $\mathbf{f}_{\text{fg}}$ closer to the $\mathbf{f}'$ while push $\mathbf{f}_{\text{bg}}$ away from $\mathbf{f}'$:

$$\mathcal{L}_{\text{Match}} = \mathbb{E}(-\log(\cos(\mathbf{f}_{\text{fg}}, \mathbf{f}'))) + \lambda_{\text{bg}}\mathbb{E}(-\log(1 - \cos(\mathbf{f}_{\text{bg}}, \mathbf{f}'))), \quad (4)$$

where $\cos(\cdot)$ denotes the cosine similarity, and λ_{bg} is a scalar hyperparameter that balances the focus between foreground/background loss components.

3.3   Stage II: Segmentation Depiction by Visual Pattern Learning

By learning the concept weight matrix, we generate the SSP prediction $\mathbf{P}$, which represents a coarse, low-resolution segmentation of the target organ, inevitably lacking high-frequency details to generalize to a full-resolution segmentation prediction. To learn detailed target organ boundary information, we train a network that has a similar structure to [28], and use $\mathbf{P}$ as a condition to guide the network learning the high-resolution predictions. Here, we use two learning objectives for visual pattern learning.

RecFlow. To get the target of Recflow, we convert the binary mask $\mathbf{G}$ into its unsigned distance transform representation $\mathbf{U}$ by:

$$\mathbf{U}_{(i,j)} = \begin{cases} \min_{(m,n)\in\partial\mathbf{G}} \|(i,j) - (m,n)\|_2, & \text{if } \mathbf{G}_{(i,j)} = 1 \\ 0, & \text{if } \mathbf{G}_{(i,j)} = 0. \end{cases} \quad (5)$$

Then, we utilize the flow matching algorithm which learns geometry mapping $\Psi : \epsilon \rightarrow \mathbf{U} \in \mathbb{R}^{H\times W}$, expressed as $\frac{d\psi}{dt} = v_\theta(t)$ from an initial Gaussian noise image ϵ, taking a series of steps t to generate the full resolution segmentation mask $\mathbf{U}$, conditioned on the shape prior $\mathbf{P}$ from Stage I. Here, $v_\theta(\cdot)$ denotes a neural network architecture with model parameters θ. Then, the learning objective is defined as:

$$\mathcal{L}_v = \|(\mathbf{U} - \epsilon) - v_\theta(\mathbf{U}_t, \mathbf{I}, \mathbf{P}, t)\|^2, \quad (6)$$

where $\mathbf{U}_t = t \cdot \epsilon + (1 - t) \cdot \mathbf{U}$ denotes the learning target at the t-th time step. Finally, the variable t represents timestamps sampled from a uniform distribution $t \sim U(0, 1000)$. During the inference time, inspired by [42], we apply mean value sampling to accelerate the inference process when computing the final prediction from the Gaussian noise. Specifically, with the time interval set as $\Delta t > 1$, we sample T time stamps $\{0 \cdot \Delta t, \cdots, T \cdot \Delta t\}$. The flow displacement can be computed as:

$$\tilde{\mathbf{U}}_{t\Delta t} = \tilde{\mathbf{U}}_{(t-1)\Delta t} + \frac{1}{T}v_\theta(\tilde{\mathbf{U}}_{(t-1)\Delta t}, \mathbf{I}, \mathbf{P}, (t-1)\Delta t), \quad (7)$$

where $\tilde{\mathbf{U}}$ denotes the full resolution segmentation prediction. In practice, we set $T = 4$ and $\Delta t = 250$.

Dice. We keep the model structure and train it by dice loss, which follows a similar expression as 2 but replace the $\mathbf{P}_{(i,j)}$ to $\tilde{\mathbf{P}}_{(i,j)}$ which is expressed as :

$$\tilde{\mathbf{P}}_{(i,j)} = v_\theta(\mathbf{I}, \mathbf{P})_{(i,j)} \tag{8}$$

4 Experiments

Datasets. We evaluate our pipeline on four public datasets to evaluate the generalization ability of our method in terms of three OOD settings. (1) Cross-Organ setting: We use the healthy lung segmentation task of the COVID-19 Radiography dataset [3,21] as our in-domain training dataset. COVID-19 contains 10192 chest X-rays with the pixel-wise annotation of left and right lungs. For the out-of-domain dataset, we choose COVID-Seg [31], which is a chest CT dataset that comprises 118 CT volumes. (2) Cross-organ: the MRI segmentation task of AMOS 2022 Multi-Modality Abdominal Multi-Organ Segmentation Challenge Dataset [8], which contains 100 MRI volumes annotating 15 different organs. (3) Cross-view: CAMUS Cardiac Acquisitions for Multi-structure Ultrasound Segmentation dataset [13], which contains the pixel-wise annotations of heart structure from two-chamber view. In the paper, we segment the left heart ventricle and the left heart atrium.

Compared Methods. Our proposed method is compared with the following approaches: (1) Baseline (DL), which trains a model of the same architecture using Dice loss. (2) MedSegDiffv2 [28], a diffusion model designed for medical image segmentation, utilizing DDPM [7]. (3) MedCLIP-SAMv2 [12], which employs BioMedCLIP and SAM for the task of medical image segmentation. (4) The approach from [20] involves training a text prompt decoder atop the BioMedCLIP image encoder for medical image segmentation. Additionally, we incorporate two more methods for a comprehensive evaluation: (5) PASS [34], learning the transformation of human-annotated shape priors for test-time adaptation, and (6) Medical SAM Adapter [29], which finetunes SAM specifically for medical imaging tasks. These evaluations collectively demonstrate the superior performance of our proposed pipeline.

Compared Metrics. we utilize the dice score to evaluate the accuracy of our method compared to other baselines, which is shown as:

$$\text{Dice}(\tilde{\mathbf{P}}, \mathbf{G}) = \frac{2 \sum_{i,j} \tilde{\mathbf{P}}_{(i,j)} \mathbf{G}_{(i,j)} + \epsilon}{\sum_{i,j} \tilde{\mathbf{P}}_{(i,j)} + \sum_{i,j} \mathbf{G}_{(i,j)} + \epsilon}. \tag{9}$$

For evaluating the model's performance on in-domain and out-of-domain datasets. we train our method along with baselines on the source domain datasets and test the in-domain dice score expressed as $\mathbf{Dice}_{in}$, then, we test the out-of-domain dice score ($\mathbf{Dice}_{out}$) of all the methods on target domain examples.

Data Preprocessing. We follows [38] to pre-process the dataset. (1) For the Cross-Modality task, we use images from the COVID-19 dataset as a training set. During test time, we utilize the COVID-19 and COVID-CT test datasets for in-domain and outside-domain testing. (2) For the cross-organ task, we calculate the average position of the organs in the training set and crop them accordingly. During training, we split the"liver" as the OOD data to test the transferability of our method. (3) For the Cross-View task, we train the model purely on 2CH or 4CH views and swap them during testing for evaluating the model's performance on out-of-distribution data.

Implementation Details. We train our stage I model on an RTX 4090 with a batch size set to 80. We employ Adam optimizer with warming up from 5e-4 to 1e-4, followed by an exponential learning rate decay with γ equal to 0.98, and train 100 epochs. For the stage II model, we train our model on images of resolution 224×224, batch size equal to 16 on 2 NVIDIA A100 40G GPUs with a batch size equal to 16, using the Adam optimizer. For the RecFlow objective, we keep the learning rate equal to $1 \times e^{-4}$, and train for 10,000 iterations. For Dice loss, we follow the same learning rate setting and train for 100 epochs until convergence.

Table 2. The Comparison results of CA-seg across three different tasks. CA-Seg Recflow and CA-Seg Dice indicates different refinement stragies by flow-matching and Dice loss $Dice_{in}$ and $Dice_{out}$ present the segmentation results on In-domain and Out-domain data, $Dice_{mean}$ indicates the average of both.

Methods	Tasks	$Dice_{in}(\%)$ ↑	$Dice_{out}(\%)$ ↑
MedSegDIffv2 [28]	Cross-Modality (X-ray ⇒ CT)	64.21	56.09
MedCLIP-SAMv2 [12]		25.00	16.58
MedVLSM [20]		95.87	84.71
CLIP-Driven-Universal [16]		**99.10**	44.86
PASS [34]		98.56	78.15
CA-Seg Recflow (Ours)		93.01	82.40
CA-Seg Dice (Ours)		97.17	**86.44**
MedCLIP-SAMv2 [12]	Cross-Organ (Liver excluded)	27.56	24.82
MedVLSM [20]		67.25	2.46
Medical SAM Adapter [29]		74.53	6.49
CA-Seg Recflow (Ours)		68.01	**32.32**
CA-Seg Dice (Ours)		**88.78**	30.37
MedSegDIffv2 [28]	Cross-View (2CH ⇔ 4CH)	56.21	47.46
CLIP-Driven-Universal [16]		90.72	85.35
MedVLSM [20]		88.73	77.58
MedCLIP-SAMv2 [12]		25.10	25.07
CA-Seg Recflow (Ours)		91.55	**91.14**
CA-Seg Dice (Ours)		**95.45**	88.92

4.1   Experiment Results

Comparison for Accuracy. The experimental results are presented in Table 2. We observed the following:

1. **In-Domain Segmentation Performance.** CA-Seg demonstrates superior in-domain segmentation performance across both cross-organ and cross-view tasks when trained using Dice loss. This suggests that SSP effectively enhances in-domain performance.
2. **OOD Performance.** Notably, our method achieves the highest Dice score compared to other approaches for OOD data. In particular, the refinement method using Dice loss exhibits the best cross-modality performance and ranks second-best for cross-organ and cross-view tasks. This indicates that Dice loss effectively learns domain-invariant features, especially when domain discrepancies arise from intensity differences.
3. **Refinement Strategy with Recflow.** The Recflow-based refinement strategy achieves optimal performance on cross-organ and cross-view tasks. This outcome is expected because, in these scenarios, domain differences often stem from shape variations. As a geometry-focused learning process, Recflow excels at capturing these variances and refining the output to high-resolution results.

Table 3. The efficiency test of our method, Latency means the time spent for a single image, and the FPS presents the number of images the model can infer per second. Our method achieves the second fastest speed among all competitors.

Methods	Latency (ms) ↓	FPS ↑
MedSegDIffv2 [28]	15473.99	0.06
CLIP-Driven-Universal [16]	**2.34**	**426.45**
MedVLSM [20]	100.96	9.90
MedCLIP-SAMv2 [12]	176.65	5.66
CA Seg Recflow (Ours)	53.19	18.80
CA-Seg Dice (Ours)	12.67	78.90

Comparison for Efficiency. To evaluate the runtime efficiency of our method, we benchmark the average inference latency and throughput on an NVIDIA RTX 4090 GPU. Each model was evaluated with a batch size of 1 and an input resolution of 224×224. We report the average runtime over 100 runs after 10 warm-up iterations. As Table 3 shows, the Recflow model achieves 53.19 ms latency and 18.80 FPS, which is remarkable as a diffusion process over the DDPM algorithm. For the dice version, because we use the GradCAM in a more straightforward way compare to MedCLIP-SAMv2, and no need for CLIP text decoder as Med-VLSM did, our model achieves 12.67 ms latency and 78.90 FPS, which can be used in real-time scenarios.

Table 4. The ablation study on (1) the number of text concepts, (2) with or without SSP. The performance is evaluated by the Dice score between the prediction and the ground-truth.

Datasets	# Text Concepts			# w./wo. SSP	
	128	64	32	Y	N
COVID-19 Radiology (X-ray, In-domain)	93.01	95.69	93.21	93.01	57.94
COVID-Seg (CT, Out-domain)	82.40	64.44	62.56	82.40	53.41

Ablation Study. We conduct ablation studies on three aspects of CA-Seg and show results in Table 4. (1) We observe that an increase in text concepts significantly enhances out-of-domain generation. This improvement is intuitive, as a greater number of text descriptions provides the model with richer semantic information. As a result, the strategy benefits by delivering more comprehensive morphological features within SSP, thereby boosting performance. (2) The use of SSP significantly enhances both in-domain and out-of-domain performance. SSP serves as prior information, offering the model an initial understanding of the object's rough location and shape. Consequently, the model focuses on learning the detailed segmentation mask rather than starting from scratch. Therefore, the performance improves by introducing the SSP.

5   Limitations

Although our method achieves remarkable performance across the three domain generalization scenarios, its effectiveness is closely tied to the quality of Grad-CAM. However, as a classification model, PMCCLIP still faces significant challenges in generating accurate heatmaps. This is primarily due to three main issues. First, the input resolution of PMCCLIP is too low to effectively localize objects in medical images due to the loss of critical edge information. Second, the original image captions utilized by PMCCLIP are often too brief, which limits the semantic richness of the concepts encoded and thus hinders effective SSP integration by GradCAM. Finally, GradCAM itself struggles to detect small organs and tissues accurately. Therefore, there remains considerable room for improvement in our method by employing more advanced VLMs.

6   Conclusion

The domain generalization problem is a common problem in medical image segmentation due to the costly pixel-wise segmentation annotation on medical images. We propose CA-seg, a universal framework that utilizes the rich semantic information in VLM and uses a two-stage training strategy that first extracts high-level semantic-attached information to concretize an object named semantic shape prior (SSP) and then refines the SSP leveraging dice or flow-matching to complete a meticulous depiction of the detailed boundary of the target organ. By achieving the best segmentation performance on three OOD tasks. We show that the shape prior plays a key role in unifying the common OOD problems existing in medical image segmentation while also extending the current OOD problems to more difficult scenarios.

Acknowledgments. We would like to thank the authors of BioParse [39] for providing the publicly available dataset used in this study.

Disclosure of Interests. The authors have no competing interests to declare that are relevant to the content of this article.

References

1. Anand, D., et al.: One-shot localization and segmentation of medical images with foundation models. arXiv preprint arXiv:2310.18642 (2023)
2. Bi, Y., Jiang, Z., Clarenbach, R., Ghotbi, R., Karlas, A., Navab, N.: Mi-segnet: mutual information-based us segmentation for unseen domain generalization. In: International Conference on Medical Image Computing and Computer-Assisted Intervention. pp. 130–140. Springer (2023)
3. Chowdhury, M.E., et al.: Can AI help in screening viral and covid-19 pneumonia? IEEE Access **8**, 132665–132676 (2020)
4. Chowdhury, T.F., et al.: Adacbm: an adaptive concept bottleneck model for explainable and accurate diagnosis. In: International Conference on Medical Image Computing and Computer-Assisted Intervention. pp. 35–45. Springer (2024)
5. Gao, Y., Xia, W., Hu, D., Wang, W., Gao, X.: Desam: decoupled segment anything model for generalizable medical image segmentation. In: International Conference on Medical Image Computing and Computer-Assisted Intervention. pp. 509–519. Springer (2024)
6. Gu, R., et al.: Cddsa: contrastive domain disentanglement and style augmentation for generalizable medical image segmentation. Med. Image Anal. **89**, 102904 (2023)
7. Ho, J., Jain, A., Abbeel, P.: Denoising diffusion probabilistic models. Adv. Neural. Inf. Process. Syst. **33**, 6840–6851 (2020)
8. Ji, Y., et al.: Amos: a large-scale abdominal multi-organ benchmark for versatile medical image segmentation. arXiv preprint arXiv:2206.08023 (2022)
9. Karani, N., Erdil, E., Chaitanya, K., Konukoglu, E.: Test-time adaptable neural networks for robust medical image segmentation. Med. Image Anal. **68**, 101907 (2021)
10. Kirillov, A., et al.: Segment anything. In: Proceedings of the IEEE/CVF International Conference on Computer Vision. pp. 4015–4026 (2023)
11. Koh, P.W., et al.: Concept bottleneck models. In: International conference on machine learning. pp. 5338–5348. PMLR (2020)
12. Koleilat, T., Asgariandehkordi, H., Rivaz, H., Xiao, Y.: Medclip-samv2: towards universal text-driven medical image segmentation. arXiv preprint arXiv:2409.19483 (2024)
13. Leclerc, S., et al.: Deep learning for segmentation using an open large-scale dataset in 2d echocardiography. IEEE Trans. Med. Imaging **38**(9), 2198–2210 (2019)

14. Lin, C.S., Wang, C.Y., Wang, Y.C.F., Chen, M.H.: Semples: semantic prompt learning for weakly-supervised semantic segmentation. arXiv preprint arXiv:2401.11791 (2024)
15. Lin, W., et al.: Pmc-clip: contrastive language-image pre-training using biomedical documents. In: International Conference on Medical Image Computing and Computer-Assisted Intervention. pp. 525–536. Springer (2023)
16. Liu, J., et al.: Clip-driven universal model for organ segmentation and tumor detection. In: Proceedings of the IEEE/CVF International Conference on Computer Vision. pp. 21152–21164 (2023)
17. Liu, Q., Chen, C., Dou, Q., Heng, P.A.: Single-domain generalization in medical image segmentation via test-time adaptation from shape dictionary. In: Proceedings of the AAAI Conference on Artificial Intelligence. vol. 36, pp. 1756–1764 (2022)
18. Lüddecke, T., Ecker, A.: Image segmentation using text and image prompts. In: Proceedings of the IEEE/CVF Conference on Computer Vision and Pattern Recognition. pp. 7086–7096 (2022)
19. Oikarinen, T., Das, S., Nguyen, L.M., Weng, T.W.: Label-free concept bottleneck models. arXiv preprint arXiv:2304.06129 (2023)
20. Poudel, K., Dhakal, M., Bhandari, P., Adhikari, R., Thapaliya, S., Khanal, B.: Exploring transfer learning in medical image segmentation using vision-language models. arXiv preprint arXiv:2308.07706 (2023)
21. Rahman, T., et al.: Exploring the effect of image enhancement techniques on covid-19 detection using chest x-ray images. Comput. Biol. Med. **132**, 104319 (2021)
22. Selvaraju, R.R., Cogswell, M., Das, A., Vedantam, R., Parikh, D., Batra, D.: Gradcam: Visual explanations from deep networks via gradient-based localization. In: Proceedings of the IEEE international conference on computer vision. pp. 618–626 (2017)
23. Su, Z., Yao, K., Yang, X., Huang, K., Wang, Q., Sun, J.: Rethinking data augmentation for single-source domain generalization in medical image segmentation. In: Proceedings of the AAAI Conference on Artificial Intelligence. vol. 37, pp. 2366–2374 (2023)
24. Wang, H., Ye, H., Xia, Y., Zhang, X.: Leveraging sam for single-source domain generalization in medical image segmentation. arXiv preprint arXiv:2401.02076 (2024)
25. Wang, J., et al.: Generalizing to unseen domains: a survey on domain generalization. IEEE Trans. Knowl. Data Eng. **35**(8), 8052–8072 (2022)
26. Wang, Y., Li, H., Chau, L.p., Kot, A.C.: Embracing the dark knowledge: domain generalization using regularized knowledge distillation. In: Proceedings of the 29th ACM International Conference on Multimedia. pp. 2595–2604 (2021)
27. Wen, R., Yuan, H., Ni, D., Xiao, W., Wu, Y.: From denoising training to test-time adaptation: Enhancing domain generalization for medical image segmentation. In: Proceedings of the IEEE/CVF Winter Conference on Applications of Computer Vision. pp. 464–474 (2024)
28. Wu, J., Ji, W., Fu, H., Xu, M., Jin, Y., Xu, Y.: Medsegdiff-v2: diffusion-based medical image segmentation with transformer. In: Proceedings of the AAAI Conference on Artificial Intelligence. vol. 38, pp. 6030–6038 (2024)
29. Wu, J., Ji, W., Liu, Y., Fu, H., Xu, M., Xu, Y., Jin, Y.: Medical sam adapter: adapting segment anything model for medical image segmentation. arXiv preprint arXiv:2304.12620 (2023)
30. Xu, Y., Xie, S., Reynolds, M., Ragoza, M., Gong, M., Batmanghelich, K.: Adversarial consistency for single domain generalization in medical image segmentation.

In: International Conference on Medical Image Computing and Computer-Assisted Intervention. pp. 671–681. Springer (2022)

31. Yang, X., He, X., Zhao, J., Zhang, Y., Zhang, S., Xie, P.: Covid-ct-dataset: a ct scan dataset about covid-19. arXiv preprint arXiv:2003.13865 (2020)

32. Yoon, J.S., Oh, K., Shin, Y., Mazurowski, M.A., Suk, H.I.: Domain generalization for medical image analysis: a survey. arXiv preprint arXiv:2310.08598 (2023)

33. Yuan, H., Li, X., Zhou, C., Li, Y., Chen, K., Loy, C.C.: Open-vocabulary sam: segment and recognize twenty-thousand classes interactively. In: European Conference on Computer Vision. pp. 419–437. Springer (2024)

34. Zhang, C., Zheng, H., You, X., Zheng, Y., Gu, Y.: Pass: test-time prompting to adapt styles and semantic shapes in medical image segmentation. IEEE Trans. Med. Imaging pp. 1–1 (2024). https://doi.org/10.1109/TMI.2024.3521463

35. Zhang, L., et al.: Motion correction in mri using deep learning and a novel hybrid loss function. arXiv preprint arXiv:2210.14156 (2022)

36. Zhang, R., Lu, W., Guan, C., Gao, J., Wei, X., Li, X.: Shan: shape guided network for thyroid nodule ultrasound cross-domain segmentation. In: International Conference on Medical Image Computing and Computer-Assisted Intervention. pp. 732–741. Springer (2024)

37. Zhang, S., et al.: Biomedclip: a multimodal biomedical foundation model pretrained from fifteen million scientific image-text pairs. arXiv preprint arXiv:2303.00915 (2023)

38. Zhao, T., et al.: A foundation model for joint segmentation, detection, and recognition of biomedical objects across nine modalities. Nat. Methods (2024). https://doi.org/10.1038/s41592-024-02499-w

39. Zhao, T., et al.: A foundation model for joint segmentation, detection and recognition of biomedical objects across nine modalities. Nat. Methods **22**(1), 166–176 (2025)

40. Zhou, K., Liu, Z., Qiao, Y., Xiang, T., Loy, C.C.: Domain generalization: a survey. IEEE Trans. Pattern Anal. Mach. Intell. **45**(4), 4396–4415 (2022)

41. Zhou, Z., Qi, L., Yang, X., Ni, D., Shi, Y.: Generalizable cross-modality medical image segmentation via style augmentation and dual normalization. In: Proceedings of the IEEE/CVF conference on computer vision and pattern recognition. pp. 20856–20865 (2022)

42. Zhu, Y., Zhao, W., Li, A., Tang, Y., Zhou, J., Lu, J.: Flowie: efficient image enhancement via rectified flow. In: Proceedings of the IEEE/CVF Conference on Computer Vision and Pattern Recognition. pp. 13–22 (2024)

TotalSegmentator 2D: A Tool for Rapid Anatomical Structure Analysis

Bertram Sabrowsky-Hirsch$^{(\boxtimes)}$ ⓘ, Ahmed Alshenoudy ⓘ, Stefan Thumfart ⓘ, and Michael Giretzlehner ⓘ

RISC Software, Research Unit Medical Informatics, Hagenberg, Austria
{bertram.sabrowsky-hirsch,ahmed.alshenoudy,stefan.thumfart,
michael.giretzlehner}@risc-software.at

Abstract. This work presents *TotalSegmentator 2D* (TS_{2D}), a novel tool for rapid anatomical structure analysis that employs 2D segmentation of coronal projection images derived from 3D CT scans. Using TS_{2D}, anatomical labels for all major structures can be extracted with minimal processing time, enabling rapid evaluation of both the presence and quantity of structures for screening or visualization purposes. In our evaluation, TS_{2D} was compared with projected segmentations from the original *TotalSegmentator* tool (TS_{Full}). Although the two-dimensional approach, due to information loss, shows reduced segmentation performance for soft-tissue structures (0.81 DSC), it achieves competitive accuracy for bone structures (0.90 DSC). Notably, TS_{2D} reduces inference times to under one second per scan, about 1% of the processing time required by TS_{Full}, rendering it highly suitable for large-scale screening and rapid image retrieval applications. Our method is freely available through our GitHub repository (http://github.com/risc-mi/totalsegmentator2D).

Keywords: segmentation · computed tomography · u-net · deep-learning

1 Introduction

With the continuous rise in CT examinations [5,11] and the increasing volume of clinical data made available through data-sharing initiatives such as *The Cancer Imaging Archive* (TCIA), medical imaging data has become more readily accessible. This growing data pool presents significant opportunities to enhance data-driven approaches in medical image analysis, particularly semisupervised methods and the development of foundation models. However, filtering large datasets for relevant information to maintain a reliable and well-curated training pool remains challenging due to the lack of labels and descriptive metadata in medical images. The DICOM standard provides basic details like the examined body part, but this data can be inconsistent, ambiguous, removed during de-identification, or incorrect [8].

S. Ali et al. (Eds.): MIUA 2025, LNCS 15918, pp. 32–43, 2026.
https://doi.org/10.1007/978-3-031-98694-9_3

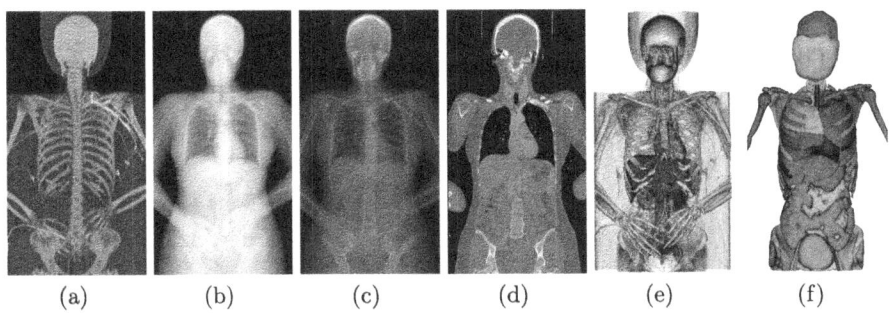

(a)   (b)   (c)   (d)   (e)   (f)

Fig. 1. From left to right: a patient of the TotalSegmentator dataset represented as (a) MIP and (b) AIP image, (c) DRR using DiffDRR (d) a coronal slice, (e) a volume and (f) a surface rendering of the anatomy segmented using TotalSegmentator, both created with 3D-Slicer using an orthogonal view.

To address these challenges, the development of automated methods for labeling and organizing medical imaging data has become a necessary task, supporting more efficient data retrieval and analysis for clinical and research purposes. In this context, semantic segmentation is an important step. For screening, segmentations can quantify the presence and localize relevant anatomical structures, or be used in visualizations to facilitate rapid decision-making by human reviewers.

While CT scans capture three-dimensional anatomical details in volumetric images, the added dimensional complexity does not necessarily improve all medical image analysis tasks equally. For initial visualization, simple 2D projection techniques like Maximum Intensity Projection (MIP) are often favored over 3D rendering or extracted 2D slices, as MIP effectively simplifies complex anatomical structures [3,7,14]. This technique is commonly applied in vascular and bone imaging.

Average Intensity Projection (AIP) is another technique that produces images that closely resemble standard X-ray (XR) images and has been utilized for computed tomography (CT) to XR comparisons [12]. More advanced methods, such as Digitally Reconstructed Radiographs (DRR), aim to further reduce the domain gap between CT and XR images. Figure 1 illustrates various visual representations of the same patient. Similar to XR images, synthetic projection images from CTs can support image analysis tasks such as identifying body regions, locating anatomical structures, and detecting abnormalities while being computationally cheaper than volumetric images.

In this paper, we evaluate the use of projected CT scans for the analysis of anatomical structures. The paper builds on our previous work, in which we introduced this approach to automatically and efficiently determine the body regions covered in medical images. This approach proved to be substantially more reliable than using DICOM metadata and was consequently adopted for image retrieval within a medical application. In the present study, we further aim to develop and thoroughly evaluate a method that enables (1) segmentation for the purpose of (2) analysis and visualization of all major anatomical structures,

(3) rapid processing of images on consumer hardware, and (4) ease of use. Finally, we outline the performance differences introduced by the loss of information in the projection step.

2   Related Work

Medical image retrieval and anatomical structure detection have been approached as classification problems, including image classification, grid-based object detection, and pixel-level semantic segmentation.

In image classification, CNNs have proven effective for detecting anatomical structures, body regions, and image properties such as the slicing axis in CT scans [13,15,17,19,20]. However, the approach is less suitable for detecting large numbers of target structures and does not directly address object localization. Grid-based classification methods, on the other hand, can simultaneously localize and classify objects within images, as demonstrated by Hammami et al. [9]. All of these methods focus on processing individual slices extracted from CT volumes, which require inference across multiple slices, or even the entire volume, along with additional logic to generate image-level decisions. However, grid-based classification has been effective on native 2D radiographs [16], suggesting that it may also perform well on synthetic images obtained through the projection of volumetric data.

In recent years, semantic segmentation methods, particularly the U-Net architecture [2], have made notable progress, especially in the segmentation of multiple organs [4]. This architecture has become a key component in modern detection methods, such as nnDetection [1]. Concurrently, the availability of publicly accessible segmentation models has grown, with TotalSegmentator [18] being the first to offer comprehensive segmentation of all major anatomical structures in body CT images. Despite these advancements, these methods face challenges when applied to medical image screening, often being limited by long processing times and high resource demands. This is primarily due to the large three-dimensional datasets they process, which result in significant memory usage and computational complexity.

In our work, we propose leveraging the superior performance of the U-Net architecture in conjunction with synthetic images generated by projecting volumetric CT data.

3   Materials and Methods

Our proposed approach is outlined as Method I in Fig. 2. Starting with the input CT image I_{3D}, we first reduce its dimensionality by computing a coronal projection image. The coronal plane provides a frontal view of the patient, spanning longitudinal structures and separating the left and right sides of the body, making it the preferred choice for detection purposes. While our approach could also be applied to the transverse or lateral planes, doing so would significantly increase the overlap of structures. The resulting 2D image, I_{2D}, is

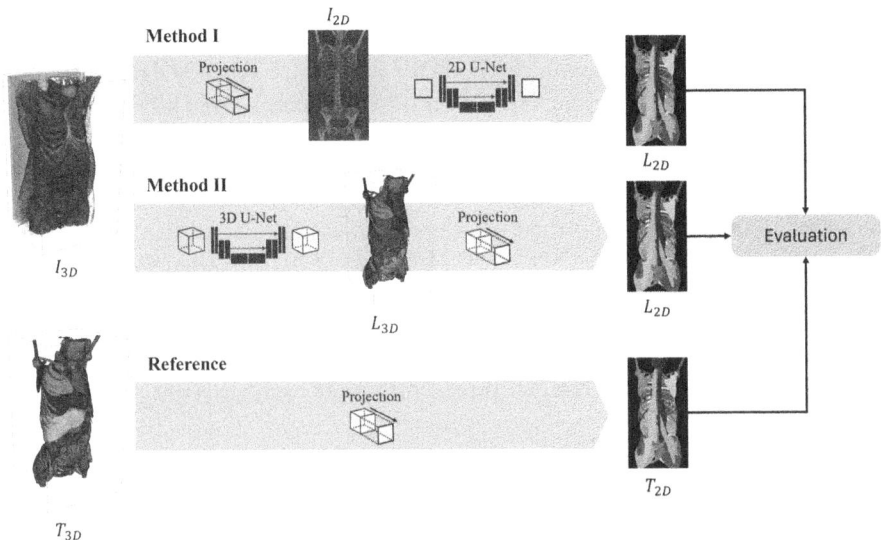

Fig. 2. Our proposed approach Method I, the competing approach Method II and the reference for evaluation of both approaches. Note that while L_{2D} and T_{2D} are visualized as single-label images, each label is mapped to a binary channel, enabling the representation of overlapping structures.

then segmented using a 2D U-Net to obtain a multi-label image, L_{2D}. Note that multi-label images assign multiple labels to each pixel to account for overlap in the projected anatomic structures.

In contrast, the competing approach, Method II, begins by segmenting the 3D image I_{3D} using a 3D U-Net, generating a 3D label image L_{3D}. This label image is then projected into 2D to produce a multi-label image L_{2D}.

As a reference, the 3D ground-truth annotations T_{3D} provided for each I_{3D} are projected into 2D to yield a multi-label image T_{2D}. In our evaluation, we compare L_{2D} with the corresponding T_{2D}.

3.1   Dataset

We conducted our experiments using the TotalSegmentator v1 dataset [18]. The newer v2 dataset was not utilized for the following reasons: The v1 dataset was used in the original publication of the dataset and tool, and there is currently no updated evaluation available for the v2 dataset. Furthermore, not all labels used for training the v2 tool have been published with the updated dataset.

Our aim was to replicate the original experiments as closely as possible to isolate the effects of performing the segmentation on 2D projection images rather than the original 3D images. The dataset consists of 1204 CT scans with annotations for 104 different anatomical structures. Our experiments use the predefined split provided with the dataset: 1082 scans for training, 57 for validation and 65 for testing.

3.2 Projection Methods

We considered three projection methods for images $p : I_{3D} \longrightarrow I_{2D}$: MIP, AIP and DRR. For the calculation of DRR images, we employed DiffDRR [6] with different attenuation levels.

For the label projection $p : L_{3D} \rightarrow L_{2D}$, we use a binary projection method as follows: For the label image $L_{3D}(i,j,k) \in C \cup \{0\}$, where $C = \{1, 2, \dots\}$ is the set of all labels and 0 represents background, we first compute a binary mask for each label $c \in C$. Each binary mask $M_c(i,j,k) \in \{0,1\}$ is then projected onto 2D using MIP along the k-axis. The resulting 2D binary masks are stacked across channels to produce a multi-label image $L_{2D}(i,j,c) \in \{0,1\}$. This channel-wise separation of labels prevents overlap between projected masks along the coronal plane, ensuring a clear and distinct representation of each class in the 2D output.

3.3 Models and Training

Just like the TotalSegmentator contribution, we rely on the nnU-Net framework [10] for the automatic configuration and training of segmentation models. For our proposed Method I, we use 2D nnU-Net models as $m_{2D} : I_{2D} \longrightarrow L_{2D}$. We adapted the framework to enable multi-label segmentation, as the original implementation only supports single channel segmentation images. Mirroring was disabled in the augmentation pipeline to enable the model to distinguish left and right anatomical structures. Another modification was the use of custom batch sizes, rather than using the one configured by the framework. In Appendix A.2, we outline how large batch-sizes inhibited the performance of the models significantly. We therefore reduced the batch size from 43 to 2, which also corresponds to the value used in the TotalSegmentator publication.

We trained five separate models, each dedicated to a specific group of anatomical structures, following the grouping defined in the original publication: Vertebrae, Ribs, Organs, Muscles and Cardiac. Each model m_g is responsible for predicting a subset of labels $C_g \subset C$, corresponding to its anatomical group. The predictions from all models are then aggregated along the channel dimension of the multi-label image $L_{2D}(i,j,c)$, where $c \in C$. Training was performed using a combination of maximum intensity projection (MIP) and average intensity projection (AIP) images, with each model trained for 4000 epochs.

4 Evaluation

We present results for our proposed Method I as TS_{2D}. The competing Method II is represented through TS_{Full} and TS_{Fast}, both employing the TotalSegmentator tool with the standard and fast options, respectively. For each evaluation, the resulting L_{2D} were compared to the respective reference T_{2D}. The following metrics were evaluated for each anatomical structure separately: the Dice Similarity Coefficient (DSC) and the Normalized Surface Distance (NSD) using a distance threshold of 3mm.

Table 1. Results for the DSC and NSD, represented by the average and the 95% CI on the test split of the TS dataset, shown for each evaluated method and group of anatomical structures.

Structures	DSC			NSD		
	TS_{Full}	TS_{Fast}	TS_{2D}	TS_{Full}	TS_{Fast}	TS_{2D}
Vertebrae	0.97 [0.96, 0.98]	0.91 [0.90, 0.93]	0.90 [0.88, 0.91]	0.99 [0.98, 0.99]	0.97 [0.97, 0.98]	0.92 [0.91, 0.93]
Ribs	0.97 [0.97, 0.97]	0.89 [0.89, 0.90]	0.89 [0.87, 0.90]	0.98 [0.98, 0.99]	0.98 [0.97, 0.98]	0.93 [0.92, 0.94]
Organs	0.96 [0.95, 0.97]	0.92 [0.90, 0.94]	0.78 [0.72, 0.84]	0.96 [0.95, 0.97]	0.94 [0.92, 0.95]	0.61 [0.54, 0.68]
Muscles	0.97 [0.96, 0.98]	0.94 [0.92, 0.96]	0.93 [0.91, 0.94]	0.99 [0.98, 0.99]	0.97 [0.96, 0.98]	0.87 [0.83, 0.91]
Cardiac	0.96 [0.95, 0.97]	0.91 [0.88, 0.94]	0.77 [0.68, 0.84]	0.98 [0.97, 0.99]	0.96 [0.94, 0.98]	0.69 [0.63, 0.74]
Soft-tissue	0.97 [0.96, 0.97]	0.93 [0.91, 0.94]	0.81 [0.77, 0.85]	0.98 [0.97, 0.98]	0.95 [0.94, 0.96]	0.69 [0.64, 0.73]
Bones	0.97 [0.96, 0.98]	0.91 [0.90, 0.92]	0.90 [0.89, 0.91]	0.98 [0.98, 0.99]	0.98 [0.97, 0.98]	0.93 [0.92, 0.94]
All	0.97 [0.96, 0.97]	0.91 [0.91, 0.92]	0.86 [0.84, 0.88]	0.98 [0.98, 0.98]	0.97 [0.96, 0.97]	0.83 [0.79, 0.86]

Through an ablation study described in Appendix A.1, we determined MIP to be most effective for the segmentation of bone structures, while AIP yielded superior results for soft tissue. Perhaps surprisingly, DRR projection was outperformed by either MIP or AIP. The combined use of MIP and AIP as a two channel input image yielded the best overall results and was therefore used for the subsequent experiments. Table 1 presents the results for various groups of anatomical structures, starting with the five groups used to train the individual models. The table includes groups for soft-tissue and bone structures, as well as an overall group encompassing all anatomical structures. Each cell reports the mean evaluation metric along with the 95% Confidence Interval (CI). Furthermore, sample predictions of the five groups of anatomical structures across different DSC results are illustrated in Fig. 3.

We observe a significant performance drop between TS_{Full} and TS_{Fast}, particularly in the DSC metric, while the NSD metric is less affected. Our approach, TS_{2D}, further reduces performance, with a particularly sharp decline in accuracy for soft-tissue structures, especially in the Organs and Cardiac groups. Notably, the NSD metric is more strongly impacted than the DSC metric. For the groups Vertebrae, Ribs and Muscles our model can still achieve excellent results, only slightly below TS_{Fast} in the DSC metric. In general, our model achieves excellent results for bone structures, with a DSC of 0.90 and NSD of 0.93, while performance for soft-tissue structures varies significantly as shown in Fig. 4. The outliers correspond to very small segmentations (often only a few voxels), which either stem from errors in the ground-truth data that were corrected in later versions of the TotalSegmentator dataset, or from small fragments of cropped structures at the image boundaries that the 2D model often fails to detect. In empirical experiments, we successfully removed all outliers by filtering the segmentations based on the 25th percentile of the average size of each respective structure, calculated across the entire dataset.

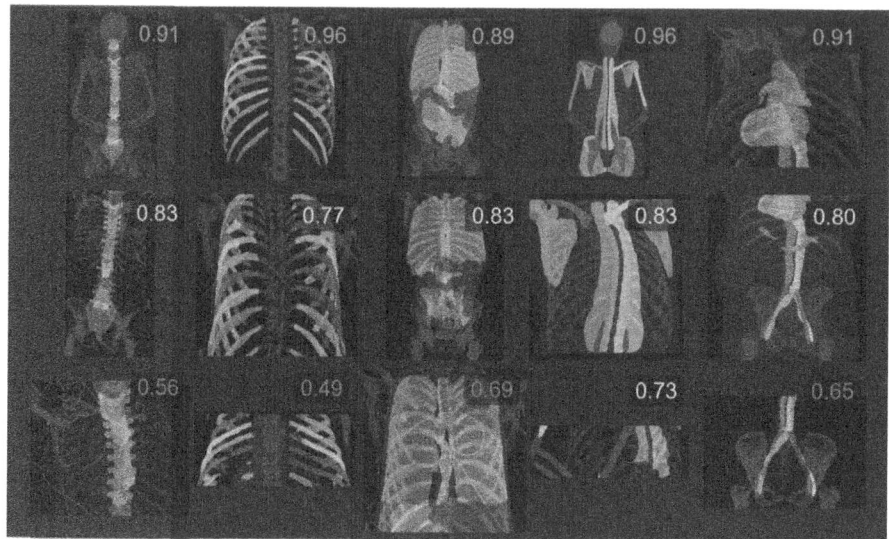

Fig. 3. Sample results for each anatomical structure group are presented. The top row showing excellent results, the middle row displaying good results (a DSC between 0.7 and 0.85), and the bottom row illustrating poor results (a DSC below 0.7). From left to right: Vertebrae, Ribs, Organs, Muscles, and Cardiac. The groupings, derived from the original TotalSegmentator publication, may not always be intuitive. For instance, the Muscles group includes not only muscles and bones, representing the musculoskeletal system, but also the brain. Also, for this group, we selected the lowest DSC result for the bottom row, as no case yielded a DSC below 0.7.

Table 2. Evaluation of processing times (in seconds) for volumes of varying sizes across all evaluated methods. Median values over 10 executions are presented. Percentage values indicate the relative time reduction compared to TS_{Full}. Inference was conducted on a workstation with an Intel Core i7-13700F CPU and Nvidia GeForce RTX4090 GPU.

ID	Study Size	Resolution	TS_{Full}	TS_{Fast}	TS_{2D}
s0105	Small	$283 \times 283 \times 59$	42.85	5.36 (12.5%)	0.47 (1.1%)
s0070	Medium	$242 \times 242 \times 270$	66.61	6.23 (9.3%)	0.51 (0.8%)
s1314	Large	$333 \times 333 \times 546$	145.97	13.76 (9.4%)	0.86 (0.6%)

We measured the inference time of all evaluated methods, as shown in Table 2. For each method, the total time required to predict all structures was recorded, with TS_{Full} and TS_{2D} requiring five inference steps. Our method consistently reduced processing time to 1% of TS_{Full}, also outperforming TS_{Fast} by a factor of 10.

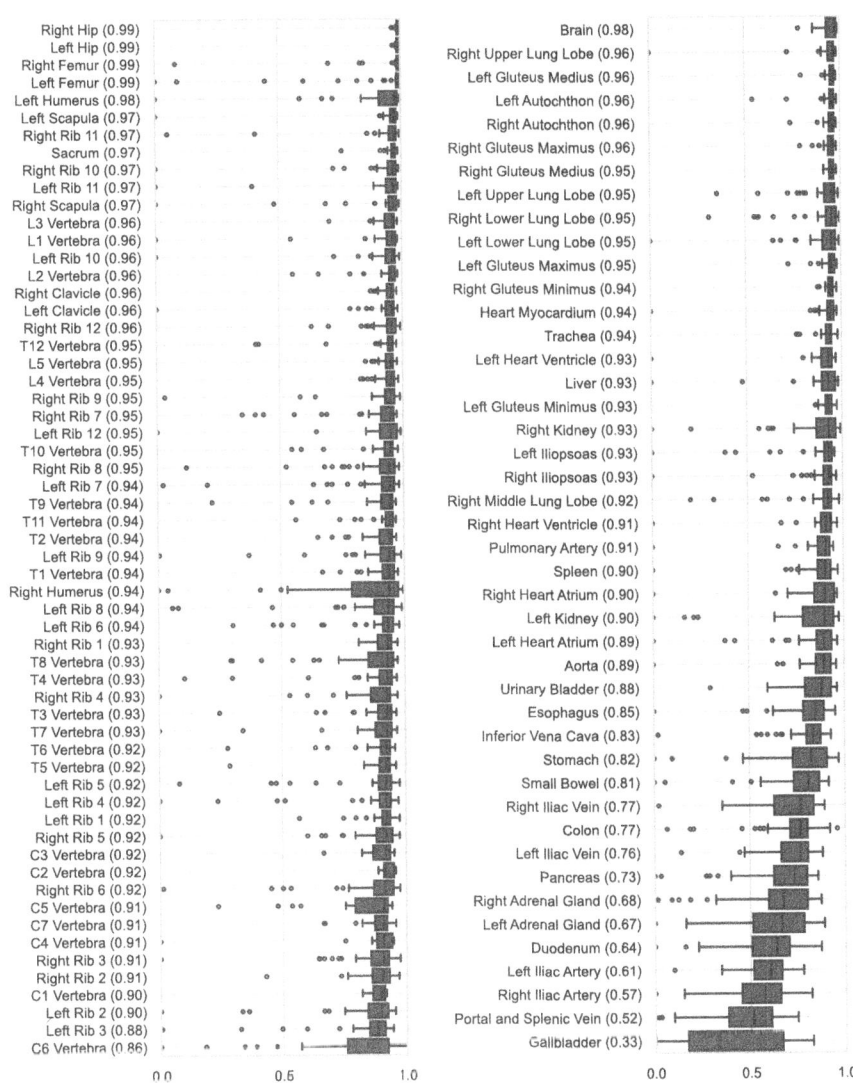

Fig. 4. DSC scores for our method TS_{2D} for each anatomical structure grouped by bone (left) and soft-tissue (right) structures, and sorted by the median score.

5   Discussion

To enable rapid detection of anatomical structures, our approach TS_{2D} addresses the high computational burden and processing time of 3D segmentation. By utilizing a coronal projection to reduce image dimensionality, we significantly decrease inference time to under one second, requiring only 1% of the processing time compared to the TotalSegmentator model (TS_{Full}). This makes TS_{2D} well-suited for large-scale screening applications or scenarios requiring rapid feedback on consumer-grade hardware.

Although the reduction to 2D inherently results in information loss, our results show that TS_{2D} performs competitively on bone structures, achieving a DSC of 0.90 and an NSD of 0.93. However, soft-tissue structures, particularly abdominal organs and vessels, are more impacted with a DSC of 0.81 and NSD of 0.69. Nevertheless, for most structures, the trade-off between speed and precision remains more than acceptable for analysis and image retrieval applications. We are currently integrating our method into an automated image retrieval pipeline that allows filtering images from large databases based on body regions or individual anatomical structures.

Our method and models are publicly available on our GitHub repository, along with a simple Python interface for inference and integration. This work also serves as the foundation for our follow-up research on XR image segmentation using models trained on synthetic projection images generated via DRR from CT scans.

To summarize, we (1) propose our method, TS_{2D}, for the segmentation of all major anatomical structures in coronal projection images, enabling accurate segmentation that (2) can be used directly for visualizations or processed further for detection and analysis of anatomical structures. Our method also (3) supports rapid processing with computation times under 1 s and (4) is publicly available and easy to use through a simple Python interface.

Acknowledgments. This work was funded by the FFG (Austrian Research Promotion Agency) under the grant 872604 (MEDUSA) and research subsidies granted by the government of Upper Austria. RISC Software GmbH is a member of UAR (Upper Austrian Research) Innovation Network.

A   Appendix: Ablation Studies

Below, we present ablation studies conducted to refine our method. All experiments followed Method I (see Fig. 2), with specific deviations in the training setup detailed for each ablation.

A.1   Projection Methods

We evaluated the impact of various projection methods $p : I_{3D} \longrightarrow I_{2D}$ separately for the different groups of anatomical structures: Vertebrae, Ribs, Organs, Muscles and Cardiac. These groups align with those used in the original TotalSegmentator paper. A separate model was trained and evaluated for each group, using only the corresponding available labels. We tested attenuation levels of 1, 3 and 6 for DRR to assess which level best corresponds to different tissue types. Additionally, we assessed the use of combinations by assigning different projections to separate channels in the input image. The model was trained for 250 epochs with a batch size of 8. Note that, although the number of epochs was reduced to keep training times manageable for the 35 combinations, the results generally do not deviate significantly from those of models trained for longer durations, as the nnU-Net framework dynamically adapts the learning rate.

The results are summarized in Table 3. The best overall performance was achieved through the combined use of AIP and MIP. MIP performed particularly well for the Vertebrae, Ribs and Muscles groups, while AIP yielded strong results for the Organs and Cardiac groups. Their combination was only slightly outperformed by individual projections in the cases of Vertebrae (MIP: 0.87) and Organs (AIP: 0.77). For DRR, we observe a similar dynamic: low attenuation performed better for Organs and Cardiac, while high attenuation was more effective for Vertebrae, Ribs, and Muscles. Overall, DRR achieved competitive results only for the Muscles group (0.92).

Table 3. Results on our experiments on different projection methods p. DSC scores on the test split are reported for each group of anatomical structures. Scores below 0.7 are highlighted in red (poor), those between 0.7 and 0.85 in yellow (moderate), and scores above 0.85 in green (excellent).

Projection p	Vertebrae	Ribs	Organs	Muscles	Cardiac
AIP	0.81	0.77	**0.77**	0.90	**0.75**
MIP	**0.87**	0.86	0.65	0.91	0.67
AIP,MIP	0.86	**0.87**	0.76	**0.92**	0.75
DRR[1]	0.80	0.75	0.69	0.91	0.68
DRR[3]	0.84	0.81	0.68	**0.92**	0.67
DRR[6]	0.85	0.82	0.67	**0.92**	0.66
DRR[1,3,6]	0.85	0.82	0.66	**0.92**	0.67

A.2 Training Batch Sizes

We evaluated the impact of different batch sizes on model training. The batch size n_B directly influences the total number of training samples n_S, which can be calculated as:

$$n_S = n_E \times n_I \times n_B. \tag{1}$$

Note that within the nnU-Net framework, the number of iterations n_I is fixed at 250. As a result, only the number of epochs n_E and the batch size n_B are configurable parameters that determine the total number of training samples n_S. Since n_S directly influences the training process, adjusting only the batch size would distort the results. For example, doubling n_B effectively doubles n_S, which increases the number of computations and the overall training time. To ensure a consistent total number of training samples n_S across all experiments with varying batch sizes n_B, the number of epochs n_E was adjusted accordingly.

Table 4 presents the results, which clearly show a decline in DSC on the test split as the batch size increases, with a significant drop occurring beyond a batch size of 8. Therefore, although nnU-Net defaults to a large batch size of 43 for our dataset, likely due to its optimization for single-class segmentation, we chose to use smaller batch sizes in our experiments.

Table 4. Results for our experiments with different batch sizes are presented, with DSC scores on the test split reported for each configuration. The number of epochs was adjusted for each configuration to ensure an equivalent number of training samples.

Batch Size	Epochs	Samples	Test DSC
2	1000	500,000	**0.877**
4	500	500,000	0.874
8	250	500,000	0.868
16	125	500,000	0.854
32	63	504,000	0.837
48	42	504,000	0.804

References

1. Baumgartner, M., Jäger, P.F., Isensee, F., Maier-Hein, K.H.: nnDetection: a self-configuring method for medical object detection. In: de Bruijne, M., Cattin, P.C., Cotin, S., Padoy, N., Speidel, S., Zheng, Y., Essert, C. (eds.) MICCAI 2021. LNCS, vol. 12905, pp. 530–539. Springer, Cham (2021). https://doi.org/10.1007/978-3-030-87240-3_51
2. Çiçek, Ö., Abdulkadir, A., Lienkamp, S.S., Brox, T., Ronneberger, O.: 3D U-net: learning dense volumetric segmentation from sparse annotation. In: Ourselin, S., Joskowicz, L., Sabuncu, M.R., Unal, G., Wells, W. (eds.) MICCAI 2016. LNCS, vol. 9901, pp. 424–432. Springer, Cham (2016). https://doi.org/10.1007/978-3-319-46723-8_49
3. Fishman, E.K., Ney, D.R., Heath, D.G., Corl, F.M., Horton, K.M., Johnson, P.T.: Volume rendering versus maximum intensity projection in ct angiography: what works best, when, and why. Radiographics **26**(3), 905–922 (2006)
4. Fu, Y., Lei, Y., Wang, T., Curran, W.J., Liu, T., Yang, X.: A review of deep learning based methods for medical image multi-organ segmentation. Physica Med. **85**, 107–122 (2021)
5. Goldfarb, J.W., Weber, J.: Trends in cardiovascular MRI and CT in the us medicare population from 2012 to 2017. Radiol. Cardiothoracic Imaging **3**(1), e200112 (2021)
6. Gopalakrishnan, V., Golland, P.: Fast auto-differentiable digitally reconstructed radiographs for solving inverse problems in intraoperative imaging. In: Workshop on Clinical Image-Based Procedures. pp. 1–11. Springer (2022)

7. Gruden, J.F., Ouanounou, S., Tigges, S., Norris, S.D., Klausner, T.S.: Incremental benefit of maximum-intensity-projection images on observer detection of small pulmonary nodules revealed by multidetector CT. Am. J. Roentgenol. **179**(1), 149–157 (2002)

8. Gueld, M.O., et al.: Quality of dicom header information for image categorization. In: Medical Imaging 2002: PACS and Integrated Medical Information Systems: Design and Evaluation. vol. 4685, pp. 280–287. SPIE (2002)

9. Hammami, M., Friboulet, D., Kechichian, R.: Cycle gan-based data augmentation for multi-organ detection in CT images via yolo. In: 2020 IEEE International Conference on Image Processing (ICIP). pp. 390–393 (2020). https://doi.org/10.1109/ICIP40778.2020.9191127

10. Isensee, F., Jaeger, P.F., Kohl, S.A., Petersen, J., Maier-Hein, K.H.: nnu-net: a self-configuring method for deep learning-based biomedical image segmentation. Nat. Methods **18**(2), 203–211 (2021). https://doi.org/10.7303/syn3193805

11. Larson, D.B., Johnson, L.W., Schnell, B.M., Salisbury, S.R., Forman, H.P.: National trends in ct use in the emergency department: 1995–2007. Radiology **258**(1), 164–173 (2011)

12. Ledda, R., et al.: Diagnostic performance of chest CT average intensity projection (AIP) reconstruction for the assessment of pleuro-parenchymal abnormalities. Clin. Radiol. **79**(7), e957–e962 (2024)

13. Li, W., et al.: Machine learning classification of body part, imaging axis, and intravenous contrast enhancement on CT imaging. Can. Assoc. Radiol. J. **75**(1), 82–91 (2024)

14. Prokop, M., Shin, H.O., Schanz, A., Schaefer-Prokop, C.M.: Use of maximum intensity projections in ct angiography: a basic review. Radiographics **17**(2), 433–451 (1997)

15. Raffy, P., et al.: Deep learning body region classification of MRI and CT examinations. J. Digit. Imaging **36**(4), 1291–1301 (2023)

16. Ragab, M.G., et al.: A comprehensive systematic review of yolo for medical object detection (2018 to 2023). IEEE Access (2024)

17. Sugimori, H.: Classification of computed tomography images in different slice positions using deep learning. J. Healthc. Eng. **2018**(1), 1753480 (2018)

18. Wasserthal, J., et al.: Totalsegmentator: robust segmentation of 104 anatomic structures in CT images. Radiol. Artif. Intell. **5**(5) (2023)

19. Yan, K., Lu, L., Summers, R.M.: Unsupervised body part regression via spatially self-ordering convolutional neural networks. In: 2018 IEEE 15th International Symposium on Biomedical Imaging (ISBI 2018). pp. 1022–1025. IEEE (2018)

20. Zhang, P., Wang, F., Zheng, Y.: Self supervised deep representation learning for fine-grained body part recognition. In: 2017 IEEE 14th International Symposium on Biomedical Imaging (ISBI 2017). pp. 578–582 (2017). https://doi.org/10.1109/ISBI.2017.7950587

Promptable Cancer Segmentation Using Minimal Expert-Curated Data

Lynn Karam[1], Yipei Wang[1,2], Veeru Kasivisvanathan[3], Mirabela Rusu[4], Yipeng Hu[1,2], and Shaheer U. Saeed[1,2(✉)]

[1] Department of Medical Physics and Biomedical Engineering,
University College London, London, UK
`shaheer.saeed.17@ucl.ac.uk`
[2] UCL Hawkes Institute, University College London, London, UK
[3] Division of Surgery and Interventional Science, University College London,
London, UK
[4] Department of Radiology and Department of Urology, Stanford University,
California, USA

Abstract. Automated segmentation of cancer on medical images can aid targeted diagnostic and therapeutic procedures. However, its adoption is limited by the high cost of expert annotations required for training and inter-observer variability in datasets. While weakly-supervised methods mitigate some challenges, using binary histology labels for training as opposed to requiring full segmentation, they require large paired datasets of histology and images, which are difficult to curate. Similarly, promptable segmentation aims to allow segmentation with no re-training for new tasks at inference, however, existing models perform poorly on pathological regions, again necessitating large datasets for training. In this work we propose a novel approach for promptable segmentation requiring only 24 fully-segmented images, supplemented by 8 weakly-labelled images, for training. Curating this minimal data to a high standard is relatively feasible and thus issues with the cost and variability of obtaining labels can be mitigated. By leveraging two classifiers, one weakly-supervised and one fully-supervised, our method refines segmentation through a guided search process initiated by a single-point prompt. Our approach outperforms existing promptable segmentation methods, and performs comparably with fully-supervised methods, for the task of prostate cancer segmentation, while using substantially less annotated data (up to 100X less). This enables promptable segmentation with very minimal labelled data, such that the labels can be curated to a very high standard. Code: https://github.com/lynnkaram/promptable-cancer-segmentation.

Keywords: Cancer · Segmentation · Prompting methods

1 Introduction

Segmentation of pathological features on medical images helps guide targeted surgical procedures. For prostate cancer, MR image localisation can aid diagnostic biopsies by improving needle placement [4,6,8,27] and enhance targeted

S. Ali et al. (Eds.): MIUA 2025, LNCS 15918, pp. 44–58, 2026.
https://doi.org/10.1007/978-3-031-98694-9_4

treatments like cryoablation and radiotherapy by minimising damage to healthy tissue [9, 11, 18, 28]. Accurate cancer localisation on medical images is thus crucial for improving diagnostic and therapeutic outcomes.

The cost associated with manually obtaining such localisations, both in terms of time and expertise, has thus far hindered a wider adoption [3, 19, 21]. Limited expert time in clinical settings is coupled with high disagreements on such cancer localisations even between experts [1, 7, 10]. Consensus or pixel-level majority votes between localisations from different observers may allow more reliable cancer segmentation. However, these consensus-based segmentations come at an even greater cost in terms of expert time. Such challenges have made adoption practically infeasible in various clinical domains, especially in resource-constrained regions [1, 23].

To mitigate the cost, recent work has proposed automated segmentation. Deep learning methods [25, 32, 33], have shown an ability to accurately delineate boundaries of prostate cancer on MR images, achieving Dice scores in the range of $0.25 - 0.35$ compared to radiologists doing the same task. However, such methods require large fully-segmented MR datasets for training, where curating high-quality consensus-based annotations is infeasible due to the associated cost. As a result, most current methods are trained with segmentations from a single institute, which may propagate the subjective biases into the final automated system. This may also be one of the reasons why Dice scores for prostate cancer segmentation have consistently remained low, compared to anatomical segmentation.

Weakly-supervised methods that aim to localise regions-of-interest (ROIs), using only classification labels of binary ROI presence, have recently been proposed for cancer segmentation [15, 24]. In these methods, segmentation is learnt solely from a weak label of binary classification indicating whether cancer is present in the image or not, without requiring any segmentations of the MR image. These sorts of weak labels can mitigate subjective biases in the pixel-level segmentation process and can also reduce the time and expertise required to annotate such labels. Objective biopsy-based histology labels indicating binary cancer presence can be used as weak labels to learn cancer segmentation on MR images, without requiring any subjective annotations. Since acquiring pixel-level histopathology labels is infeasible in vivo, such weakly-supervised approaches offer a mechanism to utilise objective information to guide clinical tasks. These approaches require large paired datasets of binary histology labels and MR images for training. However, for prostate cancer, even collecting such paired weak labels proves challenging due to a lack of standardisation in biopsy protocols, reporting, and pairing with imaging data [2].

Recently, promptable methods have emerged as mechanisms to reduce the cost associated with segmentation. Promptable segmentation allows users to specify prompts such as points [12], bounding boxes [16], or other sparse annotations [14, 31], which can then allow a full segmentation of the ROI. Most of these methods are trained across a wide variety ROIs and are intended to be usable without requiring any new data even from novel classes. However, due to the lack of pathological ROIs on medical images during training, performance remains low for ROIs such as cancer on prostate MR images (consistent with our experiments). Fine-tuning with data for pathological ROIs, such as cancer, may help to improve performance. However, this fine-tuning requires substantial data, almost equivalent to the amount of data required by conventional deep learning methods (as demonstrated in our experiments). Thus these methods suffer from the same challenges as conventional deep learning, which stem from the cost of obtaining high-quality fully-segmented pathology ROIs on medical images. Our experimental results also demonstrate that despite fine-tuning these methods cannot improve performance in challenging tasks such as cancer segmentation.

In this work, we propose a promptable segmentation that can be trained using very few full segmentations (24 segmented images) supplemented by a very small set of weakly-labelled sampled (8 pairs of weak labels and images). In expertise- and data-constrained domains such as cancer segmentation, the use of these few labels during training means that the labels can be feasibly curated to a high standard e.g., following strict protocols for acquiring weak labels based on histology and curating labels through consensus for the full segmentations. Our approach is more data-efficient compared not only to recent state-of-the-art fully-supervised methods [25,32,33] but also to other mixed supervision methods [5,20]. The minimal user interaction at inference distinguishes our method from other fully-automated methods, where the user interaction of selecting a point prompt allows our method to achieve accurate segmentation, while being data-efficient.

We propose to use two classifiers: 1) weakly-supervised classifier; and 2) fully-supervised classifier, to guide a search for the ROI within the image, such that at the end we can obtain a full segmentation. The weakly-supervised classifier is trained using image and histology-based weak label (indicating binary object presence) pairs. The fully-supervised classifier is trained using image and full segmentation pairs, where the inputs during training are image crops and the outputs are binary labels indicating ROI presence within each crop. After training, crops can be passed to both classifiers and the raw probability (logits) can indicate the likelihood of the object being present within a crop, similar to weak supervision techniques [19,24,29,34].

At inference, we require only a point prompt from the user which then leads to a full segmentation. The initial point prompt serves as the location for an initial image crop, which is passed to both the weakly-supervised and fully-supervised classifiers. The scores from the classifier are combined and thresholded to determine whether the crop should be marked as ROI presence positive or negative. The crop is then moved in a set pattern (explained in the methods), determining ROI presence at each location. The ROI-positive crops are then combined into a full segmentation. This approach allows a promptable segmentation to be trained using very limited data, such that this data can be curated to a very high standard.

The contributions of our work are summarised:

1. proposing a novel framework for promptable segmentation, which can be trained with minimal labels
2. evaluating the approach for a clinically challenging task of prostate cancer segmentation using a large real world clinical dataset
3. demonstrating superior performance compared to other promptable methods and comparable performance to fully-supervised learning which requires 100X the amount of data for training
4. presenting an open-source implementation of our approach at: https://github.com/lynnkaram/promptable-cancer-segmentation

2   Methods

2.1   Weakly-Supervised Classifier

The weakly-supervised classifier $f(\cdot; \theta) : \mathcal{X} \to [0, 1]$ takes an input image $x \in \mathcal{X}$ and outputs a probability of ROI presence in the range $[0, 1]$, where $\mathcal{X}$ represents the domain of input image samples and θ denotes the weights of the neural network.

The classifier is trained on a dataset consisting of pairs of images and binary labels $\{(x_i, y_i)\}_{i=1}^{N}$, where $y_i \in \{0, 1\}$ indicating whether the ROI is present in the image or not.

The binary cross-entropy loss is used for training the classifier:

$$\mathcal{L}_f = -\frac{1}{N} \sum_{i=1}^{N} [y_i \log(f(x_i; \theta)) + (1 - y_i) \log(1 - f(x_i; \theta))] \tag{1}$$

where the optimal weights for the neural network are given by:

$$\theta^* = \arg \min_{\theta} \mathcal{L}_f \tag{2}$$

Image Crops at Inference: A crop from the image x_i is defined as $x_{i,c}^{(w,h,d)} \subset \mathcal{X}_c$, where (w, h, d) denotes the locations of a fixed-size crop within the image, in the width, height and depth dimensions respectively, and $\mathcal{X}_c$ denotes the domain of crops. The subscript c is used to indicate the number of crops in a set of crops $\{x_{i,c}^{(w,h,d)}\}_{c=1}^{C}$, where C is the number of crops per image.

The score for the image crop can then be computed using $f(x_{i,c}^{(w,h,d)}; \theta^*) \in [0, 1]$. This strategy of training with full images and inference on crops or portions is similar to recent weak-supervision literature [19,24,29,34].

2.2   Fully-Supervised Classifier

The fully-supervised classifier $g(\cdot; \phi) : \mathcal{X}_c \to [0, 1]$ takes a crop as input $x_{i,c}^{(w,h,d)} \in \mathcal{X}_c$ and outputs a probability of ROI presence in the range $[0, 1]$, where ϕ denotes the neural network weights.

The classifier is trained on a dataset consisting of pairs of crops and binary labels $\{\{(x_{i,c}^{(w,h,d)}, z_{i,c}^{(w,h,d))})\}_{c=1}^{C}\}_{i=1}^{M}$, where C is the number of crops per image and there are a total of M images, and $z_{i,c}^{(w,h,d))} \in \{0,1\}$ indicates whether an ROI is present within the crop or not. Although a full segmentation can be used to construct such labels, other mechanisms may be used depending on data availability e.g., more dense tracked biopsies may be able to indicate crop-level presence in an objective manner as well (Fig. 1).

The binary cross-entropy loss is used for training the classifier:

$$\mathcal{L}_g = -\frac{1}{M*C}\sum_{i=1}^{M}\sum_{c=1}^{C}\left[z_{i,c}^{(w,h,d))}\log(g(x_{i,c}^{(w,h,d)};\phi)) + (1 - z_{i,c}^{(w,h,d))})\log(1 - g(x_{i,c}^{(w,h,d)};\phi))\right] \quad (3)$$

Where the optimal weights for the neural network are given by:

$$\phi^* = \arg\min_{\phi}\mathcal{L}_g \quad (4)$$

Image Crops at Inference: The score for the image crop at inference can be computed using $g(x_{i,c}^{(w,h,d)};\phi^*) \in [0,1]$.

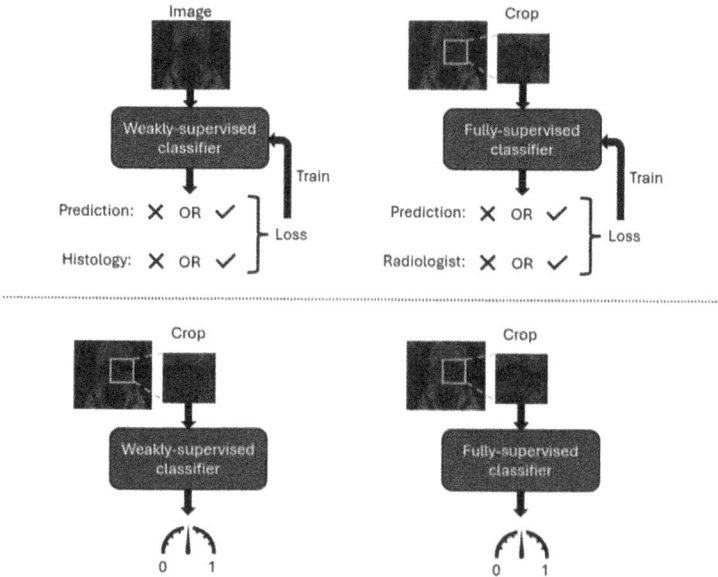

Fig. 1. The training (top) and inference (bottom) pipelines for the weakly-supervised and fully-supervised classifiers.

2.3   Point Prompt and Search

Point Prompt: During promptable segmentation, the user provides a point prompt at coordinates (w_0, h_0, d_0). The crop at these coordinates is then $x_{i,c}^{(w_0,h_0,d_0)}$. The subscripts 0 denote the initial time-step $t = 0$, which iterates as the crop moves.

Crop Scoring: We define a joint score as follows (where $\alpha \in [0,1]$ is a hyper-parameter):

$$S = \alpha \times f(x_{i,c}^{(w_t,h_t,d_t)}; \theta^*) + (1 - \alpha) \times g(x_{i,c}^{(w_t,h_t,d_t)}; \phi^*) \tag{5}$$

The score is thresholded using a threshold τ:

$$S_{\tau,t} = \begin{cases} 1, & \text{if } S > \tau, \\ 0, & \text{otherwise.} \end{cases} \tag{6}$$

Here, $S_{\tau,t}$ indicates whether a crop at step t is marked as ROI positive or negative.

Crop Movement: The crop then moves following a spline, which is a spiral in our work. The spiral strategy is more computationally efficient compared to a full sliding window approach due to a lower number of crops processed and roughly follows the spherical shape of the prostate gland. In preliminary results, this strategy showed performance improvements compared to strategies such as random search. As a crop moves, S_t is computed for each crop. The movement is defined as a spiral spline with parameters s and μ, denoting scale and total number of steps for a full circle, respectively. Steps in the spline are denoted by t, where the radius for any given step is computed as $r = t/s$ and the angle is given by $\beta = 2 \times \pi \times (t/\mu)$. The crop movement is defined by:

$$\delta w = r \times cos(\beta)$$

$$\delta h = r \times sin(\beta) \tag{7}$$

$$\delta d = 0$$

The new crop location can then be given by:

$$(w_{t+1}, h_{t+1}, d_{t+1}) = (w_t + \delta w, h_t + \delta h, d_t + \delta d) \tag{8}$$

Final Segmentation: As t iterates until a fixed number of steps T, the joint scores for each crop are collected $\{S_{\tau,t}\}_{t=0}^{T}$. Each location where $S_{\tau,t} = 1$, is combined to form the full segmentation. In practice the spiral search may be performed n times with varying parameters, and then conducting a pixel-level majority vote, such that a pixel-level segmentation map can be obtained.

The framework is summarised in Fig. 2.

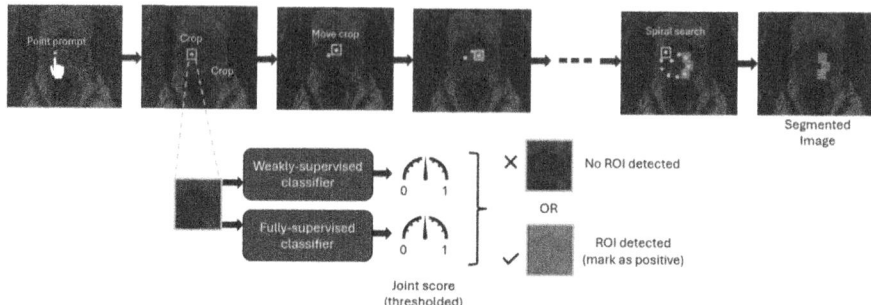

Fig. 2. The point prompt leads to a spiral search where each crop is scored by the two classifiers to determine whether to mark a crop as positive or negative. Combining all positive crops gives the final segmentation.

3 Experiments

3.1 Dataset

The dataset used in this work consists of 500 MR images from men over the age of 30, suspected of having prostate cancer. The images were bi-parametric pelvic MR scans with channels corresponding to T2-weighted and diffusion-weighted images. These images were collected as part of the [anonymous] trials. Each image had a binary histology label indicating cancer presence and a consensus-based radiologist annotation of the full segmentation of cancer.

Out of these images, 200 were reserved as the holdout set and the rest were used for development (including training other methods for comparison).

3.2 Network Architectures

Both classifiers followed a 3D convolutional neural networks (CNN) architecture [13,17]. The classifiers used 16, 32, and 64 filters in three convolutional layers, each using ReLU activation. Each convolutional layer was followed by a MaxPooling3D layer (2,2,2) to reduce spatial dimensions. The extracted features were then flattened and passed through two fully connected (dense) layers. The model was optimised using Adam. For other hyper-parameter settings please refer to experiments (specified as appropriate) or code available in open-source repository.

The training time for our method was 48 h on a single Nvidia Tesla V100 GPU.

3.3 Experimental Protocols

Comparisons: We compared our approach to a fully-supervised U-Net [22], a fine-tuned promptable SAM [30] and MedSAM [16], and recent state-of-the-art methods in prostate cancer segmentation [32,33]. The U-Net [22] was pre-trained using fully-supervised learning with 1000 samples from the PI-CAI (Prostate Imaging: Cancer AI) challenge data [26] and then fine-tuned using 200 samples from our dataset. This, along with other fully-supervised state-of-the-art methods using similar architectures [32,33], serve as upper-bound reference performance in the task of prostate cancer segmentation. SAM [30] and MedSAM [16] were fine-tuned for our dataset using 200 samples, and represent promptable segmentation methods. Note that all methods that we compared with used approximately 10X-100X the amount of data that is used for training our promptable segmentation approach.

Ablations: To investigate the impact of hyper-parameters and the amount of training data for our classifiers, we conducted ablation studies. The ablation studies investigated crop sizes, amount of training data for classifiers and the impact of the threshold τ. We also investigated variance in our method with respect to the initial point prompt location within the cancerous area.

4   Results

4.1   Comparisons

Table 1 shows that our method outperforms other promptable methods while using 100X less data for training. Compared to both SAM and MedSAM, the differences were significant (paired t-test with significance level 0.05, p-values 0.0004 and 0.0032). For the comparison with the U-Net model, which is an upper-bound performance, statistical significance was not found for the comparison (p-value 0.07). Statistical tests were not conducted for the other two methods as their test data were different from our dataset, however, the differences to these methods were small (only 0.031 Dice difference to Yi et al. [33]).

Table 1. Comparison to recent state-of-the-art methods for both promptable and non-promptable methods.

	Training Data	Dice	Variance w.r.t. prompt
Ours	8 weak + 24 full	0.3085 ± 0.1405	± 0.2163
SAM	200 full	0.2361 ± 0.1074	± 0.2359
SAM	32 full	0.1587 ± 0.1319	± 0.1729
MedSAM	200 full	0.2673 ± 0.1384	± 0.2103
MedSAM	32 full	0.1846 ± 0.1492	± 0.1837
U-Net	1200 full	0.3275 ± 0.1783	-
U-Net	32 full	0.1923 ± 0.1819	-
Yi et al. [33]	275 full	0.3392 ± 0.2358	-
Yan et al. [32]	503 full	0.3300 ± 0.1800	-

4.2   Ablations

Impact of Amount of Training Data: Table 2 presented the classifier and segmentation performances when the classifiers were trained with varying amounts of data. Convergence for the weakly-supervised classifier was observed with 8 samples and for the fully-supervised classifier with 24 samples. This low number of samples may stem from the fact that classification tasks are easier to learn due to their low-dimensional solution space compared to tasks like segmentation, which require more samples for learning. This is also in-line with recent works [24].

Table 2. Performance of classifier and segmentation based on training sample size. WSC is the weakly supervised classifier and FSC is the fully-supervised classifier.

WSC Samples	FSC Samples	WSC Acc.	FSC Acc.	Dice
4	24	0.782	0.582	0.211
8	24	0.782	0.723	0.305
12	24	0.782	0.716	0.298
16	24	0.782	0.732	0.307
8	8	0.643	0.723	0.204
8	16	0.715	0.723	0.261
8	24	0.782	0.723	0.305
8	32	0.896	0.723	0.309
8	40	0.899	0.723	0.308

Impact of Crop Sizes: As shown in Fig. 3, crop sizes substantially impact performance. A crop size of 10 pixels in the height and width dimensions (i.e. the x- and y-directions) yielded the highest dice score of 0.2621 ± 0.2106. And a crop size of 6 in the depth dimension, which corresponds to number of slices, yielded the highest dice score of 0.2621 ± 0.2106. The optimal crop size was thus selected as $10 \times 10 \times 6$.

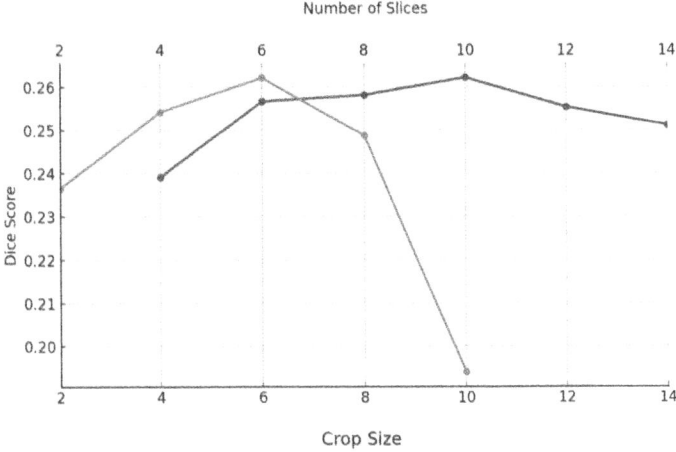

Fig. 3. Plot of crop size (w, h, d) against dice score. (w, h) on the bottom axis and d on the top axis.

Impact of Search Strategies As shown in Table 3, the spiral search strategy is both time-efficient and approaches human-level performance, compared to other common strategies.

Table 3. The time and Dice scores for different search strategies compared.

Strategy	Time	Dice
Spiral (Ours)	4.2 s	0.2967
Sliding Window	12.8 s	0.2957
Random Search	5.9 s	0.2431
Expert Human	439.6 s	0.2971

Impact of Hyper-parameters. As summarised in Table 4, the optimal value for τ was 0.05, which yielded the highest Dice. Only the difference between 0.01 to 0.05 was statistically significant (p-value 0.0312), and we did not observe statistical significance for the comparison between 0.05 and 0.10 (p-value 0.1130).

Similarly, Table 4 also presents the impact of other hyper-parameters, including the number of steps T, total number of steps for a full circle in the spiral μ, the parameter controlling the balance between weak and full supervision α and the number of times spiral search is repeated for a single sample n.

Table 4. Dice scores and standard deviation for different hyper-parameters (statistically significant performance improvement emboldened; where none or more than one emboldened, statistical significance was not found for the comparison).

τ	Dice
0.01	0.2286 ± 0.1785
0.05	**0.2689 ± 0.2163**
0.10	**0.2598 ± 0.2389**
T	
60	0.2579±0.1983
80	0.2611±0.2189
100	0.2573±0.2055
μ	
200	0.2614±0.2018
400	0.2571±0.2023
600	0.2510±0.1997
α	
0.25	**0.2753±0.1932**
0.50	**0.2749±0.2140**
0.75	0.2521±0.2276
n	
4	0.2732±0.2113
6	0.2873±0.1803
8	0.2838±0.2001

4.3   Qualitative Analysis

Figure 4 shows examples of the lesions predicted after prompting. Note that we only search a specified area in the spiral search and thus final scores were computed across different click locations to cover the entire cancerous lesion. As seen in the randomly picked examples, our method shows substantial agreement with a radiologist performing the same task.

5   Discussion

Our results show that the proposed framework allows effective prostate cancer localisation on MR images from only a point prompt. Our approach outperforms other common promptable segmentation methods while performing comparably to fully-supervised non-promptable methods, all while using substantially less data. For training, our framework only requires 8 binary histology labels indicating cancer presence, paired with MR images, and 24 radiologist segmentations of cancer. This minimal data requirement means that it is feasible to curate the

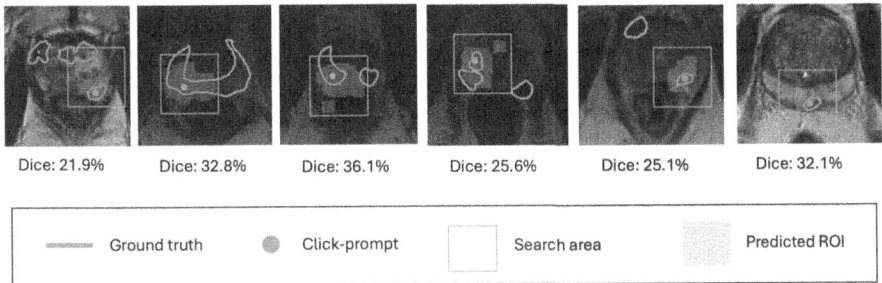

Dice: 21.9%   Dice: 32.8%   Dice: 36.1%   Dice: 25.6%   Dice: 25.1%   Dice: 32.1%

| — Ground truth | ● Click-prompt | ☐ Search area | Predicted ROI |

Fig. 4. Samples of MR scans. Ground truth is in blue, predicted is in red. (Color figure online)

data to a high standard e.g., by following strict reporting protocols for histology or curating the radiologist annotations through consensus. In other methods that we compared against, the training requires hundreds or thousands of radiologist annotated samples, which makes it infeasible to curate labels through consensus or majority votes. This means that as other methods use single observer labels for training, the subjective biases of the observers may be passed into the final trained cancer segmentation system. In contrast our method uses objective histology labels coupled with a very small set of radiologist annotations, where it is feasible to ensure that the annotations minimise the subjective biases through mechanisms such as consensus.

The over prediction is likely caused by over-representation of cancer positive cases in the data. Tuning the termination threshold τ holds potential to balance over- and under-prediction. Over-prediction may be favourable for biopsy sampling, to represent not only the most significant cancer but also surrounding areas to determine spread. Future work could explore more detailed analysis of balancing over- and under-prediction for other applications.

Our method has potential to enable promptable segmentation in a variety of domains where data is scarce or where annotations from experts are expensive. It should be noted that while the classifiers used in our framework converged with minimal examples, there may be applications where more data is required. And while the spiral search was effective for prostate cancer segmentation, possibly due to the roughly spherical shape of the gland, other strategies may need to be explored for other applications.

6   Conclusion

In this work we proposed a framework to enable promptable segmentation of complex structures such as cancer in the prostate gland, using very minimal data for training. Evaluating the approach with data from real prostate cancer patients, we found performance comparable to state-of-the-art methods while requiring a fraction of the annotated data for training. Our approach has potential to reduce the segmentation burden in a variety of applications where data or annotations are scarce including cancer localisation in other parts of the body, rare disease localisation and anomaly detection.

Acknowledgements. This work is supported by the International Alliance for Cancer Early Detection, an alliance between Cancer Research UK [EDDAPA-2024/100014] & [C73666/A31378], Canary Center at Stanford University, the University of Cambridge, OHSU Knight Cancer Institute, University College London and the University of Manchester; and National Institute for Health Research University College London Hospitals Biomedical Research Centre.

References

1. Ahmad, I., Alqurashi, F.: Early cancer detection using deep learning and medical imaging: a survey. Crit. Rev. Oncol. Hematol. 104528 (2024)
2. Ahmed, H.U., et al.: Diagnostic accuracy of multi-parametric mri and trus biopsy in prostate cancer (promis): a paired validating confirmatory study. Lancet **389**(10071), 815–822 (2017)
3. Alloghani, M., Al-Jumeily, D., Mustafina, J., Hussain, A., Aljaaf, A.J.: A systematic review on supervised and unsupervised machine learning algorithms for data science. Supervised and Unsupervised Learning for Data Science pp. 3–21 (2020)
4. Barry, M.J.: Prostate-specific-antigen testing for early diagnosis of prostate cancer. N. Engl. J. Med. **344**(18), 1373–1377 (2001)
5. Behzadi, M.M., et al.: Weakly-supervised deep learning model for prostate cancer diagnosis and gleason grading of histopathology images. Biomed. Signal Process. Control **95**, 106351 (2024)
6. Benelli, A., Vaccaro, C., Guzzo, S., Nedbal, C., Varca, V., Gregori, A.: The role of mri/trus fusion biopsy in the diagnosis of clinically significant prostate cancer. Ther. Adv. Urol. **12**, 1756287220916613 (2020)
7. Chalcroft, L.F., et al.: Development and evaluation of intraoperative ultrasound segmentation with negative image frames and multiple observer labels. In: Simplifying Medical Ultrasound: Second International Workshop, ASMUS 2021, Held in Conjunction with MICCAI 2021, Strasbourg, France, September 27, 2021, Proceedings 2. pp. 25–34. Springer (2021)
8. Chen, M., Tustison, N.J., Jena, R., Gee, J.C.: Image registration: fundamentals and recent advances based on deep learning. Machine Learning for Brain Disorders pp. 435–458 (2023)
9. Chen, Z., Meng, L., Zhang, J., Zhang, X.: Progress in the cryoablation and cryoimmunotherapy for tumor. Front. Immunol. **14**, 1094009 (2023)
10. Czolbe, S., Arnavaz, K., Krause, O., Feragen, A.: Is Segmentation Uncertainty Useful? In: Feragen, A., Sommer, S., Schnabel, J., Nielsen, M. (eds.) IPMI 2021. LNCS, vol. 12729, pp. 715–726. Springer, Cham (2021). https://doi.org/10.1007/978-3-030-78191-0_55
11. Erinjeri, J.P., Clark, T.W.: Cryoablation: mechanism of action and devices. J. Vasc. Interv. Radiol. **21**(8), S187–S191 (2010)

12. Kirillov, A., et al.: Segment anything. In: Proceedings of the IEEE/CVF International Conference on Computer Vision. pp. 4015–4026 (2023)
13. Krizhevsky, A., Sutskever, I., Hinton, G.E.: Imagenet classification with deep convolutional neural networks. Adv. Neural Inf. Process. Syst. **25** (2012)
14. Li, H., Liu, H., Hu, D., Wang, J., Oguz, I.: Prism: a promptable and robust interactive segmentation model with visual prompts. In: International Conference on Medical Image Computing and Computer-Assisted Intervention. pp. 389–399. Springer (2024)
15. Li, K., et al.: Weakly supervised histopathology image segmentation with self-attention. Med. Image Anal. **86**, 102791 (2023)
16. Ma, J., et al.: Segment anything in medical images and videos: Benchmark and Deployment. arXiv preprint arXiv:2408.03322 (2024)
17. O'shea, K., Nash, R.: An introduction to convolutional neural networks. arXiv preprint arXiv:1511.08458 (2015)
18. Peschel, R.E., Colberg, J.W.: Surgery, brachytherapy, and external-beam radiotherapy for early prostate cancer. Lancet Oncol. **4**(4), 233–241 (2003)
19. Pocius, M., et al.: Weakly supervised localisation of prostate cancer using reinforcement learning for bi-parametric mr images. In: 2024 IEEE International Symposium on Biomedical Imaging (ISBI). pp. 1–5. IEEE (2024)
20. Rajagopal, A., et al.: Mixed supervision of histopathology improves prostate cancer classification from MRI. IEEE Trans. Med. Imaging (2024)
21. Ratwani, R.M., Sutton, K., Galarraga, J.E.: Addressing AI algorithmic bias in health care. JAMA **332**(13), 1051–1052 (2024)
22. Ronneberger, O., Fischer, P., Brox, T.: U-Net: convolutional networks for biomedical image segmentation. In: Navab, N., Hornegger, J., Wells, W.M., Frangi, A.F. (eds.) MICCAI 2015. LNCS, vol. 9351, pp. 234–241. Springer, Cham (2015). https://doi.org/10.1007/978-3-319-24574-4_28
23. Rosenkrantz, A.B., Siegal, D., Skillings, J.A., Muellner, A., Nass, S.J., Hricak, H.: Oncologic errors in diagnostic radiology: a 10-year analysis based on medical malpractice claims. J. Am. Coll. Radiol. **18**(9), 1310–1316 (2021)
24. Saeed, S.U., et al.: Competing for pixels: a self-play algorithm for weakly-supervised semantic segmentation. IEEE Transa. Pattern Analy. Mach. Intell. (2024)
25. Saeed, S.U., et al.: Image quality assessment by overlapping task-specific and task-agnostic measures: application to prostate multiparametric MR images for cancer segmentation. Mach. Learn. Biomed. Imaging (MELBA) (2022)
26. Saha, A., et al.: The pi-cai challenge: public training and development dataset. (No Title) (2022)
27. Scientific, B.: Cryoablation treatment guide. Advancing Science for Life (2021)
28. Sekhoacha, M., Riet, K., Motloung, P., Gumenku, L., Adegoke, A., Mashele, S.: Prostate cancer review: genetics, diagnosis, treatment options, and alternative approaches. Molecules **27**(17), 5730 (2022)
29. Selvaraju, R.R., Cogswell, M., Das, A., Vedantam, R., Parikh, D., Batra, D.: Gradcam: visual explanations from deep networks via gradient-based localization. Int. J. Comput. Vision **128**, 336–359 (2020)
30. Wang, J., et al.: Promise: promptable medical image segmentation using sam. arXiv preprint arXiv:2403.04164 (2024)
31. Wong, H.E., Rakic, M., Guttag, J., Dalca, A.V.: Scribbleprompt: fast and flexible interactive segmentation for any biomedical image. In: European Conference on Computer Vision. pp. 207–229. Springer (2024)

32. Yan, W., et al.: The impact of using voxel-level segmentation metrics on evaluating multifocal prostate cancer localisation. In: International Workshop on Applications of Medical AI. pp. 128–138. Springer (2022)
33. Yi, W., et al.: T2-only prostate cancer prediction by meta-learning from bi-parametric MR imaging. arXiv preprint arXiv:2411.07416 (2024)
34. Zhang, H., Ogasawara, K.: Grad-cam-based explainable artificial intelligence related to medical text processing. Bioengineering **10**(9), 1070 (2023)

SPARS: Self-Play Adversarial Reinforcement Learning for Segmentation of Liver Tumours

Catalina Tan[1,2], Yipeng Hu[1,2], and Shaheer U. Saeed[1,2]([✉])

[1] Department of Medical Physics and Biomedical Engineering, University College London, London, UK
[2] UCL Hawkes Institute, University College London, London, UK
shaheer.saeed.17@ucl.ac.uk

Abstract. Accurate tumour segmentation is vital for various targeted diagnostic and therapeutic procedures for cancer, e.g., planning biopsies or tumour ablations. Manual delineation is extremely labour-intensive, requiring substantial expert time. Fully-supervised machine learning models aim to automate such localisation tasks, but require a large number of costly and often subjective 3D voxel-level labels for training. The high-variance and subjectivity in such labels impacts model generalisability, even when large datasets are available. Histopathology labels may offer more objective labels but the infeasibility of acquiring pixel-level annotations to develop tumour localisation methods based on histology remains challenging in-vivo. In this work, we propose a novel weakly-supervised semantic segmentation framework called SPARS (Self-Play Adversarial Reinforcement Learning for Segmentation), which utilises an object presence classifier, trained on a small number of image-level binary cancer presence labels, to localise cancerous regions on CT scans. Such binary labels of patient-level cancer presence can be sourced more feasibly from biopsies and histopathology reports, enabling a more objective cancer localisation on medical images. Evaluating with real patient data, we observed that SPARS yielded a mean dice score of 77.3 ± 9.4, which outperformed other weakly-supervised methods by large margins. This performance was comparable with recent fully supervised methods that require voxel-level annotations. Our results demonstrate the potential of using SPARS to reduce the need for extensive human-annotated labels to detect cancer in real-world healthcare settings. Code: https:// github.com/catalinatan/SPARS.

Keywords: Cancer · Reinforcement Learning · Weak Supervision

1 Introduction

Tumour segmentation is crucial for diagnosing and treating liver cancer, particularly in its early stages [2,7,11,31,33]. For instance, identifying cancerous lesions from medical scans can enable clinicians to estimate the tumour diameters and

S. Ali et al. (Eds.): MIUA 2025, LNCS 15918, pp. 59–72, 2026.
https://doi.org/10.1007/978-3-031-98694-9_5

volumes required for targeted radiation delivery in radiotherapies, where radiation dose varies with tumour size [31]. Currently, radiologists manually delineate tumour boundaries on each slice of 3D computed tomography (CT) and/ or magnetic resonance imaging (MRI) scans [11]. However, this manual delineation may be subjective, time-consuming and poorly reproducible [5,9,13]. The subjectivity leads to high inter- and intra-clinician variability in such tasks, which may be a result of the morphological diversity of tumour appearances on these scans as well as varying institute-specific training and expertise [5,9]. These problems underscore the need for more reproducible and objective tumour localisation for cancer interventions [12,18].

Automated segmentation methods aim to address the reproducibility of tumour localisation using fully-supervised learning, where a large number of labels that may be curated through consensus of multiple experts are used to train an automated model. However, this requires a large number of voxel-level expert-annotated labels that are very costly to obtain, especially if curated with a consensus from multiple experts [6,11,19,27].

To mitigate the challenges that plague fully-supervised learning, weakly-supervised learning has been explored for a variety of tasks. Weak supervision allows the use of weak labels (during training or model development) to perform complex tasks at inference. Examples include training neural networks to perform pixel-level segmentation using only bounding boxes [10,16], scribbles [21,24] or image-level annotations [1,17,25,29,35] during training. In particular, image-level classification labels present great promise for weakly-supervised semantic segmentation (WSSS) due to the comparatively lower cost of their acquisition [19]. However, achieving comparable performance to fully-supervised learning, especially in complex clinical tasks such as tumour localisation, remains an open challenge.

In this work we propose a novel framework for WSSS, where we use a minimal number of image-level labels of cancer presence during model development to allow a voxel-level tumour segmentation at inference. The image-level cancer presence labels are objective histopathology labels which indicate whether each patient has clinically significant cancer or not. These image-level labels are used to train an object presence classifier which can classify ROI (region-of-interest) presence within an image. At inference, we use this classifier to generate logits (classification probability) for a section or window of the image, which serves as a likelihood of object presence within the window. For localisation of ROIs, we use self-play adversarial reinforcement learning (RL) where two agents compete to localise ROIs. Each agent moves a window across an image and is rewarded based on the classifier output for the window indicating object presence likelihood. Training to maximise the reward allows each agent to improve localisation towards areas where the likelihood of object presence is maximised. Tracking the classifier outputs for each window, we can generate a voxel-level probability map (described in Sect. 2.4), where a threshold can control which voxels are to be included as positive or negative for the final segmentation. This allows greater application-specific flexibility compared to other weakly-supervised methods, with fixed localisation termination conditions [25,29,35].

The contributions of our work are summarised:

1. we propose a self-play adversarial RL framework for WSSS to minimise manual segmentation costs;
2. we propose to supervise the adversarial RL framework using a classifier trained on image-level labels of object presence to quantify ROI presence likelihood which forms the rewards for RL-based WSSS;
3. our method allows greater application-specific flexibility compared to other WSSS methods by generating a pixel-level classification map (as opposed to patch-level [25, 29]) which can be thresholded to adjust which pixels to include as positive or negative
4. we evaluate our method using data from real liver cancer patients, to localise tumours on CT scans, and compare with recent state-of-the-art weakly- and fully-supervised algorithms demonstrating superior performance to weakly-supervised, and comparable performance to fully-supervised, approaches;
5. we make our algorithm openly available: https://github.com/catalinatan/SPARS

2   Methods

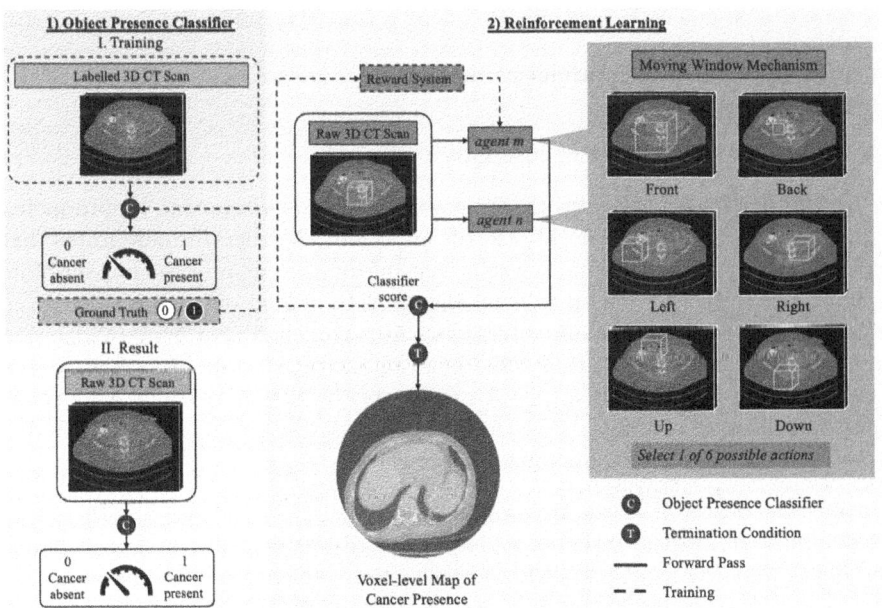

Fig. 1. An overview of the proposed method, where two agents compete to localise ROIs guided by a classifier trained only using weak classification labels.

2.1   Object Presence Classifier

The object presence classifier $f(\cdot; w) : \mathcal{X} \to [0, 1]$, generates a score for a given image sample $x \in \mathcal{X}$ where $\mathcal{X}$ is the image domain and w represents the neural network parameters. This is modelled as a mechanism to provide a linkage function between the two differing weak and full objectives, here, image-level and pixel-level classifications [4,25,28,29,32]. These network parameters are optimised using image-label pairs which indicate object presence in the sample, denoted as $\{x_i, y_i\}_{i=1}^{N}$ where $y_i \in \mathcal{Y}$ with $\mathcal{Y}$ being the label domain $\{0, 1\}$ and N is the number of samples in the set. If the region of interest (ROI) is contained in x_i, its corresponding binary label is given by $y_i = 1$. Conversely, $y_i = 0$ if the ROI is not present (Fig. 1).

The classifier is trained using the binary cross-entropy loss function:

$$l(y_i, f(x_i; w)) = -\frac{1}{N} \sum_{i=1}^{N} (y_i \log(f(x_i; w)) + (1 - y_i) \log(1 - f(x_i; w))$$

where $f(x_i; w)$ is the predicted label by the classifier and y_i is the ground truth label for an image x_i.

The network parameters w are optimised by minimising the expected loss function:

$$w^* = \arg\min_{w} \mathbb{E}_{x_i \in \mathcal{X}, y_i \in \mathcal{Y}}[l(y_i, f(x_i; w)]$$

where w^* represents the optimal parameters.

2.2   Markov Decision Process Environment

In RL, an agent (neural network) interacts with an environment by producing actions. In response to agent actions, the environment generates new states that are observed by the agent, and rewards that inform the agent of the impact of its actions. The rewards are used to train the agent to predict optimal actions given states. The agent-environment interactions are modelled as a Markov decision process that iterates sequentially, and is represented by a tuple $(\mathcal{S}, \mathcal{A}, p, r, \pi, \gamma)$, where $\mathcal{S}$ denotes the state space, $\mathcal{A}$ represents the action space, p defines the state transition probability, r is the reward, π is the agent or policy, and γ represents the discount factor for future rewards.

States: The observed states are cropped windows $x_i^{(a,b,c)}$, where x_i is the entire image and (a, b, c) denote the locations of a fixed-size crop in the height, width and depth dimensions respectively (a hyper-parameter investigated in Sect. 4.1). The state $s_t \in \mathcal{S}$ at time-step t is therefore given by $s_t = \{x_i^{(a,b,c)}\}$, where $\mathcal{S}$ denotes the state space.

Actions: The actions can move the window $x_i^{(a,b,c)}$ in any direction. The action $a_t \in \mathcal{A}$ is given by $a_t = (\delta a, \delta b, \delta c)$. The actions are modelled discretely, only allowing a movement by a fixed distance in one of 6 directions, which means that $(\delta a, \delta b, \delta c) \in \{(\pm d, 0, 0), (0, \pm d, 0), (0, 0, \pm d)\}$, where only one of δa, δb, or δc can be non-zero (i.e., $\pm d$), while the others must be zero.

State Transitions: Given the current state $s_t = \{x_i^{(a,b,c)}\}$ and action $a_t = (\delta a, \delta b, \delta c)$, the next state $s_{t+1} = \{x_i^{(a+\delta a,\ b+\delta b,\ c+\delta c)}\}$. So the action moves the window to a new location. The probability of transitioning to the next state s_{t+1}, given current state s_t and action a_t is given by $p(\cdot) : \mathcal{S} \times \mathcal{S} \times \mathcal{A} \rightarrow [0, 1]$, which can be expressed as $p(s_{t+1}|s_t, a_t)$ for a particular time-step t.

Policy: The policy or agent $\pi(\cdot; \theta) : \mathcal{S} \rightarrow \mathcal{A}$ predicts the action a_t, given the state s_t, where θ represents the parameters of the policy and $a_t = \pi(s_t; \theta)$. Note that in this work we model the policy stochastically where $\pi(\cdot; \theta) : \mathcal{S} \times \mathcal{A} \rightarrow [0, 1]$, which gives the probability whereby $a_t \sim \pi(\cdot|s_t)$, however, the notation of $a_t = \pi(s_t; \theta)$ is adopted for simplicity.

2.3 Policy Optimisation Using Self-Play Adversarial RL

The use of two competing agents to localise ROIs ensures that the impact of any errors in the object presence classifier are minimised since rewards for training are based on a comparison rather than exact object presence classifier outputs. Furthermore, using experience from two agents allows convergence with fewer time-steps compared to using only one set of experiences for training. Previous works have also shown the efficacy of using self-play in object localisation [29].

In our work we use self-play adversarial RL, where there are two versions of the policy, denoted as $\pi_m(\cdot; \theta_m)$ and $\pi_n(\cdot; \theta_n)$, where the only difference is the parameters. In further analyses subscripts m and n will denote outputs from polices m and n respectively. In this work, $\theta_m = \theta_n$. Since the policy is modelled stochastically, the actions selected by each may differ at any single time-step.

Rewards: A reward function $r(\cdot) : \mathcal{S} \times \mathcal{A} \rightarrow \mathbb{R}$ predicts a reward $R_t \in \mathbb{R}$, given the state s_t and action a_t. For policy π_m, the state, action, reward triplet is given by $(s_{m,t}, a_{m,t}, R_{m,t})$ and for policy π_n by $(s_{n,t}, a_{n,t}, R_{n,t})$. The reward for π_m is given by:

$$R_{m,t} = \begin{cases} +1 & \text{if } f(s_{m,t}; w^*) \geq f(s_{n,t}; w^*) \\ -1 & \text{otherwise} \end{cases}$$

This means that a positive reward is given for policy π_m when the likelihood of object presence as measured by the trained object presence classifier for the window $s_{m,t}$, given by $f(s_{m,t}; w^*)$, is greater than the likelihood of object presence for the window $s_{n,t}$, given by $f(s_{n,t}; w^*)$.

The reward for π_n is just the opposite of reward for π_m and is given by $R_{n,t} = -R_{m,t}$.

Despite training of the object presence classifier using only image-level labels (as outlined in Sect. 2.1), it can be used for inference on windows, where the windows can be resized to the original image size for classifier inference, similar to previous work [25,29,35]. This serves as a linkage function which links image-level labels to windows, despite training only with image-level labels. The difference in appearances between images and windows may impact classifier likelihood predictions. However, the competing mechanism described above ensures that such impact is minimised as rewards for training are only based on a comparison of window-level likelihoods rather than exact values.

Policy Optimisation: The state, action, reward triplets are collected for a total of T time-steps for both policies, giving $\tau_m = (s_{m,0}, a_{m,0}, R_{m,0}, \ldots, s_{m,T}, a_{m,T}, R_{m,T})$ and $\tau_n = (s_{n,0}, a_{n,0}, R_{n,0}, \ldots, s_{n,T}, a_{n,T}, R_{n,T})$. The return over these time-steps is given by $R(\tau) = \sum_{k=0}^{T} \gamma^k R_{t+k}$. Where $R(\tau_m)$ and $R(\tau_n)$ denote the returns for policy π_m and π_n respectively. The optimisation problem is formulated as:

$$\theta^* = \arg\max_{\theta}\{\mathbb{E}_{\tau_m}[R(\tau_m)] + \mathbb{E}_{\tau_n}[R(\tau_n)]\}$$

2.4 Segmentation of New Samples

The optimised policy $\pi(\cdot; \theta^*)$ can then be used to conduct the segmentation for a new sample x_n. The state starts out as a window in the centre of the image $s_0 = x_n^{(a_0,b_0,c_0)}$ and following the optimised policy $\pi(\cdot; \theta^*)$ produces a trajectory of states and actions $(s_0, a_0, ..., s_E, a_E)$, where E denotes the iteration at which the object presence classifier reaches a threshold $f(x_n^{a_E,b_E,c_E}; w^*) > \rho$, where ρ is the threshold that ensures localisation has reached a sufficient accuracy (configured through a grid search as outlined in experiments). The segmentation map is assembled using object presence classifier outputs for each window $(f(x_n^{a_0,b_0,c_0}; w^*), .., f(x_n^{a_E,b_E,c_E}; w^*))$ where the voxel-level probabilities for each window are denoted by $f(x_n^{a_t,b_t,c_t}; w^*)$. A full segmentation map z_n starts out with all voxel-level probabilities being 0, the probability values for a window in the segmentation map $z_n^{a_t,b_t,c_t}$ is updated as $z_n^{a_t,b_t,c_t} \leftarrow z_n^{a_t,b_t,c_t} + f(x_n^{a_t,b_t,c_t}; w^*)$. Starting with voxel-level probabilities being 0 allows the agents to minimise placing windows in locations where the ROI is extremely unlikely to exist as these voxel-level probabilities can be left unchanged throughout the localisation process. Accumulating the voxel-level probabilities for all time-steps until E, we get the final voxel-level probability map, which can be thresholded to obtain the final segmentation. The threshold for obtaining the final segmentation can be optimised per-application, which allows additional flexibility.

3 Experiments

3.1 Dataset

In our experiments we use 131 portal venous phase 3D computed tomography (CT) scans from diagnosed patients in the Liver Tumour Segmentation Benchmark (LiTS) dataset, each depicting zero to twelve clinically significant primary and secondary liver tumours [2]. Each scan is accompanied by voxel-level annotations produced by experienced radiologists with values 0 (non-hepatic tissue), 1 (non-cancerous hepatic tissue) and 2 (cancerous hepatic tissue) as ground truth labels. Binary image-level labels (0 for non-cancerous tissue and 1 for cancerous tissue) were derived from these voxel-level labels during training and testing. The development-to-testing ratio for this dataset was 3:2.

3.2 Model Architectures

The object presence classifier f consists of 4 convolutional blocks (3D convolutional layer with a $(3 \times 3 \times 3)$ kernel, 3D batch normalisation and rectified linear unit (ReLu) followed by 3D max pooling with a $(2 \times 2 \times 2)$ kernel) and 5 fully connected layers (with ReLU activations).

The RL policy follows the same architecture, with the only change being in the final output layer. The policy optimisation [30] uses only the experience from π_m for training in our experiments.

For other hyper-parameter settings please refer to experiments (specified as appropriate) or code available in open-source repository.

The classifier took approximately 12 h to train, and RL took approximately 96 h, on a single Nvidia Tesla V100 GPU. The classifier inference time on the same hardware was 126 ms and the RL inference time to obtain the final segmentation was 1.8 s on average.

3.3 Experimental Protocol and Comparisons

Ablations: In our framework, we evaluate the impact of the training dataset size for the object presence classifier as well as the impact of hyper-parameters including the window size and threshold ρ which controls the termination of the final segmentation when a sufficient accuracy has been reached.

Comparisons: We compare our method with recent state-of-the-art weakly-supervised methods based on multi-instance learning [20], class-activation maps [19], RL [29] and region-classification [6,15,34] for the same task on the same dataset and also with recent state-of-the-art fully-supervised methods including recent state-of-the-art for the task [22] and other common baselines [8,14,26].

4 Results

4.1 Ablations

Training Set Size for Object Presence Classifier: Figure 2, increasing sample size leads to a positive trend in the four performance metrics overall. This result aligns with those of Althian et al. [3], which found that their neural network performance metrics decrease with smaller training datasets. In terms of the network's true positive and negative rates, the algorithm's specificity is consistently lower than its sensitivity regardless of sample size, which suggests that it may over-predict positive cancer classes.

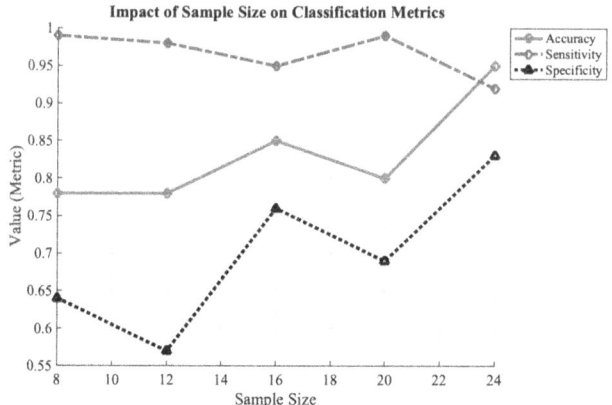

Fig. 2. Training set size against segmentation performance.

Impact of Window Size: Figure 3 shows that increasing the size of the window (state observed by an agent), tends to result in an increase in the mean dice score for the final segmentation, until it reaches a plateau after a window size of $32 \times 32 \times 16$. After this point, the mean dice score tends to stabilise.

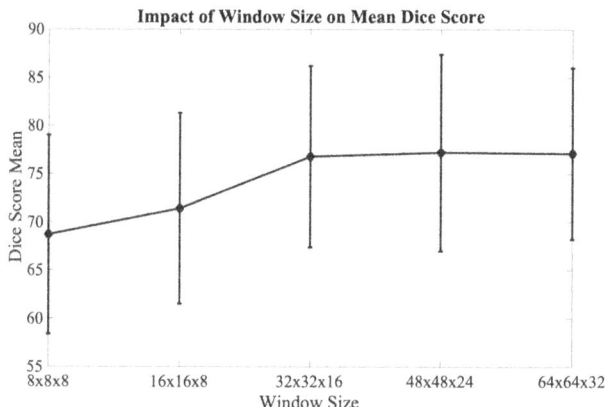

Fig. 3. Window size against segmentation performance.

Impact of Termination Threshold: Figure 4 shows that increasing the threshold that controls termination leads to an increase in mean dice score for the final segmentation, until 0.3, where the mean dice score begins to decline. This suggests that the output from the object presence classifier at a single time-step may be relatively low $f(s_{t_a}; w^*), f(s_{t_b}; w^*) \leq 0.3$. As a result, final predicted classifications primarily rely on accumulated predictions over a trajectory instead of over a single time-step.

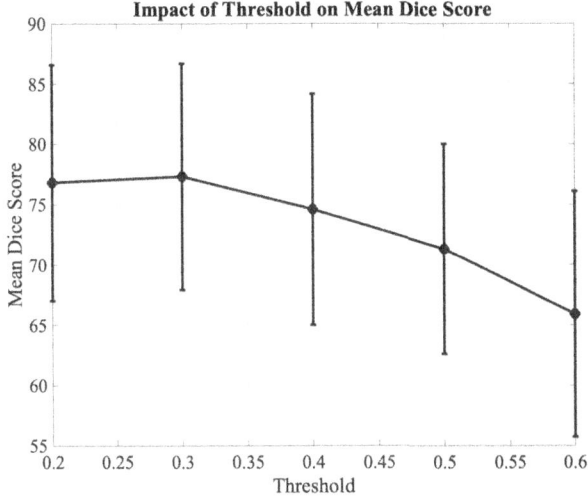

Fig. 4. Threshold against segmentation performance.

4.2 Comparisons

Comparisons with Weakly-Supervised Methods: Table 1 and Fig. 5 show
that our approach yielded in a mean dice score (Dice) 6.6% points higher than the
previous state-of-the-art method [29]. The Dice of 77.3 achieved by our method
not only outperforms the tested WSSS algorithms but aligns with recent fully-
supervised methods. Statistical tests were not conducted due to the absence of
standard deviations on reported dice scores for other methods.

Table 1. Performance compared to other models for liver tumour segmentation.
(Adapted from [29])

Method	Supervision	Dice	mIoU
SIPE [6]	Weak	66.1	49.3
MCT [34]	Weak	67.1	50.5
MIL [20]	Weak	67.4	50.8
ACR [19]	Weak	67.9	51.4
RCA [36]	Weak	68.8	52.4
MARS [15]	Weak	68.6	52.2
Patch-RLSP [27]	Weak	70.7	54.7
U-Net [26]	Full	74.5	59.3
nnU-Net [14]	Full	76.0	61.3
CLIP [22]	Full	79.4	65.8
SPARS(ours)	Weak	77.3	62.9

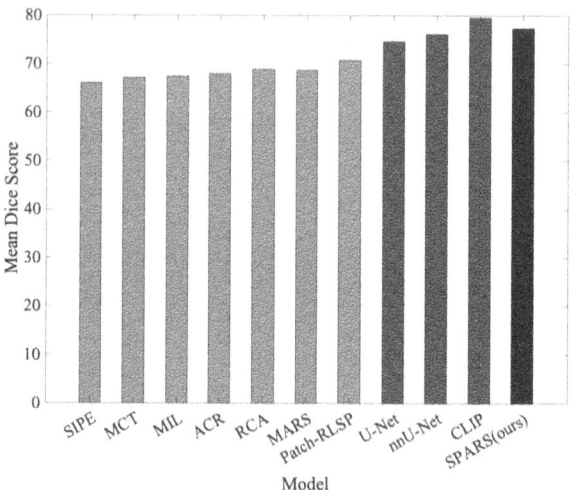

Fig. 5. Performance compared to other models for liver tumour segmentation (U-Net, nnU-Net and CLIP are fully-supervised and rest are all weakly-supervised).

Comparisons with Fully-Supervised Methods: Table 1 and Fig. 5 show that our approach outperformed several existing fully-supervised models including U-Net (Dice = 74.5) and performed comparably to CLIP which is the current state-of-the-art for the tested task (Dice = 79.4) [26], where our method only had 2.5% lower Dice (Dice = 77.3). However, the methods compared against, used the full segmentation labels for training which are much more costly to obtain compared to weak labels that are used in our method. Additionally, we only used 24 weak labels for training compared to over 64 full segmentation labels used by other methods. Statistical tests were not conducted due to the absence of standard deviations on reported dice scores for other methods.

4.3   Qualitative Results

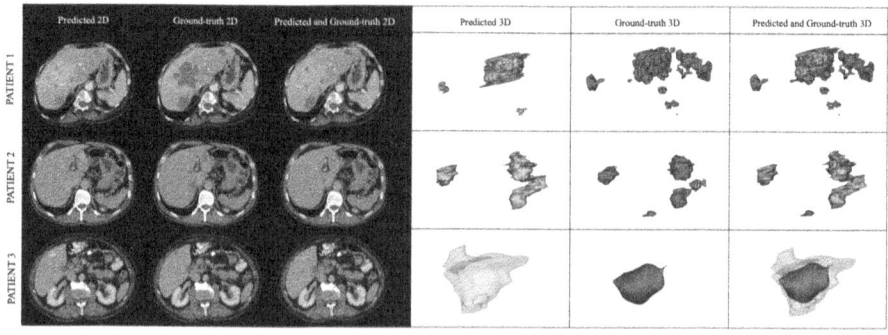

Fig. 6. Qualitative examples for a comparison between our predicted segmentations and ground-truth from radiologist annotations.

Figure 6 shows qualitative examples of predicted and ground truth liver tumour segmentations on patient data. We observed that larger tumours (volume $> 10^3$ mm^3) were under-segmented (Patient 1) compared to smaller tumours (Patients 2 and 3). We also observed a 24.5% lower average Dice for small tumours compared to their larger counterparts. Luan et al. [23] reported similar trends for their liver tumour segmentation framework where smaller tumours (< 0.2 cm) achieved a 60% lower mean dice score (Dice $= 0.32$) than larger tumours.

5   Discussion

We observed a large performance improvement for our method compared to the previous best-performing weakly-supervised method [29] for the same application. Despite both using self-play RL for WSSS, our method enables voxel level probability maps by accumulating the classifier predictions using a moving window (summarised in Sect. 2.4). This enables multiple passes over the same areas to increase segmentation confidence unlike previous patch-based approaches that only allow binary selection or rejection of patches or pixels [29]. This, along with the novel termination condition based on a thresholded classifier score, mean that our framework allows more flexibility in tuning thresholds and parameters for different applications. This application-specific tuning in our flexible framework may be the reason that we observed superior performance compared to recent state-of-the-art methods.

The ablation studies reveal the impact of key hyper-parameters on performance. The performance plateaus after a large enough window size. The performance improvement observed with increasing window size may be due to the fact that as windows become larger their appearance starts to match the appearance of full images. The performance peaks at termination threshold of 0.3, indicating that low thresholds may not be suitable as they may terminate segmentation too early (under-prediction) whereas high thresholds may terminate segmentation too late (over-prediction). The skew of the optimal threshold towards under-prediction may be because of an over representation of cancer-positive classes in the dataset.

Our method performed comparably with fully supervised approaches despite only using weak labels during training, which are much more cost-effective to obtain compared to voxel-level segmentation labels. This highlights that cost-effective training mechanisms like WSSS may be viable alternatives to fully-supervised learning when data is constrained or of poor quality.

Future investigation could explore alternative reward or termination conditions that allow greater flexibility for application-specific tuning, which may allow even further performance improvements.

6   Conclusion

In this work, we proposed self-play adversarial learning for semantic segmentation (SPARS) where agents compete to localise ROIs. Only weakly supervised labels were utilised to train an object presence classifier, which guides and scores the competition, allowing agents to move windows closer to ROIs. This approach successfully outperformed existing state-of-the-art WSSS models and performed comparably to fully-supervised method which used costly voxel-level segmentations for training. This highlights the cost-effective nature of weakly-supervised training with minimal compromise on performance compared to costly fully-supervised training.

Acknowledgements. This work is supported by the International Alliance for Cancer Early Detection, an alliance between Cancer Research UK [EDDAPA-2024/100014] & [C73666/A31378], Canary Center at Stanford University, the University of Cambridge, OHSU Knight Cancer Institute, University College London and the University of Manchester; and National Institute for Health Research University College London Hospitals Biomedical Research Centre.

References

1. Ahn, J., Kwak, S.: Learning pixel-level semantic affinity with image-level supervision for weakly supervised semantic segmentation. In: Proceedings of the IEEE Computer Society Conference on Computer Vision and Pattern Recognition, pp. 4981–4990 (2018). ISSN: 10636919. https://doi.org/10.1109/CVPR.2018.00523.
2. Bilic, P., et al.: The Liver Tumor Segmentation Benchmark (LiTS). In: Medical Image Analysis 84 (2023)
3. Althnian, A., et al.: Impact of dataset size on classification performance: an empirical evaluation in the medical domain. Appl. Sci. 11.2, 796 (2021)
4. Araslanov, N., Roth, S.: Single-stage semantic segmentation from image labels. In: Proceedings of the IEEE/CVF Conference on Computer Vision and Pattern Recognition, pp. 4253–4262 (2020)
5. Chalcroft, L.F., et al.: Development and evaluation of intraoperative ultrasound segmentation with negative image frames and multiple observer labels. In: Simplifying Medical Ultrasound: Second International Workshop, ASMUS 2021, Held in Conjunction with MICCAI 2021, Strasbourg, France, September 27, Proceedings 2. Springer. 2021, pp. 25–34 (2021)
6. Chen, Q., et al.: Self-supervised image-specific prototype exploration for weakly supervised semantic segmentation. In: Proceedings of the IEEE Computer Society Conference on Computer Vision and Pattern Recognition 2022-June, pp. 4278–4288 (2022)
7. Chierici, A., et al.: Vascular liver segmentation: a narrative review on methods and new insights brought by artificial intelligence. J. Int. Med. Res. 52.9 (2024)
8. Dan, C., et al.: Deep neural networks segment neuronal membranes in electron microscopy images (2012)
9. Czolbe, S., Arnavaz, K., Krause, O., Feragen, A.: Is Segmentation Uncertainty Useful? In: Feragen, A., Sommer, S., Schnabel, J., Nielsen, M. (eds.) IPMI 2021. LNCS, vol. 12729, pp. 715–726. Springer, Cham (2021). https://doi.org/10.1007/978-3-030-78191-0_55
10. Dai, J., He, K., Sun, J.: BoxSup: exploiting bounding boxes to supervise convolutional networks for semantic segmentation'. In: Proceedings of the IEEE International Conference on Computer Vision (2015). ISSN: 15505499. https://doi.org/10.1109/ICCV.2015.191.

11. Heimann, T., et al.: Comparison and evaluation of methods for liver segmentation from CT datasets. IEEE Trans. Med. Imaging **28**, 1251–1265 (2009)
12. Hermoye, L., et al.: Liver segmentation in living liver transplant donors: comparison of semiautomatic and manual methods1. In: Radiology 234.1, pp. 171–178 (2005)
13. Hong, T.S., et al.: interobserver variability in target definition for hepatocellular carcinoma with and without portal vein thrombus: radiation therapy oncology group consensus guidelines. Int. J. Radiat. Oncol. Biol. phys. 89.4, 804 (2014)
14. Isensee, F., et al.: nnU-Net: a self-configuring method for deep learningbased biomedical image segmentation. In: Nat. Methods 2020 18:2, **18** (2020)
15. Jo, S., Yu, I., Kim, K.: Mars: Model-agnostic biased object removal without additional supervision for weakly-supervised semantic segmentation. In: Proceedings of the IEEE/CVF International Conference on Computer Vision, pp. 614–623 (2023)
16. Khoreva, A., et al.: simple does it: weakly supervised instance and semantic segmentation. In: Proceedings - 30th IEEE Conference on Computer Vision and Pattern Recognition, CVPR 2017 2017-January, pp. 1665–1674 (2016). https://doi.org/10.1109/CVPR.2017.181.
17. Kolesnikov, A., Lampert, C.H.: Seed, Expand and Constrain: Three Principles for Weakly-Supervised Image Segmentation. In: Leibe, B., Matas, J., Sebe, N., Welling, M. (eds.) ECCV 2016. LNCS, vol. 9908, pp. 695–711. Springer, Cham (2016). https://doi.org/10.1007/978-3-319-46493-0_42
18. Krokos, G., et al.: Evaluation of manual and automated approaches for segmentation and extraction of quantitative indices from [18F]FDG PET-CT images. Biomed. Phys. Eng. Express 10.2, 025007 (2024)
19. Kweon, H., Yoon, S.H., Yoon, K.J.: Weakly supervised semantic segmentation via adversarial learning of classifier and reconstructor. In: Proceedings of the IEEE Computer Society Conference on Computer Vision and Pattern Recognition (2023)
20. Li, K., et al.: Weakly supervised histopathology image segmentation with self-attention. In: Medical Image Analysis 86 (2023)
21. Lin, D., et al.: ScribbleSup: scribble-supervised convolutional networks for semantic segmentation. In: Proceedings of the IEEE Computer Society Conference on Computer Vision and Pattern Recognition 2016-December, pp. 3159–3167 (2016). ISSN: 10636919. https://doi.org/10.1109/CVPR.2016.344
22. Liu, J., et al.: CLIP-driven universal model for organ segmentation and tumor detection. In: Proceedings of the IEEE International Conference on Computer Vision, pp. 21095–21107 (2023). https://doi.org/10.1109/ICCV51070.2023.01934
23. Luan, S., et al.: Adaptive attention convolutional neural network for liver tumor segmentation. Front. Oncol. **11** (2021)
24. Pan, Z., et al.: Scribble-supervised semantic segmentation by uncertainty reduction on neural representation and self-supervision on neural eigenspace. In: Proceedings of the IEEE International Conference on Computer Vision, pp. 7396–7405 (2021). ISSN: 15505499. https://doi.org/10.1109/ICCV48922.2021.00732
25. Pocius, M.: Weakly supervised localisation of prostate cancer using reinforcement learning for bi-parametric MR images. In: IEEE International Symposium on Biomedical Imaging (ISBI). IEEE. vol. 2024. pp. 1–5 (2024)
26. Ronneberger, O., Fischer, P.: and Thomas Brox. Convolutional networks for biomedical image segmentation. Springer, U-net (2015)
27. Saeed, S.U., et al.: Active learning using adaptable task-based prioritisation. In: Med. Image Analy. **95**, 103181 (2024)
28. Saeed, S.U., et al.: Guided ultrasound acquisition for nonrigid image registration using reinforcement learning. Med. Image Analy. **102**, 103555 (2025)

29. Saeed, S.U., et al.: Competing for pixels: a self-play algorithm for weakly-supervised semantic segmentation. IEEE Trans. Pattern Analy. Mach. Intell. (2024)
30. Schulman, J., et al.: Proximal policy optimization algorithms. In: arXiv preprint arXiv:1707.06347 (2017)
31. Wang, P.M., et al.: Stereotactic body radiation therapy in hepatocellular carcinoma: optimal treatment strategies based on liver segmentation and functional hepatic reserve. In: Reports of Practical Oncology and Radiotherapy 20.6, 417–424 (2015)
32. Wei, Y., et al.: Revisiting dilated convolution: a simple approach for weakly- and semi- supervised semantic segmentation. In: Proceedings of the IEEE Computer Society Conference on Computer Vision and Pattern Recognition, pp. 7268–7277 (2018). ISSN: 10636919. https://doi.org/10.1109/CVPR.2018.00759
33. Wu, C.C., et al.: Occlusion of hepatic blood inflow for complex central liver resections in cirrhotic patients: a randomized comparison of hemihepatic and total hepatic occlusion techniques. Archives Surgery 137.12, 1369–1376 (2002)
34. Xu, L., et al.: Multi-class token transformer for weakly supervised semantic segmentation. In: Proceedings of the IEEE Computer Society Conference on Computer Vision and Pattern Recognition 2022-June, pp. 4300–4309 (2022)
35. Yi, W., et al.: Boundary-RL: reinforcement learning for weakly-supervised prostate segmentation in TRUS images. In: International Workshop on Machine Learning in Medical Imaging. Springer. pp. 277–288 (2023)
36. Zhou, T., et al.: Regional semantic contrast and aggregation for weakly supervised semantic segmentation. In: Proceedings of the IEEE Computer Society Conference on Computer Vision and Pattern Recognition 2022-June, pp. 4289–4299 (2022)

Semantic Segmentation with Spreading Scribbles

Yeva Gabrielyan[1]($\boxtimes$) (ID), Varduhi Yeghiazaryan[1] (ID), and Irina Voiculescu[2] (ID)

[1] American University of Armenia, Yerevan 0019, Armenia
`yeva_gabrielyan22@alumni.aua.am`, `vyeghiazaryan@aua.am`
[2] University of Oxford, Oxford, OX12JD, UK
`irina@cs.ox.ac.uk`

Abstract. Hand-annotating medical images with segmentation masks requires an immense amount of time and effort from clinical experts. Replacing full masks with a simpler annotating gesture can mitigate annotation costs. This can come in the form of a scribble, and leads to weakly supervised training scenarios. Scribble-supervised segmentation typically utilises advanced neural architectures to compensate for the limited training data. Instead of just relying strictly on the pixels from each scribble, we also enhance each scribble by spreading, i.e. propagating, annotation labels through the image. We use a hierarchical partitioning of the image, produced with watershed/waterfall transforms, and propagate the individual pixel labels through the waterfall regions. We propose that a semantic label can be propagated to all other pixels in the same waterfall region. This increases the number of pixels that can be used for training supervision. We show experimentally that this technique greatly boosts the performance of established neural architectures on public semantic segmentation datasets like ACDC and MSCMRseg.

Keywords: Scribble-supervised segmentation · Waterfall transform · Spreading scribbles

1 Introduction

Training deep learning (DL) models for medical image segmentation typically requires large-scale, pixel-wise annotated datasets, which are expensive and time-consuming to obtain. To mitigate the annotation burden, various learning paradigms have been explored. Weakly supervised learning (WSL) [12,22,41] aims to train models using sparse annotations, such as image-level labels [23], bounding boxes [20], key points [1], and scribbles [17]. Among these weak annotation types, scribbles provide a compelling balance between annotation efficiency and segmentation quality [17,28]. As a result, scribble-based supervision has gained traction in medical image segmentation, offering a practical alternative to dense manual labeling [12,14].

Scribble-Supervised Segmentation. Scribble annotations provide a cost-effective alternative to pixel-wise labeling, reducing the annotation burden.

S. Ali et al. (Eds.): MIUA 2025, LNCS 15918, pp. 73–87, 2026.
https://doi.org/10.1007/978-3-031-98694-9_6

Established techniques such as GraphCuts [3], GrabCut [25], Random Walker [9], GrowCut [30], ITK-SNAP [38], Slic-Seg [39], propagate sparse annotations into dense segmentation masks. More recently, DL-based methods have used scribble annotations to train segmentation models. Lin et al. [17] propose a graphical-model-based method to expand scribbles, while Tang et al. [27] integrate conditional random field (CRF) regularisation as a loss function to refine segmentation predictions. Can et al. [4] propose to iteratively refine predictions with CRF post-processing to enhance segmentation accuracy from scribbles.

Although these methods are effective, they often require iterative relabeling or additional constraints to improve the quality of supervision. Alternative strategies include leveraging adversarial training [28] or uncertainty-aware mean teachers [18] to enforce structural consistency in segmentation masks. These strategies primarily focus on refining network predictions rather than directly enhancing the scribble annotations themselves. Consequently, the quality of the initial annotations remains a limiting factor.

Data Augmentation for Semantic Segmentation. Data augmentation plays a crucial role in mitigating overfitting and improving generalisation in DL models. Conventional augmentation techniques such as rotation, flipping, and elastic deformations have been widely employed in medical image segmentation. More advanced augmentation methods, such as mixup strategies [39], involve blending multiple images and their labels to generate new training samples. Manifold MixUp [29] extends this approach to intermediate feature representations, while CutMix [37] replaces image regions with patches from other samples to enhance diversity. In the context of weakly supervised learning, augmentation techniques have been adapted to improve performance. Chaitanya et al. [6] demonstrate that mixup augmentation can enhance semi-supervised segmentation by enforcing smooth transitions in the label space. All these methods primarily focus on image-level augmentations, rather than directly improving weak annotations such as scribbles.

Enhancement of Weak Annotations. While prior works have explored augmentation techniques for image data, fewer studies have focused on the enhancement of weak annotations. Most existing methods either attempt to refine scribble-based annotations through graphical propagation [17] or employ DL models to generate pseudo-labels [15,18]. However, these approaches often require additional supervision or iterative training, limiting their efficiency.

Our Contribution. Our algorithm directly enhances an initial set of scribble annotations before using them for model training. Instead of relying on DL-based relabelling, our method spreads scribble annotations systematically across the image, improving their spatial coverage and effectiveness as weak labels. By generating scribble-based training labels in this way, we demonstrate that deep segmentation models trained on our enhanced labels mostly outperform those using raw scribble annotations. Our approach provides a novel alternative to existing weak annotation techniques by enhancing the initial annotation quality rather than relying on iterative refinement or additional network components.

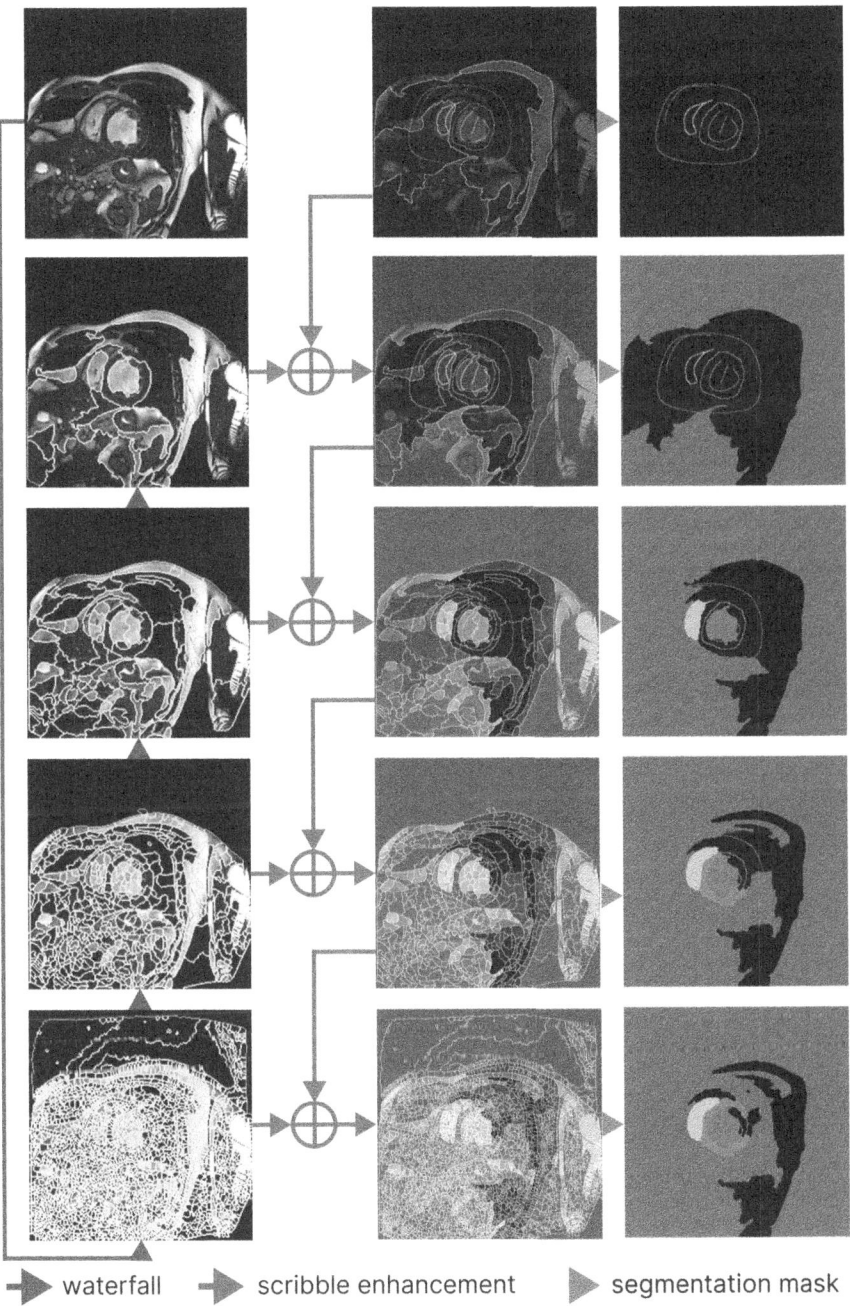

Fig. 1. Visualisation of the scribble spreading algorithm. Waterfall layers are constructed for the image. From the coarsest partitioning layer down to the finest, scribble pixel labels are propagated to all pixels in the same region, if no conflicting label is present. The bright overlay shows new labels; the pale overlay—the previous iteration.

2 Spreading Scribbles Using Hierarchical Waterfall Partitioning

We propose a novel technique for spreading scribbles across an image to construct a spatially enhanced set of labels. The scribble spreading process is visualised in Fig. 1. Our approach relies on hierarchical partitioning of the image into semantically meaningful regions using the waterfall transform. The waterfall transform [2,8] is a hierarchical image partitioning approach that is based on the watershed transform [2,24]. These transforms utilise the variations in the gradient magnitude values across the image to partition it into regions of similar-intensity pixels. There are fast parallel algorithms for the GPU execution of the watershed and waterfall transforms [7,34,36].

Algorithm 1. Scribble Spreading Using Waterfall Transform

1: **Input:** Image I with pixel domain Ω and scribble mask S
2: **Output:** Enhanced mask E
3: Let value *unknown* indicate unlabelled pixels in S
4: Initialise $E = S$
5: Construct hierarchical waterfall partitioning $WF = \{L_0, L_1, L_2, L_3, L_4\}$
6: Reverse layer sequence $\overline{WF} = \{L_4, L_3, L_2, L_1, L_0\}$
7: **for each** $L \in \overline{WF}$ **do**
8:     Initialise an empty region-to-label map Map
9:     **for each** pixel $p \in \Omega$ **do**
10:         **if** $S(p) \neq unknown$ **then**
11:             **if** $L(p) \notin Map$ **then**
12:                 $Map(L(p)) = S(p)$
13:             **else if** $Map(L(p)) \neq S(p)$ **then**
14:                 $Map(L(p)) = unknown$
15:             **end if**
16:         **end if**
17:     **end for**
18:     **for each** pixel $p \in \Omega$ **do**
19:         **if** $E(p) = unknown$ **and** $L(p) \in Map$ **and** $Map(L(p)) \neq unknown$ **then**
20:             $E(p) = Map(L(p))$
21:         **end if**
22:     **end for**
23: **end for**
24: **return** E

The proposed approach for constructing enhanced labels by spreading scribbles is presented in Algorithm 1. For each 2D slice in a 3D medical image volume, our approach constructs a hierarchical partitioning of the image into regions of decreasing granularity by applying the waterfall transform for five layers. The layers are then considered in reverse order—from coarsest to finest. Per partitioning layer L, for each pixel p with a scribble label $S(p)$, its label is considered for spreading throughout the whole partitioning region. If there is another pixel

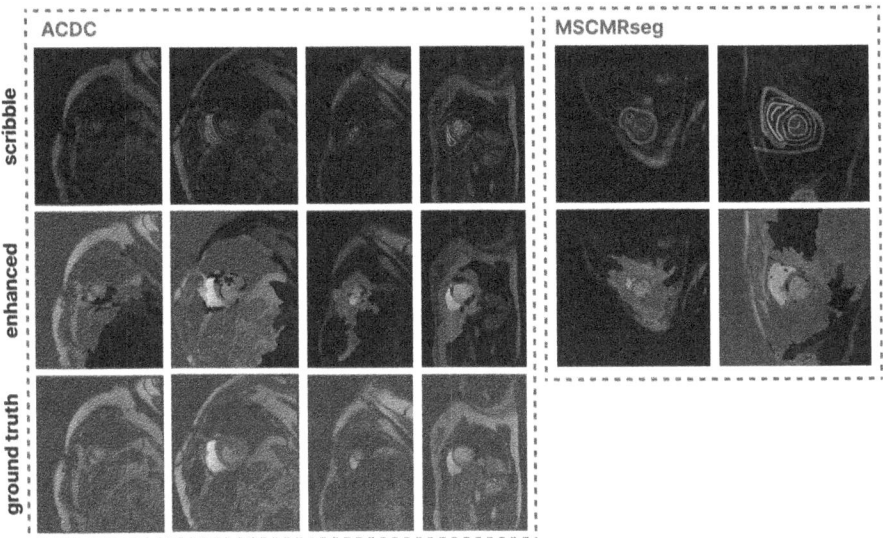

Fig. 2. Scribble spreading results from sample images from the ACDC and MSCMRseg datasets, compared against the ground truth where possible. Ground-truth masks are not available for the training images in MSCMRseg. Enhanced labels are only approximations of the expected masks. They may contain inaccurate labels on a portion of pixels.

in the same region with a *different* scribble label, then none of the labels is spread. An efficient implementation of this logic is achieved by maintaining a mapping from regions into corresponding label candidates. Eventually, regions with a *unique* label candidate are 'flooded' with that label. By considering the layers in reverse order, we spread scribbles across larger regions first, then complement those with further incremental spreading in smaller regions. Figure 2 illustrates several examples of scribble spreading on slices from the ACDC and MSCMRseg datasets.

2.1 Limitations

The proposed scribble spreading algorithm has two main limitations.

- When no labels are present or multiple conflicting labels are present in the same partitioning region, no label propagation is performed. This may result in swathes of the image left without labels. This effect can be seen especially in the third, fourth, and fifth columns of Fig. 2.
- Since partitioning region boundaries do not necessarily align with semantic boundaries, enhanced labels only approximate the expected masks and may contain inaccurate labels on a portion of pixels. In Fig. 2, inaccuracies around region boundaries can be easily traced when comparing the enhanced labels and ground-truth masks for ACDC samples.

3   Experimental Setup

3.1   Datasets

We evaluate the performance of our label enhancement framework on the two scribble-based datasets below.

ACDC dataset consists of cine-MRI scans of 150 patients. Scribble annotations are provided for 100 patients and used to generate the training and validation sets. We use a five-fold cross-validation method, allocating 80 scans for training and 20 for validation. The remaining 50 cases, which do not have scribble annotations, are used as the test set.

MSCMRseg dataset consists of late gadolinium enhancement MRI scans, from 45 patients diagnosed with cardiomyopathy. The dataset is split into 25 scans for training, 5 scans for validation, and 15 scans for testing. We aggregate and report results from five different runs.

Both datasets are annotated for three classes: left ventricle (LV), right ventricle (RV), and myocardium (MYO). All reported results are averages across the three classes.

3.2   Scribble-Supervised Segmentation Algorithms

To demonstrate the effectiveness of our scribble-spreading method, we conduct a comprehensive comparison of the performance of different state-of-the-art (SOTA) methods trained on the original scribbles versus those trained on the enhanced labels produced by spreading scribbles with our algorithm. In this experiment we include the following methods.

A Baseline fully-supervised segmentation methods including ENet [21], CCT-UNet [33], DS-UNet [11], Efficient UNet [26], PNet [31] and SwinNet [5]. All of these methods are created for the task of medical image segmentation and use either UNet-like architectures or transformers.
B Several scribble-supervised loss strategies for UNet from the literature, such as partial cross entropy (UNet$_{pce}$) [17], uncertainty-aware self-ensembling and transformation-consistent loss (UNet$_{ustr}$) [18], or Mumford–Shah loss (UNet$_{mloss}$) [13], entropy minimization (UNet$_{em}$) [10], and gated conditional random field (UNet$_{crf}$) [40].
C Pseudo-label-based methods such as ScribbleToLabel (S2L) [15], dynamically mixed pseudo labels supervision (DMPLS) [19], dense combinations of dense pseudo-labels (DCDPL) [32], and ScribbleVC [16].

3.3   Evaluation Measures

For evaluation purposes during the testing phase, the 2D slice-by-slice predictions are stacked into a 3D volume. The model used for inference is the one that achieved the best validation score during training, ensuring optimal performance.

To ensure a fair comparison, no post-processing methods are applied. We use the 3D Dice similarity coefficient (DSC), the 95th percentile of the Hausdorff distance (HD95), and Average surface distance (ASD) [35] to evaluate the similarity and differences between the predicted mask and the ground truth. HD95 and ASD are measured in mm. Good performance is reflected in large DSC and small HD95 and ASD.

3.4 Implementation Details

For the experimental setup, we followed the approach proposed in [19]. As a pre-processing step, the intensities of each slice were re-scaled to the range $[0, 1]$. Subsequently, data augmentation techniques such as random rotation, random flipping, and random noise were applied to enhance the training set. The batch size was set to 12, and the total number of iterations was 60K. All methods were implemented using PyTorch and executed on machines equipped with GeForce RTX 3060 and GTX 1080 GPUs.

4   Results and Discussion

4.1   Qualitative Results Analysis

A qualitative comparative analysis of the performance of six segmentation methods (UNet$_{crf}$, DCDPL, S2L, UNet$_{em}$, ENet, CCT-UNet) on the ACDC dataset is presented in Fig. 3. For each image and each method, results for both original scribbles and enhanced labels are shown. Clear false-positive mistakes with the original setup, but not the enhanced setup, can be seen for S2L, UNet$_{em}$, ENet, CCT-UNet. Across most architectures, enhanced labels lead to improvement in boundary delineation, evident by the improved ASD score. However, the degree of improvement significantly varies depending on the model.

Models like CCT-UNet and ENet exhibit the most substantial improvements when using enhanced labels, reducing ASD and HD95 by over 100 mm for all three example volumes and increasing DSC by at least 30%. This indicates that these architectures are highly dependent on the amount of provided scribbles to achieve high-quality segmentation. Similar performance improvements are observed with the UNet$_{em}$ and S2L models, especially in examples (b) and (c). Although for volume (a) enhanced labels show slightly worse performance, the reduction is marginal.

For models UNet$_{crf}$ and DCDPL, enhancement of labels leads to degradation of scores, in particular DSC. This implies that these models are more robust to the amount of scribble labelling provided. However, UNet$_{crf}$ still generally benefits from spreading scribbles, due to improvements in boundary precision (lower ASD). In case of DCDPL, scribble spreading worsens performance on all three volumes, possibly due to the introduction of inaccurate labels during the enhancement process.

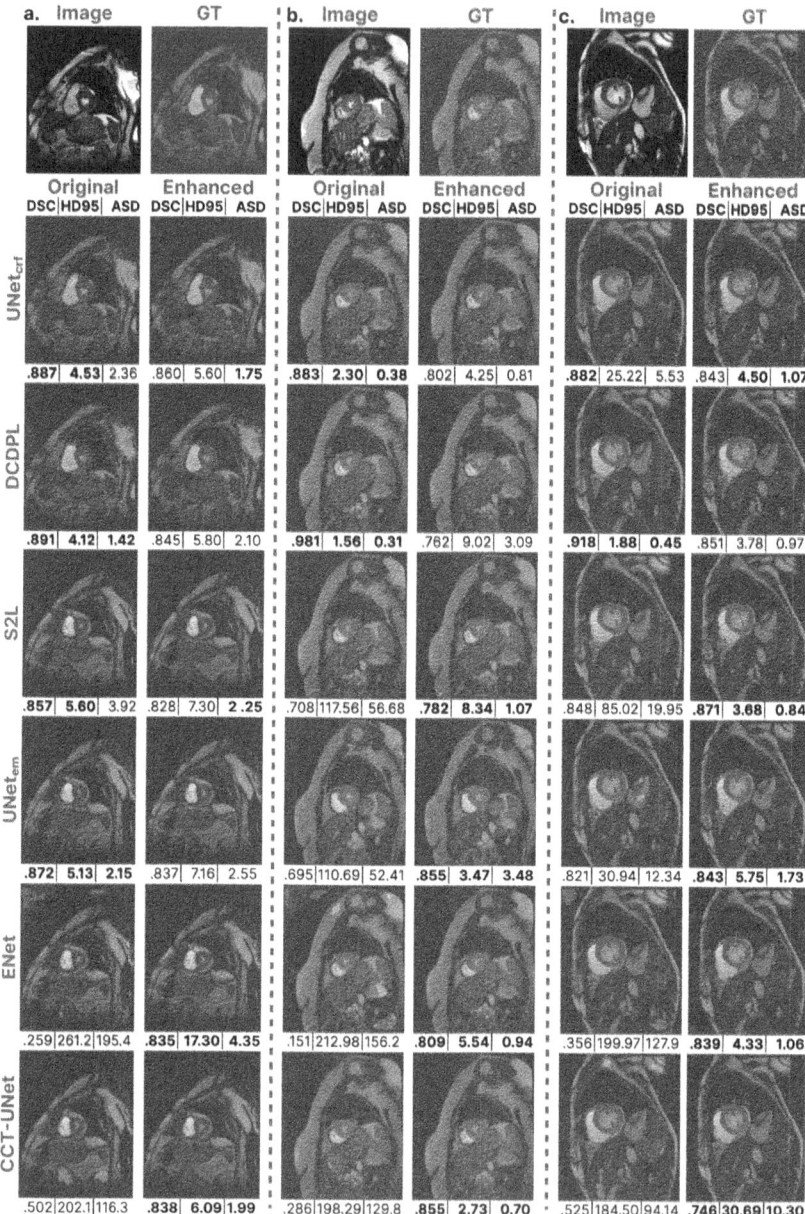

Fig. 3. Comparison of segmentation performance using original scribbles and enhanced labels on three scans (a, b, c) from ACDC. The first row displays the original MRI slice and ground truth (GT), while subsequent rows show segmentation results from different models: UNet$_{crf}$, DCDPL, S2L, UNet$_{em}$, ENet, and CCT-UNet. DSC, ASD, and HD95 scores for the whole 3D scan are reported for both original and enhanced training setups. Clear false-positive mistakes with the original setup, but not the enhanced setup, can be seen for S2L, UNet$_{em}$, ENet, CCT-UNet.

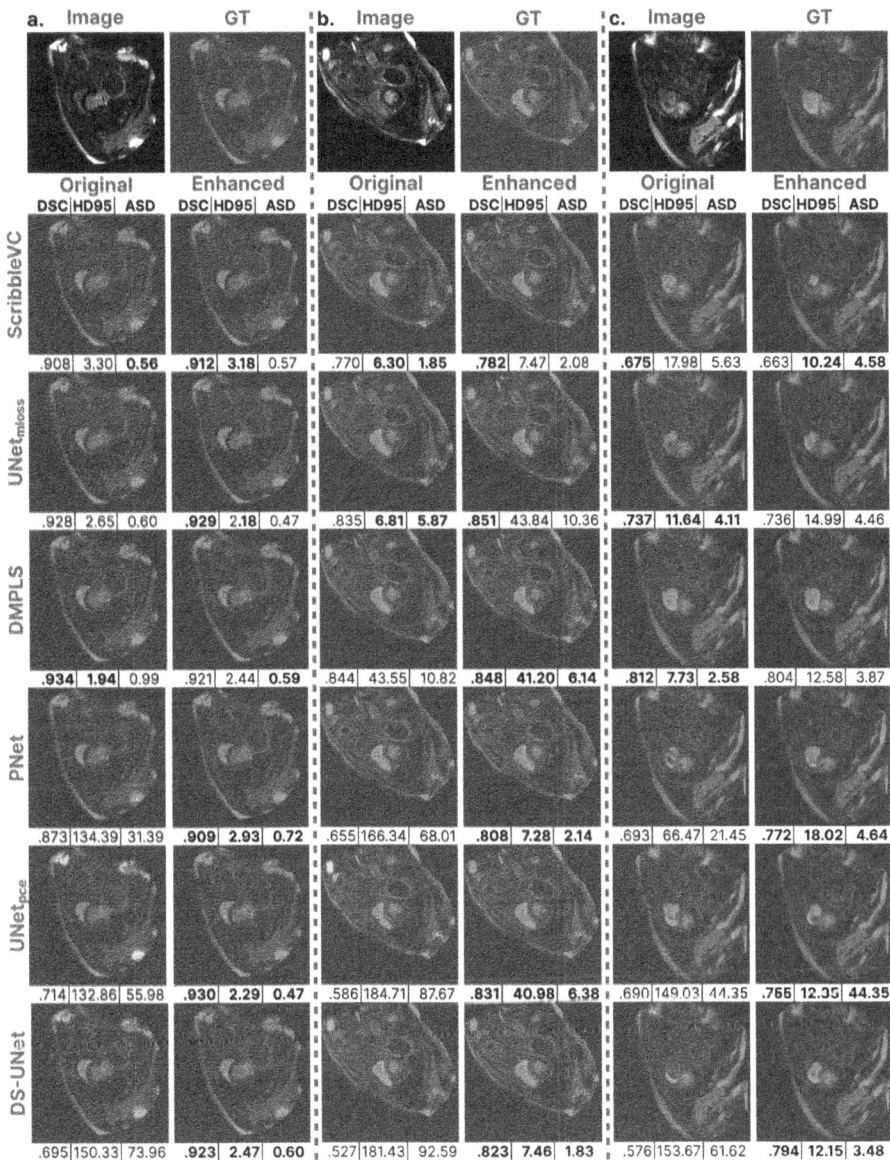

Fig. 4. Comparison of segmentation performance using original scribbles and enhanced labels on three scans (a, b, c) from MSCMRseg. The first row displays the original MRI slice and ground truth (GT), while subsequent rows show segmentation results from different models: ScribbleVC, UNet$_{mloss}$, DMPLS, PNet, UNet$_{pce}$, and DS-UNet. DSC, ASD, and HD95 scores for the whole 3D scan are reported for both original and enhanced training setups. Clear false-positive mistakes with the original setup, but not the enhanced setup, can be seen for PNet, UNet$_{mloss}$, DS-UNet.

The qualitative results on the MSCMRseg dataset (Fig. 4) show six more methods (ScribbleVC, UNet$_{mloss}$, DMPLS, PNet, UNet$_{pce}$, DS-UNet), complementary to those in Fig. 3 on ACDC. Notably, for most image–method combinations the performance in the enhanced setup shows a clear performance improvement over the original scribble setup. Compared to ACDC, fewer cases show performance degradation for MSCMRseg. This can be potentially explained by the MSCMRseg training set consisting of around three times fewer MRI volumes than the ACDC training set. The enhancement of labels through spreading scribbles boosts the amount of supervision data, even if not completely reliably.

While UNet$_{mloss}$ does exhibit some regression of boundary measures (HD95 and ASD) in volume (b), the effects are not severe but are isolated. This may suggest that the relationship between scribble quality and model performance varies across different medical imaging modalities and anatomical targets.

4.2   Quantitative Results Analysis

The full performance of all segmentation methods, with the original and enhanced setups, is reported in Table 1 for ACDC and Table 2 for MSCMRseg. It can be seen that using the enhanced setup improves performance according to at least two of the three performance measures for twelve and ten methods for ACDC and MSCMRseg, respectively. In some cases, the DSC improvement reaches more than 35%; HD95 and ASD go down from three-digit to single-digit numbers.

In general, in the enhanced setup, the performance scores of the different algorithms are very close: most DSC are above 0.8, HD95 is around 6–9 mm and ASD is around 1–3 mm.

Using the enhanced labels mostly degrades the performance of UNet$_{crf}$, DCDPL, and ScribbleVC. The latter two are SOTA pseudo-label-based methods. We can hypothesise that the training guidance provided by the pseudo-labels does not align with the enhanced labels in these particular cases. More effort is required to identify how these two techniques can be combined to improve performance. In case of UNet$_{crf}$, the assumption is that the potential presence of mislabelled pixels in the enhanced setup misleads the network when used with the *crf* loss.

For ACDC, the best DSC score of .883 is achieved with the original setup of DMPLS; HD95 of 5.48 mm and ASD of 1.39 mm with the original setup of DCDPL. For MSCMRseg, the original setup of DMPLS gets the best DSC of .886; the best HD95 of 6.26 mm is achieved with the *enhanced* setup of ENet. The best two ASD scores of 1.69 mm and 1.71 mm are observed for the original ScribbleVC and the *enhanced* Efficient UNet, respectively. Thus, baseline methods originally proposed for fully supervised segmentation can outperform pseudo-label-based methods specifically designed for scribble-supervised learning, if enhanced labels, produced by spreading scribbles with our algorithm, are used for training.

Table 1. Comparison of various segmentation methods on the ACDC dataset using original scribbles and enhanced labels. The performance of the models is evaluated using DSC, HD95, and ASD scores. The models are categorised into three groups: general segmentation models, scribble-supervised UNet variants, and models utilising pseudo-labeling to enhance weak supervision. In each row, the bold number indicates the best performance.

	Original			Enhanced		
	DSC	HD95	ASD	DSC	HD95	ASD
ENet [21]	.508	178.16	91.31	**.818**	**7.49**	**2.17**
	±.152	±31.39	±33.56	±.028	±1.91	±0.72
CCT-UNet [33]	.602	168.83	77.48	**.835**	**8.55**	**2.54**
	±.046	±6.27	±7.90	±.005	±2.01	±0.67
DS-UNet [11]	.628	169.80	75.07	**.832**	**11.09**	**2.95**
	±.041	±8.09	±10.25	±.013	±6.30	±1.68
Efficient UNet [26]	.780	85.01	27.86	**.839**	**6.78**	**1.94**
	±.003	±11.27	±3.24	±.007	±0.92	±0.30
PNet [31]	.813	79.87	22.27	**.827**	**8.43**	**2.57**
	±.010	±10.64	±4.09	±.008	±1.91	±0.55
SwinUNet [5]	**.855**	25.67	7.51	.745	**12.00**	**4.04**
	±.012	±5.63	±1.15	±.055	±3.29	±1.70
Different scribble-supervised strategies on UNet						
$UNet_{pce}$ [17]	.631	165.13	72.35	**.837**	**9.58**	**2.62**
	±.003	±5.14	±5.56	±.006	±2.04	±0.56
$UNet_{ustr}$ [18]	.815	77.68	23.48	**.826**	**10.41**	**2.72**
	±.020	±21.29	±6.52	±.009	±3.42	±0.87
$UNet_{mloss}$ [13]	**.864**	13.33	3.61	.834	**8.00**	**2.03**
	±.010	±4.55	±1.12	±.009	±1.45	±0.30
$UNet_{em}$ [10]	**.853**	37.36	10.52	.837	**9.58**	**2.62**
	±.010	+5.03	±1.27	±.006	⊥1.17	±0.37
$UNet_{crf}$ [40]	**.869**	**6.00**	**1.92**	.829	8.39	2.34
	±.001	±1.25	±0.31	±.006	±2.86	±0.83
Pseudo-label-based methods						
S2L [15]	**.846**	44.16	12.81	.838	**7.30**	**1.97**
	±.001	±8.40	±2.43	±.011	±1.53	±0.49
DMPLS [19]	**.883**	9.19	2.41	.837	**6.84**	**1.95**
	±.001	±1.40	±0.21	±.008	±0.76	±0.26
DCDPL [32]	**.874**	**5.48**	**1.39**	.824	6.56	1.88
	±.020	±1.07	±0.33	±.014	±1.50	±0.45
ScribbleVC [16]	**.860**	**5.94**	**1.42**	.817	6.49	1.58
	±.009	±0.57	±0.21	±.010	±0.66	±1.58

Table 2. Comparison of various segmentation methods on the MSCMRseg dataset using original scribbles and enhanced labels. The performance of the models is evaluated using DSC, HD95, and ASD scores. The models are categorised into three groups: general segmentation models, scribble-supervised UNet variants, and models utilising pseudo-labeling to enhance weak supervision. In each row, the bold number indicates the best performance.

	Original			Enhanced		
	DSC	HD95	ASD	DSC	HD95	ASD
ENet [21]	.473	185.76	110.82	**.836**	**6.26**	**1.95**
	±.030	±1.89	±0.98	±.034	±1.41	±0.63
CCT-UNet [33]	.682	138.44	58.73	**.858**	**10.04**	**2.71**
	±.019	±11.93	±7.78	±.016	±3.71	±1.05
DS-UNet [11]	.666	143.57	64.57	**.871**	**9.89**	**2.81**
	±.016	±3.55	±4.12	±.005	±3.70	±1.02
Efficient UNet [26]	.735	95.88	35.93	**.868**	**6.49**	**1.71**
	±.017	±22.35	±9.55	±.003	±0.11	±0.07
PNet [31]	.794	112.02	34.26	**.853**	**7.61**	**2.26**
	±.012	±18.10	±6.98	±.005	±1.79	±0.57
SwinUNet [5]	**.726**	36.66	10.26	.712	**10.15**	**3.34**
	±.003	±2.61	±0.05	±.007	±0.36	±0.07
Different scribble-supervised strategies on UNet						
UNet$_{pce}$ [17]	.670	143.67	65.00	**.869**	**8.30**	**2.39**
	±.026	±4.47	±8.87	±.006	±3.91	±0.90
UNet$_{ustr}$ [18]	.758	130.84	50.49	**.866**	**7.30**	**2.40**
	±.004	±5.95	±1.42	±.003	±1.52	±0.69
UNet$_{mloss}$ [13]	**.870**	**9.01**	**2.47**	.865	9.96	2.61
	±.004	±3.88	±0.62	±.004	±3.35	±0.89
UNet$_{em}$ [10]	.859	34.38	9.57	**.864**	**8.45**	**2.58**
	±.005	±6.73	±2.15	±.004	±1.98	±0.42
UNet$_{crf}$ [40]	**.877**	**6.72**	**1.85**	.864	7.10	1.98
	±.004	±2.05	±0.31	±.003	±1.54	±0.37
Pseudo-label-based methods						
S2L [15]	.840	67.98	21.08	**.846**	**59.61**	**17.95**
	±.015	±14.19	±5.97	±.008	±12.46	±3.61
DMPLS [19]	**.886**	**8.81**	**2.69**	.877	10.54	3.05
	±.002	±0.99	±0.60	±.005	±2.56	±1.00
DCDPL [32]	**.854**	**8.63**	2.51	.777	9.24	**2.38**
	±.022	±0.95	±0.20	±.014	±1.88	±0.38
ScribbleVC [16]	**.851**	**6.58**	1.69	.820	7.19	1.85
	±.022	±0.95	±0.20	±.014	±1.88	±0.38

5   Conclusion

Since gesture-based scribble annotations are more lax and less time-consuming than contour drawing, these make semantic segmentation tasks more easily achievable with less effort. The additional cost is that of pre-processing the images into waterfall regions, which is a fully automated task requiring minimal (parallel) compute. Scribble-based segmentation is best suited to tasks where the boundary of the feature is clear and without further aleatoric uncertainty.

Our waterfall-based enhancement of scribble labels proved most effective for classic deep learning architectures with simpler loss functions, not specifically designed for scribble supervision. These models, trained on the enhanced labels, performed in par with the pseudo-label-based models targeted for the scribble-supervised segmentation task. The architectures with multiple loss functions for weakly supervised learning, on the other hand, did not benefit much, or not at all, from the proposed enhancement.

Future work will explore how our scribble-spreading method can be better utilised in pseudo-label-based models to further improve performance.

Acknowledgments. This study was funded by the Afeyan Family Foundation Seed Fund for Collaborative Grants.

Disclosure of Interests. The authors have no competing interests to declare that are relevant to the content of this article.

References

1. Bearman, A., Russakovsky, O., Ferrari, V., Fei-Fei, L.: What's the point: semantic segmentation with point supervision. In: Computer Vision – ECCV 2016. pp. 549–565. Springer (2016)
2. Beucher, S.: Watershed, hierarchical segmentation and waterfall algorithm. In: Mathematical Morphology and Its Applications to Image Processing, pp. 69–76. Springer (1994)
3. Boykov, Y.Y., Jolly, M.P.: Interactive graph cuts for optimal boundary & region segmentation of objects in N-D images. In: Proceedings Eighth IEEE International Conference on Computer Vision. ICCV 2001. vol. 1, pp. 105–112 (2001)
4. Can, Y.B., Chaitanya, K., Mustafa, B., Koch, L.M., Konukoglu, E., Baumgartner, C.F.: Learning to segment medical images with scribble-supervision alone. In: Deep Learning in Medical Image Analysis and Multimodal Learning for Clinical Decision Support. DLMIA ML-CDS 2018. pp. 236–244. Springer (2018)
5. Cao, H., et al.: Swin-unet: Unet-like pure transformer for medical image segmentation. In: Computer Vision – ECCV 2022 Workshops. pp. 205–218. Springer (2023)
6. Chaitanya, K., Karani, N., Baumgartner, C.F., Becker, A., Donati, O., Konukoglu, E.: Semi-supervised and Task-Driven Data Augmentation. In: Chung, A., Gee, J.C., Yushkevich, P.A., Bao, S. (eds.) IPMI 2019. LNCS, vol. 11492, pp. 29–41. Springer, Cham (2019). https://doi.org/10.1007/978-3-030-20351-1_3
7. Gabrielyan, Y., Yeghiazaryan, V., Voiculescu, I.: Parallel partitioning: path reducing and union–find based watershed for the GPU. In: 2022 IEEE International Conference on Image Processing (ICIP). pp. 1501–1505 (2022)

8. Golodetz, S.M., Nicholls, C., Voiculescu, I.D., Cameron, S.A.: Two tree-based methods for the waterfall. Pattern Recogn. **47**(10), 3276–3292 (2014)
9. Grady, L.: Random walks for image segmentation. IEEE Trans. Pattern Anal. Mach. Intell. **28**(11), 1768–1783 (2006)
10. Grandvalet, Y., Bengio, Y.: Semi-supervised learning by entropy minimization. Adv. Neural Inf. Process. Syst. vol. 17. MIT Press (2004)
11. Huang, Y., Bian, S., Li, H., Wang, C., Li, K.: DS-UNet: a dual streams UNet for refined image forgery localization. Inf. Sci. **610**, 73–89 (2022)
12. Khoreva, A., Benenson, R., Hosang, J., Hein, M., Schiele, B.: Simple does it: weakly supervised instance and semantic segmentation. In: Proceedings of the IEEE Conference on Computer Vision and Pattern Recognition (CVPR). pp. 876–885 (2017)
13. Kim, B., Ye, J.C.: Mumford-Shah loss functional for image segmentation with deep learning. IEEE Trans. Image Process. **29**, 1856–1866 (2019)
14. Koch, L.M., et al.: Multi-atlas segmentation using partially annotated data: methods and annotation strategies. IEEE Trans. Pattern Anal. Mach. Intell. **40**(7), 1683–1696 (2017)
15. Lee, H., Jeong, W.-K.: Scribble2Label: Scribble-Supervised Cell Segmentation via Self-generating Pseudo-Labels with Consistency. In: Martel, A.L., Abolmaesumi, P., Stoyanov, D., Mateus, D., Zuluaga, M.A., Zhou, S.K., Racoceanu, D., Joskowicz, L. (eds.) MICCAI 2020. LNCS, vol. 12261, pp. 14–23. Springer, Cham (2020). https://doi.org/10.1007/978-3-030-59710-8_2
16. Li, Z., Zheng, Y., Luo, X., Shan, D., Hong, Q.: ScribbleVC: scribble-supervised medical image segmentation with vision-class embedding. In: Proceedings of the 31st ACM International Conference on Multimedia. pp. 3384–3393. ACM (2023)
17. Lin, D., Dai, J., Jia, J., He, K., Sun, J.: ScribbleSup: scribble-supervised convolutional networks for semantic segmentation. In: Proceedings of the IEEE Conference on Computer Vision and Pattern Recognition (CVPR). pp. 3159–3167 (2016)
18. Liu, X., et al.: Weakly supervised segmentation of COVID19 infection with scribble annotation on CT images. Pattern Recogn. **122**, 108341 (2022)
19. Luo, X., et al.: Scribble-supervised medical image segmentation via dual-branch network and dynamically mixed pseudo labels supervision. In: Medical Image Computing and Computer Assisted Intervention – MICCAI 2022. pp. 528–538. Springer (2022)
20. Papandreou, G., Chen, L.C., Murphy, K.P., Yuille, A.L.: Weakly- and semi-supervised learning of a deep convolutional network for semantic image segmentation. In: Proceedings of the IEEE International Conference on Computer Vision (ICCV). pp. 1742–1750 (2015)
21. Paszke, A., Chaurasia, A., Kim, S., Culurciello, E.: ENet: a deep neural network architecture for real-time semantic segmentation. arXiv preprint arXiv:1606.02147 (2016)
22. Pathak, D., Krahenbuhl, P., Darrell, T.: Constrained convolutional neural networks for weakly supervised segmentation. In: Proceedings of the IEEE International Conference on Computer Vision (ICCV). pp. 1796–1804 (2015)
23. Pathak, D., Shelhamer, E., Long, J., Darrell, T.: Fully convolutional multi-class multiple instance learning. arXiv preprint arXiv:1412.7144 (2014)
24. Roerdink, J.B., Meijster, A.: The watershed transform: definitions, algorithms and parallelization strategies. Fund. Inform. **41**(1–2), 187–228 (2000)
25. Rother, C., Kolmogorov, V., Blake, A.: "GrabCutâĂİ interactive foreground extraction using iterated graph cuts. ACM Trans. Graph. **23**(3), 309–314 (2004)

26. Tan, M., Le, Q.: EfficientNet: rethinking model scaling for convolutional neural networks. In: Proceedings of the 36th International Conference on Machine Learning. vol. 97, pp. 6105–6114. PMLR (2019)
27. Tang, M., Perazzi, F., Djelouah, A., Ben Ayed, I., Schroers, C., Boykov, Y.: On regularized losses for weakly-supervised CNN segmentation. In: Proceedings of the European Conference on Computer Vision (ECCV). pp. 507–522 (2018)
28. Valvano, G., Leo, A., Tsaftaris, S.A.: Learning to segment from scribbles using multi-scale adversarial attention gates. IEEE Trans. Med. Imaging **40**(8), 1990–2001 (2021)
29. Verma, V., et al.: Manifold mixup: better representations by interpolating hidden states. In: Proceedings of the 36th International Conference on Machine Learning. vol. 97, pp. 6438–6447. PMLR (2019)
30. Vezhnevets, V., Konouchine, V.: GrowCut: interactive multi-label ND image segmentation by cellular automata. In: Proceedings of GraphiCon. pp. 150–156 (2005)
31. Wang, G., et al.: DeepIGeoS: a deep interactive geodesic framework for medical image segmentation. IEEE Trans. Pattern Anal. Mach. Intell. **41**(7), 1559–1572 (2019)
32. Wang, Z., Voiculescu, I.: Weakly supervised medical image segmentation through dense combinations of dense pseudo-labels. In: MICCAI Workshop on Data Engineering in Medical Imaging (DEMI 2023). pp. 1–10. Springer (2023)
33. Yan, Y., Liu, R., Chen, H., Zhang, L., Zhang, Q.: CCT-Unet: A U-shaped network based on convolution coupled transformer for segmentation of peripheral and transition zones in prostate MRI. IEEE J. Biomed. Health Inform. **27**(9), 4341–4351 (2023)
34. Yeghiazaryan, V., Gabrielyan, Y., Voiculescu, I.: Parallel watershed partitioning: GPU-based hierarchical image segmentation. arXiv preprint arXiv:2410.08946 (2024)
35. Yeghiazaryan, V., Voiculescu, I.: Family of boundary overlap metrics for the evaluation of medical image segmentation. J. Med. Imaging **5**(1), 015006 (2018)
36. Yeghiazaryan, V., Voiculescu, I.: Path reducing watershed for the GPU. In: 2018 IEEE Winter Conference on Applications of Computer Vision (WACV). pp. 577–585 (2018)
37. Yun, S., Han, D., Oh, S.J., Chun, S., Choe, J., Yoo, Y.: CutMix: Regularization strategy to train strong classifiers with localizable features. In: Proceedings of the IEEE/CVF International Conference on Computer Vision (ICCV). pp. 6023–6032 (2019)
38. Yushkevich, P.A., et al.: User-guided 3D active contour segmentation of anatomical structures: significantly improved efficiency and reliability. Neuroimage **31**(3), 1116–1128 (2006)
39. Zhang, H., Cisse, M., Dauphin, Y.N., Lopez-Paz, D.: mixup: Beyond empirical risk minimization. arXiv preprint arXiv:1710.09412 (2017)
40. Zheng, S., et al.: Conditional random fields as recurrent neural networks. In: Proceedings of the IEEE International Conference on Computer Vision (ICCV). pp. 1529–1537 (2015)
41. Zhuang, X.: Multivariate Mixture Model for Cardiac Segmentation from Multi-Sequence MRI. In: Ourselin, S., Joskowicz, L., Sabuncu, M.R., Unal, G., Wells, W. (eds.) MICCAI 2016. LNCS, vol. 9901, pp. 581–588. Springer, Cham (2016). https://doi.org/10.1007/978-3-319-46723-8_67

A Hybrid Transformer-Graph Model for Multi-Class Lymph Node Segmentation in Histopathology

Elzbieta Budginaite[1,2], Derek R. Magee[3], Maximilian Kloft[1,4], Matthew Nankivell[5], Ruth E. Langley[5], David Cunningham[6], William H. Allum[7], Gayatri Raghuram[8,9], Takaki Yoshikawa[10], Takashi Oshima[11], Henry C. Woodruff[2(✉)], and Heike I. Grabsch[1,9(✉)]

[1] Department of Pathology, GROW – Research Institute for Oncology and Reproduction, Maastricht University Medical Center+, Maastricht, The Netherlands
h.grabsch@maastrichtuniversity.nl
[2] Department of Precision Medicine, GROW – Research Institute for Oncology and Reproduction, Maastricht University Medical Center+, Maastricht, The Netherlands
h.woodruff@maastrichtuniversity.nl
[3] School of Computing, University of Leeds, Leeds, UK
[4] Institute of Clinical Cancer Research, Krankenhaus Nordwest, Frankfurt, Germany
[5] MRC Clinical Trials Unit at UCL, University College London, London, UK
[6] Gastrointestinal and Lymphoma Unit, Royal Marsden Hospital, London, UK
[7] Department of Surgery, Royal Marsden Hospital, London, UK
[8] Department of Pathology, Nottingham University Hospitals, Nottingham, UK
[9] Pathology and Data Analytics, Leeds Institute of Medical Research at St James's, University of Leeds, Leeds, UK
[10] Department of Gastric Surgery, National Cancer Center, Tokyo, Japan
[11] Department of Gastrointestinal Surgery, Kanagawa Cancer Center, Yokohama, Japan

Abstract. Automatic accurate identification of a lymph node (LN) in digitised Haematoxylin/Eosin stained tissue sections from surgical resection specimens is challenging due to the structural variability of LNs, the presence of metastatic and non-metastatic regions, therapy-induced tissue changes, and the variability in tissues surrounding the individual LN, including fat and part of the organ wall with or without the primary tumour. These complexities pose challenges for accurately determining LN size and microarchitecture in an automated manner, underscoring the need for robust methods to unlock their prognostic potential. To address these challenges, we introduce GTFuse, a novel deep learning framework that combines SegFormer-based multi-class tissue segmentation with a graph convolutional network (GCN) for a more accurate LN segmentation. GTFuse is able to distinguish between primary tumour regions and tumour regions within LNs by multi-class segmentation, where tumour is a single class, based on local appearance with contextual information provided by a graph neural network. We evaluated GTFuse on

H. C. Woodruff and H. I. Grabsch—Joint last authors.

Supplementary Information The online version contains supplementary material available at https://doi.org/10.1007/978-3-031-98694-9_7.

S. Ali et al. (Eds.): MIUA 2025, LNCS 15918, pp. 88–101, 2026.
https://doi.org/10.1007/978-3-031-98694-9_7

independent internal and external datasets, demonstrating a performance comparable to or surpassing existing state-of-the-art methods, including foundation model MedSAM. Notably, GTFuse significantly reduced false positive detection in slides without LN tissue, thereby improving specificity and minimizing classification errors.

By addressing tissue heterogeneity and enhancing segmentation accuracy, GTFuse presents a promising solution for both clinical and research applications in digital pathology.

Keywords: Computational pathology · Lymph node detection · Histopathology segmentation · Transformer-Graph convolutional network fusion

1 Introduction

The assessment of tumour-draining lymph nodes (LNs) is essential for cancer diagnosis and staging as LN status (N category) is part of the Tumour Node Metastasis (TNM) staging system. LN status is used to determine patient treatment and has a strong relationship with survival in most cancer types [1]. Accurate TNM staging in resection specimens relies on the identification of metastatic LNs, driving research efforts towards automated LN detection techniques.

Key initiatives such as Camelyon16 and Camelyon17 [2, 3] have contributed significantly to this field offering extensive, multi-centre datasets of digitized whole-slide images (WSIs) from H&E-stained axillary LNs of breast cancer patients. While research using these datasets has primarily centered around detecting metastases, a crucial preliminary step—identifying LN-containing slides and segmenting LNs—was not necessary in these datasets due to their design. These datasets featured LN tissue while omitting primary tumours and/or other benign structures, thereby enabling the application of relatively straightforward methods like Otsu thresholding for segmentation [4].

However, automatic identification of metastatic LNs in routine histopathology practice remains complex. WSIs from surgical resection specimen often include tissue from tumour and adjacent normal tissue, resection margins, as well as tissue with the primary tumour that can appear histologically similar to metastatic tumours within LNs when analyzing zoomed-in tissue patches with limited contextual information. Beyond the detection of metastatic LNs, metastasis-free LN (LNnegs) size and LN microarchitectural features such as presence of secondary lymphoid follicles and/or sinus histiocytosis have been linked to patient survival [5–9]. To reliably evaluate LNnegs and exclude non-LN regions in resection specimens, segmentation models must be able to deal with the morphological similarity between tumour in LN and primary tumour. Relying solely on binary segmentation classifying regions as either LN or non-LN may oversimplify this challenge. A multi-class approach that accounts for diverse tissue types may offer a more context-aware and effective solution for LN segmentation in WSI data.

Advanced segmentation models have demonstrated potential in addressing this complexity. Transformer-based architectures, such as SegFormer, have emerged as powerful tools in digital pathology due to their ability to extract multi-scale features and accommodate the variable resolution of WSI data [10]. By integrating local and global tissue context, SegFormer has shown success in applications such as organ segmentation [11], breast cancer detection [12], and nuclei segmentation [13]. However, analyzing gigapixel WSIs remains challenging, as existing approaches often prioritize either fine-grained feature extraction or high-level tissue context, resulting in trade-offs that hinder model generalizability.

Graph-based methods offer a promising solution by capturing both localized tissue details and broader spatial relationships within WSIs. These methods typically define graph nodes at various levels, from WSI patches to individual cell nuclei, enabling the integration of hierarchical contextual information [14–18]. Combining multi-class segmentation with graph-based modeling bridges the gap between detailed tissue analysis and global tissue organization, improving the delineation of complex LN tissue in histopathological images.

In this work, we present GTFuse, an innovative deep learning framework developed to tackle the complexities of LN segmentation in diverse histopathological environments. By integrating a SegFormer-based multi-class segmentation model with a graph convolutional network (GCN), GTFuse effectively balances fine-grained tissue characterization with broader contextual understanding. Unlike traditional binary segmentation approaches, GTFuse frames LN segmentation as a multi-class problem, allowing for more precise differentiation between various tissue types while leveraging graph-based node classification to refine spatial compartmentalization. To assess its effectiveness, we benchmarked the multi-class strategy against leading binary segmentation models, analyzing the trade-off between contextual awareness and histological detail. Our results demonstrate that GTFuse achieves segmentation performance on par with or exceeding state-of-the-art binary models, while reducing false positives in primary tumour regions—a key limitation of existing approaches.

This study lays the groundwork for integrating multi-class segmentation and graph-based fusion in histopathological analysis, paving the way for LN evaluations in clinical practice.

2   Methods

2.1   Dataset Description

Training and Validation Datasets. Model development utilized images from the OE02 [19] and OE05 [20] trials, while external validation was conducted on datasets from the ST03 trial [21] and the Kanagawa Cancer Center Hospital (KCCH) gastric cancer slide collection. These datasets comprised digitised H&E-stained slides from resection specimens of oesophageal, junctional, or gastric cancer patients, including both metastatic and metastasis-free lymph nodes (LNs). For OE02 and OE05, patient-level splits were made into training (64%), validation (16%), and testing (20%) subsets.

OE02 Dataset. The OE02 trial dataset includes 4,240 H&E-stained tissue sections from 530 oesophageal cancer resections, scanned at 40 × magnification (0.24 microns per pixel, MPP) using an Aperio XT Scanner. LN contours were manually annotated in 761 images using ImageScope (Aperio ImageScope v11.2.0.780, Leica, Milton Keynes, UK). Non-LN tissue classes were annotated in 100 additional slides using QuPath (v0.3.2), covering muscle, stroma with fat tissue, vessels, fibroblasts, normal mucosa, and primary tumour regions. Non-LN annotations were extended via a DeepLabv3+ model trained for non-LN tissue segmentation, applied to 800 resection slides.

OE05 Dataset. This dataset comprises 20,048 H&E-stained sections from 697 oesophageal and junctional cancer resections, scanned at 20 × (0.49 MPP) or 40 × (0.24 MPP) magnification. Annotated slides include 6,082 LN-containing and 5,600 LN-absent slides. Non-LN annotations were generated using the DeepLabv3+ model trained on Non-LN OE02 tissue data, while LN annotations were accelerated by a DeepLabv3+ model trained on OE02 manual LN annotations followed by manual refinement of segmentation results. All LN annotations were quality-controlled and refined using HeteroGenius Medical Image Manager (MIM) software.

KCCH Gastric Cancer Slide Collection. For external validation, we utilized 561 H&E-stained tissue sections from gastric cancer resections scanned at 40 × magnification (0.24 MPP) using an Aperio XT Scanner. LN contours were manually annotated in 113 slides using MIM.

ST03 Dataset. This multi-center dataset included 23,323 H&E-stained sections from 809 oesophageal, junctional, or gastric cancer resections, scanned at 20 × (0.49 MPP) or 40 × (0.24 MPP) magnification. Of the 9,128 LN-containing slides, 214 were randomly selected for manual annotation using MIM for external validation.

2.2 GTFuse Model Overview

The proposed GTFuse model comprises two stages (Fig. 1):

1. SegFormer-based multi-class segmentation: The WSI is downsampled to a 0.625 × magnification thumbnail, tiled into 512 × 512 pixel patches, and segmented into six classes (lymph node, primary tumour, stroma tissue consisting of fat, vessels and fibroblasts, muscle, non-cancerous mucosa and background (no tissue/empty space)).
2. Graph Convolutional Network (GCN): The SegFormer output is processed to create graph nodes representing tissue regions with shared class labels. Node embeddings are constructed from mean SegFormer logits and used as input features for GCN classification into LN or non-LN regions.

Model Architecture. *SegFormer.* The SegFormer model, implemented using Tensor-Flow v2.10.1 and the Hugging Face Transformers library [10], was fine-tuned from the MiT-B0 base model. The model was trained to segment six tissue classes and then used in a sliding window manner with 50% overlap between WSI tiles.

Graph Convolutional Network (GCN). The GCN architecture, based on the design proposed by Kipf et al. [22], consists of two graph convolution layers with ReLU activation, dropout (rate 0.5), and a softmax output layer. Its implementation utilized the Spektral Python library. The GCN processes segmentation masks generated by the SegFormer model to classify WSI regions as LN or non-LN.

To prepare the GCN input, we first collected the SegFormer output logits for each slide in the WSI training set. These outputs, downsampled to 25% of the original input size due to SegFormer's intrinsic resolution reduction, resulted in six-layer matrices. We then applied the argmax operation to assign predicted classes to regions within the WSI, grouping pixels with the same predicted class. For each region, we computed the mean logit values across all six layers, forming a feature vector of size six to serve as the graph node embedding. Edges were established between nodes representing WSI regions that shared a border, creating a graph structure. This graph was then fed into the GCN model for classification of WSI regions as LN or non-LN.

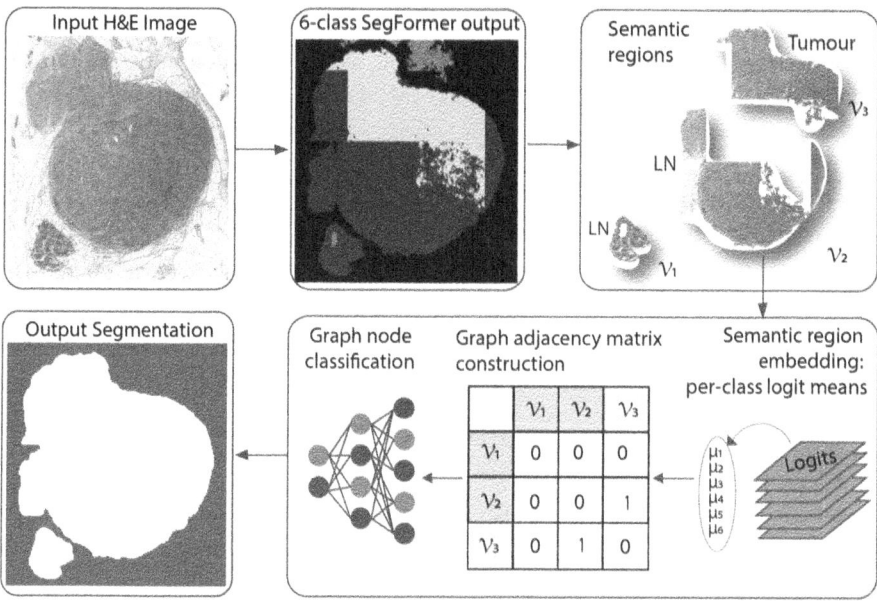

Fig. 1. Overview of the GTFuse model system. An input H&E-stained WSI (top left) is processed by a SegFormer model to generate a 6-class mask (center top), segmenting LN (blue) and misclassifying metastatic regions as primary tumour (green). Predicted regions are split into semantic segments (top right), embedded using per-channel mean logits, and represented as nodes in a spatially-connected graph (bottom right). A graph neural network classifies nodes (bottom center), and the results are fused into the final LN segmentation mask (bottom left)

2.3 Baseline Models

MedSAM-T and MedSAM-P. For these binary foundation models, LN-containing slides from the training dataset were used, ensuring consistency with the data utilized across our study. The same image augmentation strategies described earlier, including geometric, color, and brightness adjustments, were applied to enhance data diversity. Both models were implemented in PyTorch v2.0.1.

MSDenseNet. The MSDenseNet architecture integrates two DenseNet models operating at $1.25 \times$ and $5 \times$ magnifications. The outputs from these models are concatenated to generate a unified prediction. Each DenseNet model was initialized with ImageNet-trained weights and fine-tuned on the CRC Kather dataset, which comprises 100,000 patches from colorectal cancer slides [23]. The fine-tuned model achieved 99% accuracy on the Kather dataset's test set and was subsequently employed for binary patch classification in MSDenseNet. For this task, patches were extracted from LN-containing and non-LN tissue slides from the OE02 trial and augmented using the same data augmentation strategy described earlier.

UNet. We used the original implementation of UNet model published by Beuque et al. [24]. The model was trained on annotated LN-containing slides from OE02 trial. This subset was identical to the data used for training other models in our study, ensuring consistency and fairness in model comparisons.

2.4 Hardware and Training Environment

All models were implemented and trained on the same hardware setup, consisting of 4 NVIDIA RTX A6000 GPUs, ensuring consistency in computational performance across experiments.

Data Augmentation. To enhance training data diversity, the following augmentations were applied:

- Geometric augmentations: rotation and axis flipping.
- Color augmentations: channel augmentation as per Salz et al. [25].
- Brightness adjustment: using Python's PIL ImageEnhance, with brightness values ranging from 0.9 to 1.3.

Training configuration. The training hyperparameters for each AI model used in our study are summarized in Supplementary Table 1.

2.5 Overview and Benchmark Framework

To handle the histological complexity present in oesophageal cancer resection slides, we annotated a subset of H&E-stained images from two clinical trials (OE02 [19] and OE05 [20]). We categorized tissues into six classes: (I) lymph nodes, including metastases, (II) primary tumours, (III) stromal tissue (fat, vessels, fibroblasts), (IV) muscle, (V) non-cancerous mucosa, and (VI) background (non-tissue regions). Based on these annotations, we developed a SegFormer-based segmentation model to classify tissue regions, which was subsequently refined using a graph convolutional network (GCN) to improve spatial coherence and resolve ambiguous areas. This sequential hybrid approach defines our proposed GTFuse framework.

To benchmark GTFuse against existing LN segmentation methods, we evaluated two established architectures: the U-Net model proposed by Beuque et al. [24] and the multi-scale DenseNet (MSDenseNet) followed by Otsu thresholding [26], architecture of which was originally introduced as part of the multi-magnification organ network MMO-Net [27]. Using our training data, we also fine-tuned the foundational Segment Anything Model for medical images (MedSAM) [28] using a binary segmentation approach. Two

MedSAM variants were tested: MedSAM-T (thumbnail-based), which processes whole-slide images (WSIs) as single-pass 1024 × 1024 pixel thumbnails, and MedSAM-P (patch-based), which scans WSIs in a sliding window approach at 0.625 × magnification, similar to GTFuse's SegFormer. Both U-Net and MSDenseNet models were trained on images from the OE02 trial, ensuring a like-for-like comparison across methods.

3 Results

GTFuse demonstrated robust segmentation performance across diverse datasets, surpassing state-of-the-art approaches in several key areas. The evaluation included both internal and external datasets, focusing on dice scores for LN-containing test slides and specificity for LN-absent slides. GTFuse produced a consistently low number of false positives on LN-absent slides in our test set, reflecting its high specificity to LN tissue in these samples. In this context, false positives refer to regions incorrectly predicted as LN tissue in WSI areas confirmed to contain no lymph nodes. A minimum threshold of 0.5 mm in diameter (longest axis length) was applied to distinguish segmentation artefacts from the smallest LNs, selected to match the smallest segmented LN object in the training dataset. These findings set the stage for a detailed analysis of GTFuse's performance across specific test sets to highlight its strengths and limitations in various clinical scenarios.

3.1 Performance on Internal LN-Containing Test Set

GTFuse achieved high segmentation accuracy on the internal test set, comprising 1,568 slides (160 from the OE02 trial and 1,408 from the OE05 trial; see Table 1). On the OE02 subset (160 slides), the fine-tuned MedSAM-T model achieved the highest mean dice score. However, this result was driven by a subset of slides with markedly divergent scores across models, highlighting MedSAM-T's variability in handling complex images where the lymph node is closely juxtaposed with the primary tumour, making it challenging to delineate their boundaries (Fig. 2f). GTFuse performed consistently across the OE02 dataset and ranked second in terms of mean dice score.

On the larger OE05 subset (1,408 slides), GTFuse outperformed all other models. The multi-class segmentation approach was particularly effective in reducing false positives in primary tumour tissue regions, addressing a key limitation of binary models (Fig. 2d–e). The superiority of GTFuse's segmentation was also demonstrated in the analysis of dice score variance, which revealed that it maintained consistently high performance even in challenging cases with low inter-model agreement, where most other models showed significantly lower dice scores (see Fig. 3b).

The analysis of false negatives (FNs) on LN-containing slides highlighted challenges in detecting small LNs, where model sensitivity played a critical role. The UNet model had the highest number of slides with false negatives, with FNs detected on 433 slides (mean diameter $\pm$ SD of missed LNs: 2.25 $\pm$ 2.05 mm) (Supplementary Fig. 1b). In contrast, MSDenseNet had the fewest slides with FNs, with only 66 affected slides (1.27 $\pm$ 1.07 mm), benefiting from its multi-scale approach. GTFuse performed moderately,

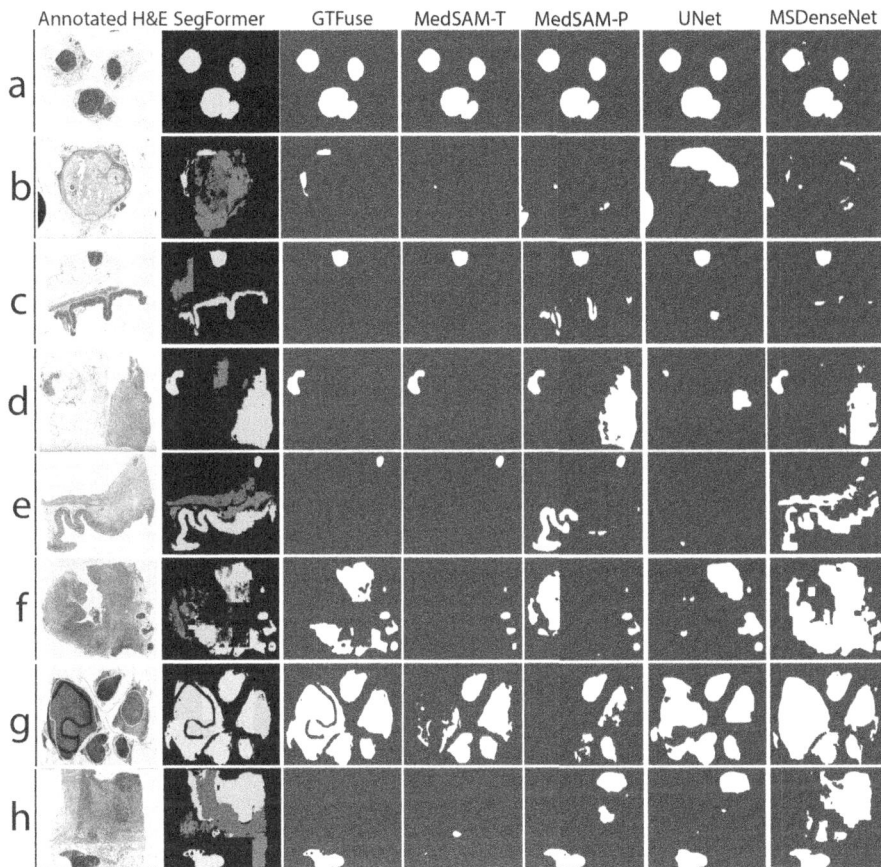

Fig. 2. Example LN segmentation outputs from the different model architectures. SegFormer predictions show six-class outputs (cyan: LN, green: primary tumour, gray: submucosa, red: muscle), all other models have a binary output (white: LN, grey: background). Image rows illustrate a range of segmentation scenarios: (A) easy case; (B) challenging due to fibrosis or mucin in LN (C) slide with both LN and complex gastric wall tissue; (D–F) Examples where both LN and primary tumour are present in the same slide; (E, F) Examples where very small LNs are located immediately adjacent to tumour tissue; (G) External KCCH slide with pen-marking artefacts; (H) representative case from the ST03 external set.

with 235 slides containing FNs (2.3 ± 2.8 mm), reflecting a trade-off between sensitivity to small structures and overall segmentation robustness.

In contrast to false negatives, false positive (FP) analysis on LN-containing slides revealed notable differences in model specificity. The UNet model exhibited the lowest FP rate, with false positives detected in 289 slides (Supplementary Fig. 1a illustrates largest per-slide FP size distribution). MedSAM-P, however, had the highest FP rate, with false positives detected in 729 slides, likely stemming from limited tile spatial context during inference at 0.625 × magnification. This is further supported by the performance of MedSAM-T, a thumbnail-based counterpart, which produced 36% fewer

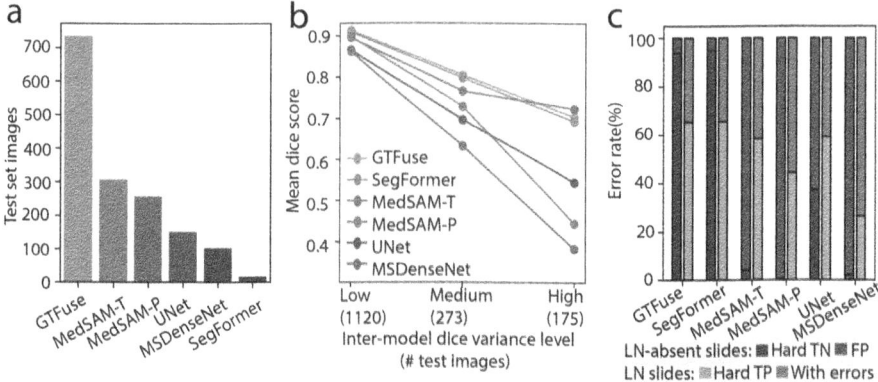

Fig. 3. Comparative performance analysis of segmentation models on LN-containing (A-B) and LN-absent/LN-containing slides (C) from the test set (OE02 and OE05 trials; 1568 LN-containing, 1338 LN-absent slides). (A) Bar plot showing the distribution of test set images where each model achieved the highest Dice coefficient, identifying the best-performing model per image. (B) Mean Dice scores for each model across inter-model variance levels (low < 0.02, medium 0.02–0.05, high > 0.05), illustrating the impact of prediction variability on segmentation accuracy. (C) Stacked bar plots displaying classification outcomes for 1568 LN-containing and 1338 LN-absent slides, with hard true positives for LN slides (no false positives or false negatives) and hard true negatives for LN-absent slides (no predicted false positives).

false positive slides compared to MedSAM-P. GTFuse produced false positives in 353 LN-containing slides, striking an effective trade-off between reducing erroneous predictions and maintaining high segmentation accuracy, ranking second only to UNet in FP reduction for LN-containing slides. These results underscore the role of spatial context in reducing false positives, particularly for complex LN-containing slides, which is also evident in false positive analysis in LN-absent slides.

3.2   Specificity of LN Detection in LN-Absent Slides

To evaluate performance in terms of the models' specificity to LN tissue, we analyzed their ability to correctly classify 1,338 LN-absent slides from the test patient subset sampled from the OE02 and OE05 trials. In this context, specificity was defined as the ability to identify non-LN slides without producing false positives. GTFuse demonstrated the highest specificity, correctly classifying 1,256 slides (93.4%) as true negatives (Fig. 3c), significantly outperforming the binary segmentation models, which exhibited notably higher number of false positives. Among the binary models, UNet correctly identified 37.6% of LN-absent slides as true negatives, followed by MedSAM-T, which correctly classified only 4.2% of LN-absent slides (Fig. 3c). Binary models, in particular those operating at higher magnifications, such as MSDenseNet and MedSAM-P, tended to generate larger false positive objects in LN-absent slides (Supplementary Fig. 1a). In contrast, GTFuse and SegFormer minimized false positives, with the majority of their LN-absent slides containing no false positive objects (Fig. 3c and Supplementary Fig. 1a).

3.3 Impact of GCN Integration on LN Segmentation

To assess the contribution of the graph convolutional network (GCN) to LN segmentation, we analyzed per-image dice score differences (dice deltas) between the standalone SegFormer and the full GTFuse model, the results are shown in Supplementary Table 2. Across the combined OE02 and OE05 test sets, the mean dice delta was small (0.005 ± 0.048), indicating minimal overall differences in performance. However, when stratifying the dataset based on dice delta ranges, GTFuse outperformed the standalone SegFormer on 85 slides (5.4% of the test set). Most of the improvements were observed in the fusion of metastatic tissue regions. Conversely, poorer performance was noted in 20 slides (1.2%), primarily due to SegFormer's small LN false positive objects fused to adjacent tissue. Performance on the remaining 93.4% of slides remained consistent.

On the KCCH dataset, the integration of the GCN had a more pronounced impact. Among slides with metastatic LNs, the GCN enhanced LN segmentation dice score in 20.3% of cases, while only 3.7% of slides showed poorer performance, underscoring its ability to refine predictions in challenging datasets. This improvement is particularly relevant in clinical scenarios where accurate segmentation of metastatic LNs might have an impact on patient management plans.

3.4 LN Segmentation Performance on External LN-Containing Test Sets

GTFuse's generalizability was evaluated on two external datasets: a subset of the ST03 clinical trial [21] (214 annotated LN-containing slides) and LN-containing subset of Kanagawa Cancer Center Hospital (KCCH) gastric cancer slide collection (113 LN-containing slides). On the ST03 subset, GTFuse achieved the highest mean dice score, reinforcing the hypothesis that multi-class segmentation reduces false positive LN detections in slides containing non-LN tissues. Representative segmentation outputs are shown in Fig. 2h, highlighting GTFuse's ability to distinguish primary tumour regions from LNs, which seems to be most problematic for binary segmentation models.

On the KCCH dataset, which predominantly contained metastatic LN slides (91% of LN-containing slides), the MSDenseNet model achieved the highest mean Dice score, with GTFuse ranking second. As can be seen in Fig. 2g, the KCCH slides contained heavy felt-tip pen markings, which likely was more detrimental to pixel-level segmentation models compared to MSDenseNet relying on patch-based classification. Despite this challenge, GTFuse demonstrated substantial dice score improvements in metastatic LN segmentation when the GCN was integrated, with 20.3% of images exhibiting moderate to strong improvements compared to the standalone SegFormer model (see Supplementary Table 2).

3.5 Inter-model Variance and Agreement

We further investigated inter-model variance in dice scores to explore the intrinsic difficulty of segmentation tasks. Inter-model variance was assessed using an internal test set of LN-containing images by calculating the dice score for each model's output against the ground truth, and then computing the variance across these scores. Across the six models tested (GTFuse, SegFormer, MedSAM-T, MedSAM-P, UNet, and MSDenseNet),

Table 1. Performance metrics comparing different model architectures tested on internal (OE02 and OE05) and external (KCCH and annotated subset of ST03 trial) datasets.

Model	Mean dice coefficient, % (±SD, %)				
	OE02 (n = 160)	OE05 (n = 1408)	KCCH (n = 133)	ST03 (n = 214)	Slide processing time, sec
UNet	71.84 ± 26.8	79.86 ± 22.66	76.45 ± 21.16	82.47 ± 19.76	**1.05**
MSDenseNet	66.12 ± 31.68	74.75 ± 25.63	**83.37** ± 22.86	77.46 ± 23.46	153.4
MedSAM-T	**80.46** ± 24.05	85.56 ± 17.74	71.26 ± 30.41	84.19 ± 19.15	2.23
MedSAM-P	70.40 ± 30.34	81.01 ± 24.53	68.70 ± 27.95	82.01 ± 23.21	6.74
SegFormer(1.25 ×)	66.6 ± 28.18	87.9 ± 15.32	-	-	20
GTFuse(1.25 ×)	67.3 ± 27.65	**87.9** ± 15.28	-	-	25.47
SegFormer	71.8 ± 29.27	87.26 ± 18.56	76.05 ± 26.21	85.6 ± 21.31	4.44
GTFuse	73.01 ± 30.01	87.78 ± 18.46	79.48 ± 24.69	**86.4** ± 20.38	5

the mean inter-model variance was 0.025 ± 0.04, indicating strong overall agreement on most slides. However, a subset of challenging images exhibited higher variance (273 and 175 images with medium and high inter-model variance, respectively out of 1568 slides), reflecting the complexity of distinguishing LN from histologically similar looking tissues. GTFuse, SegFormer, and MedSAM-T maintained high dice scores even in high-variance cases, whereas MedSAM-P, UNet, and MSDenseNet showed a notable decline in per-image dice score under these conditions (Fig. 3b).

To further investigate inter-model relationships, we performed a pairwise comparison of dice scores for each combination of the six models tested. For each model pair, this analysis evaluated (I) the mean absolute difference (MAD) in dice scores per image to assess the similarity of their absolute performance levels and (II) the correlation of dice scores to explore prediction consistency across images. The results revealed complementary strengths between models (results shown in Supplementary Fig. 2). GTFuse and MedSAM-T showed the lowest MAD (0.009), indicating similar overall segmentation accuracy. However, the moderate dice score correlation coefficients between these models (0.52–0.54) suggest prediction diversity, likely stemming from differences in feature extraction strategies. These findings highlight how combining models with diverse but complementary prediction patterns could offer opportunities for ensemble approaches or uncertainty estimation in segmentation tasks.

3.6 Time Efficiency and Magnification Considerations

The time efficiency of each model was evaluated in the OE02 and OE05 test sets. The UNet model proposed by Beuque et al. was the fastest, processing slides in 1.05 s on average, followed by MedSAM-T at 2.23 s and SegFormer at 4.44 s per slide. GTFuse, with the added GCN module, required 5.00 s per slide whereas MSDenseNet was significantly slower model, averaging 2.5 min per slide. The choice of 0.625x magnification for GTFuse and SegFormer enabled efficient processing while maintaining high segmentation accuracy. Training and evaluation at $1.25 \times$ magnification did not result in significant performance gains (Table 1).

4   Discussion

The task of automating lymph node (LN) identification in whole-slide images (WSIs) remains challenging in histopathology. Routine slides from resection specimens frequently contain a mixture of LN and non-LN tissues, making it crucial for AI models to incorporate contextual histological awareness to enhance segmentation accuracy while minimizing specificity issues and false positives. Previous methods, such as Wang et al.'s U-Net autoencoder for gastric cancer LN segmentation [29] and Beuque et al.'s UNet model applied to low-resolution thumbnails [24], have primarily relied on binary segmentation approaches. More recently, Gamez Serna et al. [27] explored a multi-scale DenseNet framework for segmenting various mouse organs, including mandibular LNs. However, these methods have limitations for large-scale WSI analysis—either due to the computational burden of multi-scale DenseNet models or related to an increased rate of false positives in complex histological images where LNs coexist with non-LN structures. To address these challenges, GTFuse leverages multi-class segmentation combined with graph-based contextual refinement, allowing it to more effectively differentiate LN metastases from histologically similar primary tumours and adjacent tissues.

Our inter-model comparisons emphasized the critical role of contextual information in segmentation. MedSAM-T leveraged low-resolution WSI thumbnails to achieve dice scores comparable to GTFuse, highlighting the importance of broader spatial context over fine-grained detail. The significance of contextual information is evident when comparing MedSAM-T, which leverages broader spatial context, to MedSAM-P, whose limited contextual awareness resulted in a higher number of false positives and lower dice score. GTFuse's ability to model tissue relationships with a graph convolutional network (GCN) further enhances its segmentation performance, particularly in datasets with metastatic LNs.

Furthermore, our analysis of mean absolute dice differences (MAD) revealed that MedSAM-T was the closest model to GTFuse, but the moderate dice correlation between the two suggests they likely leverage different image features in their decision-making processes. This divergence, paired with their strong individual performances, points to the potential benefit of combining GTFuse and MedSAM-T in an ensemble model or leveraging their complementary strengths as a quality or uncertainty checking mechanism—a promising avenue for future exploration.

Despite its strengths, GTFuse has some limitations. Its reliance on SegFormer's output logits restricts scalability to higher magnifications due to memory demands, making it more suited for tasks requiring broader spatial context, like organ segmentation. Additionally, the specificity of its training classes may hinder generalization to other organ systems, potentially leading to false positives in non-target tissues. Testing on the Camelyon17 dataset demonstrated GTFuse's high sensitivity, detecting lymph nodes in 99% of slides. However, because Camelyon17 lacks histological diversity and does not include non-LN tissues such as primary tumours or normal tissue, further testing on more diverse datasets is needed to fully evaluate its generalizability. Future work should explore integrating high-magnification multi-class models with thumbnail-based approaches to balance accuracy and contextual awareness.

In summary, GTFuse demonstrates the advantages of combining multi-class segmentation with graph-based contextual refinement for LN segmentation in complex histopathological contexts. Our findings show that a) multi-class segmentation reduces false positives, b) graph-based modeling effectively merges metastatic LN components with the main LN structure, and c) broader spatial context enhances segmentation accuracy compared to patch-based methods. By addressing challenges of contextual ambiguity and patch-level limitations, GTFuse provides a robust foundation for advancing automated LN segmentation in clinical workflows.

Acknowledgments. This study was funded by the Hanarth Fonds. HG and DM are supported in part by the National Institute for Health and Care Research (NIHR) Leeds Biomedical Research Centre (BRC) (NIHR203331). The views expressed are those of the author(s) and not necessarily those of the NHS, the NIHR or the Department of Health and Social Care. GR has received funding from The Jean Shanks Foundation. DC has received funding from the National Institute for Health funding from The Royal Marsden and Institute of Cancer Research Biomedical Research Center. The funder had no role in the study design, experiments, interpretation of the results, or writing of this manuscript. We acknowledge the clinical centers that provided material for this study.

Disclosure of Interests. HW has minority shares in the company Radiomics SA. D.C. declares grants from Medimmune/AstraZeneca, Clovis, Eli Lilly, 4SC, Bayer, Celgene, Leap, and Roche, and Scientific Board Membership for OVIBIO. Author DRM is a director of HeteroGenius Limited. Other authors declare that they have no known competing financial interests or personal relationships that could have appeared to influence the work reported in this paper.

References

1. Gusterson, B.A.: The new TNM classification and micrometastases. Breast **12**(6), 387–390 (2003)
2. Budginaite, E., et al., Computational methods for metastasis detection in lymph nodes and characterization of the metastasis-free lymph node microarchitecture: A systematic-narrative hybrid review. J. Pathol. Inform. 100367 (2024)
3. Litjens, G., et al.: 1399 H&E-stained sentinel lymph node sections of breast cancer patients: the CAMELYON dataset. GigaScience, **7**(6) (2018)
4. Wang, L., et al.: Deep regional metastases segmentation for patient-level lymph node status classification. IEEE Access **9**, 129293–129302 (2021)
5. Riegrova, D., Jansa, P.: Prognostic significance of reactive changes in regional lymph nodes in gastric and mammary carcinomas. Neoplasma **29**(4), 481–486 (1982)
6. Black, M.M., Barclay, T.H.C., Hankey, B.F.: Prognosis in breast cancer utilizing histologic characteristics of the primary tumour. Cancer **36**(6), 2048–2055 (1975)
7. Oka, M.: Immunological studies on esophageal cancer. Cellular immunocompetence and histological responses in main tumour and regional lymph nodes in esophageal cancer patients. Archiv fur Japanische Chirurgie, **50**(1), 29–44 (1981)
8. Kloft, M., et al.: Prognostic significance of negative lymph node long axis in esophageal cancer: results from the randomized controlled UK MRC OE02 trial. Ann. Surg. (2022)
9. Verghese, G., et al.: Multiscale deep learning framework captures systemic immune features in lymph nodes predictive of triple negative breast cancer outcome in large-scale studies. J. Pathol. **260**(4), 376–389 (2023)
10. Xie, E., et al.: SegFormer: simple and efficient design for semantic segmentation with transformers. Adv. Neural. Inf. Process. Syst. **34**, 12077–12090 (2021)

11. Jain, Y., et al.: Segmenting functional tissue units across human organs using community-driven development of generalizable machine learning algorithms. Nat. Commun. **14**(1), 4656 (2023)
12. Hamnett, L., et al.: Enhancing transformer-based segmentation for breast cancer diagnosis using auto-augmentation and search optimisation techniques (2023)
13. Khaled, M., et al.: Efficient semantic segmentation of nuclei in histopathology images using segformer. In: Annual Conference on Medical Image Understanding and Analysis. Springer (2023)
14. Levy, J., et al.: Topological feature extraction and visualization of whole slide images using graph neural networks. Pac. Symp. Biocomput. **26**, 285–296 (2021)
15. Anklin, V., et al.: Learning whole-slide segmentation from inexact and incomplete labels using tissue graphs. In: Medical Image Computing and Computer Assisted Intervention–MICCAI 2021: 24th International Conference, Strasbourg, France, September 27–October 1, 2021, Proceedings, Part II 24. Springer (2021)
16. Zheng, Y., et al.: A graph-transformer for whole slide image classification. IEEE Trans. Med. Imaging **41**(11), 3003–3015 (2022)
17. Lu, W., et al.: SlideGraph+: whole slide image level graphs to predict HER2 status in breast cancer. Med. Image Anal. **80**, 102486 (2022)
18. Pati, P., et al.: Hierarchical graph representations in digital pathology. Med. Image Anal. **75**, 102264 (2022)
19. Allum, W.H., et al.: Long-term results of a randomized trial of surgery with or without preoperative chemotherapy in esophageal cancer. J. Clin. Oncol. **27**(30), 5062–5067 (2009)
20. Alderson, D., et al.: Neoadjuvant cisplatin and fluorouracil versus epirubicin, cisplatin, and capecitabine followed by resection in patients with oesophageal adenocarcinoma (UK MRC OE05): an open-label, randomised phase 3 trial. Lancet Oncol. **18**(9), 1249–1260 (2017)
21. Cunningham, D., et al.: Peri-operative chemotherapy with or without bevacizumab in operable oesophagogastric adenocarcinoma (UK medical research council ST03): primary analysis results of a multicentre, open-label, randomised phase 2–3 trial. Lancet Oncol. **18**(3), 357–370 (2017)
22. Kipf, T.N., Welling, M.: Semi-supervised classification with graph convolutional networks. arXiv preprint arXiv:1609.02907 (2016)
23. Kather, J.N., et al.: Predicting survival from colorectal cancer histology slides using deep learning: a retrospective multicenter study. PLoS Med. **16**(1), e1002730 (2019)
24. Beuque, M., et al.: Automated detection and delineation of lymph nodes in haematoxylin & eosin stained digitised slides. J. Pathol. Inform. **14**, 100192 (2023)
25. Saltz, J., et al.: Spatial organization and molecular correlation of tumour infiltrating lymphocytes using deep learning on pathology images. Cell Rep. **23**(1), 181–193 (2018)
26. Otsu, N.: A threshold selection method from gray-level histograms. IEEE Trans. Syst. Man Cybern. **9**(1), 62–66 (1979)
27. Gámez Serna, C., et al.: MMO-net (multi-magnification organ network): a use case for organ identification using multiple magnifications in preclinical pathology studies. J. Pathol. Inform. **13** (2022)
28. Ma, J., et al.: Segment anything in medical images. Nat. Commun. **15**(1), 654 (2024)
29. Wang, X., et al.: Predicting gastric cancer outcome from resected lymph node histopathology images using deep learning. Nat. Commun. **12**(1), 1637 (2021)

Exploring Context-Switching in Medical Image Retrieval Using Segmentation Models

Sai Susmitha Arvapalli[1]([ID]) and Vinay P. Namboodiri[2][ID]

[1] Department of Computer Science and Engineering, Indian Institute of Technology Kanpur, Kanpur, India
susmitha@cse.iitk.ac.in
[2] Department of Computer Science, University of Bath, Bath, UK
vpn22@bath.ac.uk

Abstract. Medical Image Retrieval (MIR) is essential for clinical workflows, enabling accurate diagnosis and advancing medical research. In this work, we aim to better understand the use of context for medical image retrieval. To this end, we propose a novel context-switching-based medical image retrieval framework. Our approach uses the MedSAM2 foundation model to extract segmentations and generate three distinct input versions of each image: the original image, the region-of-interest (ROI) image, and a bounding box around the region of interest that captures additional contextual information. We generate the corresponding embeddings using a contrastive loss-based metric learning approach. A selective backpropagation mechanism enables the model to dynamically identify and utilize the most informative feature embedding for retrieval. Our results suggest that the general context is often more beneficial than a specific context for accurate image retrieval. Our proposed method is evaluated on the ISIC17 and COVID-QU-Ex chest X-ray datasets and demonstrates superior performance compared to strongly related baselines.

Keywords: Content-Based Medical Image Retrieval · Swin Transformers · MedSAM2 · Contrastive Learning

1 Introduction

Medical image retrieval (MIR) is a fundamental task in medical image analysis, enabling efficient access to relevant images by identifying similar case histories. With the growing volume of medical imaging data, MIR plays a vital role in helping physicians to streamline image analysis and improve diagnostic accuracy [1,6,15]. Early MIR systems often relied on convolutional neural networks (CNNs) [17,20], and [8] addressed interpretability concerns in MIR using CNNs with their X-MIR method. However, CNN-based methods struggled to capture long-range dependencies and contextual relationships. Recent works, such as

S. Ali et al. (Eds.): MIUA 2025, LNCS 15918, pp. 102–114, 2026.
https://doi.org/10.1007/978-3-031-98694-9_8

[22] and [7], highlight the potential of Vision Transformers (ViTs) [5] for better performance in content-based image retrieval (CBIR) tasks. Furthermore, [23] analyzed various ViT architectures, demonstrating that MIRViT-based architectures outperform CNNs in medical retrieval tasks.

All these MIR methods used the whole image(Full) features, rather than a specific region of interest(ROI). Although some studies such as [10,11,27], have investigated the use of a region-of-interest (ROI) to enhance retrieval performance, these were not using vision transformers. We first investigated whether region-of-interest-based segmentation could aid transformers to provide better retrieval. This turns out to not be the case. As context turns out to be important, We therefore devised a method where the learning algorithm could choose whether a particular region-of-interest, the whole image, or a bounding box around the region-of-interest that captures additional contextual information is useful to obtain better image retrieval. Providing this choice to the learning algorithm enables it to provide the highest performance. In most cases, the method chose the whole image, but, by having to choose between the different observations, we observed that the learning algorithm obtained significantly improved performance. Our Multi-input context-based switching MIR framework begins by using MedSAM2, a fine-tuned version of SAM2 [14], to generate segmentation masks that delineate key anatomical features and ROIs in medical images. This segmentation is used to create three variants, full-image, region-of-interest, and bounding-box context, and we generate feature embeddings for these three variants. We employ a network selection mechanism that dynamically chooses the most informative image version and its corresponding feature embedding for similarity matching. This mechanism is trained using contrastive learning with regularization techniques, alongside a specialized network selection loss function.

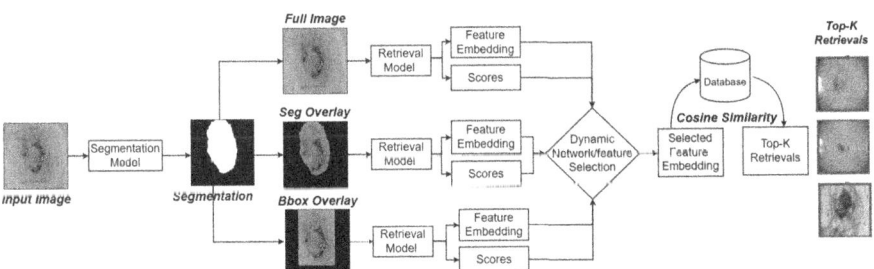

Fig. 1. Context-switching based Medical Image Retrieval Framework. This framework utilizes three networks, each processing different image representations: the original image (full image), the region-of-interest image (Seg Overlay), and a bounding box around the region of interest that captures additional contextual information (bbox Overlay). The system dynamically selects the optimal feature embedding for each query, which is then used to retrieve similar images based on cosine similarity.

During inference, the same procedure is used to generate three feature embeddings for a given query image, and the model dynamically selects the best embedding, allowing it to adaptively choose the most informative representation for each image. We show that this approach leads to enhanced retrieval accuracy. The key contributions of our work are as follows:

- We developed a Novel Context-switching MIR framework using segmentation (with MedSAM2) to create multiple image versions for more focused and clinically relevant retrieval.
- Our method is evaluated on two medical imaging datasets, including ISIC17 (skin lesion) and COVID-QU-Ex(chest X-ray) datasets, demonstrating comparable or superior performance to regular retrieval approaches. We also provide ablations on the context-switching and architecture variation.

2   Related Works

Recent advancements, especially leveraging machine learning and pre-trained models, have significantly improved retrieval accuracy and efficiency. For instance, [9] used pre-trained models for retrieval at the modality, body region, and organ levels, achieving high recall rates without additional training. Similarly, [18] combined DenseNet with FAISS for efficient breast cancer image retrieval, improving precision and recall. [16] proposed a hybrid medical image classifier named MedViT, which combines CNN and ViT networks. Deep convolutional neural networks (CNNs) and Vision Transformers (ViTs) have also been widely utilized. ViTs, in particular, overcome CNN limitations by capturing long-range dependencies. For instance, [7] demonstrated that Vision Transformers (ViTs) paired with metric learning outperform CNNs in CBIR. Similarly, [8] integrates deep metric learning with similarity-based saliency maps to provide visual explanations of retrieved images, addressing the interpretability challenges in CNN-based retrieval. [25] proposed a binary cross-entropy-based content-based Medical image retrieval(CBMIR) method using a modified ViT for chest X-rays. Meanwhile, [23] highlighted the superior accuracy of MIRViT, a contrastive loss-based Vision Transformer architecture.

Segmentation-based retrieval approaches, although promising, remain underexplored. For instance, [21] introduced MIPS, employing perceptual region growing for segmentation and feature extraction. [2] used multithresholding segmentation to create partitions for CBIR, while [29] adapted segmentation criteria for block-based feature extraction. More recent studies, such as [11] combined the Bag-of-Visual-Words (BoVW) with shape and texture features, utilizing the Dynamic Delaunay Triangulation (DDT) Segmentation algorithm to extract regions of interest, and then building hybrid bag-of-features using BoVWs and low-level features. Similarly, [10] improved retrieval accuracy using Delaunay triangulation for precise lung segmentation in CT images. They extracted shape and texture features from segmented regions, forming hybrid feature vectors for MIR. However, these approaches focus on extracting features from segmented regions and comparing different feature extractors best for retrieval. In contrast, our framework introduces a context-switching approach for MIR, enabling the network to dynamically select the context that is most relevant for retrieval.

3   Method

Our overall context-switching MIR framework first performs segmentation, followed by retrieval. In the segmentation task, masks are generated using Med-SAM2, a fine-tuned version of the Segment Anything Model 2 (SAM2) [4,14]. We fine-tuned SAM2 specifically for medical datasets by freezing the prompt encoder and updating the image encoder and mask decoder. Detailed fine-tuning steps are provided in Sect. 6. In the retrieval task, we utilize the Swin Transformer [12], a hierarchical network, as the backbone, which addresses the scalability limitations of Vision Transformer (ViT) [5] models by incorporating window-based attention mechanisms. We use the Swin-Tiny architecture consisting of four stages with 2, 2, 6, and 2 Swin Transformer blocks. We extend this model with an auxiliary head that outputs class scores along with the feature embeddings as shown in Fig. 2.

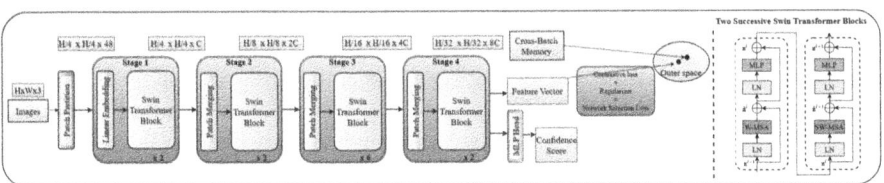

Fig. 2. Retrieval Network for our MIR Framework

Training Phase: For each image, three versions are created using the MedSAM2 segmentation: the original full image, the segmentation-overlayed image(ROI), and a bounding box around the segmentation that captures more contextual information. The bounding box was defined by the minimum and maximum coordinates of the segmentation mask, expanded with a margin to include the surrounding context, and this bounding box ROI was then overlayed on the full image to generate the bbox overlayed image. Three independent networks are trained for each version using a selective backpropagation-based metric learning approach. A cross-batch memory mechanism [28] is employed to store feature embeddings from previous batches and utilize them as hard negatives in the current batch. This approach increases the diversity of negative samples, providing more challenging examples during training. Additionally, differential entropy loss [19] is applied as a regularizer to enhance the distinctiveness of embeddings, as demonstrated in [7,23].

Each Swin-Tiny retrieval network generates a feature embedding along with the class probabilities (nevi, melanoma, seborrheic keratosis for ISIC17, and COVID-19, Normal, or Pneumonia class labels for COVID_QU_Ex). Three networks are trained on three different types of inputs - full image, ROI, and bounding box ROI. Each network outputs its corresponding feature embedding and class scores as in Fig. 1.

The training process is guided by contrastive loss, which is essential for retrieval-based tasks as it ensures intra-class similarity (pulling embeddings of the same class closer together) while maximizing inter-class separation (pushing apart embeddings from different classes). Unlike standard classification losses such as cross-entropy, which focuses on assigning discrete labels, contrastive loss directly optimizes the distance between learned embeddings, making it particularly effective for retrieval tasks where the goal is to rank and compare images based on similarity. The contrastive loss function used in our framework is given by:

$$L_{\text{contr}} = \sum_{l:c_k=c_l} \left[1 - e_k^T e_l\right] + \sum_{l:c_k \neq c_l} \left[e_k^T e_l - \gamma\right]$$

Here, e_k represents the feature embedding of sample k, and c_k is its corresponding class label. The margin γ defines the threshold for negative pairs, ensuring that embeddings from different classes remain sufficiently separated in the feature space. To ensure that the embeddings are well separated we also include a regularization using a differential entropy loss L_{reg} is calculated as: $L_{\text{reg}} = -\log(\nu_k)$. Here, ν_k is the minimum distance between the embedding vector e_k of the current image and any other embedding vector e_l, where $l \neq k$. The regularization term is integrated into the final loss with a weighting coefficient λ.

One could train each network (Full Image, ROI, or bounding box ROI) using a combination of contrastive loss and the regularization term. During training, since the true class labels are available, it is possible to determine which network performs best for each image. However, at inference, this information is not available, so a mechanism is required to predict the most suitable network for a given image. To achieve this, we introduce a network selection loss, which is formulated using cross-entropy. This loss ensures that the model learns to choose the network that minimizes the regularized contrastive loss during training. The loss is given as: $L_{\text{Sel}} = \text{cross\_entropy}(\text{logits}_i, \text{net\_label}_i)$. Here, logits_i are the raw class logits (i.e., scores from the network output) for each image i, and net_label_i indicates the network with the lowest regularized contrastive loss.

The final total loss used for training is computed as $L_{\text{Total}} = L_{\text{contr}} + \lambda L_{\text{reg}} + L_{\text{Sel}}$. Once L_{Total} is computed, selective backpropagation is applied to train the networks efficiently. For each image, the network to be updated is determined dynamically. During the first half of the total training iterations, the network that achieved the lowest regularized contrastive loss is selected for backpropagation. In the remaining iterations, the network with the highest class score among the three is chosen instead. This ensures that backpropagation is applied only to the most relevant network for each image, allowing each network to specialize in handling the input type it performs best on, leading to improved retrieval performance.

Testing Phase:
During inference, the network with the highest class score among the three networks is selected for each input query image. The feature embedding from the selected network is used to compute the cosine similarity with the embeddings of

the database images. The cosine similarity between two embeddings, e_i (query image embedding) and e_j (database image embedding), is calculated as: $\frac{e_i \cdot e_j}{\|e_i\|\|e_j\|}$ The top-k most similar images are retrieved based on these cosine similarity scores. The retrieval performance is then evaluated using Recall@k(R@K) which measures the proportion of relevant images in the top-k results, mean Precision@k(mP@K) which reflects retrieval relevance within the top-k, and mean Average Precision (mAP) captures overall ranking quality. These metrics ensure robust performance and high-quality retrieval results by quantifying the accuracy and relevance of the retrieved images.

4 Datasets Used

We utilized two diverse datasets for the MIR task, each tailored to distinct medical imaging challenges. The ISIC Skin Lesion Dataset [3] includes dermoscopic images categorized into three classes: benign nevi, seborrheic keratosis, and melanoma. Specifically, the dataset includes 2,000 training images distributed as follows: 1,372 benign nevi, 254 seborrheic keratosis, and 374 melanoma cases. This dataset is widely recognized in dermatological research and provides a robust foundation for analyzing skin lesion patterns, differentiating between non-cancerous and malignant cases. The second dataset, we employed the COVID-QU-Ex dataset [24], a comprehensive collection curated by researchers at Qatar University. This dataset comprises 33,920 chest X-ray (CXR) images divided into three categories: 11,956 COVID-19 cases, 11,263 cases of non-COVID infections (viral or bacterial pneumonia), and 10,701 normal cases. The dataset provides ground-truth lung segmentation masks, enabling precise lung isolation for advanced retrieval tasks and making it the largest lung mask dataset available. For the segmentation part in our MIR framework, we fine-tuned the SAM2 model using the HAM10000 [26], which consists of 10,015 dermatoscopic images from diverse populations and part of the COVID-QU-Ex dataset.

5 Results and Discussion

The performance of our proposed context-switching MIR framework using Med-SAM2 segmentations was evaluated on the ISIC17 and COVID-QU-Ex datasets, as shown in Table 1. The results indicate that Context_MIR achieves the best performance, particularly in terms of mAP, with improvements over MIRViT [23], DenseNet121 [8], ResNet50 [8] on both datasets. ViT with cross-entropy [25] and MedViT [16] (where the classifier was used as a feature extractor for retrieval) performed the weakest on both datasets. This is likely because these methods are optimized for classification tasks rather than retrieval. These results also highlight the advantages of metric learning loss functions, which align better with retrieval tasks by optimizing embedding similarity. The optimal λ value, calculated using a validation dataset, was found to be $\lambda = 0.7$ for both ISIC17 and COVID-QU-Ex, as shown in the hyperparameter analysis section

Table 1. The performance evaluation of different existing models on the ISIC17 and COVID-QU-Ex datasets is presented. The first row for both datasets is based on the work by [23]. The next two rows represent X-MIR, utilizing DenseNet121 [8] and ResNet50 [8] embeddings with triplet loss for metric learning. The fourth row is derived from the work of [25], the fifth row from [16], and the sixth row showcases the performance of our proposed Context Switching MIR framework.

Dataset	Model	R@K[1,5,10]	mAP	mP@K[1,5,10]
ISIC17	MIRViT	[74.17 88.17 91.33]	70.96	[74.17 73.80 73.72]
	DenseNet121	[70.00 88.00 92.00]	69.82	[70.00 72.27 72.13]
	ResNet50	[71.33 92.67 96.00]	69.22	[71.33 70.67 71.00]
	ViT + Cross Entropy	[72.00 94.00 96.67]	62.08	[72.00 69.87 67.67]
	MedViT	[46.00 90.00 96.67]	42.54	[46.00 44.80 44.67]
	Context_MIR (Ours)	[78.67 86.67 90.67]	**73.32**	[78.67 77.87 76.93]
COVID-QU-Ex	MIRViT	[93.34 98.03 98.44]	88.40	[93.34 93.00 92.75]
	DenseNet121	[93.08 97.10 97.97]	91.10	[93.08 92.80 92.73]
	ResNet50	[91.57 97.26 98.26]	90.59	[91.57 91.21 91.10]
	ViT + Cross Entropy	[72.08 95.37 98.34]	43.39	[72.08 69.12 67.27]
	MedViT	[77.22 93.89 97.04]	41.24	[77.24 72.91 70.74]
	Context_MIR (Ours)	[94.95 97.66 98.01]	**93.82**	[94.95 94.76 94.70]

in Sect. 7. All the reported results in Table 1 represent the test set performance using this common optimal λ setting, and the implementation details are provided in Sect. 6. An analysis of the network selection counters for the ISIC17 and COVID-QU-Ex datasets revealed that the best-performing models predominantly selected full images, followed by bounding-box ROIs and then standalone ROIs. This indicates a strong preference for full-context inputs during retrieval. Despite the dominance of full images, the context-switching mechanism significantly improved retrieval performance compared to single-input networks trained solely on full images without any context-switching(MIR(Full)).

5.1   Ablation Study

The ablation results shown Table 2 highlight the effectiveness of the proposed context-switching MIR framework (Fig. 1), which consistently outperforms both MIR(Full) and MIR(ROI). MIR(Full) is a single-input retrieval network that uses the Swin-Tiny backbone and is trained on full images without any context switching. It is identical to the model proposed in the MIRViT study [23], with the only difference being the use of the Swin Transformer backbone same as in Context_MIR. MIR(ROI) also uses the Swin-Tiny backbone but is trained on segmentation overlaid images without context switching. The architectures of both models are shown in Fig. 3.

Incorporating segmentation overlaid (ROI) images alone as in MIR(ROI), was expected to improve retrieval performance by focusing on ROI regions instead

Table 2. Performance Evaluation of Context Switching MIR Framework on ISIC17 and COVID-QU-Ex Datasets. This table presents the performance of our proposed Context_MIR framework in comparison with two configurations: MIR(Full), which is trained on full images without context switching which shares the same architecture as the MIRViT study [23] but uses a Swin Transformer backbone, and MIR(ROI), which is trained on segmentation-overlaid images without context switching.

Dataset	Model	R@K[1,5,10]	mAP	mP@K[1,5,10]
ISIC17	Context_MIR(Ours)	[78.67 86.67 90.67]	**73.32**	[78.67 77.87 76.93]
	MIR(Full)	[78.17 89.00 92.33]	71.21	[78.17 76.53 75.32]
	MIR(ROI)	[74.50 89.50 93.33]	67.65	[74.50 72.53 72.03]
COVID_QU_Ex	Context_MIR(Ours)	[94.95 97.66 98.01]	**93.82**	[94.95 94.76 94.70]
	MIR(Full)	[94.86 97.10 97.73]	89.22	[94.86 94.30 94.13]
	MIR(ROI)	[88.07 95.55 96.71]	77.87	[88.07 87.12 86.88]

of full images. This aligns with the common assumption that removing unnecessary parts and retaining only the Region of Interest should enhance results. However, our observations show that this is not always true: isolating the ROI did not surpass the full-image baseline (MIR(Full)) as shown in Table 2. On the other hand, if the surrounding context were always crucial, then using full images (MIR(Full)) should have consistently produced the best results, yet this too did not hold across all cases. Instead, our context-switching framework, Context_MIR, bridges this gap by dynamically selecting the most suitable representations. The framework's additional task of deciding which context to prioritize forces the network to learn richer, more adaptive features, ultimately encouraging more effective representation learning and leading to improved retrieval performance, as evidenced by the superior performance of Context_MIR on both datasets.

Figure 4 presents qualitative retrieval comparisons on ISIC17 and COVID-QU-Ex respectively. Subfigures (a) and (b) show retrievals for the same query, where Context_MIR dynamically selects the segmentation overlaid representation in (a), while MIR(ROI) is trained entirely on segmentation-overlaid images. Despite both using segmentation overlaid inputs, Context_MIR achieves better retrieval. Similarly, (c) and (d) compare retrievals for another query, where Context_MIR selects the full image representation, leading to accurate retrievals, whereas MIR(ROI) fails. This highlights the advantage of context-switching in adapting to the most informative representation. Lastly, (e) and (f) illustrate consistently correct retrievals by our context-switching framework, further underscoring its effectiveness in robust and accurate retrieval.

The comparison shown in Table 3 presents an ablation study evaluating different ViT and Swin architectures as the retrieval network backbones in our proposed Context_MIR framework. The results show that Swin-Tiny outperforms across all metrics on both datasets, highlighting its effectiveness in retrieval tasks. Notably, Context_MIR (ViT-Small) uses the same backbone as the MIRViT

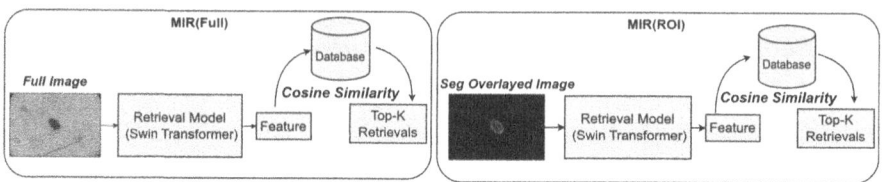

Fig. 3. MIR(Full) uses only full images and MIR(ROI) uses only segmentation-overlaid ROI images for training. Both are single networks without any context switching trained using the Swin Tiny backbone with contrastive learning.

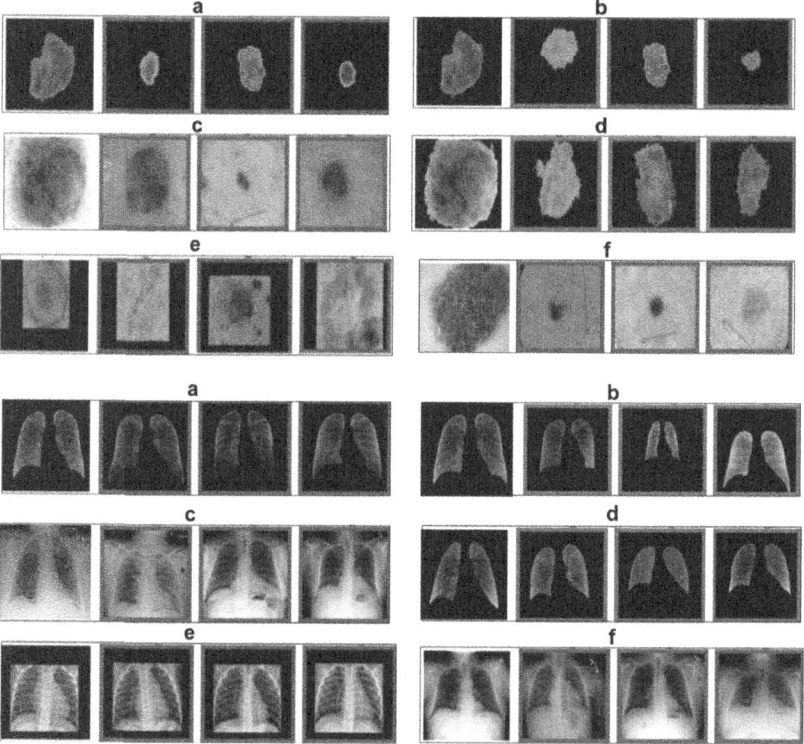

Fig. 4. Examples of image retrievals for ISIC17 and COVID-QU-Ex using Context_MIR and MIR(ROI) networks. (a) Context_MIR image where segmentation-overlaid selection gave correct retrievals. (b) MIR(ROI) with poorer retrievals for the same input as (a). (c) Context_MIR using the full image for correct retrievals. (d) MIR(ROI) with incorrect retrievals (red border) for the same input as (c). (e–f) Correct retrieval examples using our Context_MIR framework. (Color figure online)

study [23], enabling a direct comparison. These findings led to the selection of Swin-Tiny as the backbone for our framework, confirming its superiority in achieving higher performance in MIR tasks. Complete results for these two studies can be found in Tables.

Table 3. Ablation Study: Performance evaluation of different backbones for our Context_MIR framework on the ISIC17 and COVID-QU-Ex datasets. Context_MIR(ViT-Small) employs ViT-Small backbone which is the same backbone as the MIRViT model.

Dataset	Model	R@K (1,5,10)	mAP	mP@K (1,5,10)
ISIC	Context_MIR (Swin-tiny)	[78.67 86.67 90.67]	**73.32**	[78.67 77.87 76.93]
	Context_MIR (ViT-small)	[78.67 90.00 91.33]	72.88	[78.67 77.20 76.07]
	Context_MIR (ViT-base)	[68.67 92.00 96.00]	69.45	[68.67 71.47 72.27]
	Context_MIR (Swin-small)	[74.00 91.33 96.00]	71.33	[74.00 73.33 73.87]
COVID-QU-Ex	Context_MIR (Swin-tiny)	[94.95 97.66 98.01]	**93.82**	[94.95 94.76 94.70]
	Context_MIR (ViT-small)	[93.28 97.11 97.91]	91.79	[93.28 92.85 92.71]
	Context_MIR (ViT-base)	[90.59 95.92 96.97]	86.91	[90.59 90.03 89.83]
	Context_MIR (Swin-small)	93.95 97.08 97.75	92.49	93.95 93.56 93.52

6 Implementation Details

For MIR, the optimization of these models employs the AdamW optimizer with a learning rate of 3×10^{-5}, a weight decay of 5×10^{-4}, and a total of 10,000 iterations and batch size 24. The contrastive loss margin (β) is set to 0.5. In the absence of regularization ($\lambda = 0$) and with differential entropy regularization, different variants of λ ($\lambda = 0.3, 0.7$) are employed. The bounding box was created from the segmentation mask's extent, expanded by a 10–20 pixel margin to include context, and overlaid on the full image. The margin was chosen to ensure all ROIs are captured without making the box nearly as large as the full image. Standard data augmentation techniques are applied, including resizing images to 256×256, random cropping to 224×224, and random horizontal flipping. Both datasets were partitioned to maintain balanced validation and test sets for consistent performance evaluation. For MedSAM2, the input images are resized to 1024×1024 and normalized using z-score normalization. Bounding box prompts are derived from ground truth (GT) masks by identifying the minimum and maximum x and y coordinates of the lesion pixels. Random perturbations are applied to the bounding box coordinates, with a maximum shift of 5 pixels. The GT masks are resized to 256×256 to align with the mask decoder's output resolution, ensuring high-quality segmentation for subsequent MIR tasks. The AdamW optimizer is used with a learning rate of 6×10^{-5}, aligning with [13] to ensure stable fine-tuning. A batch size of 4 was selected as it was the most feasible within GPU memory constraints. The model was trained for 300 epochs, as the loss plateaued around this point.

7 Hyperparameter Tuning

The results presented in Fig. 5 represent the validation performance obtained during the hyperparameter analysis of the Context-Switching MIR framework. The primary objective was to investigate the impact of the regularization parameter λ on key performance metrics - mean Average Precision (mAP), Recall@K

(R@K), and Mean Precision@K (mP@K), using the validation sets of the respective datasets. For the COVID_QU_EX dataset, 45% of the original training set was allocated for MedSAM2 training, while the remaining dataset was evenly split into training, validation, and test subsets for our Context-Switching MIR model.

Hyperparameter tuning was conducted on the validation sets of both ISIC17 and COVID_QU_EX. Across both datasets, $\lambda = 0.7$ consistently achieved the highest mAP, followed closely by $\lambda = 0.3$. The lowest mAP scores were observed for $\lambda = 0.0$, indicating that incorporating regularization improves retrieval performance. In addition to strong mAP performance, $\lambda = 0.7$ also demonstrated superior results across R@K and mP@K metrics, underscoring its robustness in ranking and retrieval. Based on these observations, $\lambda = 0.7$ is identified as the optimal regularization setting for the framework, offering consistent and balanced performance across both datasets.

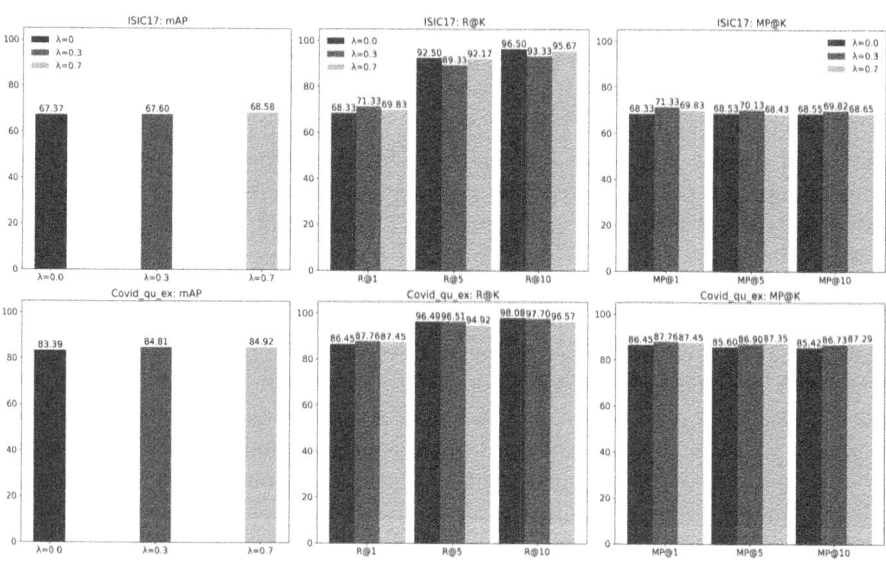

Fig. 5. Hyperparameter tuning on our Context_MIR Framework

8 Conclusion

The proposed context-switching medical image retrieval (MIR) framework, utilizing MedSAM2 for segmentation, effectively addresses the limitations of single-network approaches by dynamically adapting to the unique requirements of each query image. By enabling the network to explore multiple input contexts during both training and inference, our framework overcomes the rigid constraints of ROI-based retrievals. Notably, our findings suggest that general contextual information often provides more reliable cues for accurate image retrieval than focusing solely on ROI regions. In future work, this framework could be extended to varied segmentation inputs that precisely can provide much varied context adaptation capabilities. For instance, incorporating context obtained from radiologists would be helpful to ensure appropriate context is incorporated. One way to achieve this is by using multi-modal retrieval, expanding the framework to include clinical metadata or radiology reports alongside images. However, this would require extensive clinical studies that are beyond the scope of this present work. Further, it would be interesting to examine the difference in human and machine contexts in terms of relevance for retrieval.

Acknowledgements. This research work was partially supported by Research-I Foundation of the Department of CSE at IIT Kanpur.

References

1. Choe, J., et al.: Content-based image retrieval by using deep learning for interstitial lung disease diagnosis with chest CT. Radiology **302**(1), 187–197 (2022)
2. Chupikov, A., Kinoshenko, D., Mashtalir, V., Shcherbinin, K.: Image retrieval with segmentation-based query. In: International Workshop on Adaptive Multimedia Retrieval, pp. 207–221. Springer (2006)
3. Codella, N.C., et al.: Skin lesion analysis toward melanoma detection: a challenge at the 2017 international symposium on biomedical imaging (ISBI), hosted by the international skin imaging collaboration (ISIC). In: 2018 IEEE 15th International Symposium on Biomedical Imaging (ISBI 2018), pp. 168–172. IEEE (2018)
4. Dong, H., Gu, H., Chen, Y., Yang, J., Chen, Y., Mazurowski, M.A.: Segment anything model 2: an application to 2d and 3d medical images. arXiv preprint arXiv:2408.00756 (2024)
5. Dosovitskiy, A., et al.: An image is worth 16x16 words: transformers for image recognition at scale. In: 9th International Conference on Learning Representations, ICLR 2021. OpenReview.net (2021). https://openreview.net/forum?id=YicbFdNTTy
6. Dubey, S.R.: A decade survey of content based image retrieval using deep learning. IEEE Trans. Circuits Syst. Video Technol. **32**(5), 2687–2704 (2021)
7. El-Nouby, A., Neverova, N., Laptev, I., Jégou, H.: Training vision transformers for image retrieval. arXiv preprint arXiv:2102.05644 (2021)
8. Hu, B., Vasu, B., Hoogs, A.: X-MIR: explainable medical image retrieval. In: Proceedings of the IEEE/CVF Winter Conference on Applications of Computer Vision, pp. 440–450 (2022)
9. Jush, F.K., Truong, T., Vogler, S., Lenga, M.: Medical image retrieval using pretrained embeddings. In: 2024 IEEE International Symposium on Biomedical Imaging (ISBI), pp. 1–5. IEEE (2024)
10. Kugunavar, S., Prabhakar, C.: Content-based medical image retrieval using delaunay triangulation segmentation technique. In: Research Anthology on Improving Medical Imaging Techniques for Analysis and Intervention, pp. 439–459. IGI Global (2023)
11. Kugunavar, S., Prabhakar, C.: Medical image retrieval using ROI extraction and hybrid bag-of-features model (2024)

12. Liu, Z., et al.: Swin transformer: hierarchical vision transformer using shifted windows. In: Proceedings of the IEEE/CVF International Conference on Computer Vision, pp. 10012–10022 (2021)
13. Ma, J., He, Y., Li, F., Han, L., You, C., Wang, B.: Segment anything in medical images. Nat. Commun. **15**(1), 654 (2024)
14. Ma, J., et al.: Segment anything in medical images and videos: benchmark and deployment. ArXiv **abs/2408.03322** (2024). https://api.semanticscholar.org/CorpusID:271719837
15. Manna, A., Sista, R., Sheet, D.: Deep neural hashing for content-based medical image retrieval: a survey (2024)
16. Manzari, O.N., Ahmadabadi, H., Kashiani, H., Shokouhi, S.B., Ayatollahi, A.: Medvit: a robust vision transformer for generalized medical image classification. Comput. Biol. Med. **157**, 106791 (2023)
17. Qayyum, A., Anwar, S.M., Awais, M., Majid, M.: Medical image retrieval using deep convolutional neural network. Neurocomputing **266**, 8–20 (2017)
18. Rahman, M., Humayara, F., Rabbi, S.M.E., Rashid, M.M.: Efficient medical image retrieval using densenet and faiss for birads classification. arXiv preprint arXiv:2411.01473 (2024)
19. Sablayrolles, A., Douze, M., Schmid, C., Jégou, H.: Spreading vectors for similarity search. arXiv: Machine Learning (2018). https://api.semanticscholar.org/CorpusID:62841605
20. Shetty, R., Bhat, V.S., Handigol, S., Kumar, S., Kubasad, S., Badiger, K.: Medical image retrieval system for endoscopy images using CNN. In: 2023 International Conference on Applied Intelligence and Sustainable Computing (ICAISC), pp. 1–5. IEEE (2023)
21. Siebert, A.: Segmentation-based image retrieval. In: Storage and Retrieval for Image and Video Databases VI, vol. 3312, pp. 14–24. SPIE (1997)
22. Song, C.H., Yoon, J., Choi, S., Avrithis, Y.: Boosting vision transformers for image retrieval. In: Proceedings of the IEEE/CVF Winter Conference on Applications of Computer Vision, pp. 107–117 (2023)
23. Susmitha, A.S., Namboodiri, V.P.: Analysis of transformers for medical image retrieval. In: Proceedings of The 7nd International Conference on Medical Imaging with Deep Learning, vol. 250, pp. 1497–1512 (2024). https://proceedings.mlr.press/v250/susmitha24a.html
24. Tahir, A., et al.: Covid-qu-ex dataset. Kaggle (2022). https://doi.org/10.34740/KAGGLE/DSV/2759090
25. Thakrar, A., et al.: Semantic retrieval of similar radiological images using vision transformers. medRxiv, pp. 2023–02 (2023)
26. Tschandl, P., Rosendahl, C., Kittler, H.: The ham10000 dataset, a large collection of multi-source dermatoscopic images of common pigmented skin lesions. Sci. Data **5**(1), 1–9 (2018)
27. Vani, K., Papachary, B., Lavanya, L.: Segmentation based biomedical image retrieval with low-level feature extraction. J. Phys. Conf. Ser. **1964**, 062059 (2021)
28. Wang, T., Isola, P.: Understanding contrastive representation learning through alignment and uniformity on the hypersphere. In: International Conference on Machine Learning, pp. 9929–9939. PMLR (2020)
29. Zhang, Z., Li, W., Li, B.: An improving technique of color histogram in segmentation-based image retrieval. In: 2009 Fifth International Conference on Information Assurance and Security, vol. 2, pp. 381–384. IEEE (2009)

Segmentation in Histopathology Utilising Simulated Masked Patches

Aashay Tinaikar⬤ and Nitin Singhal⁽✉⁾⬤

AIRA Matrix, Mumbai, India
nitin.singhal@airamatrix.com
http://airamatrix.com

Abstract. Deep learning algorithms have demonstrated significant potential in segmenting diverse tissue morphologies within histopathological whole-slide images. However, the availability of these datasets is limited, and obtaining expert annotations is often time-consuming and difficult. Consequently, training precise segmentation algorithms poses a considerable challenge. To address this, we introduce Simulated Segmentation with Masked Patches (SSMP), a novel method for training segmentation models that relies on weak or incomplete labels. This approach can significantly reduce model development time from days to hours by bypassing the labor-intensive annotation process. In few-shot settings, our method has shown promising results on datasets such as Camelyon16, MSKCC Lymphnode, and BCNB, achieving fewer false positives compared to existing weakly-supervised methods. Moreover, on large lymph node metastatic datasets like Camelyon16 and MSKCC, SSMP surpasses MIL-based algorithms in whole-slide image classification tasks, particularly in scenarios with limited data.

Keywords: Segmentation · patrially supervised learning · simulated segmentation · training on limited data

1 Introduction

Histopathology images are widely regarded as the definitive and reliable method for diagnosis in clinical settings. Due to multi-scale nature, and very large image resolutions of histopathology Whole Slide Images (WSIs), their manual examination and the subsequent identification of abnormalities is a labor-intensive and time-consuming process, which hinders the timely delivery of clinical reports [1].

Deep learning (DL) models have demonstrated tremendous promise in automating WSI image analysis over the past decade. Fully-supervised, a DL method that is the most prevalent; rely on massive datasets annotated with high-quality information [2,3]. However, these types of datasets are exceedingly uncommon, and the process of developing comprehensive annotations is both arduous and time-consuming. Semi-supervised segmentation methods [4] enhance predictions by training models on a limited set of pixel-annotated images

S. Ali et al. (Eds.): MIUA 2025, LNCS 15918, pp. 115–128, 2026.
https://doi.org/10.1007/978-3-031-98694-9_9

which share similarities with a larger, unlabeled dataset. While these methods mitigate annotation burden, they are still dependent on the availability of large data pool, even though being un-labelled. On the other hand, weakly-supervised methods involve training DL models in a Multi-instance-learning (MIL) [4] environment using only WSI level labels. In the MIL framework, each WSI is considered as a bag of patches with its respective label. The goal of MIL is to learn a model that can predict the class label of the entire WSI. Later, the attention mechanism in MIL highlights the patches which are most relevant for the predicted label of a WSI. Then the attention scores are used to cluster the similar patches within a bag, which can be used for creating coarse segmentation masks.

Although MIL techniques do indeed simplify the process of annotation [5], numerous studies have highlighted the data-intensive characteristics of these methods. For accurate attention modelling, large datasets are required [6]. In the absence of large datasets, MIL methods lead to inadequate performance. Hence, training segmentation models with minimum annotation efforts remains one of the most sought after research direction. This requirement is compounded in scenarios with limited sized datasets.

This effort aims to tackle the above mentioned challenges associated with limited data and labor-intensive task of annotating histopathology images required for training segmentation models. We introduce a unique approach called Simulated Segmentation with Masked Patches (SSMP), which allows for the creation of a very efficient and accurate segmentation dataset with minimal annotation requirements. This approach is one of the first to use a simulated dataset to solve the pixel-wise annotation problem. Unlike earlier research that recommend specialised training approaches, the proposed strategy can be incorporated into standard training process. The proposed strategy showed state-of-the-art performance in multiple data constrained scenarios in regards to pixel level segmentation and WSI level classification.

2   Related Works and Comparative Methods

A considerable number of partial-annotation techniques [7–11] depend on piece wise continuity assumptions that are intrinsic to natural images. With regard to histopathology, this assumption is not valid [12]. Therefore, it is imperative to establish specialised methodologies for partial supervised training in the field of histopathology.

The most recent advancements in the domain of histopathology involve classification and segmentation techniques that operate with minimal supervision. Multi-head attention and feature clustering are utilised by CLAM [5] to deliver state-of-the-art WSI level classification performance.

Conventional strategies mentioned above use Convolutional Neural Network (CNNs) [13] architectures. An alternative approach suggested by Qian et al. [14] is the utilisation of transformers [15] to attract long-range attention. Individual patches are utilised to train MIL, and the concatenated patch attention is employed as the WSI segmentation label. The same research team (Li et al. [16])

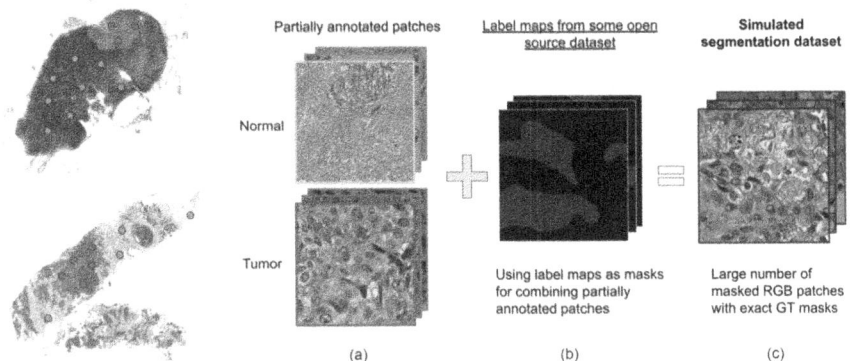

Fig. 1. Data compilation for Simulated Segmentation with Masked Patches (SSMP) is described in detail. The SSMP dataset was constructed by extracting complete normal(non-tumor) and tumor regions as depicted in (a), which are denoted by green and red dots, respectively. These complete patches are fused together by using a binary mask to generate a simulated patch as depicted in (b) and (c). (Color figure online)

later introduced a novel idea that incorporates self-attention in the Multiple Instance Learning (MIL) framework to capture long-range interdependence.

3 Method: Simulated Segmentation Using Masked Patches

The schematic representation of Simulated Segmentation using Masked Patches (SSMP) is depicted in Fig. 1. This approach involves the identification and labelling of specific areas that exhibit tissue morphologies of interest through the use of point annotations.

An in-house WSI annotation tool is used to analyze large digital images (WSI) of tissue which breaks down the WSI into smaller square patches at different magnification levels. Then, green and red markers are used to identify patches containing only either non-tumor or tumor tissue, respectively (see Fig. 1a). The marking is done manually at a desired magnification level chosen for the experiment.

Instead of labeling every single WSI, we focus on a smaller number of WSIs that clearly show both non-tumorous and tumorous tissue and covers enough tissue morphology variability. We save the patches with green and red markers in separate folders.

The key idea is that each patch primarily contains either non-tumorous or tumorous tissue, making it easier to categorize. This allows us to create a partially labeled dataset by annotating only a few key WSIs. Further this dataset is then used to generate a much larger dataset of simulated tissue segmentation patches using Algorithm 1. This generated dataset contains N patches, where N is the desired number of patches chosen for the experiment.

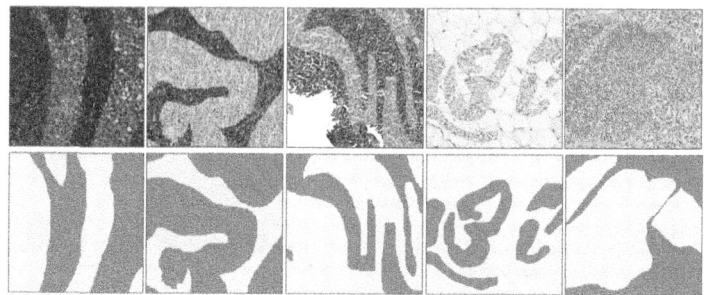

Fig. 2. Representative samples of SSMP derived simulated RGB images (top row) and their corresponding segmentation GT masks (bottom row) for Camelyon17 dataset. Yellow and Green colors in GT masks represent normal(non-tumor) and tumor tissue regions respectively. (Color figure online)

For synthesis, a patch each from normal (s_n) and tumor (s_t) sets are selected randomly. These patches are fused with the help of a random binary mask (s_m) selected from a pool of available masks. This mask serves as a proxy GT label for synthesized image generation. A synthesis of a simulated image s_{ssmp} is depicted by Eq. 1. Figure 2 shows the representative samples from simulated segmentation dataset.

$$s_{ssmp} = s_n * (s_m = 0) + s_t * (s_m = 1) \tag{1}$$

Algorithm 1. Steps for Data Creation

Inputs: Set of normal patches (S_n), tumor patches (S_t), binary masks (S_m)

Output: Set of Simulated Segmentation patches (S_{ssmp})

1: **while** $n \leq N$ **do**
2:     Randomly select normal patch $s_n \in \mathcal{S}_n$, tumor patch $s_t \in \mathcal{S}_t$
3:     Randomly select mask patch $s_m \in \mathcal{S}_m$
4:     Simulated patch:$s_{ssmp} = s_n * (s_m = 0) + s_t * (s_m = 1)$
5: **end while**

It is important to acknowledge that the labels utilised in the present analysis were sourced from the DigestPath2019 dataset [17]. Careful selection of the labels maps is important since the effectiveness of this approach remains sensitive towards the selection of label maps. Ideally, label maps should be selected such that the foreground structures closely resemble the morphologies encountered in the downstream task.

The SSMP merges different tissue classes—such as tumor and non-tumor regions—by applying a random binary mask, as described in Eq. 1. While this approach enables the blending of distinct classes during image synthesis, it can sometimes result in artificial image artifacts, such as discontinuous tissue structures or transitions that violate anatomical realism. To address these issues, one effective strategy is to apply spatial blurring to the class masks, particularly along the boundaries between regions. This technique softens the edges of the binary mask, creating gradual transitions between classes rather than abrupt boundaries. The result is a more anatomically coherent and visually realistic synthesis, better preserving tissue continuity and structural integrity in the generated images.

The utilisation of image fusion methods like CutMix and Copy-Paste to produce augmentations has been investigated in prior research [18,19]. CutMix is a data augmentation strategy which removes informative pixels from training images and replaces them with a patch of either black pixels or random noise. Whereas, in Copy-Paste augmentation, regions from one image are pasted into another. These strategies, predominantly developed for classification and object detection scenarios respectively, force the model to focus on relevant regions leading to improvements in model generalization. However, it should be noted that both of these approaches largely serve as augmentation techniques. In contrast, the SSMP method enables the construction of a semantic segmentation model by utilising patch classification labels.

4   Datasets

Camelyon 16 and 17. Camelyon16 [20] dataset consists of 399 H&E stained WSIs of Breast Lymphnode sections with presence of metastatic regions. Whole dataset is consolidated from two different labs. Detailed tumor masks are provided for all WSIs along with WSI level binary label for presence of tumor. We use this dataset for evaluation of pixel level segmentation as well as WSI level tumor prediction performance.

Likewise, Camelyon17 [21] dataset comprise of in total 1000 WSIs of Breast Lymphnode sections, collected from five different centers. Detailed tumor masks are provided for 10 WSIs from each center. We use these annotated WSIs for creating our training dataset.

MSKCC Lymphnode Metastasis. MSKCC Lymphnode dataset [22] consists of 130 de-identified WSIs of H&E stained axiliary lymph node specimens from 78 patients. Each slide is assigned a class label indicating the presence of breast cancer, denoted as positive, or the absence thereof, denoted as negative. The dataset serves as an external test set for evaluating the performance.

Breast Cancer Core-Needle Biopsy Dataset. Early Breast Cancer Core-Needle Biopsy Dataset (BCNB) [23] includes 1058 core-needle biopsy WSIs of early breast cancer patients and the corresponding clinical data. The whole slide images (WSIs) have undergone examination, and specific areas of the tumour have been annotated by two pathologists who possess extensive experience and work independently of each other.

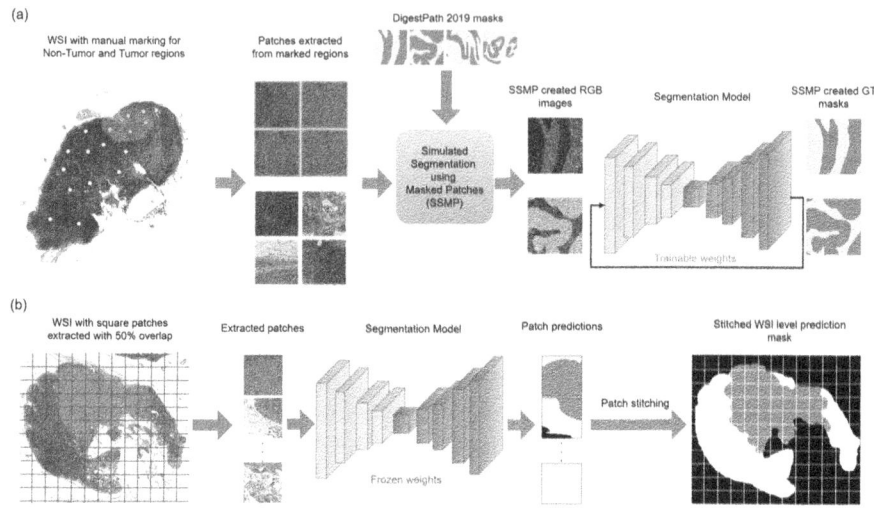

Fig. 3. Schematic of (a) Training phase using SSMP generated dataset and (b) WSI testing phase. During testing phase, the model weights obtained after training phase are used.

5   Experiments and Training Details

5.1   Camelyon 16 and 17

Experiments were conducted utilising WSIs in a few-shot setting to investigate lymph node metastasis. In each laboratory, a single malignant WSI is selected from the dataset provided by Camelyon17.

The available tumour masks were utilised to extract patches measuring 512×512 pixels at a magnification of 10x, with a pixel width of $0.9078\ \mu m/pixel$. Distribution of extracted patches in training and validation sets are given in Table 1.

Table 1. Distribution of WSIs and patches in training and validation sets for the Five shot Camelyon17 dataset

Split	Num. WSIs	Num. Patches
Training	5	2850
Validation	5	4679

5.2   BCNB Dataset

We extract 256×256 patches containing tumor pixels from annotated images, focusing on areas with tumor presence. These patches, along with their masks, form a supervised dataset from selected WSIs with significant tumor areas intentionally chosen. Additionally, fully filled tumor and normal tissue patches are included in our simulated dataset.

We also extract patches containing tumor areas from all the available WSIs. These are used for training a fully supervised segmentation model which act as a baseline for comparison of segmentation performance.

Table 2 mentions the amount of WSIs and patches utilied for training models under Fully-supervised and Few shot configuration.

The current experiments are centered on segmenting tumor and non-tumor regions. Patch sizes of 512 (for the Camelyon dataset) and 256 (for the BCNB dataset) were selected to facilitate the generation of simulated data, following the procedure described in Sect. 3. Additional considerations and rationale behind these choices are discussed in detail in Sects. 7.2 and 7.3.

Table 2. Distribution of WSIs and patches in training and validation sets for the fully supervised and Few shot BCNB dataset respectively. Originally provided training-validation splits were used.

Split	Fully supervised		Few shot	
	Num. WSIs	Num. Patches	Num. WSIs	Num. Patches
Training	630	98706	10	2997
Validation	210	33257	5	1330

5.3 Training Settings

Various model architectures, including U-Net [24] with ResNet50 encoder [25], U-Net with EfficientNetB0 encoder [26], and SegFormerB0 [27], are employed for training on both supervised and simulated segmentation datasets.

The current study focuses on proposing a novel data creation method rather than evaluating different model architectures. Moreover, in the limited data setting of this study, using larger model architectures may promote overfitting. Hence for simplicity, we have limited the experiments to base variants (B0) of EfficientNet and SegFormer.

In the context of supervised and SSMP model training, a maximum learning rate of 1e-4 is employed for CNN-based models, while a maximum learning rate of 1e-5 is utilised for Transformer-based models. The use of the OneCycle learning rate scheduler is common throughout the training phase. The model training process is conducted using the DICE loss function in conjunction with the ADAM optimizer. All models underwent training until they reached convergence.

The supervised patch dataset obtained in this study was utilised for training the Swin-MIL [14], SA-MIL [16] and DWS-MIL [28] models. The model architecture remained unaltered. To facilitate comparison with the CLAM framework, we employ the end-to-end pipeline in its original form, which encompasses patch extraction, attention calculation, and final WSI level predictions.

The models were trained with PyTorch 1.9.0, employing Python 3.9, and leveraging the computational power of an NVIDIA RTX A6000 GPU.

6   Results

The performance of every trained model is assessed through the implementation of whole slide level inference using a Python programme. Few shot segmentation and classification results are obtained using models trained on small number of WSIs. Fig. 3 shows the detailed schematic of training and inference pipelines. Inference is performed by extracting patches from the tissue region in a cartesian grid as shown in Fig. 3b, utilising patches of comparable size to those employed during the training phase of the model. For all inferences, an overlap fraction of 0.5 is utilised to reduce tiling artefacts. There are no post-processing operations performed. In the context of models trained under the CLAM framework, consistency was maintained in tile size and overlap fraction to replicate our inference configuration.

Table 3. WSI classification AUROC for predictions on Camelyon16 and MSKCC dataset. Models are trained on 5 WSIs from Camelyon17 dataset. Best values in bold.

Model type	Camelyon 16		MSKCC	
	AUROC (%)	Best Acc. (%)	AUROC (%)	Best Acc. (%)
Sup. Seg. - U-Net ResNet50	65.23	66.12	81.59	80.27
CLAM [5] (10x)	61.43	63.51	69.32	72.32
CLAM [5] (40x)	65.24	67.57	-	-
Swin-MIL [14]	53.72	54.01	68.67	66.87
DWS-MIL [28]	52.64	55.32	58.17	61.39
SA-MIL [16]	53.72	54.67	50.68	53.07
SSMP - U-Net ResNet50	**72.31**	**73.52**	**90.54**	**91.54**

6.1   Segmentation Performance

Metrics for Camelyon16 are computed by utilising the tumour masks that are supplied (Table 4). The absence of GT tumour masks for MSKCC precludes the evaluation of such segmentation performance.

For BCNB dataset, available GT masks are annotated only partially. Therefore, the segmentation masks acquired utilising the fully-supervised trained model are regarded as the baseline GT masks. Experiments show that segmentation DICE scores for models trained with the SSMP dataset are higher than those for models trained with the conventional configuration (Fig. 4 and Table 4).

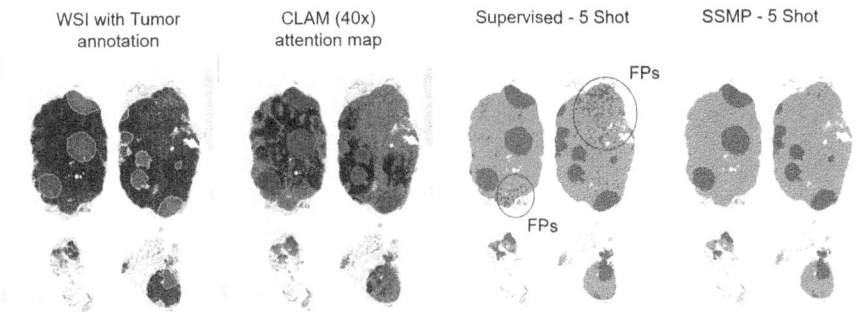

Fig. 4. Visualization of GT, CLAM [5] (40x) attention map, Few shot (5 Shot) supervised and SSMP model output for Camelyon16 Lymphnode metastasis dataset. Models were trained on 5 WSIs from Camelyon17

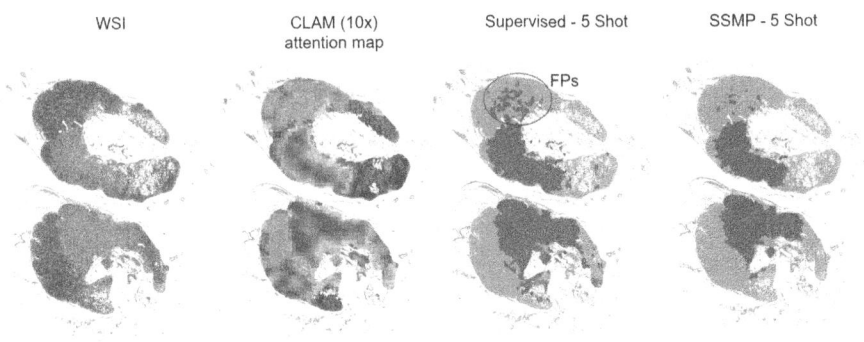

Fig. 5. Visualization of GT, CLAM [5] (10x) attention map, Few shot (5 Shot) supervised and SSMP model output for MSKCC Lymphnode metastasis dataset. Models were trained on 5 WSIs from Camelyon17

When compared to the attention maps obtained from the most effective weakly-supervised experiments, segmentation strategies have consistently demonstrated an ability to provide more accurate localization. Since other MIL setups perform very poorly at WSI level classification itself, we avoid evaluating their attention maps altogether.

6.2   WSI Classification Performance

Stitched tumor prediction masks are used to calculate percentage of tumor region wrt. tissue area for each WSI. Fig. 6a and b shows the box plot obtained for 130 WSIs from MSKCC using Unet with ResNet50 encoder. The True Positive Rate (TPR) and False Positive Rate (FPR) are computed across various anticipated tumour percentage values. The WSI level classification measure for the Camelyon16 and MSKCC datasets is computed using AUROC (Table 3, Fig. 6c).

Afterwards, the most accurate values are computed using a grid search technique. The models that have been trained using the SSMP dataset demonstrate superior performance in scenarios when there is limited data available, outperforming both CLAM and other approaches.

Table 4. DICE metrics on Camelyon16 and BNCB test datasets for models trained using fully supervised and simulated datasets. Best values are highlighted in bold.

Method	Model type	Camelyon 16 DICE (%)	BNCB DICE (%)
Supervised	U-Net EfficientNetB0	61.43	67.6
	U-Net ResNet50	45.61	59.71
	SegFormerB0	**65.28**	64.03
SSMP	U-Net EfficientNetB0	68.51	**72.96**
	U-Net ResNet50	**64.17**	**69.27**
	SegFormerB0	62.13	**72.03**

6.3   Ablation Study

For the Camelyon16 dataset, the AUROC and accuracy values for WSI level classification are displayed in Table 5. It has been demonstrated that the SSMP method produces superior results to conventional settings for all models. This observation holds true even for SegFormerB0, however the performance gains are significantly lower. Enhanced modelling of long-range dependencies in the transformer-based encoder could account for this.

Table 5. WSI classification AUROC and Accuracy for predictions on Camelyon16 dataset using different model architectures. Best values are highlighted in bold.

Method	Model type	AUROC (%)	Best Acc. (%)
Supervised	U-Net EfficientNetB0	72.62	75.10
	U-Net ResNet50	65.23	66.12
	SegFormerB0	77.17	79.37
SSMP	U-Net EfficientNetB0	**76.18**	**78.31**
	U-Net ResNet50	**72.31**	**73.52**
	SegFormerB0	**78.43**	**80.17**

Experiments in the Few-Shot configuration involve using different quantities of WSIs (whole slide images) to train the model. We analyse one, two, or three cancerous whole slide images (WSIs) from each laboratory in Camelyon17 dataset. Table 6 shows the results for different configuration.

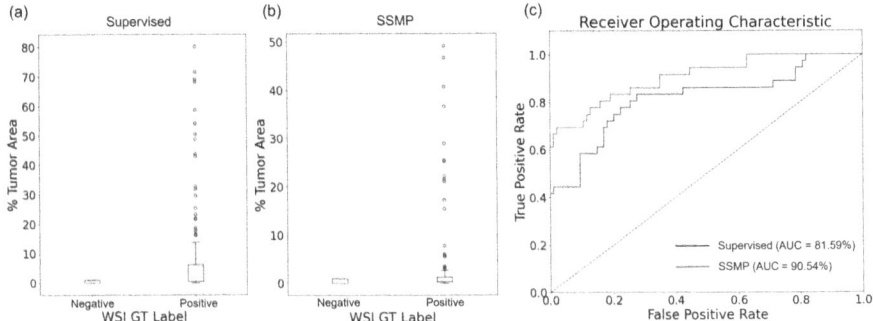

Fig. 6. Plots showing results on 130 WSIs from MSKCC obtained using Unet with ResNet50 encoder trained in a 5-shot setting. (a) and (b) show box plots of predicted % Tumor area for Negative and Positive cohorts using supervised and SSMP training strategies. (c) shows the ROC plots derived using the predicted % Tumor area for the two strategies.

Increasing benefits are observed in the regime of decreasing data when the SSMP method is used to generate the dataset. The performance of the model approaches that of one trained on a conventional supervised segmentation dataset as the size of the data increases. The specific performance improvements achieved by SSMP may differ depending on the type of dataset.

Table 6. AUROC and DICE values obtained on Camelyon16 using U-Net with ResNet50 encoder for different number of WSIs in the training set. Values are compared for supervised and SSMP dataset based model training strategies.

Method	AUROC (%)			DICE (%)		
	5-shot	10-shot	15-shot	5-shot	10-shot	15-shot
Supervised	65.23	79.91	86.14	77.17	82.29	**87.29**
SSMP	**72.31**	**82.23**	**86.21**	**78.43**	**82.61**	87.15

7 Discussion: Advantages and Limitations

In this research, we examined the efficacy of SSMP for training segmentation models in histopathology. In practical situations where the acquisition and dissemination of data on a large scale can present difficulties, few-shot approaches are considered to be incredibly desirable. Consequently, we outline the benefits and shortcomings of the SSMP method as follows:

7.1   Improved Intra-class Balancing and Reduction in False-Positives

It is evident from Fig. 4 and Fig. 5 that the SSMP approach yields a considerably smaller number of false positives (FPs) for a model trained in a few shot setting compared to a comparable model trained in a conventional setting. In the training process of a conventional, supervised segmentation model, it becomes challenging to balance this intra-class variation. The SSMP method enables intelligent sampling of various tissues, which reduces the bias of the models.

7.2   Significant Reduction in Annotation Effort

According to a number of empirical studies, annotation efforts can be reduced by as much as 95% [29,30] using weak annotations, such as those employed in SSMP. Therefore, SSMP eliminates the need to generate pixel level segmentation masks. The model behaves similarly to a segmentation model during inference, providing predictions at the pixel level.

7.3   Increased Noise in Predictions

The model's access to contextual information is limited due to the simulated nature of the dataset. Therefore, the model has a higher likelihood for acquiring local pixel-based characteristics as opposed to context-based representations. During inference time, this may translate to small-size's false positives. However, these can be handled by several proposed strategies [31,32].

7.4   Application to Specific Class of Problems

In order to generate SSMP data, regions that represent just one tissue morphology (benign or malignant)Âăare extracted. Consequently, the present approach lacks applicability to scenarios in which the region of interest is confined to a sub-patch level, such as nucleus segmentation. Additionally, accommodating glandular structures or tissue regions that are inherently thin, such as epithelial linings, poses a greater challenge when employing the SSMP method.

8   Conclusion

This study introduces a unique technique called SSMP, which aims to effectively train segmentation models using partially annotated classification datasets. Our findings from the tests done using Camelyon16 and BCNB indicate that theÂătechnique is well-suited for the development of segmentation models employing datasets of extremely small sizes (few shots). The aforementioned technique serves as an intelligent augmentation strategy that effectively addresses the issue of class imbalance across different tissue morphologies. In addition, the SSMP technique effectively minimises the labor-intensive annotation requirements for training pixel-wise segmentation models, resulting in a significant acceleration of the model development process. In general, our findings also demonstrate that the classification of whole slide images (WSI) achieved by the use of segmentation model's output mask has superior performance compared to the performance of the weakly-supervised model in situations when there is limited data available. Although the results presented in this work are limited to binary datasets, it is important to note that the SSMP approach may be readily extended to address multi-class situations. Our future work will be focused on exploring this possibility.

References

1. Fuchs, T.J., Buhmann, J.M.: Computational pathology: challenges and promises for tissue analysis. Comput. Med. Imaging Graph. **35**, 515–530 (2011)
2. Singhal, N., Soni, S., Bonthu, S., et al.: A deep learning system for prostate cancer diagnosis and grading in whole slide images of core needle biopsies. Sci. Rep. **12**, 3383 (2022)
3. Yuan, H., Chen, L., He, X.: MMUNet: morphological feature enhancement network for colon cancer segmentation in pathological images. Biomed. Signal Process. Control **91**, 105927 (2024)
4. Zhong, L., Liao, X., Zhang, S., Wang, G.: Semi-supervised pathological image segmentation via cross distillation of multiple attentions (2023)
5. Lu, M.Y., Williamson, D.F., Chen, T.Y., Chen, R.J., Barbieri, M., Mahmood, F.: Data-efficient and weakly supervised computational pathology on whole-slide images. Nat. Biomed. Eng. **5**(6), 555–570 (2021)
6. Schmidt, A., Silva-Rodriguez, J., Molina, R., Naranjo, V.: Efficient cancer classification by coupling semi supervised and multiple instance learning. IEEE Access **10**, 9763–9773 (2022)
7. Fang, Z., Chen, Y., Wang, Y., Wang, Z., Ji, X., Zhang, Y.: Weakly-supervised semantic segmentation for histopathology images based on dataset synthesis and feature consistency constraint. In: Proceedings of the AAAI Conference on Artificial Intelligence, vol. 37, pp. 606–613 (2023)
8. Kervadec, H., Dolz, J., Tang, M., Granger, E., Boykov, Y., Ayed, I.B.: Constrained-CNN losses for weakly supervised segmentation. Med. Image Anal. **54**, 88–99 (2019)
9. Liu, Q., Ramanathan, V., Mahajan, D., Yuille, A., Yang, Z.: Weakly supervised instance segmentation for videos with temporal mask consistency. In: Proceedings of the IEEE/CVF Conference on Computer Vision and Pattern Recognition, pp. 13968–13978 (2021)
10. Pu, M., Huang, Y., Guan, Q., Zou, Q.: Graphnet: learning image pseudo annotations for weakly-supervised semantic segmentation. In: Proceedings of the 26th ACM International Conference on Multimedia, pp. 483–491 (2018)
11. Zhang, B., Xiao, J., Jiao, J., Wei, Y., Zhao, Y.: Affinity attention graph neural network for weakly supervised semantic segmentation. IEEE Trans. Pattern Anal. Mach. Intell. **44**(11), 8082–8096 (2021)
12. Zhang, H., et al.: Weakly supervised segmentation with point annotations for histopathology images via contrast-based variational model. In: Proceedings of the IEEE/CVF Conference on Computer Vision and Pattern Recognition, pp. 15630–15640 (2023)

13. O'shea, K., Nash, R.: An introduction to convolutional neural networks. arXiv preprint arXiv:1511.08458 (2015)
14. Qian, Z., et al.: Transformer based multiple instance learning for weakly supervised histopathology image segmentation. In: International Conference on Medical Image Computing and Computer-Assisted Intervention, pp. 160–170, Springer (2022)
15. Vaswani, A., et al.: Attention is all you need. In: Advances in Neural Information Processing Systems, vol. 30 (2017)
16. Li, K., et al.: Weakly supervised histopathology image segmentation with self-attention. Med. Image Anal. **86**, 102791 (2023)
17. Da, Q., et al.: Digestpath: a benchmark dataset with challenge review for the pathological detection and segmentation of digestive-system. Med. Image Anal. **80**, 102485 (2022)
18. Yun, S., Han, D., Oh, S.J., Chun, S., Choe, J., Yoo, Y.: Cut-mix: regularization strategy to train strong classifiers with localizable features. In: Proceedings of the IEEE/CVF International Conference on Computer Vision, pp. 6023–6032 (2019)
19. Ghiasi, G., et al.: Simple copy-paste is a strong data augmentation method for instance segmentation. In: Proceedings of the IEEE/CVF Conference on Computer Vision and Pattern Recognition, pp. 2918–2928 (2021)
20. Bejnordi, B.E., et al.: Diagnostic assessment of deep learning algorithms for detection of lymph node metastases in women with breast cancer. JAMA **318**(22), 2199–2210 (2017)
21. Litjens, G., et al.: 1399 h&e-stained sentinel lymph node sections of breast cancer patients: the camelyon dataset. GigaScience, **7**(6), giy065 (2018)
22. Campanella, G., Hanna, M.G., Brogi, E., Fuchs, T.J.: Breast metastases to axillary lymph nodes (2019)
23. Xu, F., et al.: Predicting axillary lymph node metastasis in early breast cancer using deep learning on primary tumor biopsy slides. Front. Oncol. 4133 (2021)
24. Ronneberger, O., Fischer, P., Brox, T.: U-Net, Convolutional networks for biomedical image segmentation (2015)
25. He, K., Zhang, X., Ren, S., Sun, J.: Deep residual learning for image recognition (2015)
26. Tan, M., Quoc V. Le.: EfficientNet: rethinking model scaling for convolutional neural networks (2020)
27. Xie, E., Wang, W., Yu, Z., Anandkumar, A., Alvarez, J.M., Luo, P.: Segformer: simple and efficient design for semantic segmentation with transformers. In: Neural Information Processing Systems (NeurIPS)
28. Jia, Z., Huang, X., Eric, I., Chang, C., Xu, Y.: Constrained deep weak supervision for histopathology image segmentation. IEEE Trans. Med. Imaging **36**(11), 2376–2388 (2017)
29. Han, C., et al.: Multi-layer pseudo-supervision for histopathology tissue semantic segmentation using patch-level classification labels. Med. Image Anal. **80**, 102487 (2022)
30. Gao, Z., Puttapirat, P., Shi, J., Li, C.: Renal cell carcinoma detection and subtyping with minimalpoint-based annotation in whole-slide images (2020)
31. Lu, Z., Fu, Z., Xiang, T., Han, P., Wang, L., Gao, X.: Learning from weak and noisy labels for semantic segmentation. IEEE Trans. Pattern Anal. Mach. Intell. **39**, 486–500 (2017)
32. Liu, S., Liu, K., Zhu, W., Shen, Y., Fernandez-Granda, C.: Adaptive early-learning correction for segmentation from noisy annotations. In: Proceedings of the IEEE/CVF Conference on Computer Vision and Pattern Recognition (CVPR), pp. 2606–2616 (2022)

A Feature-Driven Acquisition Strategy Using Scale-Invariant Descriptors for Deep Active Learning in Preclinical CT Segmentation

Faye Warren[1][(✉)] , Stephen Paisey[1] , Emiliano Spezi[2] , Yu-kun Lai[3] ,
and Rhodri Smith[4]

[1] School of Medicine, Cardiff University, Cardiff, UK
`warrenf2@cardiff.ac.uk`
[2] School of Engineering, Cardiff University, Cardiff, UK
[3] School of Computer Science and Informatics, Cardiff University, Cardiff, UK
[4] Faculty of Medicine and Dentistry - Radiology and Diagnostic Imaging
Department, Alberta University, Edmonton, Canada

Abstract. Accurate medical image segmentation is essential for clinical decision-making, and while deep learning (DL) models have substantially advanced automated segmentation, their performance depends heavily on large, well-annotated datasets, which are often costly and time-consuming to produce, especially in specialised or emerging imaging scenarios. Active learning (AL) addresses this limitation by iteratively selecting the most informative samples for annotation, ensuring the training dataset is diverse and representative of the overall data distribution to maximise model performance with fewer annotations. This work proposes a novel acquisition function that, for the first time, integrates Scale-Invariant Feature Transform (SIFT) descriptors into AL. By combining entropy-based uncertainty sampling with SIFT-based keypoint matching, we introduce a hybrid strategy—*SIFT-Entropy*—that leverages both learned uncertainty and feature-driven diversity to enhance training efficiency. We validate SIFT-Entropy by comparing its performance against uncertainty and random sampling in a preclinical whole-body mouse Computer Tomography (CT) segmentation task using a Dense VNet. The experiments assess segmentation performance across multiple labels using the Dice Similarity Coefficient (DSC). SIFT-Entropy accelerates model performance improvements, achieving full dataset performance with 61% fewer annotated samples. Furthermore, interquartile range (IQR) analysis confirms the consistency of these performance gains. These findings highlight the potential of hybrid acquisition functions in AL for medical image segmentation, offering a pathway toward data-efficient DL models in resource-constrained environments.

Keywords: Deep Active Learning · Artificial Neural Network · 3D Image Segmentation

S. Ali et al. (Eds.): MIUA 2025, LNCS 15918, pp. 129–145, 2026.
https://doi.org/10.1007/978-3-031-98694-9_10

1 Introduction

Medical imaging is essential in clinical decision-making, aiding diagnosis, treatment planning, and intervention [4]. Among various modalities, Computer Tomography (CT) is widely used for its high-resolution imaging of anatomical structures. Image segmentation is essential for accurate image quantification, interpretation and for facilitating downstream tasks within clinical and research workflows, as it delineates regions of interest (ROI) to distinguish tissues and abnormalities [29]. Manual segmentation, though considered the gold standard, is time-intensive, costly and requires expert knowledge, leading to inter- and intra-observer variability [5,10,21]. To improve efficiency and accuracy, automated segmentation methods are increasingly needed in medical imaging.

Deep learning (DL) techniques have proven effective in significantly improving the accuracy of automated medical image segmentation and have shown success in segmenting various anatomical regions across different imaging modalities [17]. The use of DL in medical image segmentation has increased in recent years, incorporating various architectures and methods, including the widely used TotalSegmentator [28]. Trained on 1204 CT examinations, TotalSegmentator segments 104 individual anatomical structures using an nn-UNet approach [11], a self-adapting framework for U-Net-based medical image segmentation. This approach has shown strong performance with an average overlap via Dice Similarity Coefficient (DSC) of 0.94 (for 1.5 mm voxels) and 0.84 (for 3 mm voxels).

Despite models like TotalSegmentator demonstrating robust performance across a wide variety of clinical CT scans, their effectiveness can decline when applied to edge cases or unseen clinical scenarios. These models are typically trained on all available data from large public datasets with little or no curation based on anatomical complexity, rare conditions or acquisition variability. As a result, the training data may not fully capture the diversity of real-world clinical or research use cases, including rare diseases, abnormal anatomies, or underrepresented regions. Specialised imaging settings—such as distinct contrast phases, non-standard acquisition protocols, or uncommon body regions—further exacerbate these challenges. In such scenarios, trained or even pre-trained models may fail to generalise effectively, highlighting the limitations of conventional training pipelines and motivating the need for adaptive approaches that guide the selection of informative training samples [3,33]. This challenge extends to preclinical imaging, such as Positron Emission Tomography-Computer Tomography (PET-CT) studies used for biodistribution analysis of novel therapeutics and imaging agents. Preclinical datasets often feature smaller anatomical structures, varying acquisition parameters, and limited publicly available data, making standard DL frameworks unsuitable [1].

To overcome these challenges, Active Learning (AL) offers a promising solution. AL is an iterative process that improves model performance by identifying and prioritising the most informative cases for annotation, reducing the reliance on large annotated datasets [4,27]. Making it a viable strategy for optimising segmentation in preclinical imaging and other specialised scenarios.

In this work, we present a novel acquisition function for deep active learning that leverages a combined approach using entropy and the Scale-Invariant Feature Transform (SIFT) to guide data selection prior to annotation. By integrating these two strategies, the AL process benefits from both uncertainty-based sampling and the selection of feature-diverse samples, enhancing the representativeness and informativeness of the training set. To our knowledge, this is the first study to integrate handcrafted, scale- and rotation-invariant features into an AL acquisition function for 3D medical image segmentation. The main contributions of this paper are as follows: (1) we propose *SIFT-Entropy*, a hybrid acquisition function that unifies entropy-based uncertainty with SIFT-based feature diversity to improve training data selection during AL; (2) we demonstrate that SIFT-Entropy achieves comparable segmentation performance to full supervision using **61% fewer annotations**, significantly reducing expert annotation effort; and (3) we perform a comprehensive evaluation on a challenging whole-body preclinical CT dataset, with per-ROI analysis showing consistent or improved performance across diverse anatomical structures.

These contributions address the critical challenge of balancing uncertainty and diversity in AL, and underscore the potential of hybrid strategies in resource-constrained medical imaging scenarios. The paper is organised as follows: Sect. 2 provides an overview of AL and SIFT feature extraction. Section 3 describes the DL and AL framework and introduces our acquisition function. Section 4 outlines the implementation details and presents the numerical experiments, followed by results in Sect. 5. Finally, the discussion, future work and concluding remarks in Sects. 6 and 7.

2   Background

2.1   Active Learning

AL relies on an acquisition function to quantify the informativeness or uncertainty of unannotated samples, guiding the selection of those most valuable for annotation. Its effectiveness hinges on the design of this acquisition function.

Two main criteria are typically used: uncertainty and diversity. Uncertainty-based sampling prioritises samples where the model exhibits the highest level of uncertainty, under the assumption that these contribute the most to model improvement. Common approaches include least confident sampling, selecting samples where the model is least certain in its predictions [14], margin sampling, which targets cases where the model is uncertain between its top two predicted classes [22] and entropy-based sampling, which considers overall uncertainty across all classes [12]. Monte-Carlo (MC) dropout has also been employed to estimate uncertainty by approximating Bayesian inference [7]. Despite its effectiveness, uncertainty-based sampling alone can introduce redundancy by selecting similar uncertain samples or outliers that do not contribute to generalisation, potentially hampering performance [4].

Diversity-based approaches prioritise selecting representative samples from high-density regions or those that differ from previously annotated data to avoid redundancy. Common techniques include clustering-based selection, where data is partitioned into clusters and samples are chosen from centroids, and core-set selection, which ensures a batch of representative samples by optimising a core-set criterion [24]. These approaches often utilise distance or similarity metrics to quantify the relationship between the unannotated and annotated data. These measures include Euclidean distance, cosine similarity measures, correlation coefficient, mean squared error and mutual information (MI) [2,6]. However, purely diversity-based strategies may neglect informativeness, potentially leading to suboptimal model updates.

Hybrid methods combine uncertainty and diversity measures to improve generalisation by selecting both uncertain and representative samples [15]. These methods typically follow two main approaches: weighted sum optimisation, where uncertainty and diversity scores are combined into a single metric, and the multi stage process which is a sequential process where the model selects a broad subset of samples based on one metric and then further filtering or prioritising them based on an additional metric [32]. Various combinations have been explored including MedAL, which combines an entropy-based uncertainty strategy and a range of distance functions including Euclidean, Russellrao, City Block, Kulsinski, Cosine, and Chebyshev to maximise the dissimilarity between the chosen samples and the training pool to select diverse samples whose predictions the model is most uncertain of [25]. MI between image sets has recently been proposed for AL in medical imaging applications as a regulariser to ensure diversity in the training set alongside the use of entropy [18]. [31] introduced Suggestive Annotation, combining uncertainty sampling with representativeness-based selection by training multiple models through bootstrapping. The approach uses model variance to estimate uncertainty and applies a greedy algorithm to select the most representative samples of the unannotated dataset using cosine similarity. Similarly, [16] used the cosine similarity; they selected samples far from the annotated set and close to the unannotated set.

Many of these distance or similarity metrics, such as Euclidean or MI, assume that if the image intensities are aligned or strongly correlated, the images are well aligned [6]. Thus, misalignment can influence differences within these metrics rather than true informational differences. While image registration could address this issue, it introduces interpolation, which may affect raw intensities and alter natural features in the image. Moreover, the choice of deformation model (e.g., rigid, affine, or non-rigid/elastic) adds a confounding variable, complicating the assessment of these approaches in AL. To circumnavigate this complication, feature-based methods like the SIFT algorithm offer a robust alternative to extract key image features that are invariant to rotation and scale. Geometric misalignments and varying field-of-view are common in medical imaging; using SIFT features allows the acquisition function to remain robust to such differences without requiring explicit image registration. Matching SIFT keypoints has been used for medical image feature mapping previously [30] and can subsequently be used as a measure of similarity between datasets, lending itself well to incorporation into an acquisition function for AL. Furthermore, the rotational invariance of the SIFT features, coupled with the classification power of convolutional neural networks (CNN), has recently been proposed to improve biomedical image classification in comparison to a CNN alone [26] and serves as a means to alleviate problems associated with rotational invariance of CNNs.

Despite these advancements, a key gap remains in how acquisition functions can effectively balance uncertainty and diversity while accounting for the limitations of traditional similarity metrics in medical imaging. Existing hybrid methods typically rely on image intensities, learned embeddings, or distance measures that are sensitive to alignment and deformation. In contrast, our approach introduces a handcrafted, feature-based similarity component using SIFT keypoint matching, which captures local structures robust to scale, rotation, and misalignment. Unlike deep feature-based similarity, this measure is independent of the model's internal representations and remains stable throughout training. To the best of our knowledge, this is the first integration of SIFT features into an AL acquisition function for 3D medical image segmentation, addressing the challenge of quantifying diversity in anatomically variable data.

2.2   Scale Invariant Feature Transform

To extract important features that are invariant to rotation and scale, we utilise the 3D SIFT algorithm [20]. This method constructs a Gaussian scale-space representation of volumetric data, followed by Difference of Gaussian (DoG) computation to identify keypoints as local extrema. A keypoint is retained if it is a local maximum or minimum within its von Neumann neighbourhood, and keypoints with weak magnitudes are rejected based on a threshold fraction (α) of the maximum DoG value. This ensures robustness by filtering out low-contrast points. To enhance stability, keypoints are filtered based on curvature analysis using the Hessian matrix. Keypoints located on edges are rejected by evaluating the eigenvalue ratio, ensuring that only stable corner-like features are preserved. Specifically, a keypoint is discarded if the ratio exceeds a threshold, indicating an edge-like structure. The cosine of the angle between the gradient and eigenvectors are then tested, rejecting keypoints if this value falls below a parameter (γ), ensuring reliable directional derivatives. Once stable keypoints are confirmed, descriptors are constructed from local gradient histograms, ensuring invariance to rotation, scale, and translation. Matching between 3D volumes is performed by comparing descriptor distances, where valid matches are determined using a ratio test with a threshold (η). A higher number of matching keypoints indicates that the volumes share similar local features, resulting in a greater similarity between volumes, while a score of zero suggests no correspondence.

3   Methodology

In this section, we introduce our novel deep AL algorithm. The objective is to achieve the highest possible segmentation accuracy using as few annotated samples as possible.

3.1   Deep Learning Segmentation Framework

An implementation of Dense VNet [8], via the Niftynet API [9] was utilised. The Dense VNet consists of downsampling and upsampling subnetworks, with skip connections to propagate higher-resolution information to the final segmentation. The downsampling subnetwork consists of three layers of dense feature stacks. Which are connected by downsampling strided convolutions, whose outputs are concatenated after a single convolution in the skip connection and bilinear upsampling. Batch normalisation and "PReLU" activation were used for each layer except the last layer, which was activated by a "softmax" layer.

3.2   Active Learning Framework

Active Learning Pipeline. We use a standard pool-based AL framework shown in Fig. 1. In each AL round, the acquisition function assigns a score to each unannotated sample, and the top K samples with the highest scores are selected for annotation. These samples are then manually annotated by the oracle, added to the training set, and removed from the unannotated data pool. The model is retrained from scratch with the updated training set, and this process continues until all unannotated images are used.

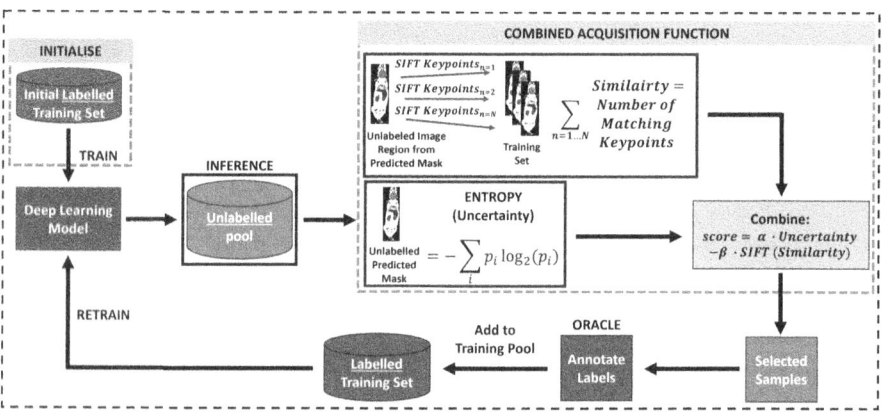

Fig. 1. Proposed Active Learning framework. Samples are selected from the unannotated data pool using an acquisition function that combines entropy-based uncertainty and SIFT-based similarity. Selected samples are annotated by an oracle and added to the training pool for model update.

Active Learning Acquisition Function. The DL model is trained on an annotated dataset, X_{train} and the candidate samples for expert annotation and incorporation into the training set are selected from an unannotated data pool U. The proposed acquisition function for AL is described in the equation:

$$\text{score}(x_l^U) = \alpha \cdot \frac{1}{n_{\text{labels}}} \sum_{j=1}^{n_{\text{labels}}} \text{Uncertainty}(\text{label}_j)$$

$$- \beta \cdot \frac{1}{n_{\text{labels}} n_{\text{train}}} \sum_{j=1}^{n_{\text{labels}}} \sum_{i=1}^{n_{\text{train}}} \text{SIFT}(X_{\text{train}}^i, \text{label}_j) \qquad (1)$$

Notation Definitions

- x_l^U: Unannotated image from the pool U with predicted label l
- n_{labels}: Number of class labels (e.g., skeleton, liver, etc.)
- n_{train}: Number of annotated training images
- α: Weight controlling the importance of uncertainty
- β: Weight controlling the importance of similarity (diversity)
- Uncertainty(label_j): Entropy-based uncertainty for predicted label j in the unannotated image
- SIFT($X_i^{\text{train}}, \text{label}_j$): SIFT-based similarity between predicted label j in the unannotated image and the same label in training image X_i

Let x_l^U denote an unannotated image from the pool U, with predicted segmentation label l. The acquisition function assigns a score by combining two components: model uncertainty and feature similarity. Uncertainty is quantified using entropy, computed per pixel for each predicted label label_j corresponding to a ROI, aggregated via the median, and normalised across the dataset. Similarity is estimated using SIFT by matching keypoints between label_j and corresponding ROIs in the annotated training set X_i^{train}, with the median similarity score taken per label, combined and normalised across the dataset. The final score is computed as the weighted difference between uncertainty and similarity, where α and β control their relative influence. Higher α prioritises uncertain predictions; higher β favours diverse, dissimilar samples. Background labels are excluded to reduce noise. For this work, we set $\alpha = \beta = 1$ to give equal importance to both components, serving as a neutral baseline. This design choice maintains flexibility in the framework, allowing future adaptation or tuning of these weights for specific tasks or datasets.

A hyperparameter grid search was conducted to optimise 3D SIFT parameters for each ROI using both the ground truth and predicted segmentation class labels. The search explored the parameters with ranges: peak threshold $\alpha \in \{0.1, 0.5, 0.7, 1.0\}$, corner threshold $\gamma \in \{0.1, 0.5, 0.7, 1.0\}$, number of pyramid levels $\in \{3, 4, 5, 6, 7\}$, scale-space parameters $\sigma_n \in \{0.5, 1.5, 2.5, 3.5, 4.5, 6.5\}$, and $\sigma_0 \in \{1.0, 2.0, 3.0, 4.0, 5.0, 6.0\}$, and matching threshold $\eta \in \{0.85, 0.90, 0.95, 0.97, 0.98, 0.99, 1\}$. Parameters were tuned per label to maximise keypoint detection within ROIs while minimising background noise. The optimal set balanced informative ROI features against irrelevant background responses. Matching threshold η was separately optimised to minimise false positives across ROIs.

4   Data and Experimental Setup

4.1   Dataset

The data set used to explore the effectiveness of SIFT-Entropy was whole-body mouse CTs obtained from a series of preclinical PET-CT investigations. The mice were scanned in a Mediso PET/CT Preclinical Imaging System (nanoScan 122S PET/CT, Mediso). Mice were injected intravenously with 1–2 MBq of Zr^{89}-labelled protein (0.5 µl) followed by iopamidol CT contrast agent (Niopam 300, Bracco, 100 µl/mouse ip). Respiration was monitored with a pressure pad connected to differential pressure transducers for low-range pressure monitoring during the entire PET-CT examination, and anesthesia was maintained through the nose cone of the bed (1–2% isoflurane in O_2 gas, 1–2 l/min). The CT scan parameters were set as follows: tube voltage 50 kVp, tube current 1 mA, exposure time 300 ms, and the maximum number of projections was 400. The reconstructed resolution of CT was 0.25 mm and the mice were scanned at 0.5, 24, 48, 72, and 140 h post injection.

The dataset includes 74 pre-clinical CT scans, each manually annotated by an experienced preclinical imaging researcher with eight ROIs: background, skeleton, liver, kidney, brain, lungs, bladder and mouse, as shown in Fig. 3. All organ classes were equally represented in the dataset, ensuring balanced training data across ROIs. Scans were converted to 3D NIfTI, cropped to $136 \times 136 \times 384$ centred around the image's centre of mass, and retained a 0.25 mm isotropic resolution. Each AL experiment begins with the same fixed initial training set of 16 scans and a validation set of 4 scans, randomly selected once and held constant across all experiments with varying acquisition functions, to ensure fair comparison. An additional 4 scans form a separate test set, also kept fixed. The remaining 50 scans comprise the unannotated pool. At each AL iteration, $K = 10$ new scans are selected from this pool using the acquisition function, manually annotated, and added to the training set. This process corresponds to the first AL iteration, which is repeated until all images within the unannotated data set are used.

To prioritise reducing annotation effort, validation and test sets were kept deliberately small—a necessary trade-off to maximise the size of the unannotated and actively learned data. As a final preprocessing step, the imaging bed was removed from each label using a pre-trained Dense VNet model, which generated binary masks to reassign bed pixels to the background.

4.2   Implementation

All models were trained from scratch on a 16 GB NVIDIA V100 Tensor Core GPU. The DL model used an initial learning rate of 0.001 with the Adam optimiser, using default parameters for $\beta_1 = 0.9$ and $\beta_2 = 0.99$, and a batch size of

6. The learning rate was selected via a hyperparameter grid search. Models optimised a Dice loss function, with evaluation of the validation set at every epoch. To alleviate overfitting, we employed a dynamic stopping criterion that detects convergence by fitting a Chebyshev polynomial to the validation loss curve and identifying when the normalised change in the smoothed loss remains below a predefined threshold for a set number of iterations. Training is halted at the earliest detected convergence point to ensure sufficient learning while preventing unnecessary overfitting. Data augmentation, including scaling and rotation, was applied during training.

To validate SIFT-Entropy, we compared its performance to two baselines: (1) Random Sampling, which selects K samples per iteration at random, serving as a lower-bound (uninformed) reference; and (2) Entropy-based Uncertainty Sampling, which selects the top K most uncertain samples using entropy alone representing a strong, widely-used uncertainty-based AL baseline for segmentation. Allowing us to isolate the added value of our feature-driven strategy. All acquisition functions were evaluated using the same dataset, model architecture, and training procedure to ensure fair comparison. Performance was assessed using the DSC across seven class labels on the test set after each AL iteration.

For reference, DSC of up to 0.98 have been reported for lung segmentation in clinical CT, and around 0.83 for tumour segmentation [19,29]. In preclinical mouse imaging, the AIMOS pipeline has achieved median DSC between 0.87 and 0.95 across multiple organs in contrast-enhanced micro-CT scans [23]. To remain competitive, our model must achieve comparably high DSC across relevant organs.

5   Results and Evaluation

Figure 2 shows the median DSC and the interquartile range (IQR) (shaded region) achieved by the different acquisition functions against the percentage of annotated data for each AL iteration. Each point represents the median DSC across four test images, with the IQR capturing the variability among them, summarising performance across different unseen cases. The proposed SIFT-Entropy acquisition function consistently outperforms both random and entropy-based sampling, particularly in earlier iterations where annotated data is limited. In the early iterations (30–45% annotated data), SIFT-Entropy shows a steeper improvement in DSC, indicating that it selects more informative samples. This demonstrates that SIFT-Entropy effectively prioritises samples that contribute the most to model learning, leading to faster performance improvements with fewer annotated instances. Notably, as the proportion of annotated images increases, the differences between the training sets diminish, as all methods utilise the same fully annotated dataset at 100%. Consequently, their DSC gradually converge. However, SIFT-Entropy maintains a slight advantage throughout the process, demonstrating its sustained effectiveness even in the later stages of AL.

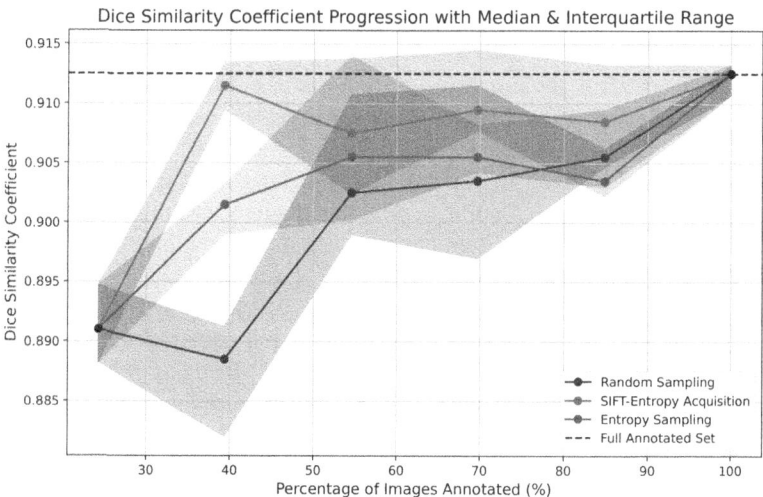

Fig. 2. Comparison of median Dice Similarity Coefficient progression across Active Learning iterations for each acquisition function - Random (blue), SIFT-Entropy (red), and Entropy (green). Each set of results includes a shaded region representing the Interquartile range. (Color figure online)

SIFT-Entropy reaches the performance of the full annotated dataset in fewer iterations compared to both random and entropy sampling. Specifically, the DSC for the fully annotated model (trained with all annotated data) is 0.913 ± 0.0025, SIFT-Entropy reaches a similar performance level 0.0912 ± 0.004 by iteration 1, while entropy sampling reaches it at iteration 2 and random sampling requires the full annotated dataset. SIFT-Entropy achieves this result using only 39% of the dataset, a 61% reduction in annotation effort. This highlights the potential of our method to significantly lower the human annotation burden in medical image segmentation. Additionally, the IQR is smaller for SIFT-Entropy in most iterations, indicating that SIFT-Entropy maintains greater stability and reduced variance in performance. Table 1 summarizes the median DSCs and IQRs across iterations, supporting the trend shown in Fig. 2. These numerical results confirm that SIFT-Entropy achieves near-optimal performance with substantially fewer annotated images.

To illustrate the segmentation performance of the proposed SIFT-Entropy acquisition strategy, Fig. 3 shows a representative test case, including the input CT image, ground truth segmentation, and the predicted segmentation produced by the SIFT-Entropy acquisition model. The prediction demonstrates strong agreement with the ground truth, particularly in the delineation of anatomical structures, highlighting the effectiveness of the proposed method.

To further assess the effectiveness of SIFT-Entropy, we analysed median DSC progression for each of the seven class labels individually. Figure 4 presents the per-ROI performance across AL iterations for each acquisition function. The

Table 1. Median Dice Similarity Coefficient ± Interquartile Range at each annotation percentage for different acquisition strategies. Each value is computed from 4 test images.

Active Learning Iteration	% Images Annotated	Random Sampling	SIFT-Entropy	Entropy Sampling
Initial	24.2% (16/66)	0.891 Âś 0.007	0.891 Âś 0.007	0.891 Âś 0.007
Iteration 1	39.4% (26/66)	0.889 Âś 0.009	0.911 Âś 0.004	0.901 Âś 0.004
Iteration 2	54.5% (36/66)	0.903 Âś 0.012	0.907 Âś 0.011	0.905 Âś 0.014
Iteration 3	69.7% (46/66)	0.903 Âś 0.014	0.909 Âś 0.007	0.905 Âś 0.004
Iteration 4	84.8% (56/66)	0.905 Âś 0.001	0.909 Âś 0.011	0.903 Âś 0.006
Iteration 5	100% (66/66)	0.913 Âś 0.002	0.913 Âś 0.002	0.913 Âś 0.002

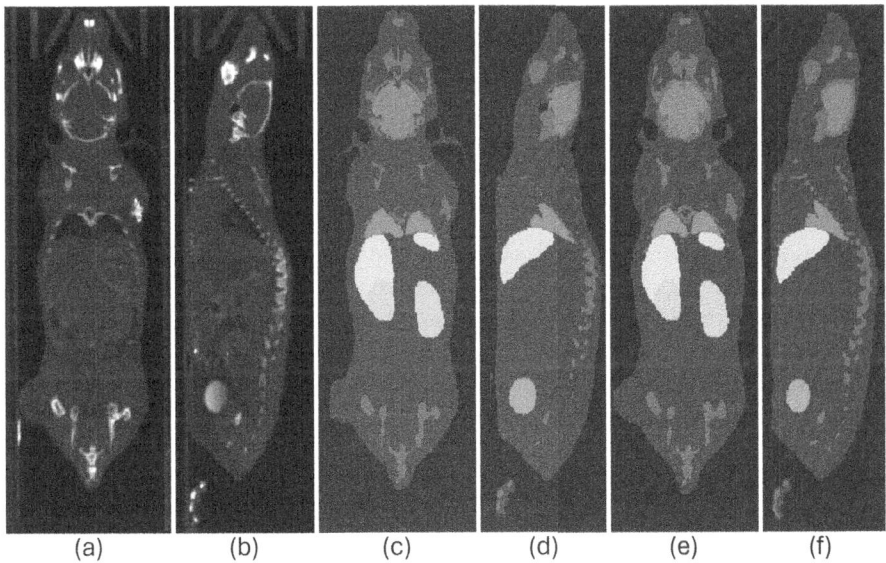

(a)   (b)   (c)   (d)   (e)   (f)

Fig. 3. Example of segmentation produced by the SIFT-Entropy acquisition model. From left to right: (a) and (b) Input CT image, (c) and (d) Ground truth annotation, and (e) and (f) Predicted segmentation. Showing background (dark blue), skeleton (mid blue), liver (light blue), kidneys (green), brain (yellow), lungs (orange), bladder (light red) and mouse (dark red). (Color figure online)

results indicate that different ROIs exhibit varying levels of sensitivity to the choice of acquisition strategy. Overall, SIFT-Entropy consistently outperforms or remains competitive with both random and entropy-based sampling. For bladder and lungs, SIFT-Entropy achieved the highest DSC, indicating superior segmentation accuracy compared to the baseline methods. In brain and mouse, all three acquisition strategies converged to a high performance early on, with minimal differences across iterations. For the liver, all methods performed similarly,

Per-Label Dice Similarity Coefficient Evolution

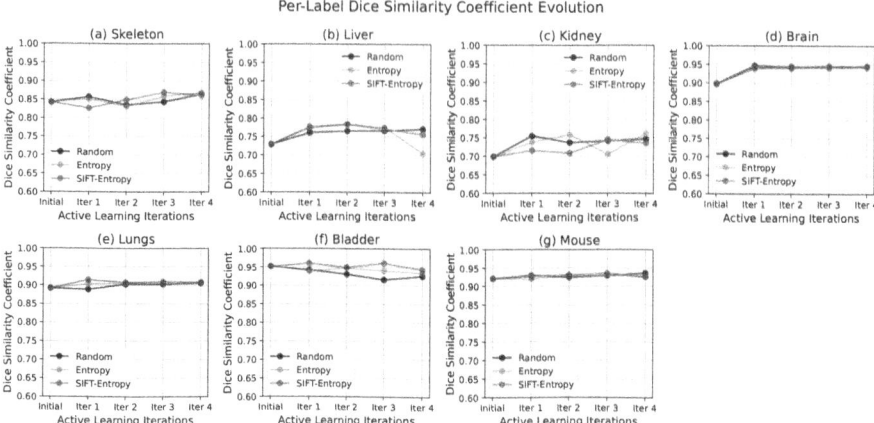

Fig. 4. Evolution of Dice Similarity Coefficients across Active Learning iterations for different anatomical labels. The performance of three acquisition strategies—Random (blue), SIFT-Entropy (red), and Entropy (green)—is shown for each label. Subplots correspond to: (a) Skeleton, (b) Liver, (c) Kidney, (d) Brain, (e) Lungs, (f) Bladder, and (g) Mouse. (Color figure online)

though both SIFT-Entropy and entropy-based sampling outperformed random sampling. In the case of the kidney, SIFT-Entropy provided more stable improvements across iterations, with entropy-based and random sampling displaying greater fluctuations. For more complex ROIs like the skeleton, which is inherently more variable due to its angular shape and potential deformation between scans, SIFT-Entropy achieved optimal DSC an iteration earlier than the other methods, despite an initial drop in performance.

These results reinforce that SIFT-Entropy provides more reliable performance improvement across all labels while avoiding the risk of performance drop seen with entropy sampling. While random sampling is stable, it lacks the efficiency required for optimal segmentation accuracy. The ROI-specific analysis further highlights that some ROIs benefit more from active selection strategies, emphasising the need for an acquisition function that effectively balances uncertainty with diversity. By combining entropy-based uncertainty with SIFT-derived feature diversity, SIFT-Entropy ensures that selected samples are uncertain and feature-distinct, leading to more informative and representative training data.

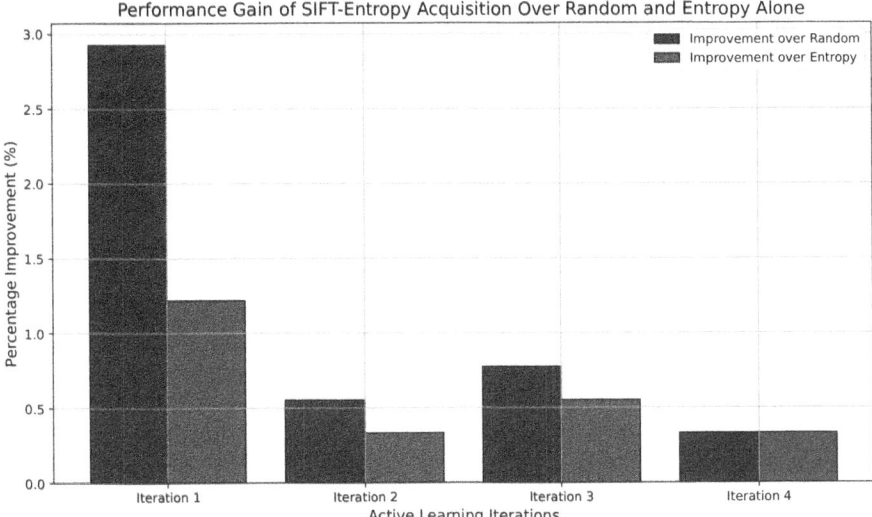

Fig. 5. Percentage improvement of the SIFT-Entropy acquisition strategy over Random and Entropy strategies across Active Learning iterations. Where the bars represent median improvement.

To quantify the overall advantage of SIFT-Entropy over both random and entropy-based sampling, Fig. 5 presents the median DSC percentage gain across AL rounds. The results show that, across multiple rounds, SIFT-Entropy consistently outperforms random and entropy sampling. The data reveals a clear trend: SIFT-Entropy yields its greatest percentage gain in iteration 1, when the annotated data is most limited. As more data is added in subsequent iterations, the performance gap gradually narrows, with all methods converging as their training sets become more similar—allowing the methods to catch up to SIFT-Entropy's early advantage.

6 Discussion

The results of our study demonstrate that the proposed SIFT-Entropy acquisition function consistently outperforms both random and entropy-based sampling in terms of DSC improvement. The overall DSC progression shows that the SIFT-Entropy approach leads to faster and more stable segmentation accuracy gains with fewer annotated samples. SIFT-Entropy reaches the full dataset performance using just 39% of the full annotated dataset, representing a 61% reduction in annotating. This demonstrates that integrating both uncertainty and diversity in AL acquisition functions enables more effective sample selection, particularly in scenarios where data is limited. The performance gain analysis further quantifies the advantage of SIFT-Entropy over both random and entropy sampling.

The inclusion of ROI-specific performance analysis reveals that the effectiveness of AL acquisition functions depends on the anatomical ROI being segmented. SIFT-Entropy achieved the highest DSCs for the bladder and lungs, indicating improved segmentation accuracy. For ROIs like the brain and mouse, all methods converged to similar high accuracy with minimal variation. The liver and kidney showed smaller performance differences, with SIFT-Entropy offering more stable improvements, particularly in the kidney. The skeleton, with its complex shape, also benefited from SIFT-Entropy, which reached optimal performance earlier. These findings highlight SIFT-Entropy's effectiveness in improving segmentation across different anatomical ROIs. While random sampling remains stable, it lacks the efficiency of AL acquisition functions like SIFT-Entropy, which balances uncertainty and diversity for better, more consistent performance. The results fall within or exceed the DSC ranges reported in existing literature. For example, the AIMOS pipeline achieved DSCs of 0.87–0.95 for key organs in preclinical CT [23]. Our model, using SIFT-Entropy, reached DSCs of 0.87 for skeleton, 0.92 for lungs, 0.95 for brain, and 0.96 for bladder— demonstrating comparable or improved performance. This supports the robustness of our approach, particularly in data-limited preclinical scenarios, and highlights its potential for efficient, high-accuracy segmentation with fewer annotations.

Despite promising results, some limitations must be acknowledged. While SIFT-Entropy improves segmentation accuracy across iterations, its effectiveness may still depend on dataset characteristics, such as class imbalance or label ambiguity. Further investigations will explore adaptive weighting between uncertainty and diversity to support dynamic, data-dependent optimisation of acquisition performance. Alternative uncertainty metrics may also help refine the acquisition strategy. While the DSC is widely used for evaluating segmentation performance, it does not account for spatial discrepancies between prediction and ground truth and is particularly sensitive to small ROIs [34]. Future work will incorporate additional metrics, such as Hausdorff Distance or Average Surface Distance, to better capture boundary accuracy and misalignment errors. More complex AL methods (e.g., core-set [24] or hybrid approaches [18,25,31]) could provide additional baseline comparisons. Although these methods employ different optimisation criteria not directly tailored to our 3D multi-organ setting, we expect SIFT-Entropy's ability to capture structural diversity would complement them. Benchmarking against such methods is a valuable direction for future work to better contextualise performance. Additional investigations will include expanding to more AL iterations to observe longer-term performance trends and applying the method to larger public datasets and additional imaging modalities to assess robustness and generalisability. As well as exploring performance in cases involving under-represented organs or the introduction of new organ classes, where acquisition strategies may need to adapt dynamically. Lastly, previous computational limitations restricted SIFT extraction speed, future work will leverage GPU-based implementations [13] to significantly reduce runtime and accelerate feature extraction.

7   Conclusion

This study proposed a SIFT-Entropy acquisition function for AL in medical image segmentation, combining uncertainty and diversity-based sampling criteria. Addressing the difficult challenge of balancing these criteria, particularly due to the limitations of traditional similarity metrics in medical imaging. Evaluation on pre-clinical CT data demonstrated that SIFT-Entropy consistently outperforms both random and traditional entropy-based sampling, achieving full dataset performance with 61% fewer annotated samples. Demonstrating more stable and efficient improvements in segmentation accuracy across multiple labels. By balancing sample uncertainty with feature diversity, SIFT-Entropy enables more effective data selection, reducing annotation requirements while maintaining high segmentation accuracy. Our findings underscore the value of intelligent hybrid acquisition strategies in minimising annotation effort and enhancing model adaptability—a crucial consideration for real-world deployment in medical imaging workflows.

Acknowledgements. This work was supported by the EPSRC Doctoral Training Partnership under grant number EP/W524682. This research was undertaken using the supercomputing facilities at Cardiff University operated by Advanced Research Computing at Cardiff on behalf of the Cardiff Supercomputing Facility and the Supercomputing Wales project. We acknowledge the support of the latter, which is part-funded by the European Regional Development Fund via the Welsh Government.

Disclosure of Interests. The authors have no competing interests to declare that are relevant to the content of this article.

References

1. Akselrod-Ballin, A., et al.: Multimodal correlative preclinical whole body imaging and segmentation **6**(1), 27940. https://doi.org/10.1038/srep27940, https://www.nature.com/articles/srep27940
2. Balluff, B., Heeren, R., Race, A.: An overview of image registration for aligning mass spectrometry imaging with clinically relevant imaging modalities. J. Mass Spectrom. Adv. Clin. Lab **23**, 26–38 (2022). https://doi.org/10.1016/j.jmsacl.2021.12.006
3. Biswas, A., Nasim, M.A.A., Ali, M.S., Hossain, I., Ullah, M.A., Talukder, S.: Active learning on medical image. https://doi.org/10.48550/ARXIV.2306.01827, https://arxiv.org/abs/2306.01827. version Number: 2
4. Budd, S., Robinson, E., Kainz, B.: A survey on active learning and human-in-the-loop deep learning for medical image analysis. Med. Image Anal. **71**, 102062 (2021). https://doi.org/10.1016/j.media.2021.102062
5. Chowdhary, C., Acharjya, D.: Segmentation and feature extraction in medical imaging: a systematic review. Procedia Comput. Sci. **167**, 26–36 (2020). https://doi.org/10.1016/j.procs.2020.03.179
6. Czolbe, S., Pegios, P., Krause, O., Feragen, A.: Semantic similarity metrics for image registration (2023). https://doi.org/10.1016/j.media.2023.102830, https://www.sciencedirect.com/science/article/pii/S1361841523000907

7. Gal, Y., Ghahramani, Z.: Dropout as a bayesian approximation: representing model uncertainty in deep learning (2016). https://arxiv.org/abs/1506.02142
8. Gibson, E., et al.: Automatic multi-organ segmentation on abdominal CT with dense V-networks. IEEE Trans. Med. Imaging **37**(8), 1822–1834 (2018). https://doi.org/10.1109/TMI.2018.2806309
9. Gibson, E., et al.: NiftyNet: a deep-learning platform for medical imaging. Comput. Methods Programs Biomed. **158**, 113–122 (2018). https://doi.org/10.1016/j.cmpb.2018.01.025, https://www.sciencedirect.com/science/article/pii/S0169260717311823
10. Isaksson, L.J., et al.: Automatic segmentation with deep learning in radiotherapy. Cancers **15**(17) (2023). https://doi.org/10.3390/cancers15174389, https://www.mdpi.com/2072-6694/15/17/4389
11. Isensee, F., Jaeger, P.F., Kohl, S.A., Petersen, J., Maier-Hein, K.H.: nnU-Net: a self-configuring method for deep learning-based biomedical image segmentation. Nat. Methods **18**(2), 203–211 (2021). https://doi.org/10.1038/s41592-020-01008-z
12. Joshi, A.J., Porikli, F., Papanikolopoulos, N.: Multi-class active learning for image classification. In: 2009 IEEE Conference on Computer Vision and Pattern Recognition, pp. 2372–2379 (2009). https://doi.org/10.1109/CVPR.2009.5206627
13. K, A.A., Venkatesh Babu, R.: Speeding up SIFT using GPU. In: 2013 Fourth National Conference on Computer Vision, Pattern Recognition, Image Processing and Graphics (NCVPRIPG), pp. 1–4 (2013). https://doi.org/10.1109/NCVPRIPG.2013.6776198
14. Lewis, D.D., Catlett, J.: Heterogeneous uncertainty sampling for supervised learning. In: Cohen, W.W., Hirsh, H. (eds.) Machine Learning Proceedings 1994, pp. 148–156. Morgan Kaufmann, San Francisco (1994). https://doi.org/10.1016/B978-1-55860-335-6.50026-X, https://www.sciencedirect.com/science/article/pii/B978155860335650026X
15. Li, G., et al.: Hybrid representation-enhanced sampling for bayesian active learning in musculoskeletal segmentation of lower extremities. Int. J. Comput. Assist. Radiol. Surg. (2024). https://doi.org/10.1007/s11548-024-03065-7
16. Li, H., Yin, Z.: Attention, suggestion and annotation: a deep active learning framework for biomedical image segmentation. In: Martel, A.L. (ed.) MICCAI 2020. LNCS, vol. 12261, pp. 3–13. Springer, Cham (2020). https://doi.org/10.1007/978-3-030-59710-8_1
17. Ma, S., Wu, H., Lawlor, A., Dong, R.: Breaking the barrier: selective uncertainty-based active learning for medical image segmentation (2024). https://doi.org/10.48550/arXiv.2401.16298, https://arxiv.org/abs/2401.16298
18. Nath, V., Yang, D., Landman, B., Xu, D., Roth, H.: Diminishing uncertainty within the training pool: active learning for medical image segmentation. IEEE Trans. Med. Imaging **40**(10), 2534–2547 (2021). https://doi.org/10.1109/TMI.2020.3048055
19. Rayed, Md.E., I.S.N.S.J.J.K.M., Mridha, M.: Deep learning for medical image segmentation: state-of-the-art advancements and challenges. Inform. Med. Unlocked **47**, 101504 (2024). https://doi.org/10.1016/j.imu.2024.101504
20. Rister, B., Horowitz, M.A., Rubin, D.L.: Volumetric image registration from invariant keypoints. IEEE Trans. Image Process. **26**(10), 4900–4910 (2017). https://doi.org/10.1109/TIP.2017.2722689
21. Rizwan I Haque, I., Neubert, J.: Deep learning approaches to biomedical image segmentation. Inform. Med. Unlocked **18**, 100297 (2020). https://doi.org/10.1016/j.imu.2020.100297

22. Roth, D., Small, K.: Margin-based active learning for structured output spaces. In: Fürnkranz, J., Scheffer, T., Spiliopoulou, M. (eds.) ECML 2006. LNCS (LNAI), vol. 4212, pp. 413–424. Springer, Heidelberg (2006). https://doi.org/10.1007/11871842_40

23. Schoppe, O., et al.: Deep learning-enabled multi-organ segmentation in whole-body mouse scans **11**(1), 5626. https://doi.org/10.1038/s41467-020-19449-7, https://www.nature.com/articles/s41467-020-19449-7

24. Sener, O., Savarese, S.: Active learning for convolutional neural networks: a core-set approach (2018). https://doi.org/10.48550/arXiv.1708.00489, https://arxiv.org/abs/1708.00489

25. Smailagic, A., et al.: MedAL: accurate and robust deep active learning for medical image analysis. In: 2018 17th IEEE International Conference on Machine Learning and Applications (ICMLA), pp. 481–488 (2018). https://doi.org/10.1109/ICMLA.2018.00078

26. Tsourounis, D., Kastaniotis, D., Theoharatos, C., Kazantzidis, A., Economou, G.: SIFT-CNN: when convolutional neural networks meet dense sift descriptors for image and sequence classification. J. Imaging **8**(10) (2022). https://doi.org/10.3390/jimaging8100256, https://www.mdpi.com/2313-433X/8/10/256

27. Wang, H., Jin, Q., Li, S., Liu, S., Wang, M., Song, Z.: A comprehensive survey on deep active learning in medical image analysis. Med. Image Anal. **95**, 103201 (2024). https://doi.org/10.1016/j.media.2024.103201

28. Wasserthal, J., et al.: TotalSegmentator: robust segmentation of 104 anatomic structures in CT images. Radiol. Artif. Intell. **5**(5) (2023). https://doi.org/10.1148/ryai.230024

29. Xu, Y., Quan, R., Xu, W., Huang, Y., Chen, X., Liu, F.: Advances in medical image segmentation: a comprehensive review of traditional, deep learning and hybrid approaches. Bioengineering **11**, 1034 (2024). https://doi.org/10.3390/bioengineering11101034

30. Xu, Y., et al.: 3D-SIFT-flow for atlas-based CT liver image segmentation. Med. Phys. **43**(5), 2229–2241 (2016). https://doi.org/10.1118/1.4945021

31. Yang, L., Zhang, Y., Chen, J., Zhang, S., Chen, D.Z.: Suggestive annotation: a deep active learning framework for biomedical image segmentation. In: Descoteaux, M., Maier-Hein, L., Franz, A., Jannin, P., Collins, D.L., Duchesne, S. (eds.) MICCAI 2017. LNCS, vol. 10435, pp. 399–407. Springer, Cham (2017). https://doi.org/10.1007/978-3-319-66179-7_46

32. Zhan, X., Wang, Q., Huang, K., Xiong, H., Dou, D., Chan, A.B.: A comparative survey of deep active learning (2022). https://doi.org/10.48550/arXiv.2203.13450, https://arxiv.org/abs/2203.13450

33. Zhang, L., et al.: Generalizing deep learning for medical image segmentation to unseen domains via deep stacked transformation **39**(7), 2531–2540. https://doi.org/10.1109/TMI.2020.2973595, https://ieeexplore.ieee.org/document/8995481/

34. Zhang, Y., Liu, S., Li, C., Wang, J.: Rethinking the dice loss for deep learning lesion segmentation in medical images **26**(1), 93–102. https://doi.org/10.1007/s12204-021-2264-x

Quantifying Inter-annotator Agreement and Generalist Model Limitations in Imaging Mass Cytometry Single Cell Segmentation

Johannes Schuiki[1]([✉])(ID), Markus Steiner[2,3](ID), Heinz Hofbauer[1](ID),
Stephan Drothler[2,3,4](ID), Giulia Pessina[2,3], Richard Greil[2,3](ID),
Nadja Zaborsky[2,3](ID), and Andreas Uhl[1](ID)

[1] Department of Artificial Intelligence and Human Interfaces,
Paris-Lodron-University Salzburg, Salzburg, Austria
jschuiki@cs.sbg.ac.at
[2] Department Laboratory of Immunological and Molecular Cancer Research-Salzburg
Cancer Research Institute, Cancer Cluster Salzburg, Salzburg, Austria
[3] Department of Internal Medicine III with Haematology, Medical Oncology,
Haemostaseology, Infectiology and Rheumatology, Oncologic Center,
Paracelsus Medical University, Salzburg, Austria
[4] Department of Biosciences, Paris-Lodron-University Salzburg, Salzburg, Austria

Abstract. Accurate segmentation mask generation is critical for single-cell analysis workflows. While established semi-automated tools require expert intervention, emerging approaches aim to eliminate human guidance through fully automatic segmentation models. However, the suitability of automatically generated cell segmentation masks as reliable alternatives to expert annotations remains uncertain. This study evaluates different imaging mass cytometry (IMC) datasets by feeding them to a variety of generalist cell segmentation models and comparing the outputs with corresponding segmentation masks. Performance is assessed using instance segmentation metrics which are also viewed in the light of an upper bound determined by inter-annotator agreement.

Keywords: imaging mass cytometry · IMC · whole cell segmentation · tissue cell segmentation · generalist model · inter annotator agreement

1 Introduction

Since its introduction [12], imaging mass cytometry (IMC) has become a widely adopted imaging methodology for downstream tasks like cell phenotyping (i.e., identifying and categorizing different cell types) and analyzing the spatial landscape of cells. IMC is well suited for tissue analysis due to its ability to simultaneously detect over 40 protein markers using metal-tagged antibodies, bypassing signal from autofluorescence and spectral overlap limitations of fluorescence-based techniques like immunofluorescence microscopy. The process involves

S. Ali et al. (Eds.): MIUA 2025, LNCS 15918, pp. 146–159, 2026.
https://doi.org/10.1007/978-3-031-98694-9_11

labeling tissue samples with antibodies conjugated to rare-earth metals (e.g., Neodymium *Nd* or Iridium *Ir*), followed by laser ablation at 1 μm^2 resolution to ionize tissue regions. These ions are then quantified via mass spectrometry, generating high-dimensional spatial cell marker data. The subcellular resolution enables mapping of cellular microenvironments, used for studying tumor heterogeneity, immune cell interactions, or tissue architecture.

A crucial step in existing frameworks or pipelines [18,31] for IMC single cell analysis, is the segmentation of cellular structures on a single cell basis (instance segmentation). While this process is increasingly recognized as prone to errors [2,22] and some approaches even try to circumvent the process of segmentation [15,29], it remains a focus for methodological advancements: a recent study [6] investigates IMC cell segmentation performance on partially labeled data. Other research is aimed to develop segmentation models specifically tailored for IMC data [26,32]. It can be derived that improving single cell segmentation using IMC is still a current topic.

This study establishes a reasonable upper bound for whole-cell segmentation on IMC data by quantifying inter-annotator agreement across cell masks independently annotated by four domain experts. This baseline reflects the inherent variability in human expert interpretations of cellular boundaries. The performance of four state-of-the-art generalist cell segmentation models is systematically evaluated on both in-house and publicly available IMC datasets, with segmentation performance compared against the established human-annotator benchmark. By comparing model performance with inter-annotator agreement, this work explores current limitations of automated segmentation methods for IMC whole cell segmentation.

The remainder of this study is structured as follows: Sect. 2 explores related works on inter-annotator agreement for cell instance segmentation, thereby positioning the current work within the context of existing research. In Sect. 3, the employed data, the segmentation models and the evaluation metrics are introduced. Section 4 presents and discusses the experimental results. Finally, Sect. 5 concludes this study.

2   Related Work on Inter-annotator Agreement for Cell Instance Segmentation

A recent work [33] provides an overview on how to assess inter-annotator agreement for medical image segmentation, including Kappa statistics, STAPLE-based and heatmap-based methods. While all of these methods constitute dedicated ways of expressing the inter-annotator agreement numerically, they are limited to semantic segmentation. A major challenge in applying similar techniques to instance segmentation problems on densely populated areas like cell tissue, is to find unambiguous element assignments between annotators, also considering over- and undersegmentation cases (i.e. one cell annotated as multiple cells or missing cell annotations). While for the two-annotator case, this could be treated as an assignment problem (as done for the sorted average precision metric described in Sect. 3.3), this becomes a practically unsolvable problem quickly as the number of annotators increases. Authors in [8] approach this by distance-based consensus matching between cell centroids across multiple annotators. However, because their approach requires the average cell size as an input parameter and also their work is centered around H&E stained samples from histopathology, its applicability to other imaging modalities, such as IMC, remains uncertain. An established way [14,34] for measuring inter-annotator agreement in the domain of cell instance segmentation is to systematically compare pairs of annotators using instance segmentation performance metrics. In [34], nuclei (as opposed to whole cells) annotations are compared using measures based on the calculation of intersection over union per element at a certain threshold. In [14], the authors evaluate the human-to-human whole cell segmentation performance for a variety of multiplexed tissue imaging modalities and tissue types, however not directly focused on IMC data. It can be deduced that assessing human-to-human performance on IMC whole cell segmentation represents a meaningful direction for systematic investigation, as current literature lacks benchmarks in this specific domain. The term *inter-annotator agreement* in the context of this work refers to the human-to-human evaluation using segmentation performance metrics described in Sect. 3.3.

3   Methods

3.1   Data

This section details the acquisition and preprocessing of a small-scale in-house IMC dataset and four employed external datasets, accompanied by a comprehensive overview of dataset statistics.

IMC Sample Generation. Samples were prepared from a high cell density lymphoid tissue according to standard IMC sample preparation techniques as suggested by the manufacturer[1]. The donor sample was collected according to the guidelines of the Declaration of Helsinki, and approved by the Institutional Review Board (or Ethics Committee) of the Province of Salzburg: Ethics statement/Ethics number: 415-E/1287/18-2018, Version 5. Written informed consent was obtained from the donor. For sample preparation, the formalin fixed paraffin embedded tissue block was sectioned into 4 μm thick slices on a HM340E microtome (Epredia, Portsmouth, New Hampshire) and mounted to superfrost plus microscopic slides (Epredia). The mounted sections were baked at 60°C for one hour and immediately transferred to coblin jars containing UltraClear solution (VWR, Radnor, Pennsylvania) and incubated for 5 min. After a second 5 min incubation in fresh UltraClear, the sample was incubated in an ethanol series of $2 \times 100\%$, 95%, 80% ethanol and incubated for 3 min (first two incubations)

---

[1] https://fluidigm.my.salesforce.com/sfc/p/#700000009DAw/a/4u000000dmhS/
avZw9iOjvvsWnYP.pqXU5au3oBAZ_xuFo0uf7pWo4Nw.

and 2 min, each, followed by incubation in water for 5 min. For epitope retrieval the sample was transferred to pre-heated pH9 EDTA epitope retrieval buffer and heated in a KOS pathological microwave (Milestone, Valbremba, Italy) for 30 min at 96°C. After retrieval, the regular protocol was continued with a one hour blocking step using Superblock blocking solution (ThermoScientific, Waltham, Massachusetts). The antibody cocktail was incubated over night at 4°C. Iridium staining was performed at a dilution of 1:100 from a 125 μM stock (Standard Biotools, Markham, Ontario) for 10 min at room temperature.

Mask Generation. After laser ablation, the data was annotated by four domain experts. During the process, each annotator manually annotated 10 crops of 50 × 50 pixels resolution which were then used to extrapolate the annotations to the whole images. Ilastik [5] was used to create pixel probability maps which are subsequently transformed to single cell segmentation masks using Cellprofiler [27].

Dataset Statistics. Additionally, four external datasets are used in this study, all of which provide IMC data and corresponding segmentation masks generated in a comparable manner as the in-house data. It should be noted, however, that the focus of these works was not to create a segmentation mask but it was merely an intermediate step towards the respective downstream task. All five datasets are listed in Table 1 along with their statistics.

Table 1. Overview datasets and their statistics. For patching, 68 samples from the Ali20 dataset and 14 samples from the Jackson20 dataset are ignored because at least one dimension is smaller than 256 pixels.

Dataset	Abbreviation	Tissue type	# Samples whole image	avg resolution whole image (y/x)	# Samples patches	# annotators per sample	avg # cell masks per patch
in-house	Annot1 – 4	Lymphoid	10	1000.0/1000.0	360	4	823.7
Ali20 [1]	A20	Breast	548	462.8/478.0	2787	1	314.0
Rendeiro21 [25]	R21	Lung	229	1108.4/1187.5	13361	1	185.3
Jackson20 [20]	J20	Breast	746	596.5/626.7	8714	1	320.5
Hoch22 [17]	H22	Melanoma	167	993.1/963.4	6361	1	467.4

Patching Strategy and Channel Aggregation. Preliminary experiments suggested unstable results in terms of segmentation performance caused by the varying resolution of the individual datasets (see column 5 in Table 1). Hence, experiments in this work analyze the data in two modes:

- *whole image*: The full image is fed into the respective segmentation model and the full mask is evaluated afterwards.

– *sliding window patches*: Patches of size 256 × 256 pixels are cropped from the original image with an overlap of 128 pixels. For evaluation, a border of 28 pixels is ignored on all four sides, reducing the evaluated field of view per patch to 200 × 200 pixels. The border removal is meant to mitigate artifacts generated by partitions of cells at the border which potentially distort the results especially when using smaller crops. It should be noted, however, that from a practical perspective smaller patching is unfavorable for analysis of larger data because stitching masks is prone to errors caused by border cells.

Because all the models described in the upcoming section require both a nucleus channel and a membrane channel, IMC channels are aggregated using the arithmetic mean over a selection of markers on a per pixel basis. Table 2 presents a breakdown what markers are aggregated to which channel, along with additional details (used clone and dilution for the generation of the in-house data is also mentioned for better reproducibility) on the employed markers. To ensure a consistent and fair comparison across all experiments, the markers for channel aggregation were carefully selected based on analysis of all the datasets used in this study and their available markers.

Table 2. Aggregated channels and their corresponding antibody markers.

Category	Marker	Clone	Channel	Dilution (1:n)
Membrane Channel	CD19	6OMP31	Nd142	100
	TOMM20	EPR1581-54	Nd144	100
	CD5	CLDA5-1	Nd145	30
	CD4	EPR6855	Gd156	400
	CD68	KP1	Tb159	1000
	CD20	H1	Dy161	150
	CD8a	C8/144B	Dy162	800
	CD14	EPR3653	Dy163	1000
	CD45RA	HI100	Er166	600
	B2M	B2M/961	Yb171	200
	CD45RO	UCHL1	Yb173	1000
Nucleus Channel	DNA	–	Ir191	100
	DNA	–	Ir193	100

3.2 Segmentation Models

In total, four generalist single cell segmentation models are employed in this work without further fine-tuning of internal parameters. In the following, each model is briefly introduced:

- Cellpose v3 [28]: Cellpose was introduced as an early generalist cell segmentation model. The Cellpose model got progressively enhanced by adding more training data. Currently, the "cyto3" model is its latest iteration for whole cell segmentation, which is also the one used in this work. Unlike other segmentation models at the time, which mostly employed a U-Net architecture and trained to directly yield a semantic segmentation map of nuclei, cell borders, and background, Cellpose predicts gradient vector fields that guide pixel assignments toward cell centers, enabling instance segmentation of diverse cell morphologies.
- DeepCell [14]: The DeepCell model employs a ResNet-50 architecture as its core that is connected to a feature pyramid network. It is especially aimed at nucleus and whole cell segmentation for tissue data. The version used in this work is *0.12.10*.
- CellSAM [19]: CellSAM is based on the Segment Anything Model (SAM) [21]. It automates segmentation via a transformer-based object detector that generates bounding box prompts. CellSAM is still in development at the time of this study. The used version number is *0.0.dev1*.
- VISTA-2D [24]: VISTA-2D is a recent generalist cell segmentation model developed by NVIDIA, which also uses the SAM as its core. The model is part of the MONAI framework [9]. The model delivers gradient vector fields similarly to the Cellpose model. The final segmentation masks are derived from these vector fields using Cellpose's postprocessing implementation. While the other models come with their internal way of contrast enhancement, the data was manually rescaled using histogram percentile clipping with limits 1% and 99%.

Models differ in the way the nucleus and membrane channels are arranged as an input tensor. Cellpose and DeepCell provide exemplary usages of the order to feed the channels into the model. Because CellSAM stems from the same lab as the DeepCell model, similar usage is assumed. VISTA-2D does not come with a defined way how the nucleus and membrane channel should be assigned to the expected RGB input. Based on preliminary experimental validation, the three input channels are ordered as follows: an empty channel (all zeros), the membrane channel, and the nucleus channel.

3.3   Segmentation Evaluation Metrics

The right evaluation metric to choose for segmentation experiments heavily depends on the specific scenario. Existing works on cell instance segmentation rely on various metrics such as F1 score [14] (also reported as the technically identical dice score [6]) or mean average precision [7]. While the term mean average precision is widely used for evaluating object detection/newly trained models, it can be unclear how this metric translates to masks without confidence scores per object. A recent work [16] unravels this confusion by giving an overview on how different variants of "average precision" metrics are calculated. For evaluation of segmentation masks in this work, three metrics are employed, all of which rely on the calculation of the intersection over union (IoU) of cell areas on a per object basis. In coherence with [7,16], the calculation for the "average precision" (AP) for a specific IoU threshold t_{IoU} is shown in Eq. 1. Note that this formula is closely related to the F1/Dice score. After assigning cell elements from the ground truth mask to cell elements on the prediction mask (TP), leftover (without counterpart) cells on the ground truth mask are viewed as false negatives (FN) and leftover cells on the prediction mask are treated as false positives (FP).

$$AP(t_{IoU}) = \frac{TP(t_{IoU})}{TP(t_{IoU}) + FN(t_{IoU}) + FP(t_{IoU})} \tag{1}$$

The metric ap50 corresponds to AP from Eq. 1 at threshold $t_{IoU} = 0.5$. The metric map computes the arithmetic mean of AP values at t_{IoU} points 0.5 to 0.95 with a step size of 0.05. The sortedAP [10] (sap) metric uses linear assignment optimization for finding corresponding segmentation objects based on their IoU, thereby allowing for IoU values below 0.5 to be included in the calculation. Further, the AP metric is calculated at every available IoU point. This is the equivalent of calculating the area on the whole AP/IoU curve. In fact, this metric is similar to the map metric, but instead of calculating the AP only at points {0.5, 0.55, ..., 0.95}, the AP is calculated at every step and also the arithmetic mean is used between steps. Figure 1 illustrates how the different metrics can be visually represented. The three metrics were chosen to assess performance not only at one fixed threshold but also over a spectrum of IoU values, providing a more comprehensive evaluation. Since ap50 already provides a single-threshold score (and F1/Dice would similarly focus on one cutoff), F1/Dice was excluded to avoid redundant evaluations.

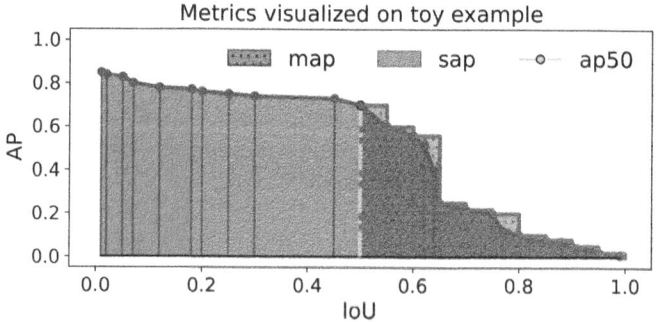

Fig. 1. Exemplary depiction of the three metrics. The map metric constitutes the area under the AP/IoU curve over the interval [0.5, 1.0]. The sap metric corresponds to an approximation of the whole area under the AP/IoU curve. All values are exemplary.

4   Results and Discussion

This section covers the experimental results. In Sect. 4.1, the inter-annotator agreement is determined. Section 4.2 evaluates the performance of automatic segmentation via generalist models against the four expert-annotated masks obtained in a semi-automatic fashion. Section 4.3 evaluates the performance of the models on publicly available IMC datasets. The generalist models are used out-of-the-box without further fine tuning. Finally, Sect. 4.4 states limitations of the present study. For significance testing in Figs. 4 and 5, data was checked for normality using the Shapiro-Wilk test and for homogeneity of variances using Bartlett's test. Based on these preliminary checks, if the data were normally distributed and variances were equal, an independent t-test was used; if normality was met but variances were unequal, Welch's t-test was applied; and if normality was not satisfied, the non-parametric Mann-Whitney U test was chosen. For all experiments significance tests yield p-values $< 10^{-6}$, i.e. statistically significant.

4.1   Inter-annotator Agreement

Employing the evaluation metrics from Sect. 3.3 and the cell masks from the in-house dataset annotated by four experts, the inter-annotator agreement is determined as a baseline. Figure 3 presents a direct comparison of each pair of annotators by displaying manually annotated single cell mask boundaries from a single patch. Although this work deals with single cell areas, the boundary is depicted here for better visualization of the differences. The first named annotator is depicted in blue, annotations from the second annotator are visualized in gold. Overlapping annotations are depicted in white. For visual context, a contrast enhanced version of the Ir191 metal tag channel is used as a background image. The patch, originally of resolution 50×50 pixels, is upscaled to 300×300 pixels using nearest neighbor interpolation for better visibility. While large parts of the respective cell boundaries are overlapping in a pixel-perfect manner, we can also observe a subjective bias where each annotator draws cellular borders. This results in minor spatial offsets (acceptable errors) but also leads to under- and oversegmentation, which constitute unfavorable errors.

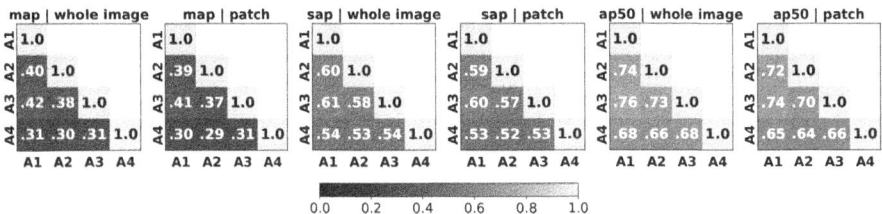

Fig. 2. Pairwise inter-annotator comparison across different metrics and patch modes. Abbreviations A1 – A4 denote Annotators 1 to 4, respectively.

Table 3. Average inter-annotator agreement over all annotators.

average map		average sap		average ap50	
whole	patch	whole	patch	whole	patch
.353	.345	.566	.557	.708	.686

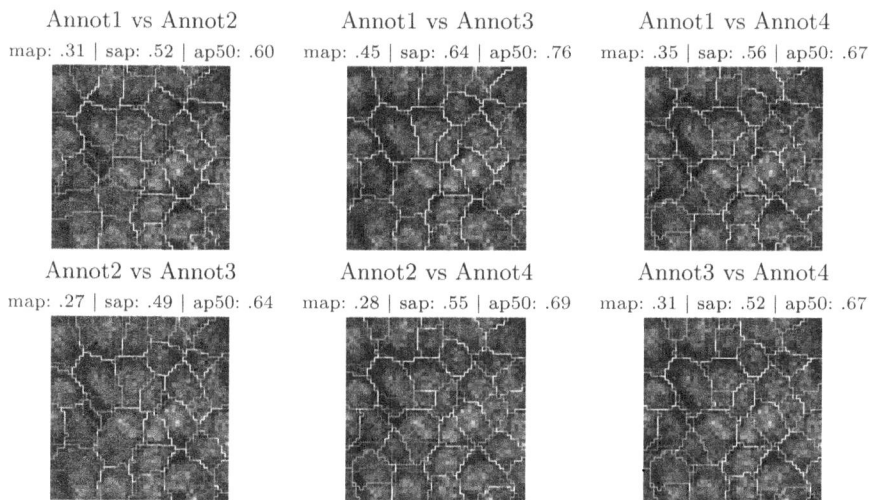

Annot1 vs Annot2
map: .31 | sap: .52 | ap50: .60

Annot1 vs Annot3
map: .45 | sap: .64 | ap50: .76

Annot1 vs Annot4
map: .35 | sap: .56 | ap50: .67

Annot2 vs Annot3
map: .27 | sap: .49 | ap50: .64

Annot2 vs Annot4
map: .28 | sap: .55 | ap50: .69

Annot3 vs Annot4
map: .31 | sap: .52 | ap50: .67

Fig. 3. Visualization of annotation agreement between two annotators and the corresponding metrics per patch. Only cell borders are displayed for better visibility. Annotators colored in blue and golden. Annotation overlap in white. Best viewed in color. (Color figure online)

Figure 2 lists detailed results for pairwise comparisons between expert annotators using an agreement matrix. Numbers in *whole image* matrices therefore show the arithmetic mean of 10 mask comparisons, numbers in the *patch* matrices represent the arithmetic mean of 360 mask comparisons. Finally, Table 3 shows the overall average over all pairwise comparisons per evaluation metric.

The averaged inter-annotator values from Table 3 can be viewed as a reasonable upper bound for automatic segmentation models. Because if a model would perform better on a set of annotated masks from a specific annotator, discrepancies would increase when evaluated against masks from other annotators. To achieve results that more accurately reflect reality, methods beyond manual annotation would be required for ground truth generation to mitigate human biases. Hence, average performance metrics are used as upper bounds in the following diagrams, with average values indicated by dashed lines. Note that these lines represent the arithmetic mean from all inter-annotator calculations and should thus be compared with the mean values from the boxplot diagrams to ensure a fair comparison.

4.2   Automatic Segmentation Using Generalist Models

Figure 4 shows the results for model performance on the in-house dataset for both modes, whole images and sliding window patches. Model outputs are always compared against segmentation masks from one annotator, indicated via abbreviations A1–A4. The SAM based models appear to face difficulties with the rather small cellular structures on the whole-image resolution. For smaller patches, the performance aligns well with the other two approaches. However, when compared to the human-to-human baseline, model output results in inferior segmentation performance across all three evaluation metrics.

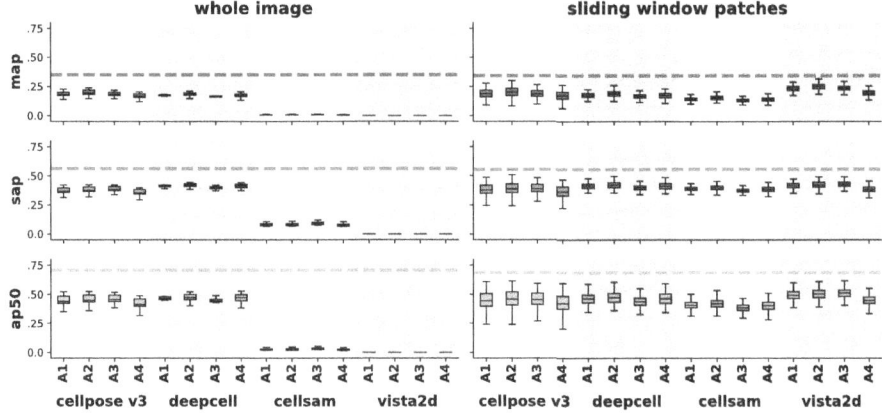

Fig. 4. Model outputs evaluated against annotation masks on a per annotator basis.

4.3   Automatic Segmentation on Public Datasets

Figure 5 presents the results of the model performance on the four external datasets. Here, it is assumed that the determined inter-annotator agreement from Sect. 4.1 can also be applied to the external datasets, although the used tissue types differ. The performance of VISTA-2D varies across datasets for the whole-image mode, which can be attributed to differences in average resolution per dataset as outlined in Table 1. The better performance of CellSAM on the whole images in comparison to the previous experiment using the in-house data can also be explained by the differences in image resolution. For the patching approach, all models perform best on the H22 dataset, yet none reach the reasonable upper bound established by inter-annotator agreement metrics, indicating systematic limitations in current segmentation algorithms. The results on external data reveal a larger variance in results compared to previous experiments, likely due to increased sample size capturing a broader biological heterogeneity.

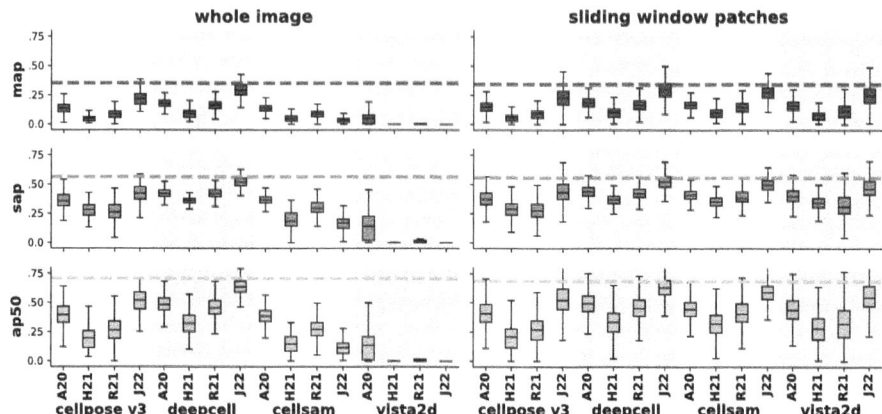

Fig. 5. Model outputs evaluated on their available segmentation masks.

4.4 Limitations of this Study

While this work advances understanding of inter-annotator agreement and generalist model cell segmentation on IMC data, several constraints merit consideration for future research:

– Antibody channel aggregation: The impact of channel selection for nucleus & membrane/cytoplasm aggregation remains unexplored. While multi-channel IMC data inherently captures diverse biomarkers, the interplay between channel combinations could influence segmentation robustness. Future studies should systematically evaluate how channel aggregation strategies affect model performance. Another recent approach [13] tries to process all channels separately, thereby avoiding the channel aggregation step entirely.

– Specialized IMC segmentation models: This study focused on generalist models. While generalist models provide a convenient way due to their out-of-the-box usage potential, IMC specific cell segmentation approaches such as [32] also hold great potential.

– IMC specific pre-processing: Optional processing steps such as hot pixel removal, spillover correction [4] and denoising [23] were not incorporated into the evaluation pipeline.

– Scale sensitivity in large images: Discrepancies between whole-image and sliding-window analyses suggest resolution-dependent detection challenges for small cells. Optimal crop sizing and super-resolution techniques (e.g. SpiDe-Sr [11]) could address this limitation by preserving fine-grained structures without sacrificing contextual information.

– Emerging generalist architectures: Some advances in foundation models like μSAM [3] and SAMCell [30], were not included in this study. Incorporating these models would strengthen the findings of this work due to their SAM based nature.

These limitations, however, do not undermine the core findings regarding inter-annotation agreement and IMC segmentation performance using generalist models but highlight pathways to refine segmentation pipelines.

5   Conclusion

This study first assessed the inter-annotator agreement for IMC single cell segmentation by comparing cell masks independently obtained by semi-automatic annotation from four domain experts. This presents a reasonable upper bound for automatic segmentation approaches. Afterwards, four generalist models are utilized to apply single cell segmentation of the same data. Results indicate that there is room left for improvement in the light of this upper bound. Additionally, models also were tasked to segment publicly available IMC data. Under assumption that this upper bound still holds true for the external data, similar conclusions regarding the demand for further improvement of the accuracy can be drawn. While this study includes a systematic analysis of inter-annotator agreement and generalist model performance on IMC data, there are things yet to be addressed such as employing specialized segmentation models.

Acknowledgements. This work has been partially supported by the Salzburg State Government WISS 2025 Research and Transfer Lab on " Artificial Intelligence in BioMedical Image Analysis (AIBIA)"; the Austrian Science Fund (FWF) doc.funds.connect programme " Artificial Intelligence-Driven Biomedical Imaging Innovation (REVELATION)" Grant-DOI 10.55776/DFH4791124; the WISS 2025 Cancer Cluster Salzburg, CCSII-IOS; the Province of Salzburg and FWF Grant-DOI 10.55776/P32762 to N. Zaborsky.

Data Availibility Statement. External data sets can be found through their corresponding citations. The newly generated data and the accompanied annotations are publicly available at https://zenodo.org/records/15511299. The code is available at https://gitlab.cosy.sbg.ac.at/wavelab/imc-interannotator-agreement

Disclosure of Interests. The authors have no competing interests to declare that are relevant to the content of this article.

References

1. Ali, H.R., et al.: Imaging mass cytometry and multiplatform genomics define the phenogenomic landscape of breast cancer. Nat. Cancer **1**(2), 163–175 (2020). https://doi.org/10.1038/s43018-020-0026-6
2. Amitay, Y., Bussi, Y., Feinstein, B., Bagon, S., Milo, I., Keren, L.: Cellsighter: a neural network to classify cells in highly multiplexed images. Nat. Commun. **14**(1), 4302 (2023). https://doi.org/10.1038/s41467-023-40066-7
3. Archit, A., et al.: Segment anything for microscopy. Nat. Methods **22**(3), 579–591 (2025). https://doi.org/10.1038/s41592-024-02580-4

4. Bai, Y., et al.: Adjacent cell marker lateral spillover compensation and reinforcement for multiplexed images. Front. Immunol. **12** (2021). https://doi.org/10.3389/fimmu.2021.652631

5. Berg, S., et al.: ilastik: interactive machine learning for (bio)image analysis. Nat. Methods **16**(12), 1226–1232 (2019). https://doi.org/10.1038/s41592-019-0582-9

6. Bird, K.M., Ye, X., Race, A.M., Brown, J.M.: Pushing the limits of cell segmentation models for imaging mass cytometry. In: 2024 IEEE International Symposium on Biomedical Imaging (ISBI), pp. 1–5 (2024). https://doi.org/10.1109/ISBI56570.2024.10635782

7. Caicedo, J.C., et al.: Nucleus segmentation across imaging experiments: the 2018 data science bowl. Nat. Methods **16**(12), 1247–1253 (2019). https://doi.org/10.1038/s41592-019-0612-7

8. Capar, A., et al.: An interpretable framework for inter-observer agreement measurements in tils scoring on histopathological breast images: A proof-of-principle study. PLoS ONE **19**(12), e0314450 (2024). https://doi.org/10.1371/journal.pone.0314450

9. Cardoso, M.J., et al.: Monai: an open-source framework for deep learning in healthcare (2022). https://arxiv.org/abs/2211.02701

10. Chen, L., Wu, Y., Stegmaier, J., Merhof, D.: Sortedap: rethinking evaluation metrics for instance segmentation. In: Proceedings of the IEEE/CVF International Conference on Computer Vision (ICCV) Workshops, pp. 3923–3929 (2023)

11. Chen, R., et al.: SpiDe-Sr: blind super-resolution network for precise cell segmentation and clustering in spatial proteomics imaging. Nat. Commun. **15**(1), 2708 (2024). https://doi.org/10.1038/s41467-024-46989-z

12. Giesen, C., et al.: Highly multiplexed imaging of tumor tissues with subcellular resolution by mass cytometry. Nat. Methods **11**(4), 417–422 (2014). https://doi.org/10.1038/nmeth.2869

13. Goldsborough, T., et al.: A novel channel invariant architecture for the segmentation of cells and nuclei in multiplexed images using instanseg. bioRxiv (2024). https://doi.org/10.1101/2024.09.04.611150

14. Greenwald, N.F., et al.: Whole-cell segmentation of tissue images with human-level performance using large-scale data annotation and deep learning. Nat. Biotechnol. **40**(4), 555–565 (2021)

15. Gutwein, S., Lazic, D., Walter, T., Taschner-Mandl, S., Licandro, R.: Interpretable embeddings for segmentation-free single-cell analysis in multiplex imaging (2024). https://arxiv.org/abs/2411.03341

16. Hirling, D., et al.: Segmentation metric misinterpretations in bioimage analysis. Nat. Methods **21**(2), 213–216 (2024). https://doi.org/10.1038/s41592-023-01942-8

17. Hoch, T., Schulz, D., Eling, N., Gómez, J.M., Levesque, M.P., Bodenmiller, B.: Multiplexed imaging mass cytometry of the chemokine milieus in melanoma characterizes features of the response to immunotherapy. Sci. Immunol. **7**(70), eabk1692 (2022)

18. Hunter, B., et al.: Optimal: an optimized imaging mass cytometry analysis framework for benchmarking segmentation and data exploration. Cytometry A **105**(1), 36–53 (2023). https://doi.org/10.1002/cyto.a.24803

19. Israel, U., et al.: A foundation model for cell segmentation (2023). https://doi.org/10.1101/2023.11.17.567630

20. Jackson, H.W., et al.: The single-cell pathology landscape of breast cancer. Nature **578**(7796), 615–620 (2020). https://doi.org/10.1038/s41586-019-1876-x

21. Kirillov, A., et al.: Segment anything (2023). https://arxiv.org/abs/2304.02643
22. Lee, Y., et al.: Segmentation aware probabilistic phenotyping of single-cell spatial protein expression data. Nat. Commun. **16**(1), 389 (2025). https://doi.org/10.1038/s41467-024-55214-w
23. Lu, P., et al.: IMC-denoise: a content aware denoising pipeline to enhance imaging mass cytometry. Nat. Commun. **14**(1) (2023). https://doi.org/10.1038/s41467-023-37123-6
24. NVIDIA: VISTA-2D: A foundational model for cell segmentation in spatial omics workflows. (2024). https://github.com/Project-MONAI/VISTA/tree/main/vista2d. version 0.3.0
25. Rendeiro, A.F., et al.: The spatial landscape of lung pathology during covid-19 progression. Nature **593**(7860), 564–569 (2021). https://doi.org/10.1038/s41586-021-03475-6
26. Scuiller, Y., et al.: Youpi: your powerful and intelligent tool for segmenting cells from imaging mass cytometry data. Front. Immunol. **14** (2023). https://doi.org/10.3389/fimmu.2023.1072118
27. Stirling, D.R., Swain-Bowden, M.J., Lucas, A.M., Carpenter, A.E., Cimini, B.A., Goodman, A.: Cellprofiler 4: improvements in speed, utility and usability. BMC Bioinform. **22**(1), 433 (2021). https://doi.org/10.1186/s12859-021-04344-9
28. Stringer, C., Pachitariu, M.: Cellpose3: one-click image restoration for improved cellular segmentation (2024). https://doi.org/10.1101/2024.02.10.579780
29. Sultan, S., et al.: Immunet: a segmentation-free machine learning pipeline for immune landscape phenotyping in tumors by multiplex imaging. Biol. Methods Protoc. **10**(1), bpae094 (2024). https://doi.org/10.1093/biomethods/bpae094
30. VandeLoo, A.D., Malta, N.J., Aponte, E., van Zyl, C., Xu, D., Forest, C.R.: Samcell: generalized label-free biological cell segmentation with segment anything. bioRxiv (2025). https://doi.org/10.1101/2025.02.06.636835
31. Windhager, J., et al.: An end-to-end workflow for multiplexed image processing and analysis. Nat. Protoc. **18**(11), 3565–3613 (2023)
32. Xiao, X., et al.: Dice-xmbd: deep learning-based cell segmentation for imaging mass cytometry. Front. Genet. **12** (2021). https://doi.org/10.3389/fgene.2021.721229
33. Yang, F., et al.: Assessing inter-annotator agreement for medical image segmentation. IEEE Access **11**, 21300–21312 (2023). https://doi.org/10.1109/ACCESS.2023.3249759
34. Yapp, C., et al.: Unmicst: deep learning with real augmentation for robust segmentation of highly multiplexed images of human tissues. Commun. Biol. **5**(1) (2022). https://doi.org/10.1038/s42003-022-04076-3

Subcortical Masks Generation in CT Images via Ensemble-Based Cross-Domain Label Transfer

Augustine X. W. Lee[✉][iD], Pak-Hei Yeung[iD], and Jagath C. Rajapakse[iD]

College of Computing and Data Science, Nanyang Technological University,
Singapore, Singapore
{alee067,pakhei.yeung}@ntu.edu.sg

Abstract. Subcortical segmentation in neuroimages plays an important role in understanding brain anatomy and facilitating computer-aided diagnosis of traumatic brain injuries and neurodegenerative disorders. However, training accurate automatic models requires large amounts of labelled data. Despite the availability of publicly available subcortical segmentation datasets for Magnetic Resonance Imaging (MRI), a significant gap exists for Computed Tomography (CT). This paper proposes an automatic ensemble framework to generate high-quality subcortical segmentation labels for CT scans by leveraging existing MRI-based models. We introduce a robust ensembling pipeline to integrate them and apply it to unannotated paired MRI-CT data, resulting in a comprehensive CT subcortical segmentation dataset. Extensive experiments on multiple public datasets demonstrate the superior performance of our proposed framework. Furthermore, using our generated CT dataset, we train segmentation models that achieve improved performance on related segmentation tasks. To facilitate future research, we make our source code, generated dataset, and trained models publicly available at https://github.com/SCSE-Biomedical-Computing-Group/CT-Subcortical-Segmentation, marking the first open-source release for CT subcortical segmentation to the best of our knowledge.

Keywords: CT Subcortical Segmentation Dataset · MRI-Derived Segmentation Labels · Automated Segmentation Label Generation

1 Introduction

The human subcortex contains numerous crucial structures and regions that play crucial roles in various physiological functions underlying basic human activities [14]. For example, the thalamus facilitates the transmission of all sensory and motor signals to the cerebral cortex [29] while the hippocampus is responsible

---

A. X. W. Lee and P-H Yeung—These authors contributed equally to this work.

Supplementary Information The online version contains supplementary material available at https://doi.org/10.1007/978-3-031-98694-9_12.

S. Ali et al. (Eds.): MIUA 2025, LNCS 15918, pp. 160–174, 2026.
https://doi.org/10.1007/978-3-031-98694-9_12

for memory persistence and creation of long-term memories [19]. Besides their key physiological responsibilities, these anatomical structures have also been found to exhibit volumetric and morphological changes during the development of neurodegenerative disorders like Alzheimers' disease [31] and Parkinson's Disease [20]. Therefore, neuroimaging, which enables the analysis of the volume and morphology of the subcortical anatomies, is crucial to advance our understanding of the brain and facilitate computer-aided diagnosis of neurological conditions.

Thanks to the high contrast resolution of Magnetic Resonance Imaging (MRI) [22] that allows for better visualization of tissues, it has been widely adopted in subcortical analysis [9,26]. Specifically, there have been numerous research and methods developed for automated subcortical segmentation for MRI, with a mix of both probabilistic methods [8,23] and deep-learning methods [2,11, 25]. In contrast, Computed Tomography (CT), another primary neuroimaging modality, has received relatively little attention in this area of research. Despite its potential to deliver much faster (5–7 min *vs.* 30–60 min for MRI) and more affordable scanning at half the cost, the limited studies on automatic subcortical segmentation for CT have constrained its utilization in computer-aided diagnosis and treatment planning of emergent conditions, such as acute stroke or traumatic brain injuries, where CT scans are readily available.

The primary obstacle hindering the development of automated CT subcortical segmentation is the scarcity of labelled datasets. In contrast to the abundance of publicly available labelled MRI subcortical segmentation datasets, such as the IBSR-18 [6] and Mindboggle-101 [17], which have greatly facilitated the creation of various tools and models for this task, there is a notable lack of similar publicly available datasets for CT subcortical segmentation. In this work, we aim to fill in this gap by transferring the rich resources from the MRI community to CT, creating open-source and publicly available labels and pre-trained models for CT subcortical segmentation.

To achieve this goal, this paper presents a novel framework for automated CT subcortical segmentation label generation. Our framework leverages on the performance of existing MRI subcortical segmentation models and introduces a robust ensembling pipeline to integrate them. This pipeline is then applied to a publicly available, unannotated paired MRI-CT brain dataset [28], generating subcortical masks for the corresponding paired images. Specifically, we make the following contributions:

- We propose an ensemble pipeline that integrates predictions from off-the-shelf MRI subcortical segmentation tools and models. Through benchmarking on multiple publicly available MRI subcortical segmentation datasets, our ensemble approach demonstrates superior performance to various state-of-the-art standalone models.
- We apply our proposed framework to an open-source MRI-CT brain dataset [28] to generate CT subcortical segmentation masks that are made publicly available. To the best of our knowledge, this constitutes the first open-access subcortical segmentation dataset for the CT modality.

– We train multiple segmentation models on our generated dataset and make the models and weights openly accessible. Extensive experiments show that the trained models exhibit accurate and robust performance in CT subcortical segmentation, as well as other tasks via transfer learning.

As the first study to make all our source codes, generated labels, and trained models publicly available for CT subcortical segmentation, this will greatly facilitate performance benchmarking and, hence, drive development in this research area. Although our generated subcortical segmentation labels may not be perfectly accurate due to the lack of expert manual correction, they serve as a strong prior for further refinement as future work. By releasing our trained models alongside these labels, we aim to significantly reduce the manual efforts required to annotate subcortical structures in CT images, ultimately facilitating the development of computer-aided solutions for various CT-based downstream neuroimaging applications.

2   Related Works

2.1   Whole Brain Segmentation

Whole brain segmentation involves the partition and delineation of the brain into its respective tissue types and anatomical labels, and allows for quantitative analysis of brain tissues and structures in downstream tasks. Given MRI's superior ability to visualize tissue contrast, whole brain segmentation algorithms are predominantly developed for MRI. Conventional probabilistic algorithms, such as FreeSurfer [8] and FIRST [15], make use of priors from brain atlases and likelihoods from the voxel's intensity to estimate the Maximum A Posteriori (MAP) label for each voxel, but are often limited to T1-weighted MRI. More recent probabilistic algorithms like SAMSEG [23] also adopt the Bayesian framework to estimate MAP labels, which are able to adapt to multiple domains like both T1 and T2-weighted MRI.

While newer probabilistic algorithms have improved generalization abilities, they tend to be computationally intensive and require long processing times. The advent of deep-learning has led to the development of models for whole brain segmentation with shorter processing time. In particular, Convolutional Neural Network (CNN)-based models like FastSurfer [11] and QuickNAT [25] have demonstrated commendable segmentation performance on MRI scans. Novel CNN-based methods like SynthSeg [2] which synthetically generates multi-contrast training data from an atlas has also shown improved generalization ability, including the capacity to segment different modalities. Our proposed framework is designed to be applicable and agnostic to both probabilistic models and deep learning models, ensuring its generalizability.

2.2   CT Subcortical Segmentation

There is much fewer research done on brain segmentation in CT modality due to the poorer tissue contrast in CT scans compared to MRI. Recent developments in

CT brain segmentation include development of a 2D UNet by Cai et al. [3] which segments 11 intracranial structures and a DenseVNet by Wang et al. [30] which segments 8 brain regions. Despite their remarkable performance, they primarily focus on segmenting non-subcortical structures, with only a limited subset of subcortical structures being targeted, such as the ventricles, caudate, lentiform nucleus, internal capsule and hippocampus. Thus, it would be meaningful to develop deep-learning models catered to subcortical segmentation. Additionally, these studies utilized private datasets that are not publicly available, making reproducibility and performance benchmarking challenging. In this work, we trained deep-learning models for CT subcortical segmentation, and open-sourced them and our generated dataset.

2.3 Labelled Neuroanatomy Datasets

The training of deep-learning models often requires large, labelled datasets. However, open-source neuroanatomy datasets are scarce due to patient privacy concerns and also the significant manual efforts required from expert annotators to curate these dataset. For MRI modality, some open-source segmentation datasets include the IBSR-18 [6] and the MindBoggle-101 [17]. In contrast, to the best of our knowledge, there is currently no open-source subcortical segmentation dataset available for CT modality. A study by Srikrishna et al. [27] shows the potential for cross-domain label propagation from MRI to CT scans. Using co-registered MRI-CT scan pairs, they carried out inference on the MRI scan using a probabilistic model and propagated the labels to the CT scan to curate a CT dataset for deep-learning training. Drawing inspiration from these prior works, we propose that open-source CT subcortical segmentation datasets can be curated using a similar approach, leveraging the extensive research conducted on MRI subcortical segmentation.

3 Methods and Materials

Given a dataset of N pairs of unlabelled MRI-CT scans, $\mathcal{I} = \left\{ \mathbf{I}_i^{MR}, \mathbf{I}_i^{CT} \right\}_{i=1}^{N}$, where each pair consists of an ith MRI scan, $\mathbf{I}_i^{MR}$, and a CT scan $\mathbf{I}_i^{CT}$, acquired from the same patient, we propose an automated pipeline to generate subcortical segmentation labels without requiring any manual intervention. Our framework utilizes a set of arbitrary number, M, of off-the-shelf MRI segmentation models, $\{ \mathcal{S}_j(\cdot; \theta_j) \}_{j=1}^{M}$, where each model, $\mathcal{S}_j(\cdot; \theta_j)$, is parameterized by θ_j. The proposed ensembling framework, detailed in Sect. 3.1, generates robust segmentation masks, $\mathbf{L}_i^{MR}$ for the corresponding $\mathbf{I}_i^{MR}$.

The generated labels are then propagated across modality from $\mathbf{I}^{MR}$ to $\mathbf{I}^{CT}$, as described in Sect. 3.2. The selection and details of the MRI segmentation models, $\mathcal{S}(\cdot; \theta)$, are outlined in Sect. 3.3. Finally, using our proposed framework, we generate subcortical segmentation labels, $\mathbf{L}^{CT}$ for an open-source unannotated MRI-CT paired dataset (Sect. 3.4), which are then used to trained different deep segmentation models (Sect. 3.5). All the generated labels and models will be made publicly available.

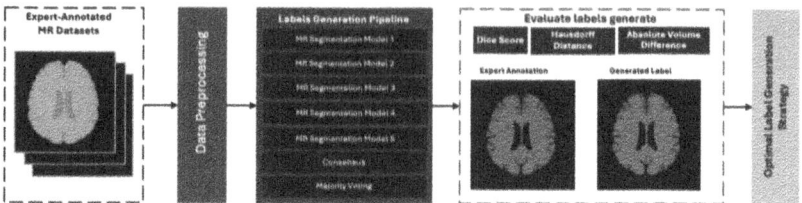

Fig. 1. The workflow of our label generation strategy. It involves ensembling an arbitrary number of off-the-shelf MRI segmentation models to develop the optimal label generation strategy

3.1 Label Generation Strategy

To leverage the strength of publicly available MRI subcortical segmentation tools and models, as illustrated in Fig. 1, we propose a label generation strategy that combines the predictions of multiple models. For each MRI image, $\mathbf{I}^{MR} \in \mathbb{R}^{C_m \times H \times W \times D}$, where C_m, H, W and D denote the number of channels, height, width and depth, respectively, we utilize a set of M MRI segmentation models, $\{\mathcal{S}_j(\cdot; \theta_j)\}_{j=1}^{M}$. Each model outputs a subcortical predicted mask:

$$[\mathbf{y}_i^1, \mathbf{y}_i^2, ..., \mathbf{y}_i^M] = [\mathcal{S}_1(\mathbf{I}_i^{MR}; \theta_1), \mathcal{S}_2(\mathbf{I}_i^{MR}; \theta_2), ..., \mathcal{S}_M(\mathbf{I}_i^{MR}; \theta_M)], \tag{1}$$

where each prediction, $\mathbf{y} \in \mathbb{R}^{C_c \times H \times W \times D}$ has C_c classes, height H, width W and depth D. We then integrate these predicted masks into the final labels using our proposed ensembling approaches. Noted that many off-the-shelf MRI subcortical segmentation models only provide hard segmentation outputs (*i.e.* 0 and 1) without access to the inner layers of the model (*i.e.* soft probability scores). To ensure the model-agnostic nature and generalizability of our proposed framework, we perform ensembling on the hard segmentation outputs of the models. We explore two ensembling methods: consensus and majority voting in this work.

Both approaches require getting a count map, $\mathbf{C}_i \in \mathbb{R}^{C_c \times H \times W \times D}$, for its corresponding $\mathbf{I}_i^{MR}$ by:

$$\mathbf{C} = \sum_{j=1}^{M} \mathbf{y}_i^j. \tag{2}$$

For every voxel, $\mathbf{v} = \mathbf{C}(:, x, y, z)$, where $\mathbf{v} \in \mathbb{R}^{C_c}$, we identify the class with the most predictions, c_{max}, as:

$$c_{max} = \arg\max_{c \in C_c} \mathbf{v}(c). \tag{3}$$

The consensus ensembling, $f_{concensus}(\cdot)$, classifies each voxel $\mathbf{v}$ as a particular class only if all models, $\{\mathcal{S}_j(\cdot; \theta_j)\}_{j=1}^{M}$ agree on that class; otherwise it is classified as the background class, bg. This is formulated as:

$$f_{\text{consensus}}(\mathbf{v}) = \begin{cases} c_{max} & \text{if } \mathbf{v}(c_{max}) = M, \\ bg & \text{else.} \end{cases} \tag{4}$$

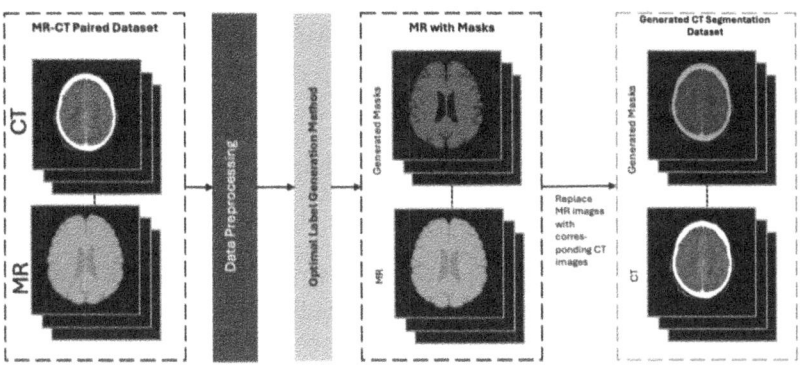

Fig. 2. The workflow of our label propagation method. For an MRI-CT scan pair, the optimal label generation strategy is applied on an MRI scan, $\mathbf{I}_i^{MR}$ and subsequently propagated to the co-registered CT scan, $\mathbf{I}_i^{CT}$

However, this approach can be overly strict, resulting in a strong bias towards the background class. To address this, we propose majority voting as an improvement by imposing a less strict rule. This method classifies each voxel $\mathbf{v}$ as the class that receives the most votes, namely c_{max}. In cases of ties where multiple classes have the same maximum count, the voxel is classified as the background class. The final subcortical mask, $\mathbf{L}_i^{MR} \in \mathbb{R}^{H \times W \times D}$, corresponding to $\mathbf{I}_i^{MR}$ is generated by combining the prediction of every voxel $\mathbf{v}$.

3.2 Label Propagation from MRI to CT

Given that each MRI-CT scan pair, $\mathbf{I}_i^{MR}$ and $\mathbf{I}_i^{CT}$, is from the same patient, we can infer that they share identical regions of interest. Therefore, the generated segmentation label, $\mathbf{L}_i^{MR}$, obtained in Sect. 3.1 for the MRI scan, $\mathbf{I}_i^{MR}$, can be transferred to the corresponding CT scan, $\mathbf{I}_i^{CT}$, as illustrated in Fig. 2.

To achieve this, we first compute the registration between the paired images by finding the optimal spatial transformation, $\hat{T}_i$, to align $\mathbf{I}_i^{MR}$ with $\mathbf{I}_i^{CT}$:

$$\hat{T}_i = \arg\min_T \mathcal{C}_{\mathrm{sim}} \left(\mathbf{I}_i^{CT}, \mathbf{I}_i^{MR} \circ T \right), \tag{5}$$

where $\mathcal{C}_{\mathrm{sim}}$ is the similarity cost function, such as mean square error. Equation 5 is a simplified generalization of the registration process. In practice, regularization terms that encourage smooth or diffeomorphic transformations may be added. The details of the image registration are beyond the scope of this work, and our proposed framework is agnostic to the choice of registration methods. Off-the-shelf image registration tools [18] or deep learning-based registration approaches [4] can be employed for this purpose.

Once the optimal spatial transformation, $\hat{T}_i$, is computed, the subcortical segmentation label, $\mathbf{L}_i^{CT}$, of the corresponding CT scan, $\mathbf{I}_i^{CT}$, can be generated by transforming $\mathbf{L}_i^{MR}$ with $\hat{T}_i$:

$$\mathbf{L}_i^{CT} = \mathbf{L}_i^{MR} \circ \hat{T}_i. \tag{6}$$

3.3   Choices of MRI Segmentation Models

Our proposed framework can accommodate an arbitrary number, M, of off-the-shelf MRI segmentation models, $\{\mathcal{S}_j(\cdot; \theta_j)\}_{j=1}^M$, as explained in Sect. 3.1. In this study, we implemented five publicly available MRI segmentation models, $\mathcal{S}(\cdot; \theta)$. The selected models include both probabilistic-based and deep-learning-based approaches, with their details as follows:

ASeg [8] is the default subcortical segmentation model employed by Freesurfer recon-all pipeline [7]. It is a probabilistic atlas-based segmentation model.

Sequence Adaptive Multimodal Segmentation (SAMSEG) [23] is a probabilistic model that utilizes Bayesian modelling for whole brain segmentation. It is also packaged within the Freesurfer toolkit.

FastSurfer [11] is a deep-learning-based whole-brain segmentation model built on a 2D UNet. It serves as an alternative to Freesurfer and reduces the processing time significantly.

SynthSeg [2] is a CNN-based model designed to perform segmentation on brain scans across various domains and contrasts through synthetic generation of a wide range of training data.

QuickNAT [25] is a CNN-based model optimized for fast brain segmentation. It is trained on labels from multiple segmentation softwares and fine-tuned with manually-annotated data.

3.4   Generation of CT Subcortical Segmentation Labels

Using our proposed framework, as summarized in Sects. 3.1 to 3.3, we generated CT subcortical segmentation labels, $\mathbf{L}^{CT}$, for an unannotated MRI-CT paired dataset. The dataset used was the open-access paired MRI-CT brain dataset [28] released by the **SynthRAD Grand Challenge 2023** [12]. This dataset consists of scans from 180 subjects, evenly distributed across three different medical centers.

The dataset provides both T1-weighted MRI and CT scans for each subject, with the MRI and CT scans already aligned with each other. The scans were preprocessed by cropping to the bounding box defined by the patient's outline, with a 20-voxel margin. We selected 17 subcortical regions to include in our segmentation dataset, based on their physiological significance: Lateral Ventricles (L/R), Thalamus (L/R), Caudate (L/R), Putamen (L/R), Pallidum (L/R), Hippocampus (L/R), Amygdala (L/R), Accumbens Area (L/R) and Brainstem. Although other subcortical regions, such as the Substantia Nigra, have key physiological roles, they are too small and not all MRI segmentation models provide segmentation masks for them.

Both MRI and CT scans were resampled to a resolution of $1 \times 1 \times 1\,\mathrm{mm}^3$, with a maximum image dimension of $256 \times 256 \times 256$. The MRI scans underwent additional processing using Freesurfer's autorecon1 pipeline, which includes intensity correction, Talairach transformation to the MNI305 atlas and intensity normalization.

Since the paired MRI-CT images in this dataset were already aligned using rigid image registration with Elastix [18], we could skip the registration steps described in Eqs. (5) and (6). Instead, we directly transferred the generated $\mathbf{L}^{MR}$ to obtain $\mathbf{L}^{CT}$. The resulting set of CT subcortical labels is publicly available at https://github.com/SCSE-Biomedical-Computing-Group/CT-Subcortical-Segmentation.

3.5 Training of CT Subcortical Segmentation Models

Using the CT subcortical labels generated in Sect. 3.4 and their corresponding CT images, we trained numerous CNN-based and Transformer-based segmentation models. The details of these models are as follows:

UNet [24] is a CNN-based model characterized by a series of encoders and decoders connected by skip connections, forming a U-shaped architecture. The UNet has achieved impressive performance in various medical segmentation tasks [1]. In this study, we trained both 2D and 3D versions of UNet.

SwinUNETR [10] differs from conventional UNets by using Swin Transformers [21] as its encoders instead of convolutional layers. This design enables the model to capture long-range global context more effectively.

nnUNet [13] is a state-of-the-art model that features a self-configuring pipeline that automatically trains a UNet with an optimal parameter configuration, eliminating the need for manual hyperparameter tuning.

4 Experimental Setup

4.1 Optimal Label Generation Strategy

To evaluate the performance of our proposed ensemble framework, we compared it with each of the off-the-shelf MRI segmentation models introduced in Sect. 3.3 using two publicly available expert-annotated datasets (detailed in Sect. 4.4). We implemented the two ensembling methods, consensus and majority voting, as described in Sect. 3.1 for our proposed framework and benchmarked their performance.

4.2 CT Subcortical Segmentation Models

We trained both CNN-based and Transformer-based models, as introduced in Sect. 3.5, on our generated CT subcortical segmentation dataset. The dataset was split into training (70%), validation (15%), and test sets (15%). To enhance model performance, we applied additional preprocessing steps, including skull-stripping the CT scans and combining the left and right regions of each structure.

We trained the SwinUNETR [10], imported from the MONAI library [5], and the UNets using the PyTorch framework. They were optimized using Dice loss and the Adam [16] optimizer with an initial learning rate of 0.0001. The learning rate was decayed using the ReduceLROnPlateau scheduler with a patience of 3, based on the validation loss. Early stopping was implemented with a patience of 5. The nnUNet [13] was trained using the *nnUNet v2* framework [13] with the *3d_fullres* configuration from the official source codes[1]. The training process consisted of 1000 epochs and hyperparameters tuning was automatically performed by the framework.

4.3   Transfer Learning

The scarcity of publicly available CT subcortical segmentation datasets poses a challenge in directly evaluating the quality of our generated segmentation dataset. To address this limitation, we proposed transfer learning as an indirect yet practical method of validating our segmentation labels.

Using a 3D UNet trained on our generated CT subcortical segmentation dataset, as described in Sects. 3.5 and 4.2, we froze its encoder and fine-tuned its decoder on an open-source, expert-annotated MRI dataset, OASIS-TRT-20 [17], under limited data conditions by only using 5 annotated scans for training. The details of the OASIS-TRT-20 dataset are provided in Sect. 4.4.

To assess the effectiveness of the features learned from our generated dataset, we compared the fine-tuned model with a 3D UNet trained from scratch on the same MRI dataset. This comparison allowed us to evaluate the transferability of the knowledge learned from our CT subcortical segmentation dataset to a different modality (MRI) and dataset. To ensure the results were not due to model bias, we also conducted the transfer learning experiment with ResUNet.

4.4   Evaluation Datasets

We utilized two MRI subcortical segmentation datasets in our experiments. Both datasets' voxel spacing was preprocessed to have a uniform voxel spacing of $1mm^3$ and cropped to a maximum dimension of $256 \times 256 \times 256 \, mm^3$ to standardize the outputs of various MRI segmentation models.

The IBSR-18 dataset [6] contains 18 manually-guided annotated T1-weighted MRI brain scans from 18 healthy subjects. The dataset was provided by the Center for Morphometric Analysis at Massachusetts General Hospital[2]. The original scans and masks have dimensions of $256 \times 256 \times 128$ with the voxel spacing of $0.9375 \times 0.9375 \times 1.5 \, mm^3$.

---

[1] https://github.com/MIC-DKFZ/nnUNet.

[2] http://www.cma.mgh.harvard.edu/ibsr/.

Table 1. Segmentation results on two MRI expert-annotated datasets

Label Generation Method	IBSR-18			OASIS-TRT-20		
	DSC ↑	HD (vox)↓	AVD (vox)↓	DSC ↑	HD (vox)↓	AVD (vox)↓
ASeg (FreeSurfer) [8]	0.796	4.8	415.2	0.785	6.2	602.3
SAMSEG [23]	0.796	4.9	658.8	0.758	6.7	1312.3
FastSurfer [11]	0.820	4.6	397.5	0.802	6.0	697.0
SynthSeg [2]	0.824	4.4	357.1	0.806	5.2	883.2
QuickNAT [25]	0.834	10.7	455.9	0.795	32.4	812.0
Consensus (All Models)	0.784	5.6	995.3	0.772	6.6	1579.1
Consensus (Deep Learning Models)	0.826	5.1	648.5	0.807	6.1	1040.0
Majority Voting (All Models)	0.845	4.1	312.5	0.820	5.0	544.9
Majority Voting (Deep Learning Models)	**0.852**	**4.0**	**312.5**	**0.825**	**5.0**	**500.4**

↑ *means higher values being more accurate*
Bold *indicates the best performance*

The OASIS-TRT-20 dataset [17] is part of the Mindboggle-101 project and contains 20 T1-weighted MRI brain scans from 20 healthy subjects aged between 23–29 years old.

4.5 Evaluation Metrics

The segmentation performance of different methods in our experiments was evaluated by 3 metrics: Dice-Sørensen coefficient (DSC), undirected Hausdorff Distance (HD) and Absolute Volume Difference (AVD).

5 Results

5.1 Optimal Label Generation Strategy

We compared the performance of our proposed framework with each of the off-the-shelf MRI segmentation models introduced in Sect. 3.3. The overall results are presented in Table 1, while detailed results for each subcortical structure on both datasets can be found in the Supplementary Tables 1–6.

As shown in Table 1, when used as standalone models, deep learning-based approaches like QuickNAT and SynthSeg tended to generate labels with higher overlap with the ground-truth, as evidenced by their higher average DSC for both datasets. This can be attributed to the ability of deep models to learn complex representations. However, they did not necessarily exhibit greater robustness than probabilistic models, as demonstrated by QuickNAT's significantly higher HD for both datasets. Notably, no single model consistently achieved the highest DSC and lowest HD and AVD.

Table 2. Average DSC of segmentation of different structures by various deep models trained on our generated CT subcortical segmentation dataset

Model	Ventricles	Thalamus	Caudate	Putamen	Pallidum	Hippocampus	Brainstem	Average
SwinUNETR	0.829	0.811	0.662	0.692	0.668	0.650	0.874	0.741
2D UNet	0.867	0.890	0.820	0.801	0.774	0.730	0.898	0.825
3D UNet	0.875	0.908	0.852	0.851	0.844	0.777	0.917	0.861
nnUNet	**0.912**	**0.933**	**0.892**	**0.891**	**0.880**	**0.854**	**0.946**	**0.901**

In contrast, our proposed framework, which employs majority voting ensembling, demonstrated superior and more robust and consistent performance. This was reflected in its higher DSC and lower HD and AVD compared to all other methods. While the strict rule of consensus ensembling may result in smaller integrated segmentation labels, leading to poorer results, majority voting ensembling improves on this by eliminating outliers specific to a minority of the models without significantly shrinking the segmented volume.

To further improve robustness, we evaluated the performance of majority voting ensembling using only deep learning models. As expected, given their higher DSC values, this approach generated labels with the highest average DSC and lowest HD and AVD for both datasets. Our results demonstrated that our proposed framework, which leverages majority voting ensembling, produces more robust segmentation masks than any individual model, proving the effectiveness of our proposed framework.

5.2 CT Subcortical Segmentation Models

We further evaluated the performance of different models trained on our generated CT subcortical segmentation dataset. The qualitative results are shown in Fig. 3, while the quantitative results are presented in Table 2.

As shown in Table 2, CNN-based models, namely UNet and nnUNet, outperformed Transformer-based model, SwinUNETR. This is likely attributed to the limited amount of training data, which may not be sufficient to fully leverage the capabilities of the transformer-based architecture. Nevertheless, our trained models have established a performance baseline for future works aiming to improve the performance of segmentation models for CT subcortical segmentation.

5.3 Validating Dataset's Utility Through Transfer Learning

Finally, we assessed the utility of our generated CT subcortical segmentation dataset by pretraining a 3D UNet and a ResUNet on our CT dataset and finetuning them with a small amount (*i.e.* 5) of annotated MRI images, followed by comparing them to the same networks which were trained from scratch.

As illustrated in Fig. 4, the training curves of 3D UNet reveal that the pretrained model converged significantly faster at 65 epochs, whereas the model

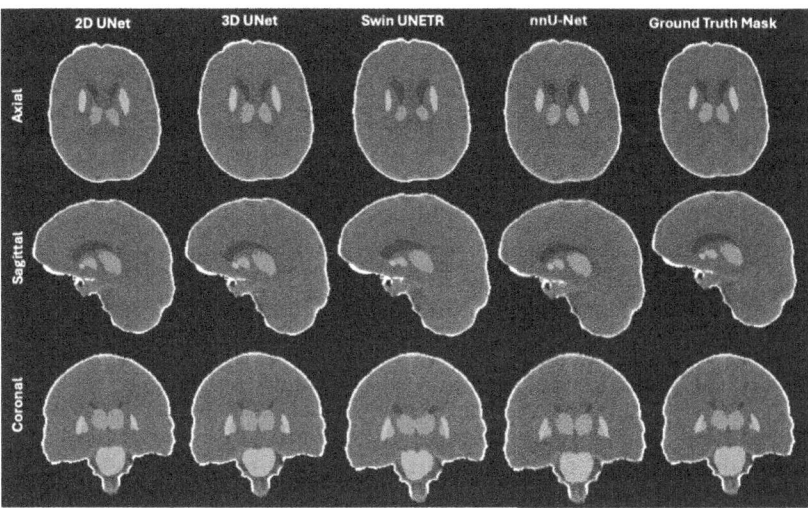

Fig. 3. Qualitative results by various CT subcortical segmentation models. The results and ground-truth across the axial, sagittal and coronal axes.

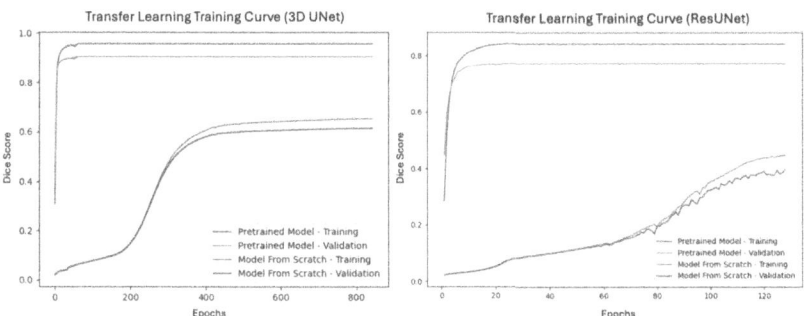

Fig. 4. Training and Validation Dice Scores of both pretrained models and models trained from scratch.

trained from scratch required more than 840 epochs to converge. Similarly, the pretrained ResUNet converged much faster at 28 epochs while the ResUNet trained from scratch required more than 130 epochs. Additionally, the validation Dice score for the pretrained models is significantly higher, suggesting its better performance. To further evaluate their segmentation capabilities, we applied the models to the test dataset, and the results are presented in Table 3. Notably, for the three smallest structures, Pallidum, Amygdala and Accumbens Area, the pretrained model performed significantly better than the model trained from scratch, leading to higher overall segmentation accuracy.

The faster convergence speed and superior segmentation performance of the pretrained model indirectly validate the quality and utility of our generated CT subcortical segmentation labels, suggesting that it can serve as a strong reference

Table 3. Evaluation of segmentation performance of both pretrained model and model trained from scratch using transfer learning

Subcortical Structure	Pretrained UNet			UNet from Scratch			Pretrained ResUNet			ResUNet from Scratch		
	DSC ↑	HD (vox)↓	AVD (vox)↓	DSC ↑	HD (vox)↓	AVD (vox)↓	DSC ↑	HD (vox)↓	AVD (vox)↓	DSC ↑	HD (vox)↓	AVD (vox)↓
Ventricles	0.905	21.3	1921.2	0.936	18.2	636.1	0.853	55.5	3922.0	0.810	48.8	4796.1
Thalamus	0.931	5.3	551.9	0.943	2.6	416.3	0.906	21.8	929.9	0.021	75.7	1908400.0
Caudate	0.896	15.8	504.3	0.935	19.3	146.5	0.856	24.8	621.9	0.798	45.2	1174.2
Putamen	0.912	37.1	541.5	0.939	6.8	155.9	0.861	39.0	704.9	0.814	45.4	2516.0
Pallidum	0.896	3.9	370.2	0.622	24.8	5388.1	0.849	3.1	452.9	0.000	30.9	4882.0
Hippocampus	0.868	14.3	533.3	0.882	6.2	440.6	0.774	38.6	1163.9	0.000	46.1	10100.1
Brainstem	0.947	11.6	392.8	0.957	4.4	317.8	0.899	27.9	2506.8	0.754	38.3	8514.2
Amygdala	0.857	8.9	140.5	0.001	230.9	6920161.5	0.004	102.6	1968550.2	0.000	98.0	3576.4
Accumbens Area	0.839	23.7	168.7	0.000	5.6	1477.7	0.736	17.0	154.4	0.000	10.4	1477.8
Average	**0.895**	**15.8**	**569.4**	0.691	35.4	769904.5	**0.749**	**36.7**	219889.7	0.355	48.8	**216159.6**

↑ *means higher values indicate better segmentation performance*

standard for training deep-learning models. Our transfer learning experiments further demonstrate the potential of our dataset to facilitate the training of deep models for related medical image analysis tasks with limited annotated data. This is particularly useful in practice, where acquiring expert-annotated data can be resource-intensive and challenging.

6   Conclusion

In summary, we have proposed an automated ensemble framework that leverages existing MRI segmentation models to generate robust and accurate segmentation labels for CT scans. This framework effectively addresses the data scarcity problem in CT subcortical segmentation and greatly reduces the manual annotation effort required by clinical experts. As a model-agnostic pipeline, it can be easily extended to incorporate future improvements in segmentation, further enhancing its robustness. By utilizing this pipeline, we have generated an open-source CT subcortical segmentation dataset and trained reliable segmentation models on it, providing a strong foundation for future research and performance benchmarking. Potential avenues for future work include extending the framework to generate labels for additional subcortical anatomies beyond the 17 classes currently addressed, as well as exploring its applicability to other imaging modalities. Semi-automated and community-driven label correction methods can also be explored and incorporated to further enhance the labels' robustness.

Acknowledgments. PH. Yeung is funded by the Presidential Postdoctoral Fellowship from Nanyang Technological University.

Disclosure of Interest. The authors have no competing interests to declare.

References

1. Azad, R., et al.: Medical image segmentation review: the success of u-net. IEEE Trans. Pattern Anal. Mach. Intell. (2024)
2. Billot, B., et al.: Synthseg: segmentation of brain MRI scans of any contrast and resolution without retraining. Med. Image Anal. **86**, 102789 (2023)
3. Cai, J.C., et al.: Fully automated segmentation of head CT neuroanatomy using deep learning. Radiol. Artif. Intell. **2**(5), e190183 (2020)
4. Cao, X., Yang, J., Wang, L., Xue, Z., Wang, Q., Shen, D.: Deep learning based inter-modality image registration supervised by intra-modality similarity. In: Machine Learning in Medical Imaging: 9th International Workshop, MLMI 2018, Held in Conjunction with MICCAI 2018, Granada, Spain, September 16, 2018, Proceedings 9, pp. 55–63. Springer (2018)
5. Cardoso, M.J., et al.: Monai: an open-source framework for deep learning in healthcare. arXiv preprint arXiv:2211.02701 (2022)
6. Center for Morphometric Analysis, Massachusetts General Hospital: Internet brain segmentation repository (ibsr-18) (2006). https://www.nitrc.org/projects/ibsr
7. Fischi, B., et al.: Whole brain segmentation: automated labeling of neuroanatomical structures in the human brain. Neuron **33**(3), 341–355 (2002)
8. Fischl, B.: Freesurfer. Neuroimage **62**(2), 774–781 (2012)
9. Greve, D.N., et al.: A deep learning toolbox for automatic segmentation of subcortical limbic structures from MRI images. Neuroimage **244**, 118610 (2021)
10. Hatamizadeh, A., Nath, V., Tang, Y., Yang, D., Roth, H.R., Xu, D.: Swin unetr: swin transformers for semantic segmentation of brain tumors in MRI images. In: International MICCAI Brainlesion Workshop, pp. 272–284. Springer (2021)
11. Henschel, L., Conjeti, S., Estrada, S., Diers, K., Fischl, B., Reuter, M.: Fastsurfer-a fast and accurate deep learning based neuroimaging pipeline. Neuroimage **219**, 117012 (2020)
12. Huijben, E.M., et al.: Generating synthetic computed tomography for radiotherapy: Synthrad 2023 challenge report. Med. Image Anal. **97**, 103276 (2024)
13. Isensee, F., Jaeger, P.F., Kohl, S.A., Petersen, J., Maier-Hein, K.H.: nnU-net: a self-configuring method for deep learning-based biomedical image segmentation. Nat. Methods **18**(2), 203–211 (2021)
14. Janacsek, K., Evans, T.M., Kiss, M., Shah, L., Blumenfeld, H., Ullman, M.T.: Subcortical cognition: the fruit below the rind. Annu. Rev. Neurosci. **45**(1), 361–386 (2022)
15. Jenkinson, M., Beckmann, C.F., Behrens, T.E., Woolrich, M.W., Smith, S.M.: Fsl. Neuroimage **62**(2), 782–790 (2012)
16. Kingma, D.P., Ba, J.: Adam: a method for stochastic optimization. arXiv preprint arXiv:1412.6980 (2014)
17. Klein, A., Tourville, J.: 101 labeled brain images and a consistent human cortical labeling protocol. Front. Neurosci. **6**, 171 (2012)
18. Klein, S., Staring, M., Murphy, K., Viergever, M.A., Pluim, J.P.: Elastix: a toolbox for intensity-based medical image registration. IEEE Trans. Med. Imaging **29**(1), 196–205 (2009)
19. Knierim, J.J.: The hippocampus. Curr. Biol. **25**(23), R1116–R1121 (2015)
20. Li, J., et al.: Cortical and subcortical morphological alterations in motor subtypes of parkinson's disease. NPJ Parkinson's Dis. **8**(1), 167 (2022)
21. Liu, Z., et al.: Swin transformer: hierarchical vision transformer using shifted windows. In: Proceedings of the IEEE/CVF International Conference on Computer Vision, pp. 10012–10022 (2021)

22. Müller, N.: Computed tomography and magnetic resonance imaging: past, present and future. Eur. Respir. J. **19**(35 suppl), 3s–12s (2002)

23. Puonti, O., Iglesias, J.E., Van Leemput, K.: Fast and sequence-adaptive whole-brain segmentation using parametric Bayesian modeling. Neuroimage **143**, 235–249 (2016)

24. Ronneberger, O., Fischer, P., Brox, T.: U-net: Convolutional networks for biomedical image segmentation. In: Medical Image Computing and Computer-Assisted Intervention–MICCAI 2015: 18th International Conference, Munich, Germany, October 5-9, 2015, Proceedings, Part III 18, pp. 234–241. Springer (2015)

25. Roy, A.G., Conjeti, S., Navab, N., Wachinger, C., Initiative, A., et al.: Quicknat: a fully convolutional network for quick and accurate segmentation of neuroanatomy. Neuroimage **186**, 713–727 (2019)

26. Rushmore, R.J., et al.: Anatomically curated segmentation of human subcortical structures in high resolution magnetic resonance imaging: an open science approach. Front. Neuroanat. **16**, 894606 (2022)

27. Srikrishna, M., et al.: Deep learning from MRI-derived labels enables automatic brain tissue classification on human brain CT. Neuroimage **244**, 118606 (2021)

28. Thummerer, A., et al.: Synthrad 2023 grand challenge dataset: generating synthetic CT for radiotherapy. Med. Phys. **50**(7), 4664–4674 (2023)

29. Vertes, R.P., Linley, S.B., Groenewegen, H.J., Witter, M.P.: Thalamus. In: The rat Nervous System, pp. 335–390. Elsevier (2015)

30. Wang, T., et al.: Deep learning-based automated segmentation of eight brain anatomical regions using head CT images in PET/CT. BMC Med. Imaging **22**(1), 99 (2022)

31. Yi, H.A., et al.: Relation between subcortical grey matter atrophy and conversion from mild cognitive impairment to Alzheimer's disease. J. Neurol. Neurosurg. Psychiatry **87**(4), 425–432 (2016)

DRASU-Net: Dual-Backbone and Residual Atrous Squeeze Module-Aided U-Net Model for Polyp Segmentation

Utathya Aich[1,2], Ritabrata Roy[1], Alexander Eroshkin[3], Dmitrii Kaplun[4,5(✉)], and Ram Sarkar[1]

[1] Department of Computer Science and Engineering, Jadavpur University,
Kolkata, India
[2] CNH Industrial ITC, Gurgaon, India
[3] Department of Automation and Control Processes, St. Petersburg Electrotechnical
University "LETI", St. Petersburg, Russia
[4] Artificial Intelligence Research Institute, China University of Mining
and Technology, Xuzhou, China
[5] Intelligent Devices Institute, St. Petersburg Electrotechnical University "LETI",
St. Petersburg, Russia
dikaplun@etu.ru

Abstract. Polyp segmentation in colonoscopy images is essential for the early detection and treatment of colorectal cancer. Accurate segmentation aids in diagnosis and reduces risks of malignancy. Existing deep learning models often struggle with the trade-off between semantic understanding and spatial precision, requiring extensive computational resources that limit their deployment in real-world, resource-constrained clinical settings. The need for an optimized yet high-performing segmentation model remains an open challenge. To bridge this gap, we propose Dual-backbone and Residual Atrous Squeeze module-aided U-Net (DRASU-Net), optimized for low-resource environments. Our model features a dual-backbone and multi-scale feature learning approach, integrating EfficientNetB4 and MobileNetV2 to balance feature richness and spatial details. We introduce the RAS module, which leverages Atrous Convolutions, Residual Connections, and Squeeze-and-Excite (SE) blocks to enhance feature recalibration and improve segmentation accuracy. Experiments on the CVC-ClinicDB and Kvasir-SEG datasets demonstrate that DRASU-Net outperforms other methods, with a dice score of 0.9540 on CVC-ClinicDB and 0.9525 on Kvasir-SEG, while maintaining only 10.72 million parameters. DRASU-Net exhibits strong generalization when evaluated across multiple polyp segmentation datasets. The code for our proposed model is available on Github.

Keywords: Medical Image Processing · Colorectal Cancer · Polyp Segmentation · U-Net · Deep Learning

---

U. Aich and R. Roy—Equal contribution.

© The Author(s), under exclusive license to Springer Nature Switzerland AG 2026
S. Ali et al. (Eds.): MIUA 2025, LNCS 15918, pp. 175–189, 2026.
https://doi.org/10.1007/978-3-031-98694-9_13

1 Introduction

Colorectal cancer (CRC) is the second leading cause of cancer-related deaths in the United States, with over 50,000 fatalities annually. Early polyp detection is crucial to reducing CRC incidence, but optical colonoscopy, the gold standard for screening, has a polyp miss rate of 14%–30%. Research shows that improving the adenoma detection rate (ADR) by just 1% can lower CRC risk by 3% [1,2]. This underscores the urgent need for advanced computational techniques to enhance polyp detection accuracy.

Medical image segmentation is crucial for automating clinical workflows by accurately locating polyps, aiding in their removal, and ensuring complete excision while preserving healthy tissue. For instance, polyps can be obscured, making detection difficult. Recent advancements in deep learning, particularly semantic segmentation techniques, have demonstrated promising results in medical imaging [3]. Traditional models such as U-Net [4] have achieved competent performance in biomedical image segmentation tasks, yet their high computational cost limits their deployment in real-time clinical settings. Colonoscopy procedures demand efficient, low-latency inference to support affordable decision-making systems. Reports indicate that between 17%–28% of colon polyps are missed during screenings [5,6], emphasizing the need for more reliable and accessible segmentation models.

To address these challenges, we propose a novel deep learning-based polyp segmentation model, called **DRASU-Net** (Dual-backbone and Residual Atrous Squeeze module-aided U-Net). Our model outperforms exisitng methods while utilizing fewer parameters, making it suitable for integration into Computer-Aided Detection (CAD) systems. This approach enables real-time inference on medical hardware, assisting endoscopists in segmenting polyps more effectively. The **key contributions** of this study are as follows:

1. **Dual-backbone Multi-scale Learning**: In the encoder, a novel architecture is proposed by integrating the features of EfficientNetB4 and MobileNetV2 to balance semantic richness and spatial precision.
2. **RAS Module for Context-Aware Refinement**: Our model combines Atrous Convolutions, Residual Connections and Squeeze-and-Excite (SE) blocks to enhance feature recalibration, detail preservation and spatial awareness.
3. **Hierarchical Feature Fusion & Progressive Reconstruction**: The proposed model aligns multi-scale features using summation and transformation layers, with a decoder employing bilinear upsampling, skip connections, and spatially-aware refinement for high-resolution predictions.
4. **Optimized for Low-Resource Environments**: DRASU-Net achieves competent segmentation performance by using lesser parameters than many state-of-the-art models on Kvasir-SEG and CVC-ClinicDB datasets, ensuring superior boundary retention without compromising accuracy.

2   Related Work

Polyp segmentation in medical imaging, particularly in colonoscopy, has gained significant attention due to its critical role in early detection and diagnosis of CRC. Traditional methods relied on manual annotation by radiologists, which is time-consuming and prone to variability. With the advancement of computer vision and deep learning, automated polyp segmentation techniques have emerged, leveraging convolutional neural networks (CNNs), transformers, and hybrid architectures.

CNN-based architectures, such as U-Net [4], have become a cornerstone for medical image segmentation tasks. It's encoder-decoder structure, has been widely adopted for polyp segmentation due to its ability to capture both global and local features through skip connections. However, while U-Net has shown promising results, its performance may degrade when handling complex or diverse polyp appearances. To address these challenges, variants like ResUNet++ [7] have been proposed, integrating residual blocks and advanced feature extraction techniques such as SE blocks and atrous spatial pyramidal pooling (ASPP).

While CNN-based approaches have been successful, they often struggle with capturing long-range dependencies and global contextual information. Parallel Reverse Attention Network, PraNet [3] is one such example that incorporates attention to address the challenges in polyp segmentation. By using a parallel decoder and reverse attention mechanism, it aggregates both global and local features, which improves the segmentation of polyps with unclear boundaries. Transformer models, such as Polyp-PVT [8], further enhance this approach by capturing multi-level features and incorporating modules like Cascaded Fusion and Camouflage Identification.

Despite the success of both CNN and transformer models, a hybrid approach that combines the strengths of both paradigms has gained attention. DUCK-Net [9] is one such hybrid model, which combines CNN-based convolutional blocks with residual downsampling to improve local feature extraction. This approach allows the network to work effectively even with limited annotated data, thus making it more applicable for clinical environments where large annotated datasets are scarce. Similarly, models like FCB-SwinV2 Transformer [10] combine the power of CNNs and transformers in parallel, with the SwinV2 transformer replacing the traditional transformer branch, leading to improved generalization and better performance on diverse colonoscopy datasets. DuAT [11] introduces Global-to-Local Spatial Aggregation and Selective Boundary Aggregation modules, which effectively enhance the segmentation of small polyps and those with unclear boundaries, showing significant improvements in performance. The RAPUNet [12] model, a hybrid of MetaFormer and CNN, uses a custom convolutional block (RAPU) to better capture local features and improve the robustness of polyp segmentation.

These innovations tackle key challenges in polyp segmentation, such as small object detection, boundary ambiguity, and generalization across clinical conditions. However, despite their strong dice score, these models are computationally intensive and require significant memory, limiting their use in clinical settings with limited computational resources. This highlights the need for models that are both high-performing and parameter-efficient, ensuring they maintain accuracy while being computationally light enough for deployment in resource-constrained clinical environments. In response to this, we propose **DRASU-Net**, a dual-backbone architecture that balances semantic richness and spatial precision using a RAS module, achieving state-of-the-art segmentation with efficient upsampling and fewer parameters, optimized for low-resource environments.

3   Proposed Model: DRASU-Net

We have proposed a novel U-Net model, called **DRASU-Net** (Dual-backbone Residual Atrous Squeeze Network), that integrates a dual-backbone encoder with a Residual Atrous Squeeze (RAS) module and an efficient upsampling strategy. It integrates EfficientNetB4 and MobileNetV2, extracting multi-scale features from three spatial levels in each of the three encoder blocks. These six feature maps at different depths are refined using the Residual Atrous Squeeze (RAS) module, containing atrous convolutions for multi-scale context capture, residual connections for stable gradient flow, and SE attention to emphasize relevant structures while suppressing irrelevant details. By leveraging EfficientNetB4 and MobileNetV2 architectures as complementary feature extractors, DRASU-Net captures both fine-grained spatial details and high-level semantic features, ensuring robust segmentation. RAS module enhances boundary delineation and suppresses irrelevant information. It preserves fine-grained spatial details while effectively capturing global information. The decoder employs a three-level upsampling process to ensure smooth feature reconstruction while preventing artifacts. A final 1×1 convolution with sigmoid activation produces the segmentation map, ensuring accurate pixel-wise classification with computational efficiency.

In Fig. 1, our proposed model starts with two stacked 3×3 convolutions to pressively extract features, thus improving nonlinearity and efficient gradient flow. Stacking two 3×3 convolutions instead of using a single large kernel (e.g., 5×5 or 7×7) achieves a larger receptive field while maintaining a lower parameter count, thereby improving computational efficiency. This approach also prevents excessive information loss that may occur with a single-strided convolution, allowing for a more structured feature encoding process, which is critical for downstream segmentation tasks. Additionally, this approach ensures that the output feature maps align in spatial dimensions with the first stage of the dual-backbone encoder, facilitating seamless feature fusion from both backbone networks.

Dual-backbone Encoder: A core architectural advancement of DRASU-Net lies in its multi-layer feature extraction strategy, which enables precise polyp segmentation by incorporating multi-scale hierarchical information. Traditional single-backbone models often struggle to simultaneously preserve spatial granularity and deep semantic abstraction. In contrast, DRASU-Net's dual-backbone architecture combines MobileNetV2, a lightweight and computationally efficient

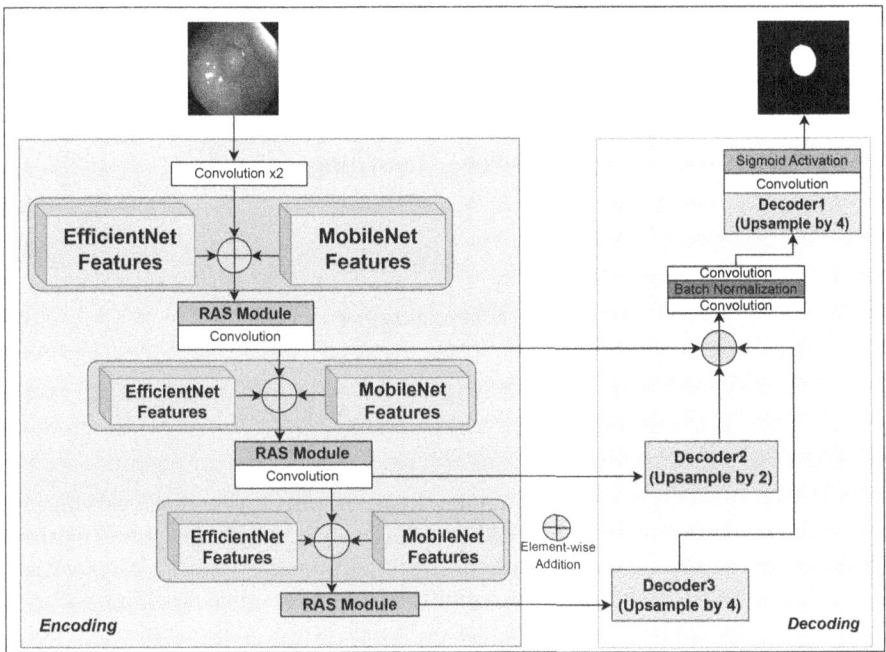

Fig. 1. Architecture of the proposed model, called DRASU-Net

feature extractor, with EfficientNetB4, a high-capacity semantic model, achieving an optimal trade-off between accuracy and inference speed. By systematically fusing multi-depth feature representations, this dual-backbone encoder enhances boundary precision, texture understanding, and generalization, making it distinctly more robust than conventional single-backbone approaches. Extracted layers as encoders are strategically selected to capture a hierarchical representation of the input data, ensuring a progressive multi-scale feature extraction process. Shallow layers capture fine details, while deeper layers encode high level features, both vital for accurate segmentation.

The extracted feature maps are processed through convolutional layers for dimensional alignment before being aggregated through additive fusion.

Residual Atrous Squeeze (RAS) Module: Inspired by the architecture of DUCK-Net [9] and RAPU-Net [12], the Residual Atrous Squeeze (RAS) module is a key addition to our proposed model, designed to enhance feature representation by integrating residual learning, Atrous Convolutions, and channel attention through mechanisms. This module refines the integrated multi-scale features extracted from EfficientNetB4 and MobileNetV2, ensuring effective feature encoding across multiple depth levels. It preserves fine-grained spatial details while enriching high-level contextual information, leading to a more discriminative feature representation.

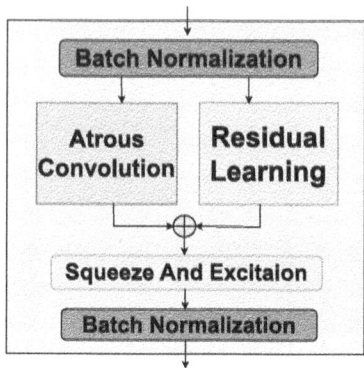

Fig. 2. Architecture of the RAS module

One of the primary challenges in polyp image segmentation is the varying size and morphology of polyps. The **RAS** module in Fig. 2 incorporates **Residual Connections**, ensuring stable gradient flow and improved feature propagation. By preserving spatial details across multiple layers, residual learning prevents the degradation of fine-grained information, which is crucial for delineating polyp boundaries. This enhancement enables DRASU-Net to maintain structural consistency, ensuring that both low-level texture and high-level semantic representations are retained throughout the network.

To further enrich feature extraction, the **Atrous Convolution** mechanism is employed, allowing the model to capture both local and global contextual information, making it particularly effective in segmenting polyps of varying sizes. Atrous Convolutions adjust dynamically to capture fine details and maintain structural coherence, enhancing multi-scale feature representation and improving model robustness across varied polyp morphologies.

The **Squeeze-and-Excitation (SE)** mechanism refines the extracted features by dynamically recalibrating channel-wise activations. By emphasizing the most relevant feature responses while suppressing irrelevant background noise, the SE module enhances the network's ability to focus on polyp regions with high precision. This selective attention mechanism allows DRASU-Net to achieve superior segmentation performance, effectively distinguishing polyps from surrounding tissues. The integration of Residual learning, Atrous Convolutions, and SE attention within the RAS module establishes a powerful feature refinement framework, ensuring accurate boundary delineation and robust segmentation across diverse scenarios.

The implementation of **RAS** module in Fig. 2 begins with batch normalization on the existing features. To stabilize input feature distributions, an Atrous Convolution block is used, which applies three convolutional layers with increasing dilation rates of 1, 2 and 3, respectively to capture features at multiple receptive fields without reducing spatial resolution. Simultaneously, a Residual block processes the same input using a ResNet-style structure. The outputs from the Atrous and Residual paths are then combined using an additive fusion mechanism, ensuring complementary feature integration. Finally, a SE module performs global feature recalibration, dynamically adjusting channel-wise activations to prioritize informative regions.

Decoder Module: The decoder in our proposed model is meticulously designed to reconstruct high-resolution segmentation maps by leveraging hierarchical feature fusion, progressive upsampling, and residual refinement. Unlike conventional decoder architectures that rely solely on simple bilinear upsampling or transposed convolutions, our approach integrates deep multiscale contextual information extracted from the dual encoder while ensuring that spatial details and boundary precision are preserved. A key novelty in our decoder design is the multi-scale feature aggregation strategy, where refined deep features from the RAS module are progressively fused and upsampled to ensure smooth information propagation across different resolution levels. Instead of directly concatenating encoder and decoder features, we introduce an adaptive fusion mechanism, where feature maps from different hierarchical depths are selectively combined using element-wise addition. This ensures that only discriminative features are retained while suppressing redundant activations that may lead to false positives. Furthermore, DRASU-Net employs residual learning in the upsampling pathway, where each upsampling stage is followed by a refinement block consisting of 3×3 convolutions. Additionally, to further refine the segmentation boundaries, the decoder integrates skip connections from earlier encoder layers, allowing the model to recover fine-grained spatial details while maintaining high-level semantic consistency.

At the final stage, a 1×1 convolutional layer is applied to project the feature maps into the required segmentation space, followed by a sigmoid activation function for pixel-wise classification. To prevent grid-like artifacts commonly introduced by transposed convolutions, the decoder employs bilinear interpolation-based upsampling, which ensures a spatially smooth and artifact-free reconstruction. This approach preserves feature continuity while avoiding the uneven activation patterns often observed with deconvolution operations.

4 Datasets

In this study, we primarily utilize the CVC-ClinicDB [1] and Kvasir-SEG [2] datasets for training and evaluating our polyp segmentation model. These datasets consist of high-quality endoscopic images with pixel-wise annotated ground truth masks, making them well-suited for developing and benchmarking deep learning-based segmentation models. The CVC-ClinicDB [1] dataset comprises 612 polyp images extracted from 31 colonoscopy sequences, each accompanied by corresponding binary ground truth masks, with a fixed resolution of 384×288 pixels. The Kvasir-SEG [2] dataset contains 1,000 annotated polyp images with varying resolutions ranging from 332×487 to 1920×1072 pixels, capturing a diverse set of polyp appearances under different imaging conditions.

To ensure a standardized comparison with prior work, we adopt the dataset-splits used in DUCK-Net[1]. Specifically, for training, validation, and testing, we use 800, 100, and 100 images from Kvasir-SEG [2], and 488, 62, and 62 images from CVC-ClinicDB [1], respectively.

To further benchmark our model's performance, we also evaluate our model on ETIS-LaribPolypDB [13] and CVC-ColonDB [14] datasets, which contain more challenging cases, making it a valuable resource for evaluating segmentation models. These datasets serve as unseen test datasets to evaluate the model's generalization capability, demonstrating its performance on previously unseen data. The CVC-ColonDB [14] dataset comprises 380 polyp images extracted from 15 short colonoscopy sequences, each provided with corresponding segmentation masks at a resolution of 574×500 pixels. The ETIS-LaribPolypDB [13] dataset contains 196 high-resolution endoscopic images, each with a resolution of 1255×966 pixels, along with corresponding binary segmentation masks. It is considered one of the most challenging benchmarking datasets due to the presence of polyps with various types and sizes, posing significant challenges for segmentation models.

5   Implementation Details

The model is trained in Kaggle's 16 GB NVIDIA P100 GPU for accelerated computation. Our implementation uses the TensorFlow framework, with input images resized to 352×352 pixels. Training is conducted with a batch size of 8, using the AdamW optimizer with learning rate of 1×10^{-4} for a total of 150 epochs. However, instead of training continuously, inspired by the technique followed in Stochastic Gradient Descent with Warm Restarts (SGDR) [15], we divide the training process into staged-training cycles, where the model trains for 50 epochs, resets the optimizer, and resumes training afterwards.

To enhance generalization and robustness, we follow the same runtime data augmentation used in DUCK-Net [9]. The augmentation strategy includes horizontal and vertical flipping to ensure orientation invariance, color jittering to simulate diverse imaging conditions, and affine transformations (scaling, translation, rotation, shearing). Our training objective minimizes a hybrid loss, composed of the Dice loss and the Focal loss. The Dice loss reduces overlap-related errors by maximizing the agreement between the predicted probabilities ($\hat{k}$) and the ground truth labels (k):

$$\mathcal{L}_{\text{dice}} = 1 - \frac{2\sum(k \cdot \hat{k}) + \varepsilon}{\sum k + \sum \hat{k} + \varepsilon} \tag{1}$$

The focal loss mitigates class imbalance by reducing the relative loss for well-classified examples and emphasizing challenging ones:

$$\mathcal{L}_{\text{focal}} = -\beta(1 - \hat{k})^{\gamma} k \log(\hat{k}) - (1 - \beta)\hat{k}^{\gamma}(1 - k) \log(1 - \hat{k}) \tag{2}$$

---

[1] https://github.com/RazvanDu/DUCK-Net.

After extensive experimentation with different parameter values, the study used $\beta = 0.25$ and $\gamma = 2$ in the focal loss, this improved generalization, enhances boundary precision, and effectively segments small or irregular structures.

6   Evaluation Metrics

We majorly utilize two key metrics for image segmentation evaluation: Mean Dice Coefficient (mDice) and Mean Intersection over Union (mIoU).

Mean Dice Coefficient (mDice): The Dice Coefficient is a measure of the spatial overlap between the predicted mask and the ground truth mask. We followed the Mean Dice Coefficient (mDice) calculation from [10], which is defined as:

$$P_{\text{total}} = \sum_{i=1}^{N} P_i, \quad Q_{\text{total}} = \sum_{i=1}^{N} Q_i, \quad R_{\text{total}} = \sum_{i=1}^{N} R_i \tag{3}$$

$$\text{mDice} = \frac{2 \cdot P_{\text{total}}}{2 \cdot P_{\text{total}} + Q_{\text{total}} + R_{\text{total}}} \tag{4}$$

Here, P_i, Q_i, and R_i denotes the number of true positive, false positive, and false negative pixels for the ith image, respectively. The metric mDice denotes the mean Dice coefficient computed across the dataset.

Mean Intersection over Union (mIoU): The Intersection over Union (IoU) measures the ratio of the intersection to the union of the predicted and ground truth segmentation masks. The Mean IoU (mIoU) is defined as:

$$\text{mIoU} = \frac{P_{\text{total}}}{P_{\text{total}} + Q_{\text{total}} + R_{\text{total}}} \tag{5}$$

Hausdorff Distance (IID): This is used to evaluate how closely the predicted segmentation aligns with the ground truth. A smaller HD value indicates greater similarity, reflecting more accurate segmentation results.

$$\text{HD}(A, B) = \max \left\{ \max_{a \in A} \min_{b \in B} \|a - b\|_2, \ \max_{b \in B} \min_{a \in A} \|b - a\|_2 \right\} \tag{6}$$

Here, A and B represent the sets of boundary points from the predicted and ground truth segmentation masks, respectively. The function $\|a - b\|_2$ denotes the Euclidean distance between points a and b. The Hausdorff Distance captures the maximum distance of a point in one set to the closest point in the other set. We report the median Hausdorff Distance (mHD) across the dataset to ensure robustness against outliers.

7   Experimental Results and Discussion

In this section, we analyze the performance of our proposed model, DRASU-Net, on the CVC-ClinicDB [1] and Kvasir-SEG [2] datasets following the dataset partitioning of DUCK-Net [9].

Our Result: DRASU-Net achieves an *mDice* of 0.9540 and an *mIoU* of 0.9138 on CVC-ClinicDB [1], demonstrating its ability to accurately segment polyp structures with high boundary precision. The model effectively captures fine-grained details, ensuring minimal segmentation errors. Similarly, on Kvasir-SEG [2], the model attains an *mDice* of 0.9525 and an *mIoU* of 0.9094. The *median Hausdorff distance (mHD)* is 8.11 on the CVC-ClinicDB dataset [1], while it increases to 10.19 on the Kvasir-SEG dataset [2], reflecting greater boundary variability in the latter.

Table 1. Performance comparison of the DRASU-Net with existing models following the DUCK-Net [9] data splits

Model	CVC-ClinicDB [1]		Kvasir-SEG [2]	
	mDice	mIoU	mDice	mIoU
SegNET [16], 2015	0.8728	0.7744	0.8936	0.8077
DoubleU-Net [17], 2020	0.9422	0.8907	0.9301	0.8694
DUCK-Net [9], 2023	0.9478	0.9009	0.9502	0.9051
RAPUNet [12], 2024	0.9454	0.8965	0.9503	0.9054
FCB-SwinV2 Transformer [10], 2024	0.9489	0.9028	**0.9577**	**0.9188**
DRASU-Net, 2025	**0.9540**	**0.9121**	0.9525	0.9094

The effectiveness of DRASU-Net is evaluated by comparing its performance against existing models, including DUCK-Net [9], FCB-SwinV2 Transformer [10], DoubleU-Net [17], RAPUNet [12] and SegNet [16], and results are presented in Table 1. FCB-SwinV2 Transformer [10], leveraging hierarchical feature extraction, demonstrates strong results but lacks explicit boundary refinement modules, making DRASU-Net superior in CVC-ClinicDB for precise polyp segmentation. DRASU-Net outperforms DUCK-Net on CVC-ClinicDB with an improvement of +0.0062. Similarly, on Kvasir-SEG, it surpasses DoubleU-Net by +0.0224.

These results confirm that DRASU-Net establishes a new benchmark in polyp segmentation by effectively capturing boundary details and achieving robust generalization across diverse datasets. One of the key highlights of DRASU-Net is its ability to achieve a lightweight architecture while outperforming in most cases and achieving competitive results otherwise. The comparison in terms of computational complexity, as detailed in Table 2, highlights the efficiency of the DRASU-Net over existing models in terms of both parameter count and FLOPs. DRASU-Net exhibits a significantly lower parameter count of 10.72M, which is

Table 2. Computational complexities of various models with DRASU-Net

Model	Parameters (MB)	Parameters (M)	FLOPs (G)
SegNet, 2015 [16]	127.39	33.37	154.15
DoubleU-Net, 2020 [17]	117.16	29.28	101.86
DUCK-Net, 2023 [9]	592.84	155.30	365.34
FCB-SwinV2 Transformer, 2024 [10]	429.29	129.31	230.51
RAPUNet, 2024 [12]	177.82	46.61	43.69
DRASU-Net, 2025	**40.89**	**10.72**	**21.04**

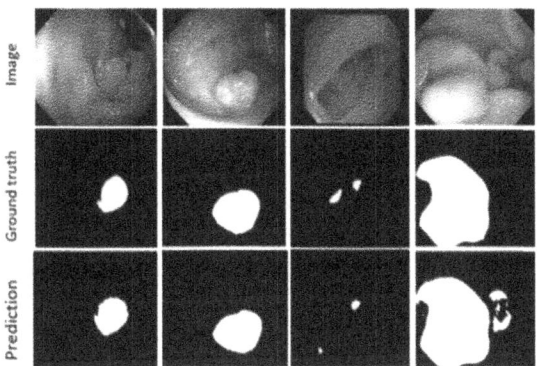

Fig. 3. Sample predicted masks

approximately 14× fewer than DUCK-Net [9] and 12× fewer than FCB-SwinV2 Transformer [10]. Furthermore, DRASU-Net requires only 21.04G FLOPs, which is 17× lower than DUCK-Net [9] and 11× lower than FCB-SwinV2 Transformer [10], demonstrating its computational efficiency. Even compared to more compact architectures like DoubleU-Net [17] and RapuNet [12], DRASU-Net achieves a ∼4× and ∼2× reduction in parameters, respectively, while maintaining strong segmentation performance. Sample predicted segmentation masks are presented in Fig. 3, demonstrating the efficiency of our model in accurately segmenting polyps of varying shapes and sizes. This substantial reduction in model size enhances memory efficiency and reduces computational overhead, making DRASU-Net more suitable for deployment in resource-constrained environments. Reproducing the exact performance reported in original studies is inherently challenging due to variations in dataset splits or other training parameters, as minor differences can lead to fluctuations in segmentation performance. To ensure a fair and comprehensive evaluation, we also assessed DRASU-Net using an alternative, well-established dataset split provided by PraNet[2]. The training process utilizes 1,450 images by combining samples from CVC-ClinicDB [1] and Kvasir-SEG [2] datasets. For testing, it includes 62 images from Kvasir-SEG [2] and 100 images from CVC-ClinicDB [1] datasets.

---

[2] https://github.com/DengPingFan/PraNet.

Our Result: DRASU-Net demonstrated high segmentation performance, achieving a *mDice* of 0.9520, *mIoU* of 0.9084, and *mHD* of 7.24 on the CVC-ClinicDB [1], and a *mDice* of 0.8974, *mIoU* of 0.8139, and *mHD* of 10.44 on the Kvasir-SED [2] dataset. These results highlight DRASU-Net's effectiveness in delivering precise and reliable polyp segmentation across diverse datasets.

The model successfully delineates polyp structures even in challenging cases, as indicated in Table 3. Our model achieves superior performance compared to six existing models, surpassing the top-performing model, MSFFNet, in the CVC-ClinicDB [1] dataset benchmark by a margin of 0.0030. Additionally, it demonstrates competitive results on the Kvasir-SEG [2] dataset while maintaining the lowest parameter count of only 10.72 million, highlighting its efficiency and effectiveness.

For generalization evaluation, we use unseen data comprising 380 images from CVC-ColonDB [14] and 196 images from ETIS-LaribPolypDB [13] datasets.

Generalization: DRASU-Net is trained on a combined dataset of CVC-ClinicDB [1] and Kvasir-SEG [2], following a similar approach to PraNet [3], which also utilizes a merged dataset for training and evaluates on unseen datasets. In contrast, DUCK-Net [9] follows a different split strategy. To ensure a fair comparison, we adapted DUCK-Net's approach by integrating the same combined dataset and assessed our model using PraNet's training methodology, Evaluating entirely on unseen datasets, such as CVC-ColonDB [14] and ETIS-LaribPolypDB [13], is crucial for assessing the true generalization ability of the model. Unlike random data splits, which can introduce bias due to overlapping feature distributions between training and test sets, testing on completely

Table 3. Performance comparison of the DRASU-Net with existing methods following the dataset partitioning of PraNet [3] split

Method	Parameters (M)	FLOPs(G)	CVC-ClinicDB [1]		Kvasir-SEG [2]	
			mDice	mIoU	mDice	mIoU
MSFFNet, 2024 [18]	64.48	15.56	0.9490	0.9040	**0.9310**	0.8840
UMF-Net, 2025 [19]	–	–	0.9150	0.8910	0.9090	0.8570
BMANet, 2025 [20]	30.59	18.23	0.9420	0.8960	0.9250	0.8790
SAFE-Net, 2025 [21]	28.48	13.70	0.9370	0.8890	0.9170	0.8650
CPSNET, 2025 [22]	–	–	0.9460	0.9030	0.9300	**0.8870**
FMCA-Net, 2025 [23]	28.601	14.36	0.9440	0.8980	0.9190	0.8660
DRASU-Net, 2025	**10.72**	**21.04**	**0.9520**	**0.9084**	0.8974	0.8139

Table 4. Performance evaluation on unseen ETIS-LaribPolypDB [13] and CVC-ColonDB [14] datasets using DRASU-Net

Dataset used for Training	ETIS-LaribPolypDB [13]			CVC-ColonDB [14]		
	mDice	mIoU	mHD	mDice	mIoU	mHD
DRASU-Net on PraNet training data [3]	0.8884	0.7993	8.39	0.7560	0.6077	8.97
DRASU-Net on DUCK-Net training data [9]	0.8835	0.7914	9.21	0.7433	0.5915	10.53

independent datasets ensures that the model does not merely memorizing dataset-specific features but learns robust representations applicable to real-world scenarios. CVC-ColonDB [14] and ETIS-LaribPolypDB [13] datasets present considerable variations in polyp size, complex backgrounds, and high-resolution images, making them ideal benchmarks for assessing the model's adaptability. It is observed from Table 4. that DRASU-Net when trained on the DUCK-Net [9] combination achieves an mDice score of 0.7560 and an mIoU of 0.6077 on CVC-ColonDB [14], demonstrating its robustness in handling complex polyp structures. Likewise, on ETIS-LaribPolypDB [13], known for its high-resolution images and diverse polyp characteristics, the model attains an mDice of 0.8884 and an mIoU of 0.7993. Additionally, when evaluated following PraNet's train split, DRASU-Net achieves 0.8884 mDice and 0.7993 on ETIS-LaribPolypDB [13], and 0.7560 mDice and 0.6077 on CVC-ColonDB [14], respectively. Despite having only 10.72 million parameters, DRASU-Net maintains strong segmentation performance, highlighting its efficiency and effectiveness in generalization for polyp segmentation tasks.

Ablation Study: The ablation study on CVC-ClinicDB [1] dataset in Table 5 shows that removing the RAS module and relying solely on standard convolutions results in a significant performance drop, yielding an mDice score of 0.9454 and an mIoU score of 0.8965. When integrating the RAS module with MobileNetV2 alone, the model achieves an improved mDice of 0.9197 and mIoU of 0.8514, while combining it with EfficientNetB4 further enhances performance to 0.9465 (mDice) and 0.8985 (mIoU). Notably, DRASU-Net, which integrates both EfficientNet and MobileNet with the RAS module, achieves the highest segmentation accuracy, with a mDice of 0.9540, a mIoU of 0.9525 and 8.11 in mHD. A similar trend is observed in the Kvasir-SEG dataset [2], where the integration of both CNN models and the RAS module in DRASU-Net yields the best performance, achieving the highest mIoU of 0.9525, the highest mDice of 0.9094, and the lowest mHD of 10.19. These results underscore the powerful synergy between EfficientNet, MobileNet, and the RAS module.

Table 5. Results of the ablation study performed on the CVC-ClinicDB [1] and Kvasir Seg [2] datasets using the DUCK-Net [9] split

Method	CVC-ClinicDB [1]			Kvasir-Seg [2]		
	mDice	mIoU	mHD	mDice	mIoU	mHD
Only Convolution (No RAS module)	0.9383	0.8837	8.02	0.9512	0.9069	12.02
Only MobileNet V2 + RAS module	0.9197	0.8514	15.23	0.9267	0.8667	18.19
Only EfficientNetB4 + RAS module	0.9465	0.8985	8.30	0.9432	0.8926	13.61
DRASU-Net	**0.9540**	**0.9052**	**8.11**	**0.9525**	**0.9094**	**10.19**

8   Conclusion and Future Work

We introduced DRASU-Net, a novel polyp segmentation model, which integrates EfficientNetB4, MobileNetV2 and the RAS module for multi-scale feature learning and context-aware refinement. Our model achieves state-of-the-art performance on the CVC-ClinicDB dataset by using only 10.72 million parameters, delivers comparable results on Kvasir-SEG, and demonstrates strong generalization on CVC-ColonDB and ETIS-LaribPolypDB datasets, ensuring high-resolution segmentation with minimal computational cost. The results demonstrate the effectiveness of DRASU-Net in preserving spatial details, enhancing feature recalibration, and achieving accurate segmentation with minimal computational overhead. One limitation remains in sensitivity to small-scale features; despite hierarchical feature fusion, extremely small polyps or subtle texture variations may still pose challenges, requiring further refinement.

For future work, we plan to extend DRASU-Net to both medical and non-medical image segmentation tasks, evaluating its generalizability across diverse datasets and applications. Further optimizations will focus on memory efficiency and real-time deployment on edge devices, ensuring it real-life usage in resource-constrained environments.

Acknowledgement. The authors are grateful for the resource and infrastructural support provided by the Centre for Microprocessor Applications for Training, Education and Research (CMATER) Laboratory of the Computer Science and Engineering Department, Jadavpur University, Kolkata, India.

References

1. Bernal, J., Sánchez, F.J., Fernández-Esparrach, G., Gil, D., de Miguel, C.R., Vilariño, F.: Wm-dova maps for accurate polyp highlighting in colonoscopy: validation vs. saliency maps from physicians. Comput. Med. Imaging Graph. **43** (2015)
2. Jha, D., et al.: Kvasir-seg: a segmented polyp dataset, November 2019
3. Fan, D.-P., et al.: Pranet: Parallel reverse attention network for polyp segmentation. In: International Conference on Medical Image Computing and Computer-Assisted Intervention. Springer, pp. 263–273, 2020
4. Ronneberger, O., Fischer, P., Brox, T.: U-net: convolutional networks for biomedical image segmentation, 2015. https://arxiv.org/abs/1505.04597
5. Kim, N.-H., et al.: Miss rate of colorectal neoplastic polyps and risk factors for missed polyps in consecutive colonoscopies. Intest. Res. **15**, 411 (2017)
6. Lee, J., et al.: Risk factors of missed colorectal lesions after colonoscopy. Medicine **96**, 07 (2017)
7. Jha, D., et al.: Resunet++: an advanced architecture for medical image segmentation. In: 2019 IEEE International Symposium on Multimedia (ISM), pp. 225–2255, 2019
8. Dong, B., Wang, W., Fan, D.-P., Li, J., Fu, H., Shao, L.: Polyp-pvt: polyp segmentation with pyramid vision transformers. CAAI Artif. Intell. Res. **2**, 9150015 (2023)

9. Dumitru, R.-G., Peteleaza, D.: Using duck-net for polyp image segmentation. Sci. Rep. **13**, 06 (2023)
10. Fitzgerald, K., Bernal, J., Histace, A., Matuszewski, B.J.: Polyp segmentation with the fcb-swinv2 transformer. IEEE Access **12**, 38 927–38 943 (2024)
11. Tang, F., et al.: Duat: dual-aggregation transformer network for medical image segmentation, 2023
12. Lee, H., Yoo, J.: Metaformer and cnn hybrid model for polyp image segmentation. IEEE Access **12**, 133 694–133 702 (2024)
13. Bernal, J., et al.: Comparative validation of polyp detection methods in video colonoscopy: results from the MICCAI 2015 endoscopic vision challenge. IEEE Trans. Med. Imaging (2017)
14. Vázquez, D., et al.: A benchmark for endoluminal scene segmentation of colonoscopy images. J. Healthc. Eng. **2017**, 07 (2017)
15. Loshchilov, I., Hutter, F.: Sgdr: stochastic gradient descent with warm restarts, 2017. https://arxiv.org/abs/1608.03983
16. Badrinarayanan, V., Kendall, A., Cipolla, R.: Segnet: a deep convolutional encoder-decoder architecture for image segmentation. IEEE Trans. Pattern Anal. Mach. Intell. **PP** (2015)
17. Jha, D., Riegler, M.A., Johansen, D., Halvorsen, P., Johansen, H.D.: Doubleu-net: a deep convolutional neural network for medical image segmentation. In: 2020 IEEE 33rd International Symposium on Computer-Based Medical Systems (CBMS), pp. 558–564, 2020
18. Zhang, Y., Zhang, T., Wu, C., Tao, R.: Multi-scale spatiotemporal feature fusion network for video saliency prediction. IEEE Trans. Multimed. **26**, 4183–4193 (2024)
19. Wan, Y., Zhou, D., Wang, C.: UMF-Net: a UNet-based multi-branch feature fusion network for colon polyp segmentation. Biomed. Signal Process. Control **99**, 106851 (2025)
20. Wu, Z., Chen, H., Xiong, X., Wu, S., Li, H., Zhou, X.: Bmanet: boundary-guided multi-level attention network for polyp segmentation in colonoscopy images. Biomed. Signal Process. Control **105**, 107524 (2025)
21. Yu, J., Qi, L.: Safe-net: shape-aware and feature enhancement network for polyp segmentation. Biomed. Signal Process. Control **99**, 106906 (2025)
22. Cai, J., Liu, X., Yang, H., Ding, Y., Zhong, T., Qin, Z.: CPSNet: comprehensive enhancement representation for polyp segmentation task. In: ICASSP 2025
23. Li, W., Nie, X., Li, F., Huang, Z., Zeng, G.: FMCA-Net: a feature secondary multiplexing and dilated convolutional attention polyp segmentation network based on pyramid vision transformer. Expert Syst. Appl. **260**, 125419 (2025)

PolypDINO: Adapting DINOv2 for Domain Generalized Polyp Segmentation

Mansoor Ali[1] , Raneem Toman[2] , Gilberto Ochoa-Ruiz[1] ,
and Sharib Ali[2(✉)]

[1] School of Engineering and Sciences, Tecnologico de Monterrey,
64700 Monterrey, Nuevo Leon, Mexico
{mansoor.ali,gilberto.ochoa}@tec.mx
[2] School of Computer Science, University of Leeds, Leeds LS2 9JT, UK
{scrmat,S.S.Ali}@leeds.ac.uk

Abstract. Despite the effectiveness of colonoscopy as a screening method for lesion detection, there is still a high polyp missing rate due to operator dependence as well as complex polyp morphology variations. Deep learning (DL)-based solutions have demonstrated their potential in assisting clinicians to improve this issue through the use of computer vision-based CAD tools. One of the major bottlenecks in applying these methods in real-world scenarios is their lack of generalizability under domain shifts due to the failure to capture the most salient features from the source training domain. In this work, we propose PolypDINO to exploit the learned parameters of the pre-trained visual foundation model (DINOv2) and adapt with Low-Rank adaption (LoRA) for domain generalized polyp segmentation. Precisely, we fine-tune DINOv2 with LoRA on the Kvasir-SEG dataset and perform generalizability tests on the out-of-distribution (OOD) PolypGen dataset containing data comprising six independent centers. Quantitative results show a consistent improvement in all test data, for instance, outperforming baseline state-of-the-art (SOTA) method by nearly 4% and 3% in terms of mean Intersection-over-Union and mean Dice scores, respectively. Code is available at https://github.com/Mansoor-at/PolypDINO.

Keywords: Visual foundational models · DINOv2 · Convolutional neural networks · PolypGen · Colorectal cancer

1 Introduction

Colorectal cancer (CRC) is the third leading cause of cancer-related mortality, with 9.4% deaths reported worldwide [25]. Accurate polyp location and boundary details are crucial for efficient polyp removal. Colonoscopy is the gold standard technique for reducing the risk of occurrence and related mortality. Despite colonoscopy being the widely used technique for detecting CRC, it remains highly operator dependent due to constant organ deformations, ambiguity in prioritization, complex organ topology, and, in most cases lack of identifiable contrast

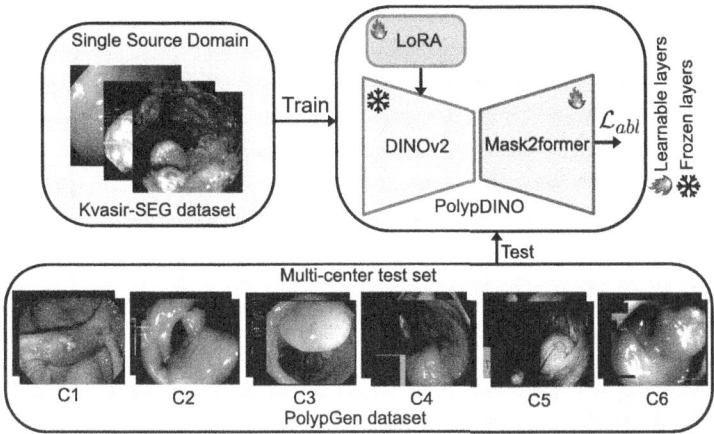

Fig. 1. General overview of our proposed approach (PolypDINO) with active boundary loss ($\mathcal{L}_{abl}$). Our PolypDINO is trained on Kvasir-SEG [11] and individually tested on the six-center PolypGen dataset [2] to assess the generalizability performance.

between polyp boundaries and the surrounding mucosa. Flat or sessile polyps are among the most commonly missed types and contribute significantly to the missed adenoma detection rate [1]. A case was reported where a 1 cm polyp was missed by the conventional system, and was later detected by a physician [27]. Moreover, post-colonoscopy recurrence of polyps, especially adenomatous polyps, can occur, and in certain cases, the recurrence risk can be moderate to high (over 30%) [14]. These challenges and risks of recurrence can be reduced by developing computer-assisted methods to aid gastroenterologists in accurately detecting and delineating polyps efficiently.

Recent advances in deep learning have enabled the development of state-of-the-art (SOTA) polyp segmentation methods including PraNet [7], HardM-SEG [10], PraDSHNet [29], TransNetR [12], showing improved performance over previous approaches. However, these methods still lack generalizability and robustness capabilities which can be due to methodological failures (models struggling to capture sufficient diverse patterns from the training data) or the data-related factors (high variability in polyp size, shape, color, texture, and blurry polyp boundaries etc.)

Prior works in domain generalized polyp segmentation has used illumination-enhancement [32], style diversification [22] or domain-invariant learning [26] with classical backbones (such as ResNet or EfficientNet), or vision transformers [17]. The main drawback of these methods is either they train on mix of datasets [17], or fail to preserve fine polyp boundaries [22], or suffer from higher false positives [17] or tested in very limited dataset settings [26]. In contrast, in recent years, large-scale Vision Foundation Models (VFMs) like DINOv2 [19], EVA-02 [8], SAM [31] have further pushed the boundaries in terms of performance. Few SAM-based approaches [16,24] have been reported to study their general-

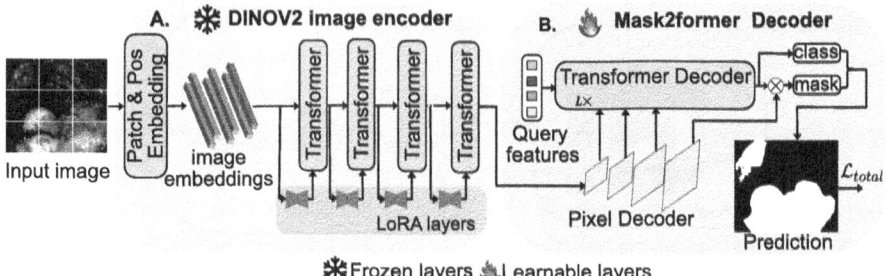

Fig. 2. Overview of PolypDINO: A. The input image in the DINOv2 encoder is transformed into tokens by extracting scaled-down patches followed by a linear projection. To enhance the embedding ability, both a patch-independent class token and a positional embedding are incorporated (in red). We freeze the image encoder and add trainable LoRA layers to fine-tune. **B.** The trainable Mask2former segmentation head is used for final mask prediction. (Color figure online)

izability on polyp segmentation, however we are of the opinion that VFMs have largely been an underexplored topic in endoscopic domain. Given the advanced generalization capabilities of VFMs in unseen domains, particularly due to their pretraining on large-scale diverse datasets, two critical questions arise: *How do VFMs perform in the context of endoscopic datasets? And how to harness VFMs for domain generalized polyp segmentation (DGPS)?*. In this work, we attempt to answer these questions.

Training VFMs from scratch require large availability of annotated data and enormous computational resources. While few large polyp datasets exist, we aim to approach the generalizability problem from the real-world clinical settings where large, diverse datasets are unavailable. We leverage parameter-efficient fine-tuning with LoRA layers to alleviate computational burden. Specifically, we fine-tune DINOv2 [19] with LoRA layers for the generalized polyp segmentation (Fig. 1). We select DINOv2 as the backbone for our work due to its strong self-supervised visual representations and versatility across a wide range of downstream vision tasks. LoRA introduces a parallel bypass to foundation models, using low-rank decomposition (dimensionality reduction followed by projection) to approximate intrinsic model rank. To address the lack of identifiable contrast between the polyp and the anatomy boundary, we also incorporate active boundary loss (ABL) [28], which unlike cross-entropy, supervises the relationship between the prediction and ground truth boundary details. PolypDINO shows a considerable improvement in polyp segmentation on the multi-center PolypGen dataset [2] over the previous methods.

The rest of this paper is organized as follows. In Sect. 2, we discuss the recent methods for polyp segmentation, Sect. 3 presents the discussion about the proposed method, experimental setup and dataset details in Sect. 4, quantitative and qualitative results are reported in Sect. 5, ablation studies to see the impact of different variables is presented in Sect. 6 and finally the conclusion is given in Sect. 7.

2   Related Works

Parameter Efficient Fine-Tuning (PEFT). Parameter Efficient Fine-Tuning (PEFT) has emerged as a critical paradigm for adapting large pretrained models while substantially reducing computational and storage requirements. Unlike conventional fine-tuning approaches that update all model parameters, PEFT methods strategically modify only a small subset of weights, keeping the majority of the pre-trained backbone frozen. This family of techniques encompasses several distinct approaches: adapter-based methods insert compact trainable modules between transformer layers [9]; selective parameter techniques identify and update only the most critical weights [30]; and Low-Rank Adaptation (LoRA) [9] employs low-rank matrix decomposition to efficiently approximate weight updates.

While initially developed for natural language processing, PEFT techniques have demonstrated significant success when adapted to computer vision tasks. Recent work has shown that vision transformers (ViTs) can be effectively adapted using PEFT approaches with adapter-based methods [31], achieving performance comparable to full fine-tuning while using <5% of trainable parameters.

Polyp Segmentation Models. Polyp segmentation has been extensively investigated in the past literature. Traditional visual methods for polyp localization have used polyp shape, color and texture [18]. Recently, data-driven approaches have been increasingly utilized. To that end, various SOTA segmentation-based methods such as FCN [3], PraNet [7], SAN SAW [21], HardMSEG [10] have been studied for polyp segmentation. Other approaches have addressed the problem of polyp diversity in terms of shapes, sizes and textures [17]. Although these methods have reported encouraging outcomes in polyp localization, they are still limited in terms of robustness and generalizability, resulting in substantial performance degradation in real-world scenarios. This problem was addressed by using transformer based approach in [12], showing considerable improvement in polyp segmentation on multi-center data; the method still struggled to segment polyp boundaries.

Visual Foundation Models. Recently, visual foundation models are being increasingly employed in various downstream tasks in both natural and medical image domains. While the adaptations of VFMs to medical imaging have prioritized tasks like tumor detection or organ segmentation [5], these approaches often rely on supervised pretraining optimized for high-level semantic understanding. Such frameworks may struggle with the fine-grained localization and boundary precision required for polyp segmentation, where subtle morphological features (e.g., flat or sessile polyps) demand robust pixel-wise feature discrimination. Therefore, we have selected DINOv2 [19] as the backbone for our study in this paper.

In this work, we explore the PEFT of DINOv2 with LoRA layers to fully benefit from the pretrained extensive parameters of the encoder with low additional cost for the generalized polyp segmentation. We also effectively improve the polyp boundary segmentation using the active boundary loss constraint.

3 Method

3.1 General Overview

This work aims to learn a domain-agnostic model for polyps segmentation that generalizes well from a single source domain to an arbitrary target domain. We train an encoder-decoder architecture (Fig. 2), where DINOv2 serves as an image encoder and Mask2former is a segmentation decoder. We adapt DINOv2 training with LoRA to alleviate the computation cost without compromising on the performance.

3.2 DINOv2

In natural language processing, learning pretrained representations without particular task considerations has proven very effective [23]. In computer vision, a similar effort yielded a model named DINOv2 [19] which can be applied to several image processing tasks. The method consisted of building a large curated dataset with the ability to learn robust vision features in an unsupervised manner. A ViT model with 1B parameters was trained without supervision and then distilled into various smaller encoders that surpassed existing benchmarks on image and pixel levels.

3.3 LoRA Layers

LoRA allows for training very large pre-trained models but using fewer parameters. This is achieved through the introduction of trainable rank decomposition matrices into each frozen layer of the backbone architecture, thus saving considerable memory and reducing the computational cost. Specifically, for a frozen pre-trained weight matrix $W_0 \in \mathbb{R}^{d \times k}$, LoRA adds a bypass with two linear layers $A \in \mathbb{R}^{r \times k}$ and $B \in \mathbb{R}^{d \times r}$ to restrict the weight update by $W_0 + \Delta W = W_0 + BA$, with rank $r \ll (d, k)$, with only A and B as trainable parameters. The updated forward with x as an encoded token embedding can be written as:

$$h = W_0 x + \Delta W x = W_0 x + BAx \qquad (1)$$

3.4 Network Architecture of PolypDINO

As illustrated in Fig. 2, our proposed network for polyp segmentation is based on an encoder-decoder arrangement, where DINOv2 serves as an image encoder and Mask2former as the segmentation head. Given an endoscopic image $\mathcal{X} \in \mathbb{R}^{C \times H \times W}$, where $H \times W$ is the spatial size and C is the channels, the final task is to predict a segmentation mask $\hat{\mathcal{M}} \in H \times W$ as close to ground truth mask as possible.

Image Encoder. In this work, we used a pre-trained ViT-Base model from DINOv2 as our backbone image encoder, with 12 transformer blocks and a feature dimension of 784. DINOv2 splits the input image into non-overlapping patches, followed by a flattening operation with a linear projection layer. Positional embedding is used to preserve spatial structure, while learnable class tokens are prepended to the sequence of patch embeddings, allowing the model to aggregate global information. The image embeddings are then passed through multiple Transformer blocks to produce updated token representations. All DINOv2 parameters are frozen during training, whereas additional LoRA layers are attached to each Transformer block to capture the learnable information. We adopted the LoRA scheme from [31], where the low-rank approximation is applied for q and v projection layers for improved performance. The LoRA layers first compress the Transformer features into a low-rank space; then, these features are re-projected to frozen transformer blocks (after re-sampling) to match the respective Transformer block output feature dimensions. Each LoRA layer works independently.

Segmentation Decoder: We use Mask2former as the decoder segmentation head. The image embeddings from the encoder are passed to the pixel decoder, from which the first three feature maps are injected into the transformer decoder to generate the mask and class corresponding to each query. The mask and final feature maps from the pixel decoder are multiplied to obtain the foreground feature maps, followed by multiplication with the class to obtain the final segmentation output.

Active Boundary Loss: Polyp boundaries in endoscopic images are often faint, irregular, or texture-less, making them poorly represented in DINOv2's feature space. Therefore, without explicit boundary supervision, segmentation models using DINOv2 tend to produce misaligned or poorly segmented polyp boundaries. To this end, we propose to incorporate a specific boundary loss constraint named active boundary loss to penalize the discrepancies between predicted and ground truth polyp boundaries.

The ABL ($\mathcal{L}_{abl}$) [28] aims to improve alignment between ground truth and predicted boundaries gradually during training. It works by taking a pixel on a prediction boundary and then determining the direction vector towards the closest pixel on the ground truth boundary:

$$\mathcal{L}_{abl} = \frac{1}{N_p} \sum_{i}^{N_p} w(M_i)\mathcal{L}_{ce}(D_i^p, D_i^g) \tag{2}$$

where w is the weight function, M is the ground truth boundary distance transform, D_i^p and D_i^g are the prediction and ground truth boundary direction vectors. The overall pipeline of ABL computation is illustrated in Fig. 3.

Overall Cost Function

PolypDINO uses a combination of three losses: cross entropy ($\mathcal{L}_{ce}$), dice loss ($\mathcal{L}_{dice}$) and active boundary loss ($\mathcal{L}_{abl}$):

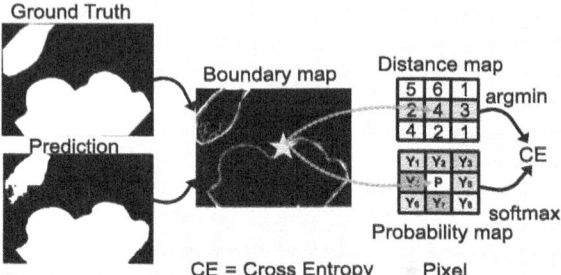

Fig. 3. The overall flow of the ABL computation shown on an example mask from Kvasir-SEG [11] data. The loss is computed using the distance transform of ground truth boundaries. The overlayed red and white lines indicate the prediction and ground truth boundaries, respectively. The probability map values indicate the closest distance to a ground truth boundary. (Color figure online)

$$\mathcal{L}_{total} = \mathcal{L}_{ce} + \mathcal{L}_{dice} + \mathcal{L}_{abl} \tag{3}$$

where $\mathcal{L}_{ce}$ focuses on per-pixel classification, whereas the goal of $\mathcal{L}_{dice}$ is to improve the segmentation of small and large polyps. Finally, $\mathcal{L}_{abl}$ enforces better boundary details in the segmentation mask.

4   Experimental Setup

4.1   Datasets

Kvasir-SEG. We use Kvasir-SEG [11] for training PolypDINO. Kvasir-SEG is an open-access dataset of gastrointestinal polyp images and their corresponding manually annotated segmentation masks. The dataset consists of 1000 images. We follow the standard splits of 80%, 10%, 10% for training, validation and testing.

PolypGen. PolypGen [2] is one of the comprehensive public multi-center polyp datasets. It contains 1537 still polyp images. It incorporates data from six different centers and varied populations from Asia and Europe, varied endoscopic systems and surveillance experts from Europe and Africa. We use the entire center-wise images of PolypGen for model evaluations.

4.2   Implementation Details

We use the MMSegmentation codebase for PolypDINO implementation. The AdamW optimizer is employed for training with a learning rate (lr) of 1e-5 for both the backbone and the decoder on a V100-PCIE-16 GB GPU. We use a batch size of 4 and crop images to 512 × 512 resolution. We only use some standard data augmentations following Mask2former. We used early stopping criteria for the best model selection. LoRA rank is set at 8 for performance optimization and efficiency. We run SOTA methods with the same batch size and lr with early stopping for the best model selection.

Table 1. Evaluation results in terms of mean Intersection over Union (mIoU), mean Dice (mDSC), and F_2 scores for the SOTA and PolypDINO trained on Kvasir-SEG [11] and tested on PolypGen data [2]. The best scores are highlighted in bold.

Train: Kvasir-SEG		Test: PolypGen (C1)			Test: PolypGen (C2)		
Backbone	Methods	mIoU	mDSC	F_2	mIoU	mDSC	F_2
CNN	DeepLabv3+ [4]	74.75	85.55	84.45	50.44	67.06	72.59
	IBN-Net [20]	74.64	85.48	84.73	63.12	77.39	80.47
	RobustNet [6]	75.99	86.36	86.50	64.56	78.46	**83.12**
	SAN-SAW [21]	73.00	84.39	83.98	57.89	73.33	78.00
	TransNetR [12]	65.38	72.04	72.69	66.08	72.32	73.66
	SNR [13]	78.26	87.80	87.23	68.77	81.50	81.00
	MLMI'24 [26]	79.54	88.61	87.59	**69.73**	**82.17**	81.00
VFM	SAMed [31]	78.28	87.82	87.42	64.50	78.42	76.00
	EVA-02 [8]	77.47	87.31	85.77	56.22	71.98	79.33
	MaskDINO [15]	67.08	80.31	73.74	37.50	54.55	44.71
	PolypDINO (Ours)	79.50	88.58	91.07	66.50	79.88	76.63
	PolypDINO (w/ ABL)	**83.48**	**91.00**	**91.90**	65.59	79.22	**81.68**
Train: Kvasir-SEG		**Test: PolypGen (C3)**			**Test: PolypGen (C4)**		
CNN	DeepLabv3+ [4]	78.50	87.95	87.34	30.84	47.14	37.32
	IBN-Net [20]	75.92	86.31	86.13	32.48	49.04	39.50
	RobustNet [6]	77.08	87.06	87.86	38.45	55.54	48.05
	SAN-SAW [21]	74.26	85.23	85.30	41.07	58.23	66.30
	TransNetR [12]	72.17	78.74	78.63	46.01	50.42	50.96
	SNR [13]	79.16	88.37	89.43	36.44	53.42	45.34
	MLMI'24 [26]	80.10	88.95	89.28	41.48	58.64	50.78
VFM	SAMed [31]	11.11	20.00	20.15	40.06	57.21	49.89
	EVA-02 [8]	78.15	87.74	86.19	46.60	63.58	71.46
	MaskDINO [15]	11.17	20.08	18.17	22.11	36.20	26.83
	PolypDINO (Ours)	78.91	88.21	89.10	45.19	62.25	65.13
	PolypDINO (w/ ABL)	**82.39**	**90.34**	**92.65**	**48.76**	**65.56**	**71.90**
Train: Kvasir-SEG		**Test: PolypGen (C5)**			**Test: PolypGen (C6)**		
CNN	DeepLabv3+ [4]	60.93	75.72	73.42	50.55	90.98	58.03
	IBN-Net [20]	56.78	72.44	68.20	58.58	73.88	67.39
	RobustNet [6]	58.73	74.00	72.54	65.63	79.25	78.03
	SAN-SAW [21]	48.03	64.90	68.21	65.46	78.28	80.26
	TransNetR [12]	35.97	42.14	42.32	63.35	69.17	68.03
	SNR [13]	64.50	78.42	80.36	67.00	80.24	79.94
	MLMI'24 [26]	60.73	75.57	74.01	67.11	80.32	79.19
VFM	SAMed [31]	48.40	65.23	61.23	65.49	79.15	82.34
	EVA-02 [8]	62.94	77.26	79.43	56.04	71.83	78.41
	MaskDINO [15]	38.06	55.12	46.98	53.35	69.61	60.00
	PolypDINO (Ours)	66.52	79.89	**84.88**	66.14	79.62	79.08
	PolypDINO (w/ ABL)	**69.55**	**82.04**	82.31	**69.78**	**82.20**	**88.79**

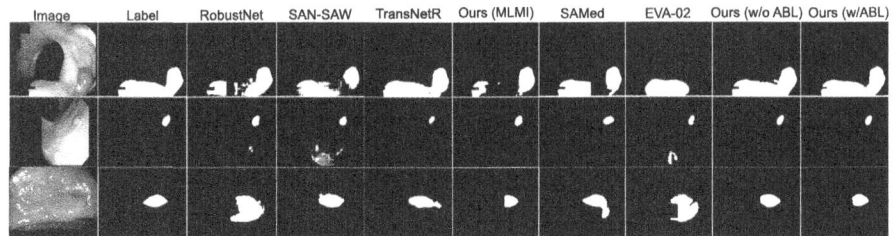

Fig. 4. Qualitative results for models trained on Kvasir-SEG and tested on PolypGen (C6)- top 2 rows - and (C1)- third row.

5   Results

We conduct a comprehensive generalizability assessment of PolypDINO with CNN and VFM-based SOTA as detailed in Table 1. Specifically, we train all the models on Kvasir-SEG [11] data and test on the OOD PolypGen multi-center dataset [2]. Results with widely used standard metrics are reported, including mIoU, mDSC, and F_2 scores. We compare our approach with ResNet50-backbone (CNN) SOTA such as DeepLabv3+ [4], IBN-Net [20], RobustNet [6], SAN-SAW [21], SNR [13], MLMI'24 [26], a transformer based approach TransNetR [12], and VFM backbones, SAMed [31], EVA-02 [8] and MaskDINO [15].

To compare PolypDINO and CNN backbone methods, MLMI'24 [26] and SNR [13] show a robust performance, especially on C2 datasets, getting 4% and 3% higher IoU score. They also work considerably well on other datasets in comparison to other CNN-backbone frameworks. PolypDINO, on the other hand, demonstrates robust generalizability across the PolypGen centers, outperforming all methods. For example, PolypDINO outperforms the best CNN performer MLMI by 9%, and 7% on C1 in terms of mIoU and mDSC.

On VFM backbone side, SAMed collapses entirely on C3 (mDSC: 20.00), while MaskDINO does poorly on most evaluation metrics, highlighting the challenges of adapting generic VFMs to endoscopic imaging. ABL consistently improves mIoU and mDSC scores, which are sensitive to segmentation performance. For example, in C1, PolypDINO with ABL achieves a 4% higher mIoU (83.48 vs. 79.50) and 3% higher mDSC (91.90 vs. 88.58) over the baseline PolypDINO.

The qualitative results (Fig. 4) show that PolypDINO performs well in segmenting small, diminutive and regular polyps. Among the SOTA methods reported, PolypDINO presents the following advantages on the qualitative results.

1. Boundaries of the masks are clear and the prediction is much closer to the ground truth (row 1).
2. There are no cavities inside the prediction masks. (row 1).
3. Improved generalizability and smooth predictions even in the cases of uneven lighting conditions (row 2).
4. Less affected by the challenging texture-less surfaces (row 3).

Table 2. Table showing mean Intersection over Union (mIoU), mean Dice (mDSC), Precision, Recall, and F_2 scores for the various ablation experiments on segmentation decoders. Results are reported on Kvasir-SEG [11] validation set. The best scores are highlighted in bold.

Backbone	Decoder	mIoU	mDSC	Recall	Precision	F_2
DINOv2	PSP	78.11	87.71	84.09	91.66	85.50
DINOv2	Deeplabv3+	82.72	90.54	91.42	89.69	91.06
DINOv2	FCN	79.22	88.12	86.72	92.34	86.94
DINOv2	Mask2former	**85.43**	**91.30**	**94.81**	**93.25**	**94.66**

Table 3. Table showing ablation study on the rank size of the LoRA layer. The best scores are highlighted in bold.

Rank Size	mIoU	mDSC	Recall	Precision	F_2
1	84.93	90.75	93.68	92.58	93.46
4	85.37	91.22	94.59	**93.37**	94.52
8	**85.43**	**91.30**	**94.81**	93.25	**94.66**
16	85.25	91.04	94.62	93.03	94.21

6   Ablation Study

We conduct an extensive ablation study on various settings to study the impact of each variable on model performance. We present ablations on using different segmentation heads such as Mask2former, Deeplabv3+, PSP and Fully convolutional neural network (FCN). The results of all the ablations are reported on the Kvasir-SEG validation set.

Effect of Decode Heads. We evaluate the impact of different segmentation decoders using a fixed DINOv2 backbone on the Kvasir-SEG validation set. As shown in Table 2, Mask2Former achieves the best performance across all metrics (mIoU: 85.43, mDSC: 91.30, Recall: 94.81, Precision: 93.25, F_2: 94.66), surpassing other decoders by a significant margin. The DeepLabv3+ decoder stood second, with competitive scores (mIoU: 82.72, mDSC: 90.54), while PSP and FCN exhibit lower but still produce robust results. Notably, Mask2Former's superior recall (94.81) and F_2 score (94.66) suggest its effectiveness in capturing fine-grained polyp structures, critical for medical segmentation. The results indicate strong performance of query-based transformers (Mask2Former) over traditional convolutional decoders (PSP, FCN) and even hybrid architectures (DeepLabv3+) in this task.

Effect of Rank Size on LoRA Layer. Table 3 shows a set of comparative experiments indicating the effect of rank size on the LoRA layer. We can observe that the increase in rank size increases the evaluation metric up to a certain range, however, the performance starts to drop as the rank size goes higher than

Table 4. Table showing ablation study on the size of pre-trained DINOv2 models. The best scores are highlighted in bold.

Model type	Model size	mIoU	mDSC	Recall	Precision	F_2
ViT-Small	~ 21M	84.92	90.87	94.03	93.08	94.27
ViT-Base	~ 86M	85.24	90.56	94.31	93.11	94.42
ViT-Large	~ 300M	85.43	91.30	94.81	93.25	94.66
ViT-Giant	~ 1100M	**85.64**	**91.47**	**94.90**	**93.87**	**94.88**

a certain range. This implies that although LoRA is intended to use low-rank decomposition for approximation, it still needs a specific number of trainable parameters to adapt effectively to downstream tasks. However, an excessive number of trainable parameters can distort the original weights, leading to a decline in performance. The best performance is obtained when the rank size is set to 8.

Effect of the Size of the Pre-trained DINOv2. There are four variants of DINOv2 based on their size. We investigated the impact of DINOv2 model size on the overall performance of PolypDINO in Table 4. We notice that larger models perform better than their adjacent smaller ones owing to their stronger vision feature integration and generalization capabilities, enabling better adaptation to downstream tasks. However, they also demand higher memory usage and training expenses. To balance performance and efficiency, we selected ViT-Large in PolypDINO for the polyp segmentation.

Effect of the Size of the Pretrained DINOv2. To evaluate the efficiency of our proposed PolypDINO, we conduct a comprehensive ablation study comparing model complexity and inference speed against state-of-the-art segmentation frameworks. As illustrated in Table 5, conventional methods such as Deeplabv3+, IBN-Net, and RobustNet employ full parameter updates (100% trainable parameters), resulting in high computational demands, but also showing higher inference speeds (5.1âĂŞ7.7 ms inference time). While SAN-SAW reduces parameter count (25.63M), its inference latency increases significantly (39.9 ms), indicating a trade-off between compactness and speed. In contrast, parameter-efficient approaches like SAMed and EVA-02 leverage partial fine-tuning (1.05% and 0.83% trainable parameters, respectively), substantially reducing memory overhead. However, SAMed suffers from slower inference (40.5 ms) due to its large base model (632M parameters). Our PolypDINO achieves an optimal balance, matching EVA-02's low trainable ratio (0.83%) while improving inference speed (15.7 ms vs. 15.9 ms). While PolypDINO exhibits slightly higher inference latency (15.7 ms) compared to conventional methods like Deeplabv3+ (5.1 ms) or RobustNet (7.5 ms), its performance advantages justify this trade-off. Unlike these fully fine-tuned models, PolypDINO leverages a parameter-efficient design (0.83% trainable parameters), drastically reducing memory overhead and preserving the generalization capabilities of its foundational vision transformer.

Table 5. Table showing ablation study on model complexity. Inference speed is reported on image size of 512×512 on Tesla V100-PCIE-16GB GPU.

Method	Params.	Trainable Params.	Trainable ratio	Speed
Deeplabv3+	45.06M	45.06M	100%	5.1 ms
IBN-Net	45.06M	45.06M	100%	6.3 ms
RobustNet	45.06M	45.06M	100%	7.5 ms
SAN-SAW	25.63M	25.63M	100%	39.9 ms
SNR	45.11M	45.11M	100%	7.6 ms
Ours (MLMI)	45.17M	45.17M	100%	7.7 ms
SAMed	632.00M	6.68M	1.05%	40.5 ms
EVA-02	304.24M	2.53M	0.83%	15.9 ms
PolypDINO	304.20M	2.53M	0.83%	15.7 ms

7   Discussion and Conclusion

The generalizability test results in Table 1 demonstrate the effectiveness of our PolypDINO model, a vision foundation model adapted for polyp segmentation, across the multi-center PolypGen dataset. The inclusion of active boundary loss further boosts the performance especially in challenging polyp cases and improves the boundary details (top row Fig. 4).

The CNN-based methods, especially MLMI'24 [26] and SNR [13], excel on PolypGen C2; however, their performance drops on other center datasets, showing their limited generalizability performance on diverse polyp sizes and shape variability. Conversely, PolpyDINO with ABL consistently performs better than the PolypDINO without ABL and other SOTA models. Unlike CNNs (e.g., DeepLabv3+) or generic VFMs (e.g., SAMed), which struggle with cross-domain shifts, PolypDINO achieves robust performance by combining DINOv2's semantic priors with task-specific geometric constraints such as the active boundary loss. The possible cause of the slightly inferior performance of PolypDINO on the PolypGen C2 can be due to the presence of blue dye in the whole dataset which did not get normalized in PolypDINO. Our results suggest that VFMs with boundary optimization (e.g., PolypDINO + ABL) are promising for real-world colonoscopy, where generalization across hospitals and devices is essential.

Ablation studies further show the effectiveness of our method. Mask2former outperforms other segmentation decoders with 85.43 mIoU. LoRA rank 8 achieves a balance between parameter efficiency and performance. ViT Giant shows better performance but at a cost of immense computational power. With smaller trainable parameters, PolypDINO serves as the best trade-off between inference speed and performance across both CNN and VFM backbone methods.

In this work, we harnessed a visual foundation model as a feature extraction backbone to address the out-of-distribution (OOD) domain generalization problem for polyp segmentation, using a multi-center dataset. We fine-tuned DINOv2 using Low-Rank adaptation with fewer trainable parameters, along with Mask2former as the decoder head for the final mask generation. We introduced active boundary loss in the cost function to improve the prediction segmentation boundaries. Our results with and without active boundary loss with various segmentation heads on OOD settings demonstrate the effectiveness of our framework named PolypDINO, and it can be observed that a VFM as an encoder is capable of extracting robust and generalizable image features from the endoscopic scenes.

Acknowledgments. The research was supported by the French-Mexican ANUIES CONAHCYT Ecos Nord grant (322537), the WUN Research Development Fund 2024, the Crohn's & Colitis UK (M2023-5) and the Academy of Medical Sciences (SBF0010\1191). The authors would also like to acknowledge "Secretaría de Ciencia, Humanidades, Tecnología e Innovación" (SECIHTI). The work has been endorsed by Azure Sponsorship credits granted by Microsoft's AI for Good Research Lab through the AI for Health program.

References

1. Ali, S.: Where do we stand in AI for endoscopic image analysis? Deciphering gaps and future directions **5**(1), 1–13. https://doi.org/10.1038/s41746-022-00733-3
2. Ali, S., et al.: A multi-centre polyp detection and segmentation dataset for generalisability assessment. Scientific Data **10**(1), 75 (2023)
3. Brandao, P., et al.: Fully convolutional neural networks for polyp segmentation in colonoscopy. In: Medical Imaging 2017: Computer-Aided Diagnosis, vol. 10134, pp. 101–107. Spie (2017)
4. Chen, L.C., Zhu, Y., Papandreou, G., Schroff, F., Adam, H.: Encoder-decoder with atrous separable convolution for semantic image segmentation. In: Proceedings of the European Conference on Computer Vision (ECCV), pp. 801–818 (2018)
5. Cheng, J., et al.: Sam-med2d. arXiv preprint arXiv:2308.16184 (2023)
6. Choi, S., Jung, S., Yun, H., Kim, J.T., Kim, S., Choo, J.: Robustnet: improving domain generalization in urban-scene segmentation via instance selective whitening. In: Proceedings of the IEEE/CVF Conference on Computer Vision and Pattern Recognition, pp. 11580–11590 (2021)
7. Fan, D.P., et al.: Pranet: parallel reverse attention network for polyp segmentation. In: International Conference on Medical Image Computing and Computer-Assisted Intervention, pp. 263–273. Springer (2020)
8. Fang, Y., Sun, Q., Wang, X., Huang, T., Wang, X., Cao, Y.: Eva-02: a visual representation for neon genesis. Image Vis. Comput. **149**, 105171 (2024)
9. Hu, E.J., et al.: Lora: low-rank adaptation of large language models. ICLR **1**(2), 3 (2022)
10. Huang, C.H., Wu, H.Y., Lin, Y.L.: Hardnet-mseg: a simple encoder-decoder polyp segmentation neural network that achieves over 0.9 mean dice and 86 fps. arXiv preprint arXiv:2101.07172 (2021)
11. Jha, D., et al.: Kvasir-seg: a segmented polyp dataset. In: International Conference on Multimedia Modeling, pp. 451–462. Springer (2020)
12. Jha, D., Tomar, N.K., Sharma, V., Bagci, U.: Transnetr: transformer-based residual network for polyp segmentation with multi-center out-of-distribution testing. In: Medical Imaging with Deep Learning, pp. 1372–1384. PMLR (2024)

13. Jin, X., Lan, C., Zeng, W., Chen, Z.: Style normalization and restitution for domain generalization and adaptation. IEEE Trans. Multimed. **24**, 3636–3651 (2021)

14. Lee, J.K., et al.: Long-term risk of colorectal cancer and related death after adenoma removal in a large, community-based population. Gastroenterology **158**(4), 884–894 (2020)

15. Li, F., et al.: Mask dino: towards a unified transformer-based framework for object detection and segmentation. In: Proceedings of the IEEE/CVF Conference on Computer Vision and Pattern Recognition, pp. 3041–3050 (2023)

16. Li, H., Zhang, D., Yao, J., Han, L., Li, Z., Han, J.: Asps: augmented segment anything model for polyp segmentation. In: International Conference on Medical Image Computing and Computer-Assisted Intervention, pp. 118–128. Springer (2024)

17. Lin, L., Lv, G., Wang, B., Xu, C., Liu, J.: Polyp-LVT: polyp segmentation with lightweight vision transformers. Knowl.-Based Syst. **300**, 112181 (2024)

18. Liu, G., Yan, G., Kuang, S., Wang, Y.: Detection of small bowel tumor based on multi-scale curvelet analysis and fractal technology in capsule endoscopy. Comput. Biol. Med. **70**, 131–138 (2016)

19. Oquab, M., et al.: Dinov2: learning robust visual features without supervision. arXiv preprint arXiv:2304.07193 (2023)

20. Pan, X., Luo, P., Shi, J., Tang, X.: Two at once: enhancing learning and generalization capacities via ibn-net. In: Proceedings of the European Conference on Computer Vision (ECCV), pp. 464–479 (2018)

21. Peng, D., Lei, Y., Hayat, M., Guo, Y., Li, W.: Semantic-aware domain generalized segmentation. In: Proceedings of the IEEE/CVF Conference on Computer Vision and Pattern Recognition, pp. 2594–2605 (2022)

22. Poudel, S., Lee, S.W.: Polyp generalization via diversifying style at feature-level space. Appl. Sci. **14**(7), 2780 (2024)

23. Raffel, C., et al.: Exploring the limits of transfer learning with a unified text-to-text transformer. J. Mach. Learn. Res. **21**(140), 1–67 (2020)

24. Ren, X., Zhou, W., Yuan, N., Li, F., Ruan, Y., Zhou, H.: Prompt-based polyp segmentation during endoscopy. Med. Image Anal. **102**, 103510 (2025)

25. Sung, H., et al.: Global cancer statistics 2020: globocan estimates of incidence and mortality worldwide for 36 cancers in 185 countries. CA Cancer J. Clin. **71**(3), 209–249 (2021)

26. Teevno, M.A., Ochoa-Ruiz, G., Ali, S.: Tackling domain generalization for out-of-distribution endoscopic imaging. In: International Workshop on Machine Learning in Medical Imaging, pp. 43–52. Springer (2024)

27. Trilisky, I., Dachman, A.H., Wroblewski, K., Vannier, M.W., Horne, J.M.: Ct colonography with computer-aided detection: Recognizing the causes of false-positive reader results–erratum. Radiographics **35**(2), 651–651 (2015)

28. Wang, C., et al.: Active boundary loss for semantic segmentation. In: Proceedings of the AAAI Conference on Artificial Intelligence, vol. 36, pp. 2397–2405 (2022)

29. Wang, H., et al.: Dynamic spectrum-driven hierarchical learning network for polyp segmentation. Med. Image Anal. **101**, 103449 (2025)

30. Zaken, E.B., Ravfogel, S., Goldberg, Y.: Bitfit: simple parameter-efficient fine-tuning for transformer-based masked language-models. arXiv preprint arXiv:2106.10199 (2021)

31. Zhang, K., Liu, D.: Customized segment anything model for medical image segmentation. arXiv preprint arXiv:2304.13785 (2023)

32. Zhang, Z., Li, Y., Shin, B.S.: Generalizable polyp segmentation via randomized global illumination augmentation. IEEE J. Biomed. Health Inform. (2024)

Intraoperative Segmentation Through Deep Learning and Mask Post-processing in Laparoscopic Liver Surgery

James Borgars⍟, Jibran Raja⍟, Abhinav Ramakrishnan⍟,
Abdul Karim Abbas⍟, Aodhan Gallagher⍟,
Ahmad Najmi Mohamad Shahir⍟, Theodora Vraimakis⍟, and Sharib Ali(✉)⍟

School of Computer Science, University of Leeds, Leeds, UK
s.s.ali@leeds.ac.uk

Abstract. Laparoscopic liver surgery is a popular surgical approach due to its capabilities of minimising trauma, complications, and recovery times. The use of a laparoscope allows for developments in the field of machine-assisted surgery due to the availability of intraoperative imagery. Accurate landmark detection of the liver using laparoscopic footage is a dependency to many developments, such as 3D-2D registration. In this paper, we present experimental results measuring the suitability of popular segmentation models, and their compatibility with different loss functions when handling intraoperative images; we also present a pipeline in training models for this segmentation task, including a novel step of applying post-processing techniques to maximise accuracy. Our results are evaluated using precision, Dice similarity coefficient, and a symmetric distance metric. Our results show that through the use of our proposed pipeline, models retain their ability to generalise, and can lead to noticeably improved accuracy both quantitatively and qualitatively. We demonstrate the feasibility of utilising post-processing to improve predictions. Finally, possible future directions in this field following from our results are discussed. The code from this research has been made available and can be accessed here: https://github.com/ARMADILLO-VISION/SLiPPA.

Keywords: liver laparoscopy · image segmentation · deep learning · post-processing

1 Introduction

1.1 Overview

Laparoscopic liver surgery, also known as minimally-invasive liver surgery, has emerged as a popular approach due to its reduction of patient trauma, recovery times, and complications compared to other approaches [18]. To enhance surgical precision in these procedures, machine-assisted approaches have long been an area of laparoscopy research. An example of this is 3D-2D registration [10],

© The Author(s), under exclusive license to Springer Nature Switzerland AG 2026
S. Ali et al. (Eds.): MIUA 2025, LNCS 15918, pp. 204–218, 2026.
https://doi.org/10.1007/978-3-031-98694-9_15

where a 3D preoperative liver model is deformed, and key surgical landmarks, such as tumours and vessels, are project onto intraoperative footage from a laparoscope [11]. A key component of the 3D-2D registration pipeline is that of 2D segmentation, where landmarks such as the falciform ligament and ridge [10], are detected in real-time during the surgery such that the current form of the liver is recorded. Prior research has demonstrated the efficacy of different model architectures and approaches to data augmentation with varying levels of success [2,10], however an approach achieving an acceptable level of accuracy is yet to be found [2,13]. In this paper we present ablation results into the suitability of five popular image segmentation models with prior use in surgical research [2,7,9], and propose a pipeline to train a model for liver segmentation (see Fig. 1), utilising pre-trained weights, training, fine-tuning, followed by a novel mask post-processing step, thereby facilitating improved model performance.

1.2 Challenges

Obtaining consistently accurate predictions from deep learning model is a non-trivial task due to a number of reasons. Firstly, the liver is prone to deforming based on its environment and forces applied upon it [2]. This means that the liver shape can change drastically not only from patient to patient, but also the same liver through the duration of the surgical procedure. This issue, combined with the small amounts of available annotated data and a complex visual environments, leads to the necessity of dataset augmentations when training models [10]. As this task identifies linear landmarks, this leads to heavy class imbalance (see Table 1), with over 98% being labelled as background within the P2ILF training set. To counter this imbalance, the choice of loss function and class weights in this work must be selected appropriately.

Table 1. Occurrences of each class within P2ILF training set

Class	Count	% (3 s.f.)
Background	244,679,040	98.3
Silhouette	1,872,457	0.752
Ridge	1,765,372	0.709
Ligament	515,071	0.207

2 Related Work

2.1 Medical Image Segmentation

The introduction of UNet by Ronneberger et al. allowed for developments within the field by proposing the "U-shaped architecture" for Fully Convolutional Networks [17], in which a model has a contracting path with pooling layers and an expansive path with up-convolutions, with these paths connected by a bottle-neck and skip connections. Models building upon the UNet architecture include UNet++ by Zhou et al. [22], a denser architecture with a greater number of convolution blocks and dense skip connection pathways, as well as the use of deep supervision; UNet3+ builds upon the the architecture of UNet++ [7], with its proposed use being within medical image segmentation. UNet3+ proposes full-scale skip connections where each convolution block in the contracting path has skip connections to its equivalent and below blocks in the expansive path; the bottleneck and each block in the expansive path is supervised by the ground truth, as well as having skip connections to every block further along the expansive path. The aforementioned models have all been measured against LiTS 2017 benchmark [4,7], highlighting the focus on the medical imaging field. ResUNet is a deep residual UNet model which replaces the standard Convolution-ReLU block with a residual block with batch normalisation [21]. ResUNet++ builds on top of ResUNet, adding squeeze-excitation blocks for dynamic weighting of convolutional channels, ASPP to allow for broader context when classifying a pixel, and attention to enhance feature quality [8]. Tailored for medical image segmentation, ResUNet++ outperforms both UNet and ResUNet in colonoscopy segmentation benchmarks [8].

2.2   Laparoscopic Segmentation

Anteby et al. discuss the suitability of deep learning, notably Convolutional Neural Networks (CNNs), in the segmentation of laparoscopic imagery, having already revolutionised the field of medical imagery [3]. Applications such as tool detection and anatomy recognition were found to be suitable [3], with use cases only increasing as developments are made within the field. Koo et al. successfully demonstrated semantic contour detection of the ridge and silhouette of the liver through the use of CNNs, using CASENet with a ResNet50 encoder pre-trained on the ImageNet dataset [10]. Dataset augmentation through scale, shear, brightness, contrast, rotation, and translation were applied, promoting generalisation and invariance of the model with a small dataset [10]. As part of MICCAI 2022, the Preoperative to Intraoperative Laparoscopy Fusion (P2ILF) challenge was hosted, focusing on solving the end-to-end task of 3D-2D liver registration without human annotation, including liver landmark segmentation from laparoscopic images [2]. As opposed to the work presented by Koo et al., the P2ILF dataset also contained annotations for the falciform ligament [2,10]. Teams from around the world competed in the P2ILF challenge, covering a range of different approach in terms of model, loss function, data augmentation, and pre-training [2]. Pei et al. introduce the D^2GPLAND, a depth-aware model which is guided by unified features from an estimated depth map through the use of a depth estimation network and a Segment Anything Model (SAM) encoder, as well as using the ResNet34 encoder on the original image [15], achieving best-in-class results evaluating against their L3D dataset. Pei et al. publicly released L3D, which is the collation of laparoscopic images from multiple sources [15].

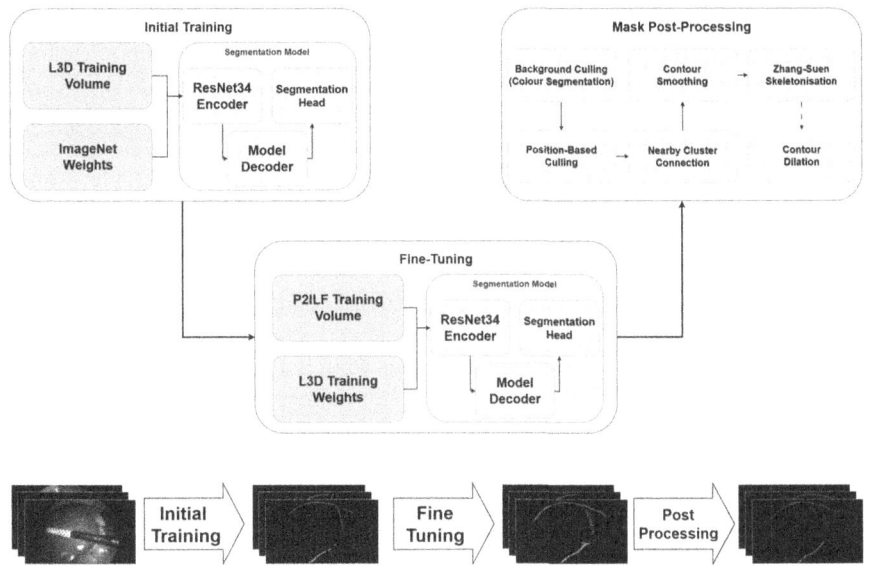

Fig. 1. Pipeline of 2D segmentation task. Dashes represent an optional process

3   Methodology

3.1   Proposed Method

Firstly, all models selected for the ablation study – UNet, UNet++, UNet3+, DeepLabV3+, and ResUNet++ – are all equipped with ResNet34 encoders that have been pre-trained on the ImageNet dataset prior to training. The ResNet family of encoders have achieved state-of-the-art Dice scores on endoscopic segmentation [6], demonstrating its suitability. ResNet34 was chosen due to its balance of accuracy when compared to larger ResNet models [14], with less computational cost. Parameters ablated over include learning rate, batch size, and loss function. The model is trained on the L3D dataset, which has been augmented flip transformations on both axes. The AdamW optimiser is used for training, and the loss functions ablated consist of different weightings of cross-entropy loss, Dice loss, Huber loss, and Focal-Tversky loss (see Eq. 2). For cross-entropy loss, the following novel modified logarithmic class weights function was used, where M is the set of all training mask pixels, and $M_i \subseteq M$ is the set of all training mask pixels of class i:

$$W_i = \max \left[1.0, \log \left(\frac{|M|}{|M_i|} \right) \right] \tag{1}$$

Once training has been completed, models were evaluated using two validation patients chosen from the P2ILF training set, using precision and Dice similarity coefficient (DSC) metrics. Candidate models are then selected to be fine-tuned on the P2ILF dataset from this evaluation.

Finally, predicted masks from the fine-tuned model are post-processed. This involved culling known false positive pixels (i.e. pixels out of camera, ligament prediction above/below both the ridge and silhouette), applying the Ramer-Douglas-Peucker algorithm [16] for smoothing landmark contours, and applying the Zhang-Suen algorithm for skeletonisation of contours [20]. This centre line can then be dilated for evaluation, or sampled into a set of points. The Ramer-Douglas-Peucker algorithm is as follows:

1. The first and last points of the curve are connected with a straight line.
2. Every other point in the line has its perpendicular distance to this straight line calculated.
3. If the furthest distance recorded is greater than some value ϵ, then the point this was found at is preserved, and two sub-curves are defined either side of this point.
4. The algorithm is recursively called for the two sub-curves that were previously defined.

3.2   Loss Function

Our proposed composite loss function using weighted cross-entropy ($\mathcal{L}_{\text{wCE}}$), Dice loss ($\mathcal{L}_{\text{D}}$), Huber loss ($\mathcal{L}_{\text{H}}$), and Focal-Tversky loss ($\mathcal{L}_{\text{FTL}}$) can be represented as:

$$\mathcal{L} = \alpha \cdot \mathcal{L}_{\text{wCE}} + \beta \cdot \mathcal{L}_{\text{D}} + \gamma \cdot \mathcal{L}_{\text{H}} + \delta \cdot \mathcal{L}_{\text{FTL}} \qquad (2)$$

Here, α, β, γ, δ are the weights (i.e. hyperparameters) which we intend to ablate to find the optimal loss function.

4   Results

4.1   Dataset

Two dataset were used for model training: the L3D dataset was used to initially training the model [15], and the P2ILF dataset was used for further fine-tuning [2]. Three landmarks are present within the segmentation masks of both datasets: the silhouette, the ridge, and the falciform ligament.

The L3D dataset contains 1,152 image frames from 39 patients (122 frames are in the validation set, and a further 109 images are within the test set). The P2ILF dataset has 197 frames from 11 patients (47 images from two patients make up a validation set, and 30 images consisting of two patients make up a holdout set).

4.2   Evaluation Metrics

To evaluate model performance, the metrics used in the P2ILF challenge 2D segmentation task [2] were also used for our evaluation, these metrics being:

- Precision (P): this metric focuses on penalising false positives within the dataset to ensure that correct predictions are made.
- Dice similarity coefficient (D): this metric is used to focus on the similarity between the predicted segmentation mask (Y_{pred}) and the ground truth segmentation mask (Y_{truth}). It is the number of true positive predicted pixels multiplied by two and divided by the sum of predicted positive pixels and actual positive pixels.

$$D = \frac{2 \cdot |Y_{\text{pred}} \cap Y_{\text{truth}}|}{|Y_{\text{pred}}| + |Y_{\text{truth}}|} \tag{3}$$

- Symmetric distance (G): Ali et al. [2] use the symmetric distance proposed by François et al. [5]. $d_{\max}$ is a threshold value for whether a predicted landmark is spurious, B_I is the set of predicted image landmarks, whilst C_I is the set of ground truth image landmarks. Q is the tolerance region around the ground truth landmarks (defined by the threshold $d_{\max}$), and d_S is a function that calculates symmetric distance.

$$G = \frac{1}{2 \cdot |C_I| \cdot d_{\max}} \left(\sum_{b_I \in B_I \cap Q} d_S(b_I, C_I \backslash \text{FN}) + \sum_{c_I \in C_I \backslash \text{FN}} d_S(c_I, B_I \cap Q) \right) \tag{4}$$

$$+ \frac{|\text{FP}|}{|I| - 2 \cdot |C_I| \cdot d_{\max}} + \frac{|\text{FN}|}{|C_I|}$$

4.3   Experimental Setup

In training, the L3D dataset was augmented with mirror augmentations across both the $x-$ and $y-$ axes, followed by resizing to 416×320 pixels. The AdamW optimiser was used with a learning rate plateau scheduler, which multiplied learning rate by 0.2 after three epochs of stagnation. Training was performed on an NVIDIA RTX 4070, except for UNet3+, where an NVIDIA L40S was used due to extra VRAM being required. For the ablation study, learning rates of $\{0.1, 0.05, 0.01, 0.005, 0.001, 0.0005, 0.0001\}$ were tested, and batch sizes of $\{2, 4, 8, 16, 32\}$ were used (UNet3+ was only ablated up to batch size 8 due to VRAM constraints). A patience of 7 was used throughout.

For loss function experimentation, 35 ablations were conducted per model on the composite loss function in Eq. 2. The loss function hyperparameters (α, β, γ, and δ) shown in Table 3 (see 5th column) are the best performing configurations from the ablation after other parameters were ablated over. Performance was evaluated using patients 1 and 2 from the training set of P2ILF as an evaluation set, providing us with candidate models for fine-tuning (see Table 3).

Table 2. P2ILF 2D segmentation challenge results [2] evaluated using our implementations of precision, Dice similarity coefficient, and the symmetric distance metric. Results are in the order of ridge, falciform ligament, and silhouette. $\bar{P}$, $\bar{D}$, $\bar{G}$ are the metric mean across all three landmarks. The best mean results are highlighted in bold.

Team	$P \uparrow$	$\bar{P} \uparrow$	$D \uparrow$	$\bar{D} \uparrow$	$G \downarrow$	$\bar{G} \downarrow$
BHL	0.24/0.41/0.46	**0.37**	0.22/0.43/0.50	**0.38**	0.70/0.43/0.40	0.51
NCT	0.20/0.31/0.41	0.31	0.24/0.32/0.52	0.36	0.52/0.51/0.32	**0.45**
UCL	0.11/0.43/0.38	0.31	0.13/0.48/0.40	0.34	0.73/0.63/0.42	0.59
VIP	0.11/0.23/0.19	0.18	0.16/0.33/0.29	0.26	0.71/0.44/0.62	0.59
VOR	0.10/0.15/0.16	0.13	0.15/0.24/0.25	0.21	0.70/0.65/0.66	0.67

Models were fine-tuned using the P2ILF training set (patients 1 and 2 were used as a validation set) with a learning rate of 0.0001, a batch size of 8, and a patience of 7. Two rounds of fine-tuning was performed: once with solely cross-entropy loss and another with a loss function consisted of weighted cross-entropy loss ($\mathcal{L}_{wCE}$) and Focal-Tversky loss ($\mathcal{L}_{FTL}$) with $\alpha = 0.75$ and $\delta = 0.25$ (see Eq. 2) A Focal-Tversky component was added to the fine-tuning loss function due to low recall of models after fine-tuning with solely cross-entropy loss (shown in Fig. 2). The Tversky index represents a generalisation of Dice loss, with the focal component promoting predictions of more difficult classes (i.e. landmarks) [1]. Lahlouh et al. achieve their best results using a combination of cross-entropy loss and Focal-Tversky when performing segmentation on cerebral angiography imagery [12], highlighting its medical suitability.

Table 3. Candidate models selected from the L3D training ablation study. Here, α, β, γ, and δ are the coefficients used in the loss function $\mathcal{L}$ in Eq. 2.

No.	Architecture	Learning Rate	Batch Size	$\alpha/\beta/\gamma/\delta$
1	UNet	0.0001	32	1.0/0.0/0.0/0.0
2	UNet	0.0001	8	1.0/0.0/0.0/0.0
3	UNet++	0.001	32	0.25/0.25/0.0/0.50
4	UNet++	0.0005	16	0.50/0.0/0.50/0.0
5	UNet++	0.0005	16	0.75/0.25/0.0/0.0
6	UNet3+	0.001	8	0.50/0.0/0.0/0.50
7	UNet3+	0.001	8	0.50/0.25/0.0/0.25
8	DeepLabV3+	0.0001	64	0.25/0.0/0.25/0.50
9	ResUNet++	0.0005	16	0.50/0.0/0.0/0.50
10	ResUNet++	0.0005	8	0.75/0.0/0.0/0.25

4.4   Quantitative Results

Firstly, testing of the cross-entropy weighting function was performed, the same model with the same parameters was trained with three different class weightings for cross-entropy loss: proportional, logarithmic weighting, and our custom weighting (see Eq. 1), fine-tuning of models and post-processing was not performed on any evaluations. As shown in Table 4, standard proportional weightings simply fails at the segmentation task, logarithmic weights provide a significant improvement, but by using our novel class weighting function, precision is doubled compared to logarithmic weights, and best performance in all three evaluation metrics.

Table 4. Evaluation of different cross-entropy class weightings on P2ILF test set. Best results are shown in bold.

Weighting	$\bar{P}\uparrow$	$\bar{D}\uparrow$	$\bar{G}\downarrow$
Proportional	0.05	0.00	1.00
Logarithmic	0.19	0.22	0.76
Ours	**0.41**	**0.29**	**0.54**

Table 3 shows the configurations of the ten best candidate models from the ablation study. For this, at least one model from each architecture was selected based on highest combined mean precision and DSC from the P2ILF evaluation set. Table 2 illustrates the P2ILF challenge results using our evaluation implementation for comparison.

Table 5 shows the performance of candidate models after initial training, fine-tuning, and post-processing, evaluating against the P2ILF test set. Fine-tuning was done with solely weighted cross-entropy loss ($\mathcal{L}_{wCE}$). 50% of models outperformed P2ILF in mean precision prior to any fine-tuning (i.e. solely trained on ImageNet followed by L3D, never having seen the P2ILF dataset), with this proportion increasing to 80% after fine-tuning. However, no model at any points outperforms the P2ILF teams in mean DSC or symmetric distance. Post-processing sees to have minimal effect on evaluation in Table 5, with slight increases in mean DSC and precision on average, but with worse performance in symmetric distance.

Table 6 shows the evaluation after the Focal-Tversky component was added to the loss function for fine-tuning. It was noted that this resulted in better performance compared to Table 5 with regards to the DSC and symmetric distance metrics after fine-tuning, but did not consistently outperform P2ILF in any metric (10% of models in mean precision and symmetric distance, and 40% of models in mean DSC) prior to post-processing.

Table 5. Results of candidate model fine-tuning using cross-entropy loss ($\mathcal{L}_{CE}$). Highlighted cells represent a result that beats all P2ILF teams in that metric, the best results are highlighted in bold.

Candidate	Initial Training			Fine-Tuning			Post-Processing		
	$\bar{P}_{\text{init}}$ ↑	$\bar{D}_{\text{init}}$ ↑	$\bar{G}_{\text{init}}$ ↓	$\bar{P}_{\text{tune}}$ ↑	$\bar{D}_{\text{tune}}$ ↑	$\bar{G}_{\text{tune}}$ ↓	$\bar{P}_{\text{post}}$ ↑	$\bar{D}_{\text{post}}$ ↑	$\bar{G}_{\text{post}}$ ↓
1	0.39	0.22	0.69	0.45	0.23	0.67	0.44	0.26	0.67
2	0.41	0.29	0.54	0.44	0.33	0.52	0.45	**0.35**	0.53
3	0.35	0.28	0.59	0.38	0.30	0.56	0.43	0.32	0.57
4	0.42	0.25	0.64	0.43	0.30	0.55	0.45	0.32	0.57
5	0.39	0.28	0.61	0.38	0.31	0.56	0.39	0.32	0.57
6	0.36	0.24	0.60	0.51	0.31	**0.51**	**0.52**	0.33	0.54
7	0.32	0.31	0.56	0.42	0.25	0.62	0.44	0.28	0.63
8	0.34	0.23	0.65	0.36	0.21	0.69	0.36	0.22	0.72
9	0.38	0.27	0.63	0.30	0.15	0.80	0.30	0.15	0.79
10	0.32	0.17	0.70	0.43	0.17	0.70	0.45	0.21	0.72

Table 6. Results of candidate model fine-tuning using a combined loss function of cross-entropy loss ($\mathcal{L}_{CE}$) and Focal-Tversky loss ($\mathcal{L}_{FTL}$). Highlighted cells represent a result that beats all P2ILF teams in that metric, the best results are highlighted in bold.

Candidate	Initial Training			Fine-Tuning			Post-Processing		
	$\bar{P}_{\text{init}}$ ↑	$\bar{D}_{\text{init}}$ ↑	$\bar{G}_{\text{init}}$ ↓	$\bar{P}_{\text{tune}}$ ↑	$\bar{D}_{\text{tune}}$ ↑	$\bar{G}_{\text{tune}}$ ↓	$\bar{P}_{\text{post}}$ ↑	$\bar{D}_{\text{post}}$ ↑	$\bar{G}_{\text{post}}$ ↓
1	0.39	0.22	0.69	0.35	0.37	0.47	0.45	0.37	0.44
2	0.41	0.29	0.54	0.38	0.40	0.40	**0.48**	**0.43**	**0.39**
3	0.35	0.28	0.59	0.35	0.37	0.47	0.47	0.39	0.45
4	0.42	0.25	0.64	0.31	0.36	0.53	0.40	0.37	0.48
5	0.39	0.28	0.61	0.36	0.39	0.46	0.44	0.39	0.45
6	0.36	0.24	0.60	0.33	0.41	0.47	0.44	0.42	0.40
7	0.32	0.31	0.56	0.33	0.40	0.54	0.45	0.42	0.43
8	0.34	0.23	0.65	0.31	0.29	0.60	0.40	0.30	0.56
9	0.38	0.27	0.63	0.31	0.29	0.66	0.35	0.28	0.56
10	0.32	0.17	0.70	0.32	0.34	0.51	0.39	0.34	0.50

It is evident that post-processing led to noticeable improvements for this model. Mean precision increased on average over 9%, from 33.5% to 42.7%, making 90% of candidate models outperform P2ILF teams in this metric. Improvements were also seen across DSC and symmetric distance. From this evaluation, there are five candidate models that match or beat all teams from P2ILF 2D segmentation task in all metrics, with three models beating in every metric outright (see Table 2 and Table 6).

Candidate 2 performed best: the model provided an 11% increase in mean precision (30% relative increase), a 5% increase in mean Dice score (over 13% relative increase), and 6% decrease in symmetric distance (over 13% relative improvement) compared to the best result in each metric in the P2ILF 2D segmentation task (see Table 2 and Table 6).

Regarding execution performance, the time taken for inference and post-processing was recorded. Inference ranged from 9–15 milliseconds, whilst post-processing added a 9–12 millisecond penalty. This results in a production frequency range of 37–56 Hz, acceptable for real-time operation.

4.5   Qualitative Results

Figure 2 shows six example images from the P2ILF test set, three from each patient within the set (patients 4 and 11). Results are shown from the two best performing teams in the reported in P2ILF challenge 2D segmentation task (BHL and NCT - see Table 2) together with our best performing model - candidate 2. Resulting inferences from initial training of the model (see TRAIN in Fig. 2), P2ILF fine-tuned models without post-processing (see CE_FT and FTL_FT), and finally with post-processing (see CE_PP and FTL_PP). Results that have the CE_ prefix is where candidate 2 was fine-tuned solely with cross-entropy loss; results that have the FTL_ prefix is where candidate 2 was fine-tuned with both a cross-entropy loss component and a Focal-Tversky loss component, as described in Sect. 4.3.

Our qualitative results demonstrate that the approaches employed by BHL and NCT can result in broken contours, particularly noticeable on images from patient 11. Sub-figure TRAIN shows that the model under-predicts landmarks, albeit with high precision when it does predict (i.e. a low false positive rate). CE_FT and PP_FT still exhibit this behaviour, but this does not seem to be present in FTL_FT. This increase does lead to thicker contours however, with some contours being disconnected or broken. Once FTL_FT has been post-processed, shown in FTL_PP, contours are now connected and consistent in thickness, cleaning up the output of the model significantly.

Figure 3 shows two failure cases for the model, it is evident that the model has difficult in predictions in cases where there is a low level of lighting, and where the liver is being manipulated such that the anterior view is not fully facing the camera. The precision in these images are still of good quality, reinforcing the idea that the model is able to generalise well, but cannot predict the full contours in extreme cases, although maintaining a low false positive rate from an qualitative perspective.

Patient 4   Patient 11

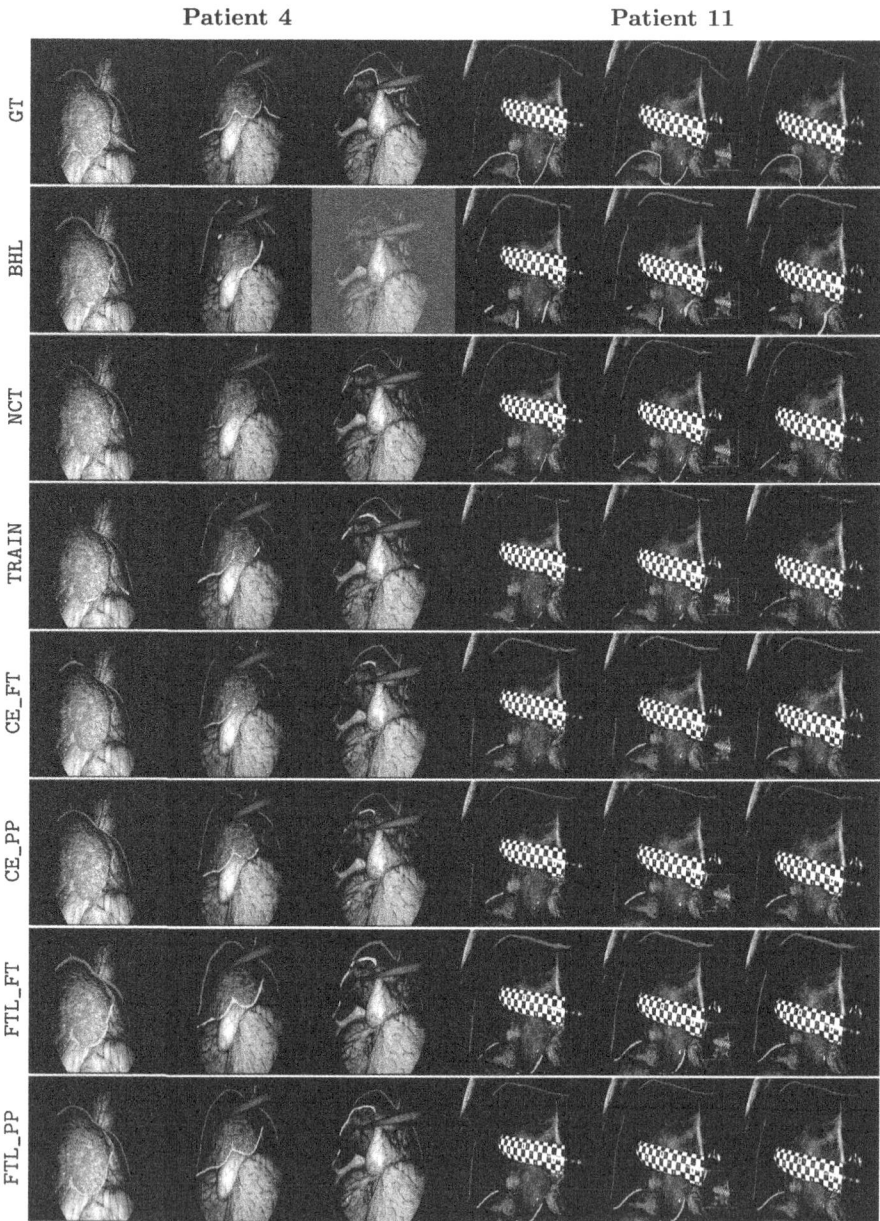

Fig. 2. Qualitative results on the P2ILF test set. GT shows ground truth annotations. BHL and NCT are the predictions made by the BHL and NCT teams from the P2ILF challenge teams respectively [2]. TRAIN is the predictions made by candidate 2 after initial training. CE_FT represents candidate model 2 being fine-tuned solely with cross-entropy loss (without post-processing). CE_PP is the same model as CE_FT but with post-processing applied. FTL_FT represents candidate model 2 being fine-tuned with both cross-entropy loss and Focal-Tversky loss (without post-processsing). FTL_PP is the same model as FTL_CE but with post-processing applied.

Ground Truth   **Prediction**

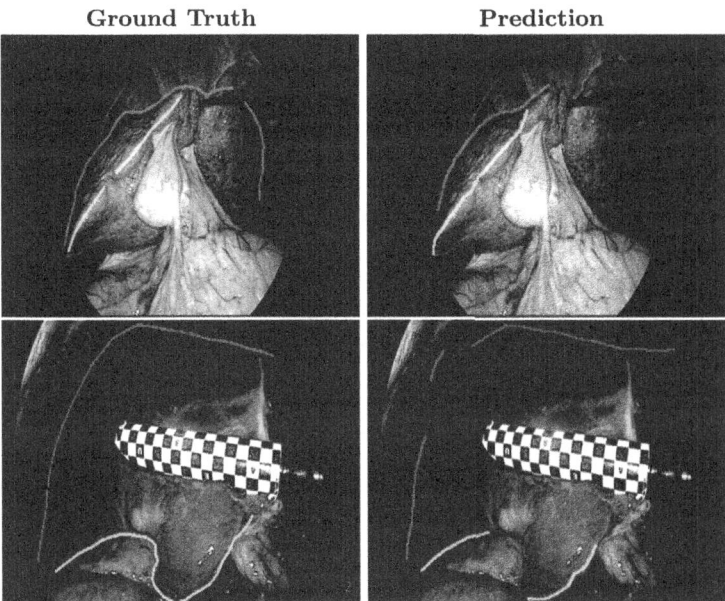

Fig. 3. Examples of failure cases of candidate 2, compared with ground truth masks.

5   Discussion and Conclusion

5.1   Discussion

Table 5 and CE_FT in Fig. 2 show that the model is precise when making a prediction, however it is visible that the recall is low. Due to this under-prediction, the advantages of post-processing is minimised (see CE_PP) due to thin and sparse predictions meaning there is little to process, the difference between FTL_FT and FTL_PP is visibly greater. This lacklustre post-processing performance is also seen quantitatively, with tune and post values being noticeably similar in Table 5, when compared to differences shown in Table 6.

Table 6 and sub-figure FTL_FT in Fig. 2 show a model that is less prone to under-prediction when compared to CE_FT, correctly predicting a greater proportion of landmarks, albeit with thicker contours. FTL_PP visualises the improvement in metrics shown in Table 6 after post-processing, with thinner contours, connection of nearby contours, whilst also leading to a more accurately predicted contour as shown by the improved DSC and symmetric distance scores.

Adding a Focal-Tversky loss component to the loss function promotes prediction of landmarks within a mask due to the focal exponent adding emphasis to landmark predictions that are of low certainty (i.e. difficult predictions). Post-processing improves evaluation metrics when there is over-prediction present by thinning contours such that they are more precise, with smoothing simplifying the contour such that the jaggedness of a contour is removed, due to it not reflecting the form shown by the landmarks of the liver that the model is attempting to predict.

The approach taken by Pei et al. in the estimation of depth masks attempts to provide more context to the model for predictions [15], an approach that we believe can be studied further. Labrunie et al. utilise distance maps as opposed to binary masks when training their 3D-2D registration model [11], allowing models to learn data that does not have harsh binary boundaries around the thin contours, and is highly transferable to the task of intraoperative segmentation of the liver through these landmarks. The mask post-processing presented in this paper lays out the fundamentals of this approach, with in-depth ablation studies, and ideas such as mask correction through deep learning yet to be explored.

There is a question concerning the appropriateness of DSC as an evaluation metric, due to the task predicting contours, rather than segments of an image; alternatives such as centre line Dice (clDice) [19] should have their suitability investigated in this field.

5.2   Conclusion

In this work, we proposed a systematic approach in training segmentation models in the context of liver laparoscopy. The methodology involves utilising pre-trained models on a large generic dataset, such as ImageNet, followed by further training on a large dataset of laparoscopic images, which can be obtained from multiple sources as demonstrated by the L3D dataset. Fine-tuning can then be performed on a high quality dataset from a single source. Furthermore, we introduce a novel post-processing pipeline that incorporates colour segmentation, skeletonisation, and contour smoothing to minimise errors from false positive predictions. We present results that outperform in all metrics used for the P2ILF challenge 2D segmentation task, on the same dataset. Research areas such as synthetic data generation and depth estimation hold promise for development in this field. The research presented in this work forms part of a 3D-2D registration pipeline, where no human annotation is required.

Acknowledgements. This project is part of the National Institute for Health and Care Research (NIHR) Leeds Biomedical Research Centre (BRC) pump-priming funding as the "ARMADILLO" project (NIHR203331). The views expressed are those of the authors and not necessarily those of the NIHR or the Department of Health and Social Care.

Disclosure of Interests. The authors have no competing interests to declare that are relevant to the content of this article.

References

1. Abraham, N., Khan, N.M.: A novel focal Tversky loss function with improved attention U-Net for lesion segmentation. In: 2019 IEEE 16th International Symposium on Biomedical Imaging (ISBI 2019), pp. 683–687 (2019). https://doi.org/10.1109/ISBI.2019.8759329

2. Ali, S., Espinel, Y., Jin, Y., Liu, P., Güttner, B., Zhang, X., et al.: An objective comparison of methods for augmented reality in laparoscopic liver resection by preoperative-to-intraoperative image fusion from the MICCAI2022 challenge. Med. Image Anal. **99**, 103371 (2025). https://doi.org/10.1016/j.media.2024.103371

3. Anteby, R., et al.: Deep learning visual analysis in laparoscopic surgery: a systematic review and diagnostic test accuracy meta-analysis. Surg. Endosc. **35**(4), 1521–1533 (2021). https://doi.org/10.1007/s00464-020-08168-1

4. Bilic, P., Christ, P., Li, H.B., Vorontsov, E., Ben-Cohen, A., Kaissis, G., et al.: The liver tumor segmentation benchmark (LiTS). Med. Image Anal. **84**, 102680 (2023). https://doi.org/10.1016/j.media.2022.102680

5. François, T., et al.: Detecting the occluding contours of the uterus to automatise augmented laparoscopy: score, loss, dataset, evaluation and user study. Int. J. Comput. Assist. Radiol. Surg. **15**(7), 1177–1186 (2020). https://doi.org/10.1007/s11548-020-02151-w

6. Ghamsarian, N., Wolf, S., Zinkernagel, M., Schoeffmann, K., Sznitman, R.: Deep-Pyramid+: medical image segmentation using pyramid view fusion and deformable pyramid reception. Int. J. Comput. Assist. Radiol. Surg. **19**(5), 851–859 (2024). https://doi.org/10.1007/s11548-023-03046-2

7. Huang, H., Lin, L., Tong, R., Hu, H., Zhang, Q., Iwamoto, Y., et al.: UNet 3+: a full-scale connected UNet for medical image segmentation. In: ICASSP 2020 - 2020 IEEE International Conference on Acoustics, Speech and Signal Processing (ICASSP), pp. 1055–1059 (2020). https://doi.org/10.1109/ICASSP40776.2020.9053405

8. Jha, D., Smedsrud, P.H., Riegler, M.A., Johansen, D., Lange, T.D., Halvorsen, P., et al.: ResUNet++: an advanced architecture for medical image segmentation. In: 2019 IEEE International Symposium on Multimedia (ISM), pp. 225–2255 (2019). https://doi.org/10.1109/ISM46123.2019.00049

9. Kojima, S., Kitaguchi, D., Igaki, T., Nakajima, K., Ishikawa, Y., Harai, Y., et al.: Deep-learning-based semantic segmentation of autonomic nerves from laparoscopic images of colorectal surgery: an experimental pilot study. Int. J. Surg. **109**(4) (2023). https://doi.org/10.1097/JS9.0000000000000317

10. Koo, B., et al.: Automatic, global registration in laparoscopic liver surgery. Int. J. Comput. Assist. Radiol. Surg. **17**(1), 167–176 (2021). https://doi.org/10.1007/s11548-021-02518-7

11. Labrunie, M., Ribeiro, M., Mourthadhoi, F., Tilmant, C., Le Roy, B., Buc, E., et al.: Automatic preoperative 3D model registration in laparoscopic liver resection. Int. J. Comput. Assist. Radiol. Surg. **17**, 1429–1436 (2022). https://doi.org/10.1007/s11548-022-02641-z

12. Lahlouh, M., Blanc, R., Piotin, M., Szewczyk, J., Passat, N., Chenoune, Y.: Cerebral AVM segmentation from 3D rotational angiography images by convolutional neural networks. Neurosci. Inform. **3**(3), 100138 (2023). https://doi.org/10.1016/j.neuri.2023.100138

13. Lin, Y., Xu, J., Hong, J., Si, Y., He, Y., Zhang, J.: Prognostic impact of surgical margin in hepatectomy on patients with hepatocellular carcinoma: a meta-analysis of observational studies. Front. Surg. **9**, 810479 (2022). https://doi.org/10.3389/fsurg.2022.810479

14. Pamungkas, Y., Triandini, E., Yunanto, W., Thwe, Y.: Impact of hyperparameter tuning on ResNet-UNet models for enhanced brain tumor segmentation in MRI scans. Int. J. Robot. Control Syst. **5**(2), 917–936 (2025). https://doi.org/10.31763/ijrcs.v5i2.1802

15. Pei, J., Cui, R., Li, Y., Si, W., Qin, J., Heng, P.A.: Depth-driven geometric prompt learning for laparoscopic liver landmark detection. In: Linguraru, M.G., et al. (eds.), Medical Image Computing and Computer Assisted Intervention – MICCAI 2024. MICCAI 2024. LNCS, vol. 15006, pp. 154–164. Springer, Cham (2024). https://doi.org/10.1007/978-3-031-72089-5_15
16. Ramer, U.: An iterative procedure for the polygonal approximation of plane curves. Comput. Graph. Image Process. **1**(3), 244–256 (1972). https://doi.org/10.1016/S0146-664X(72)80017-0
17. Ronneberger, O., Fischer, P., Brox, T.: U-net: convolutional networks for biomedical image segmentation. In: Navab, N., et al. (eds.), Medical Image Computing and Computer-Assisted Intervention – MICCAI 2015. MICCAI 2015. LNCS, vol. 9351, pp. 234–241. Springer, Cham (2015). https://doi.org/10.1007/978-3-319-24574-4_28
18. Schneider, C., Allam, M., Stoyanov, D., Hawkes, D.J., Gurusamy, K., Davidson, B.R.: Performance of image guided navigation in laparoscopic liver surgery - a systematic review. Surg. Oncol. **38**(101637), 101637 (2021). https://doi.org/10.1016/j.suronc.2021.101637
19. Shit, S., Paetzold, J.C., Sekuboyina, A., Ezhov, I., Unger, A., Zhylka, A., et al.: clDice - a novel topology-preserving loss function for tubular structure segmentation. In: 2021 IEEE/CVF Conference on Computer Vision and Pattern Recognition (CVPR), pp. 16555–16564 (2021). https://doi.org/10.1109/CVPR46437.2021.01629
20. Zhang, T.Y., Suen, C.Y.: A fast parallel algorithm for thinning digital patterns. Commun. ACM **27**(3), 236–239 (1984). https://doi.org/10.1145/357994.358023
21. Zhang, Z., Liu, Q., Wang, Y.: Road extraction by deep residual U-Net. IEEE Geosci. Remote Sens. Lett. **15**(5), 749–753 (2018). https://doi.org/10.1109/LGRS.2018.2802944
22. Zhou, Z., Rahman Siddiquee, M.M., Tajbakhsh, N., Liang, J.: UNet++: a nested U-Net architecture for medical image segmentation. In: Stoyanov, D., et al. (eds.), Deep Learning in Medical Image Analysis and Multimodal Learning for Clinical Decision Support. DLMIA ML-CDS 2018 2018. LNCS, vol. 11045, pp. 3–11. Springer, Cham (2018). https://doi.org/10.1007/978-3-030-00889-5_1

Retinal and Vascular Image Analysis

Hessian-Based Deep Retinal Vessel Segmentation with Extremely Few Annotations

Benjamin Chivet[ID], Noémie Debroux[(✉)][ID], Manuel Grand-Brochier,
and Antoine Vacavant[ID]

Université Clermont Auvergne, Clermont Auvergne INP, CNRS, Institut Pascal,
63000 Clermont–Ferrand, France
noemie.debroux@uca.fr

Abstract. Segmentation of retinal blood vessels is essential in medical image analysis and plays a central role in eye disease diagnosis. Deep learning approaches have recently emerged, providing good results in recovering the retinal vascular tree. However, it comes at the expense of numerous training-annotated datasets, which are particularly difficult and costly to obtain in the medical domain, as only experts can provide reliable annotations. We propose to lift this drawback by introducing and comparing a novel supervised modular model using information from second-order derivatives of the input image enhancing thin structures, under extremely low annotations. Firstly, we improve the LIOT (Local Intensity Order Transformation) pre-processing procedure by adding the orthogonal direction of the blood vessels. Then, a new adjustable loss function is used to train a U-Net with only a few of the available annotations. It relies on both a second-order functional for recovering thin structures such as blood vessels and the binary cross-entropy. In this work, we investigate four variants of the proposed loss function. A second, cascaded U-Net is added to polish and denoise the results. We demonstrate through numerical experiments the soundness, modularity, and practicality of our pipeline on two publicly available datasets: DRIVE and CHASEBD1.

Keywords: Blake-Zisserman functional · modified LIOT · retinal vessel segmentation · supervised learning with few annotations · U-Net

1 Introduction

The fundus retina image is a non-invasive technique that renders the microvascular system supplying blood to the eye. It is a crucial tool for ophthalmologists to diagnose vascular-related eye diseases such as diabetic retinopathy and diabetic maculopathy, which are the leading causes of global blindness. Indeed, the geometric and topological features such as vessel diameter, tree structure, and length are of great interest for diagnosing hypertension, diabetes, and atherosclerosis as they match clinical elements [12].

S. Ali et al. (Eds.): MIUA 2025, LNCS 15918, pp. 221–236, 2026.
https://doi.org/10.1007/978-3-031-98694-9_16

However, retinal blood vessel segmentation is a difficult task in image analysis due to the visual complexities of retinal fundus images, such as noise, varying contrast, uneven illumination, and variations in the blood vessels' appearance, shape, size, and location [26]. Since the advent of deep learning techniques and their outstanding results, many researchers have addressed the problem of retinal vessel segmentation using these models [4,26].

The main drawback of these techniques is that they require a large amount of accurately labeled data for the learning process, which is very costly to obtain when dealing with medical images, both financially and in human-effort [4]. Indeed, in our case, only expert ophthalmologists can provide a reliable ground truth, that is, manually assign each pixel an accurate label.

To overcome this hindrance, we introduce a novel framework for retinal vessel segmentation using a supervised setting with extremely low annotations and information from second-order derivatives of the input image, known to enhance thin structures [10]. We introduce a three-stage modular model comprising a pre-processing step followed by two cascading U-Nets, and compare four different variants. All include second-order information encoding thin structures in various ways, to prove that it is worth considering for enhancing segmentation quality while decreasing the annotation. Within this framework, we therefore propose several contributions: (i) A modified Local Intensity Order Transformation (LIOT) [24] pre-processing step by duplicating it with an inverted comparison order and adding the direction of the eigenvector associated with the largest eigenvalue of the original image Hessian matrix. Indeed, it encodes the orthogonal direction of the blood vessel, leading to 10-channel images that are contrast-invariant and enhance blood vessels as shown in Fig. 2. That task-oriented improved image then serves as input in our first U-Net architecture [22] to better guide the segmentation process. (ii) A U-Net network is trained with only a few labeled images from the training set, using a new modular loss function comprising two components designed to improve the segmentation accuracy of the last vascular tree branches. First, we consider the classic binary cross-entropy, as well as a variant that incorporates second-order image information to put more emphasis on the finest blood vessels. Second, a modified Blake-Zisserman functional dedicated to crease point and thin structure detection with a supervised and an unsupervised version, exploits the second derivatives of the original image. (iii) A second cascaded U-Net, taking the outputs of the first U-Net as inputs, is trained using the standard binary entropy to suppress noise and artifacts introduced by the second-order features. Figure 1 summarises our workflow. (iv) We compare those strategies with state-of-the-art fully-supervised, semi-supervised, and partially-supervised models. The implementation of our model is available at https://github.com/benjaminchivet/retinal-vessel-seg-few-anno.

2   Related Works

Pre-processing for Vessel Enhancement. Local intensity transformations have been widely used as pre-processing steps to enhance and make the inputs

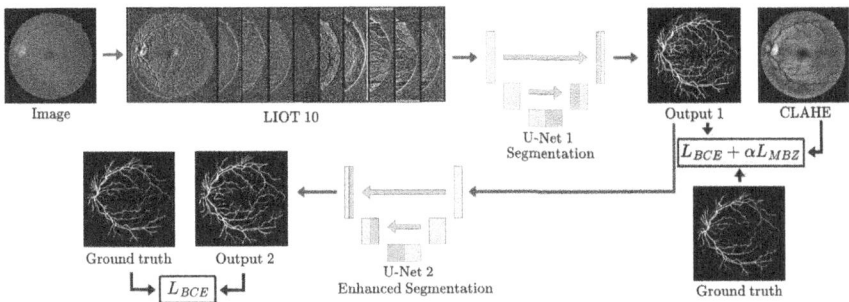

Fig. 1. The overall framework of the three-stage proposed model: modified LIOT pre-processing, first U-Net trained with a novel modular loss function encompassing four different versions and relying on two main components being the Binary Cross-Entropy and a modified Blake-Zisserman functional, and a second U-Net in cascade to clean the segmentation.

contrast-invariant. The Star-Census Transform (SCT) [16], extending [29], compares symmetrically the neighboring pixels forming a star-shaped pattern instead of evaluating them with the central pixel. In [17], Li *et al.* used a local rotation invariant transformation that compares the pixel intensity in a circular region without weighting according to distance, generating a single-channel image. Unlike LIOT (see Sect. 3.1), these transformations are not designed to capture curvilinear structures and are invariant to rotation. Other local transformations are used as LIOT for the segmentation task. The Relative Intensity Order Transformation (RIOT) [14] is derived from LIOT, where only 2 directions are considered, producing a 2-channel image instead of a 4-channel image. An edge feature map is also added to form a 3-channel image. Peng et al. [21] proposed ODoS filter by using the average intensity along 3 sticks in a multi-step strategy and a transform domain, resulting in a 4-channel image as input.

Semi and Partially Supervised Learning. Deep learning techniques have been effectively applied to retinal vessel segmentation in recent years, providing better results than traditional methods. A large number of fully supervised state-of-the-art frameworks use U-Net as a backbone [1,6,11,17,22,26]. However, providing labeled datasets with accurate annotations can be challenging and expensive, especially for medical applications [4]. Therefore, some research focuses on training deep learning algorithms with few annotations. Semi-supervised learning allows the model to learn from a smaller set of labeled data while using unlabeled data. Chen *et al.* [4] proposed a semi-supervised learning strategy based on the U-Net architecture using unlabeled images as pseudo-labels to improve the segmentation. [23] introduces SCANet, a model composed of 3 interconnected branches creating synergies between them. The training process of SCANet includes a fully supervised pre-training stage and an alternate semi-supervised training stage. Generative Adversarial Network (GAN) [5] frameworks are also employed for semi-supervised retinal vessel segmentation to take advantage of unlabeled data. The authors of [15] used a structured prediction (SP) method by viewing segmentation as a multi-label inference problem in a GAN framework. Huo [9] adopted a U-Net model as a generator and a fully convolutional network as a discriminator. LeakGAN [8] employs a U-Net network dedicated to discrimination and segmentation. The U-Net skip connections also take layers from the generator. Moreover, they used a mean teacher model [27] with unlabeled data to train the consistency of the discriminator according to a novel loss function derived from the focal loss. The authors of [7] extend the mean teacher methodology by proposing an adaptive uncertainty estimation (AUE) method at a pixel-wise level. To further reduce the number of annotated pixels, Xu et al. [28] proposed a partially supervised approach in which they annotated the training images with partial labels. They selected annotated patches using an active learning strategy based on the probability output map. The authors consider the most uncertain patches to be the most informative. Both annotated and unannotated data are used for training with a latent MixUp inspired by [30].

3   Methodology

In this section, we detail our three-stage model.

3.1   Pre-processing Step with a Modified LIOT

We now focus on our pre-processing step. Inspired by the improved performance of deep learning architectures using Local Intensity Order Transformation (LIOT) [24] for blood vessel segmentation, we propose to use a modified version of this transformation. We first recall the principles of this contrast-invariant image modification before diving into our adaptations. LIOT is a transformation designed for images containing curvilinear objects darker than the background, such as the vascular network of fundus images. It compares the intensity between each pixel of a grayscale image and its 8 neighboring pixels in four directions, resulting in an image composed of 4 channels. The 4-channel image produced by LIOT is invariant to changes in contrast. LIOT also characterizes the implicit properties of curvilinear structures. Let I be a grayscale image and $I_{i,j}$ the intensity at coordinate (i, j), for each direction $d \in \{left, right, top, bottom\}$, we compute

$$J_{i,j}^-(d) = \sum_{k=1}^{8} 2^{k-1} H(I_{i,j} - I_{i,j}(d_k))$$

(1)

where H denotes the Heaviside function that is $H(x) = \begin{cases} 1 & \text{if } x > 0 \\ 0 & \text{else} \end{cases}$, and $I_{i,j}(d_k)$ denotes the intensity of the k-th pixel from the central pixel (i, j) in the direction d. LIOT is the concatenation of $J^-(left)$, $J^-(right)$, $J^-(top)$ and $J^-(bottom)$ into a 4-channel image.

For each direction of the transformation, the power of 2 multiplying H increases with the distance to the neighboring pixel. In their implementation[1], Shi et al. suggest multiplying H by a decreasing power of 2 according to the distance from the current pixel. By using this other transformation with LIOT, we add more information in the pre-processing step while holding the properties of LIOT. The transformation becomes

$$J_{i,j}^+(d) = \sum_{k=1}^{8} 2^{8-k} H(I_{i,j} - I_{i,j}(d_k))$$ (2)

With the concatenation of J^- and J^+ we have an 8-channel image. Figure 2 shows the resulting channel of J^- and J^+ for the *left* direction. In both images, the blood vessels are enhanced to facilitate the segmentation.

We now propose to add a fifth direction corresponding to the eigenvector direction associated with the largest eigenvalue of the original image Hessian matrix to further bring the thinnest blood vessels out. This direction changes for each pixel in contrast to the four previous directions, which remain constant throughout the image. Consider a pixel belonging to a blood vessel and sufficiently close to an edge. We denote the eigenvalues of the Hessian λ_{max} and λ_{min} such that $\lambda_{max} \geq \lambda_{min}$. Since vessels are darker than the context, the greatest curvature λ_{max} is largely positive, and the smallest λ_{min} is near 0. The orthonormal eigenvectors v_{max} and v_{min} represent the orthogonal direction and the direction along the blood vessel, respectively. Applying (1) and (2) with the direction v_{max} leads to another representation of the image. In particular, the value of pixels belonging to the vascular network is 0 in $J^-(v_{max})$, as shown in Fig. 2. Since vessels aligned exactly with the fixed directions are not highlighted, this new per-pixel direction can stand alone and replace all other fixed orientations. However, using the concatenation of all directions as input provides more information to the network and leads to better performance. The pre-processing step in our model therefore consists of concatenating J^- and J^+ for the five directions $\{left, right, top, bottom, v_{max}\}$ into a 10-channel image.

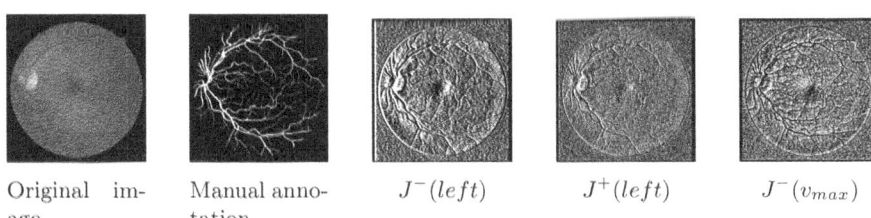

| Original image | Manual annotation | $J^-(left)$ | $J^+(left)$ | $J^-(v_{max})$ |

Fig. 2. Example of order intensity transformations computed on a fundus image.

---

[1] https://github.com/TY-Shi/LIOT.

3.2 Four Variants of a Modular Loss Function Encompassing in Various Ways Original Image Second-Order Information

In this section, we propose a modular loss function comprising a mathematically-sound functional highlighting the vessels and a binary cross-entropy-like supervised loss function. It results in four different versions. We first recall the Blake-Zisserman functional that is the second-order counterpart [3] of the Mumford-Shah [19] functional with the elliptic approximation introduced by Ambrosio, Faina, and March [2] that inspires our work. We then present our two modified versions in a supervised or unsupervised way L_{MBZ}, which will significantly improve the segmentation of thin blood vessels.

Let Ω be an open bounded subset of $\mathbb{R}^2$ of class $\mathcal{C}^1$, the spatial image domain, and $I : \Omega \to [0, 1]$ the image. Since the first-order Mumford-Shah functional fails to capture the second-order discontinuities that are crease points and one-pixel-wide features, and the "gradient limit" effect also leads to over-segmentation in the regions with steep gradients, Blake and Zisserman [3] proposed to minimize a second-order variational functional

$$BZ(u, K_0, K_1) = \mu \int_{\Omega \setminus (K_0 \cup K_1)} |u - I|^2 \, dx + \int_{\Omega \setminus (K_0 \cup K_1)} |\nabla^2 u|^2 \, dx \tag{3}$$
$$+ \alpha \mathcal{H}^1(K_0 \cap \Omega) + \beta \mathcal{H}^1((K_1 \setminus K_0) \cap \Omega)$$

over K_0, K_1 with $K_0 \cup K_1 \in \overline{\Omega}$ closed, $u \in C^2(\Omega \setminus (K_0 \cup K_1))$, u approximately continuous on $\Omega \setminus K_0$, $\mu, \alpha, \beta > 0$, and $\mathcal{H}^1$ denoting the one-dimensional Hausdorff measure so that $\mathcal{H}^1(K_0 \cap \Omega)$ measures the length of the edge set K_0. K_0 is the set of discontinuity points, and $K_1 \setminus K_0$ represents the set of gradient discontinuity points. The gradient discontinuities are crucial to the finest blood vessel segmentation. Indeed, the very weak thickness of these structures makes them invisible to first-order methods and results in low contrast.

To solve this problem numerically, Ambrosio, Faina, and March [2] approximate (3) with a family of elliptic functionals in the sense of Γ-convergence. The key idea is to reformulate the functional (3) with respect to two new variables (u, s), u still being a smooth approximation of the original image and s relates to $K = K_1 \setminus K_0$ so that s is close to 1 almost everywhere except on the set K where it is close to 0. They have shown that under certain conditions the following functionals Γ-converge to (3) as $\epsilon \to 0^+$

$$F_\epsilon(u, s) = \int_\Omega (s^2 + \kappa_\epsilon) |\nabla^2 u|^2 + \mu |u - I|^2 + \beta \left(\epsilon |\nabla s|^2 + \frac{(s-1)^2}{4\epsilon} \right) dx \tag{4}$$

where $\kappa_\epsilon = o(\epsilon^4)$ and the unknown s simulates the first and second-order discontinuities of u. By minimizing (4), the first term forces s to be close to zero where the Hessian norm of u is high and the gradient presents discontinuities. In the last term, $|\nabla s|$ prevents oscillations in the function s while $\frac{(s-1)^2}{4\epsilon}$ in opposition to the first term forces s to be 1 almost everywhere on Ω.

Inspired by (4), we construct a new loss function for fine structure segmentation by considering only the variable s as the segmentation result in a supervised $(^S)$ or unsupervised $(^{US})$ setting. In a discrete setting, let us consider I a grayscale fundus image, a non-mixed second partial derivative (*i.e.* $\frac{\partial^2 I}{\partial x^2}$ or $\frac{\partial^2 I}{\partial y^2}$) computed with a Sobel operator applied twice, and a blood vessel whose direction is not parallel to the direction of the second derivative. Since blood vessels in the fundus image have a lower intensity than the background, pixels close to the inner and outer edges of blood vessels have a great positive/negative second partial derivative. respectively. On the contrary, pixels in homogeneous regions have low values of second partial derivatives. It motivates the use of the following transformation instead of the Hessian norm:

$$
\underset{max,2}{\Delta} I_{i,j} = \max\left(\frac{\partial^2 I_{i,j}}{\partial x^2}, 0\right)^2 + \max\left(\frac{\partial^2 I_{i,j}}{\partial y^2}, 0\right)^2, \tag{5}
$$

where $I_{i,j}$ denotes the intensity of the pixel at coordinate (i,j). The square reduces background noise. To further reduce it, we propose a supervised version of our modified Blake-Zisserman loss function in which we multiply the proposed transformation (5) by a smooth version of the ground truth. It relies on the hypothesis that if the ground truth is missing a vessel, then it must be close to the ones annotated in it due to the vascular tree structure and be detected by the second-order information of the original image. Transformation (5) gives a thinner representation of the vessels, as shown in Fig. 3, especially on the finest blood vessels, and the supervised version gives a cleaner version. Inspired by (4), we define the modified Blake-Zisserman loss function in a discrete setting as follows

$$
L_{MBZ}(P) = \beta \frac{1}{NM} \sum_{i,j=1}^{N,M} \epsilon |\nabla P_{i,j}|^2 + \frac{P_{i,j}^2}{4\epsilon} + \frac{1}{NM} \sum_{i,j=1}^{N,M} ((P_{i,j}-1)^2 + \kappa_\epsilon) \tag{6}
$$

$$
\times \left| \begin{array}{ll} \underset{max,2}{\Delta} \text{CLAHE}(I)_{i,j} & \text{unsupervised version } L_{MBZ}^{US}(P) \\ \underset{max,2}{\Delta} \text{CLAHE}(I)_{i,j} \times (G_\sigma * Y)_{i,j} & \text{supervised version } L_{MBZ}^{S}(P,Y) \end{array} \right.
$$

with $I : \{1,\ldots,N\} \times \{1,\ldots,M\} \to \mathbb{R}$ a grayscale fundus image, P the unknown probabilistic map generated by the model where $P_{i,j}$ is the probability that pixel (i,j) is a vessel, G_σ a Gaussian kernel with standard deviation σ and Y the ground truth of I where $Y_{i,j}$ is 1 if the pixel (i,j) is a vessel and 0 otherwise. Contrast Limited Adaptive Histogram Equalization (CLAHE) [31] is applied to the original image before computing (5) to enhance the contrast. Unlike histogram equalization, CLAHE improves contrast locally. This algorithm provides a better second-order description of small vessels but introduces significant noise into the segmentation. We apply a Gaussian blur to limit the noise, but the kernel size and standard deviation must remain small to keep the second-order information of thin structures. Again, the supervised version of our modified Blake-Zisserman loss function aims to reduce the noise by forcing the matrix to be zero outside the smooth vascular tree. Contrary to the initial Blake-Zisserman approximation and to comply with the traditional segmentation map, the first term forces P to be one inside blood vessels, and the last one to be zero outside. The ∇P term smoothes and helps P to be one in vessels so large that not all their inner pixels have a positive second derivative.

We then complement our loss function with the binary cross-entropy L_{BCE} to learn meaningful information from a few annotated data. Two versions are also studied: (i) one is the traditional binary cross-entropy between the ground truth and the produced segmentation (L_{BCE}) while (ii) the other combines the classic binary cross-entropy with a version including second-order information, that is, we compute the binary cross-entropy between a binarised version of (5) applied to the smoothed CLAHE image (L^H_{BCE}). The motivation for introducing the second version is to give more weight to the thinnest blood vessels that the binary cross-entropy traditionally neglects. The definitions are as follows:

$$L_{BCE}(P,Y) = -\frac{1}{NM} \sum_{i,j=1}^{N,M} Y_{i,j} \log(P_{i,j}) + (1 - Y_{i,j}) \log(1 - P_{i,j}) \tag{7}$$

$$L^H_{BCE}(P,Y) = 0.5 L_{BCE}(P,Y) + 0.5 L_{BCE}(P, \underset{max,2}{\Delta} \text{CLAHE}(I))$$

where P and Y are as in (6) the model ouput and the ground truth of I.

The objective function results in

$$L = L_{BCE} + \alpha L_{MBZ} \tag{8}$$

with $\alpha > 0$ to adjust the weight of each function and with four versions $L_{BCE} + L^{US}_{MBZ}$, $L_{BCE} + L^S_{MBZ}$, $L^H_{BCE} + L^{US}_{MBZ}$ and $L^H_{BCE} + L^S_{MBZ}$.

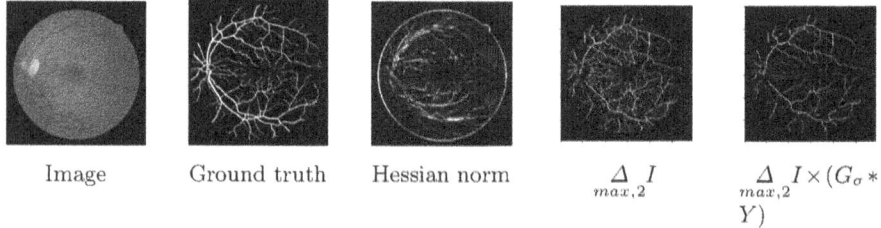

| Image | Ground truth | Hessian norm | $\underset{max,2}{\Delta} I$ | $\underset{max,2}{\Delta} I \times (G_\sigma * Y)$ |

Fig. 3. Example of the Hessian norm, the transformation $\underset{max,2}{\Delta}$ and the transformation $\underset{max,2}{\Delta}$ multiplied by a smooth version of the ground truth computed on a fundus image.

3.3   Network Architecture for the 2 Cascaded U-Nets

We use two cascaded U-Nets based on the original architecture [22]. Each network consists of a contracting encoder, where the number of feature channels doubles at each level (input channels/64/128/256/512), followed by a symmetric decoder that restores the spatial resolution. Each convolutional layer uses a ReLU activation, and the corresponding encoder-decoder feature maps are joined via skip connections. The final layer is a 1×1 convolution with sigmoid activation to produce the output probability map.

3.4   Datasets

We evaluate the performance of our model on the two most popular publicly available datasets. DRIVE [25] includes 40 fundus images of dimension 565×584 acquired with a Canon CR non-mydriatic 3CCD with a field of view (FOV) of 45 degrees. The image set is divided into 20 training images and 20 test images. Seven images show signs of mild diabetic retinopathy, while the other 33 are healthy. CHASEDB1 [20] contains images of the left and right retina of 14 children, thus forming a set of 28 images of dimension 999×960. These images, having the particularity of being centered according to the optical disc, were captured using a portable Nidek NM-200-D camera FOV of 30°C.

4   Experiments and Results

We run an ablation study and a comparison with state-of-the-art fully-supervised, semi-supervised, and partially-supervised methods to demonstrate the performance of our model.

4.1   Experimental Details

Implementation Details: Our model is implemented in Python with the PyTorch library and trained with a PNY NVIDIA V100 GPU. Training time ranges from approximately 3 to 12 min, depending on the dataset. Both U-Net are optimized using Adam [13] for 150 epochs with a learning rate of 0.001, $\beta_1 = 0.9$ and $\beta_2 = 0.999$. They have the same architecture except for the first block, which has a depth of 10 for U-Net 1 and a depth of 1 for U-Net 2. We use the LIOT implementation given by the authors for the four basic directions. We use the eight nearest neighbors to compute the transformation with the eigenvector direction. In the loss function L we set α to 0.7 for DRIVE and to 0.07 CHASEDB1. In L_{MBZ}, we set $\beta = 0.5$, $\epsilon = 0.1$ and $\kappa_\epsilon = 0$.

Setups: To evaluate our model, we use seven distinct training subsets of two images for DRIVE and six distinct subsets of four images for CHASEDB1. In addition, we used two validation images to optimize the hyperparameters of the model. Testing on DRIVE is performed on the original test set from this database. On CHASEDB1, we use 22 images for testing. We apply zero padding to convert DRIVE images from 565×584 to 592×592 and CHASEDB1 images from 999×960 to 1008×1008.

Evaluation Metrics: To evaluate the performance of our model, we use four commonly adopted metrics on the retinal vascular tree, namely Accuracy (Acc), Sensitivity (Sen), Specificity (Spe), and the Dice coefficient (Dice) [26]. Acc, Sen, Spe, and Dice are computed using a binary mask to remove artifacts on the fundus edges.

4.2   Ablation Study

In this ablation study, we exhibit the influence of each part of our model. We therefore performed experiments without the pre-processing step, with the original LIOT pre-processing , with the concatenation of the original LIOT and $(J^+(v_{max}), J^-(v_{max}))$ leading to a 6-channel image that we have named LIOT EIG, and with our 10-channel version LIOT 10, to prove the impact of our modification in the pre-processing step. We also evaluate the model without using the post-processing step. We then conducted experiments with the classic BCE loss and then with our four modular versions to show the improvement in metrics by adding second-order information in the loss function. Finally, we demonstrated interest in the second cascaded U-Net by running experiments with and without it. The quantitative results are shown in Table 4.

In Fig. 4, we draw attention to the influence of our pre-processing step on the results, especially in the reconstruction of the last branches of the vascular tree. Indeed, embedding Hessian information in the pre-processing stage improves the segmentation accuracy of the thinnest blood vessels. We also see that adding second-order information in the loss function significantly improves the segmentation of the smallest vessels with the pre-processing step.

Finally, we have studied the impact of the selected training subsets on the performance of our model. The Dice scores are reported in Table 3. We observe some variability in the results, especially on the second training subset used in DRIVE. Another important fact is that usually the best results are obtained with the version $L_{BCE} + L^{US}_{MBZ}$, and thus the visual results only report this version.

4.3   Comparison Results

We report the means and standard deviations obtained on the DRIVE subsets in Table 1. The 'Ratio' column represents the percentage of annotated images from the training set used to train the models. We recall that we trained our network fully supervised for all four proposed versions.

The metrics obtained in Table 1 show that our modular model, regardless of the chosen configuration, with only two labeled images needed for the training, gives competitive results compared to state-of-the-art methods in a semi-supervised or partially-supervised setting. It outperforms semi-supervised methods using less than 30% annotated and 70% unlabeled data. It is close to the results obtained with the partially-supervised technique using 5% annotated, and 95% unlabeled data. Furthermore, the gap with the fully supervised baseline technique is only 5% DICE. Increasing the number of annotations from 10% to 40% for training our model provides significantly better metrics, as expected with the used architecture. However, the difference is slightly lower compared to other methods. We would also like to highlight that in contrast to our model and other semi-supervised approaches, where the annotated training subset is fixed before learning, the process of Xu et al. requires manual annotation of a small portion of new images at each training iteration. This explains the difference in performance.

In Table 2, we evaluate our model on the CHASEDB1 dataset. Since all the compared models provide the number of annotated images, we replace the "Ratio" column with "Labels" corresponding to the number of labeled images for training. Using four annotated images, we obtain a higher Acc than the two semi-supervised models trained with fewer than five annotations. Adding 4 labeled images for training leads to the Dice increasing from a mean of 77.78% to 79.53%. The quantitative results obtained on CHASEDB1 corroborate those obtained on DRIVE.

Table 1. Comparison results on the DRIVE dataset. FS, SS, and PS denote fully-supervised, semi-supervised, and partially-supervised, respectively.

Method	Type	Ratio	Acc(%)	Sen(%)	Spe(%)	Dice(%)
Lahiri et al. [15]	SS	15%	90	–	–	–
		30%	93	–	–	–
		60%	95	–	–	–
SCANet [23]	SS	10%	94.23	65.47	97.06	–
		30%	95.87	71.99	97.23	–
		60%	96.62	82.08	98.00	–
LeakGAN [8]	SS	15%	93.31	88.52	94.31	–
		25%	94.69	83.14	97.00	–
		40%	95.74	86.72	97.50	–
Chen et al. [4]	SS	20%	95.53	–	–	–
		55%	96.31	–	–	–
Xu et al. [28]	PS	5%	96.18	80.20	97.68	78.75
		7.5%	96.30	80.88	97.88	79.19
FR-UNet [18]	FS	100%	97.05	83.56	98.37	83.16
Our model	FS	10%-$L_{BCE} + L_{MBZ}^{US}$	96.13±0.09	77.83±0.67	97.91±0.06	77.78±0.54
		10%-$L_{BCE}^{H} + L_{MBZ}^{US}$	96.09±0.11	77.35±0.74	97.91±0.10	77.52±0.64
		10%-L_{BCE}	95.98±0.09	76.19±0.77	97.90±0.07	76.76±0.54
		10%-$L_{BCE} + L_{MBZ}^{S}$	96.07±0.07	76.75±1.39	97.95±0.13	77.29±0.52
		10%-$L_{BCE}^{H} + L_{MBZ}^{S}$	96.07±0.08	77.22±0.86	97.90±0.13	77.41±0.37
		40%-$L_{BCE} + L_{MBZ}^{US}$	96.45	79.27	98.12	79.51

We observe by looking at the metrics in Tables 1 and 2 and visual results in Figs. 5, 6, and 4, that the inclusion of second-order information in both the pre-processing and the loss function improves the quality of the results. It, therefore, justifies the use of this relevant information. Mainly, it helps reconstruct the thinnest blood vessels, as shown in Fig. 4, and reduces false positives, as illustrated in Fig. 6.

232   B. Chivet et al.

Table 2. Comparison results on the CHASEDB1 dataset. FS, SS, and PS denote fully-supervised, semi-supervised, and partially-supervised, respectively.

Method	Type	Labels	Acc(%)	Sen(%)	Spe(%)	Dice(%)
LeakGAN [8]	SS	3	94.20	80.78	94.25	–
		5	96.65	92.03	92.25	–
		8	96.83	92.21	94.72	–
SCANet [23]	SS	2	95.73	49.55	99.32	–
		4	96.36	72.18	98.22	–
		8	97.37	82.53	98.21	–
FR-UNet [18]	FS	20	97.48	87.98	98.14	81.51
Our model	FS	4-$L_{BCE} + L_{MBZ}^{US}$	96.93±0.04	79.10±0.49	98.29±0.07	77.97±0.44
		4-$L_{BCE}^{H} + L_{MBZ}^{US}$	96.81±0.10	78.15±0.63	98.24±0.14	77.17±0.66
		4-L_{BCE}	96.84±0.04	78.28±0.71	98.26±0.08	77.31±0.32
		4-$L_{BCE} + L_{MBZ}^{S}$	96.91±0.08	78.07±0.91	98.36±0.13	77.68±0.58
		4-$L_{BCE}^{H} + L_{MBZ}^{S}$	96.86±0.07	77.39±1.09	98.35±0.14	77.23±0.50
		8-$L_{BCE} + L_{MBZ}^{US}$	97.17	79.52	98.51	79.53

Table 3. Dice score (%) evaluated on distinct image subsets: seven samples of two images for DRIVE and six samples of four images for CHASEDB1.

Method	DRIVE							CHASEDB1					
Image subset	1	2	3	4	5	6	7	1	2	3	4	5	6
$L_{BCE} + L_{MBZ}^{US}$	**78.49**	76.98	**78.16**	78.20	**78.10**	77.19	**77.38**	**77.26**	**78.24**	**78.40**	78.43	77.49	**78.00**
$L_{BCE}^{H} + L_{MBZ}^{US}$	78.04	76.63	77.70	**78.67**	77.15	**77.49**	76.96	76.26	77.62	77.84	77.94	76.43	76.96
L_{BCE}	77.42	76.55	76.40	77.67	76.10	76.89	76.30	76.98	77.17	77.49	77.94	77.25	77.04
$L_{BCE} + L_{MBZ}^{S}$	77.68	76.19	77.80	77.79	77.12	77.28	77.22	76.58	77.54	78.14	**78.44**	**77.59**	77.81
$L_{BCE}^{H} + L_{MBZ}^{S}$	77.69	**76.99**	77.78	77.98	77.31	77.20	76.95	76.78	77.81	77.27	77.35	76.40	77.79

Table 4. Ablation study on the DRIVE dataset using $L_{BCE} + L_{MBZ}^{US}$ as the loss function.

Method	Acc(%)	Sen(%)	Spe(%)	Dice(%)
No Post-processing	96.01±0.08	76.93±0.54	97.86±0.09	77.1±0.44
No Pre-processing	94.78±0.88	70.58±2.97	97.15±0.95	70.48±2.89
LIOT	95.88±0.07	76.68±0.57	97.74±0.09	76.44±0.35
LIOT EIG	96.03±0.09	77.09±0.92	97.87±0.10	77.18±0.56
LIOT 10 (Our model)	96.13±0.09	77.83±0.67	97.91±0.06	77.78±0.54

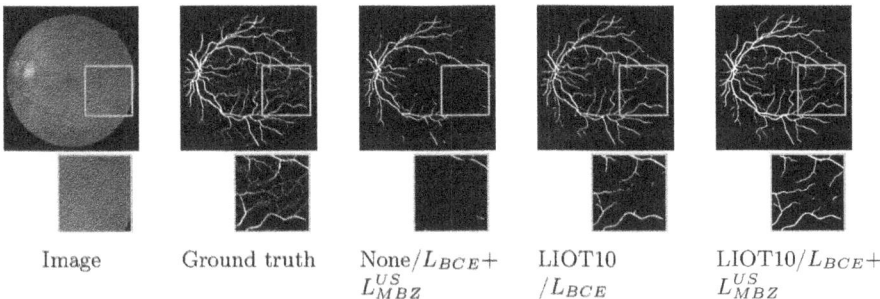

| Image | Ground truth | None/$L_{BCE}+$ L_{MBZ}^{US} | LIOT10 /L_{BCE} | LIOT10/$L_{BCE}+$ L_{MBZ}^{US} |

Fig. 4. Impact of pre-processing step in our pipeline with an image from the DRIVE dataset with a zoomed-in view in the second row. Without the pre-processing step, the vascular network is poorly segmented.

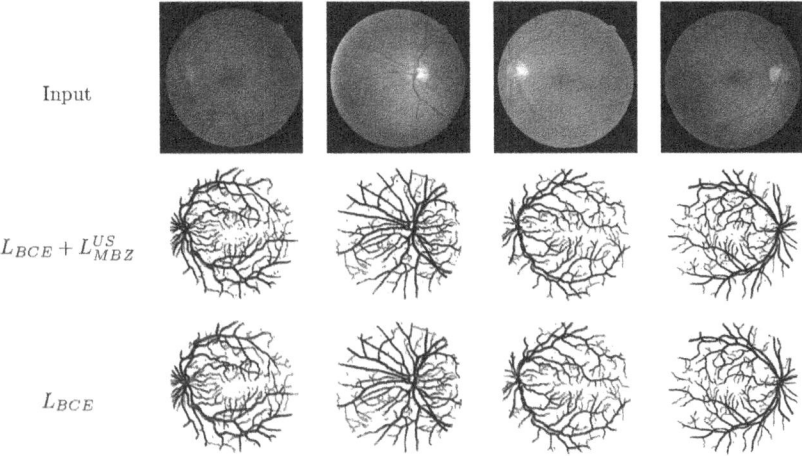

Input

$L_{BCE} + L_{MBZ}^{US}$

L_{BCE}

Fig. 5. Visualization of the segmentations on testing images from DRIVE. Colors: black$\rightarrow$ TP, white$\rightarrow$ TN, red$\rightarrow$ FP, magenta$\rightarrow$ FN. We observe that $L_{BCE} + L_{MBZ}^{US}$ yields a better segmentation of the smallest vessels in the right region of the first column images, and in the upper region of the third column images. (Color figure online)

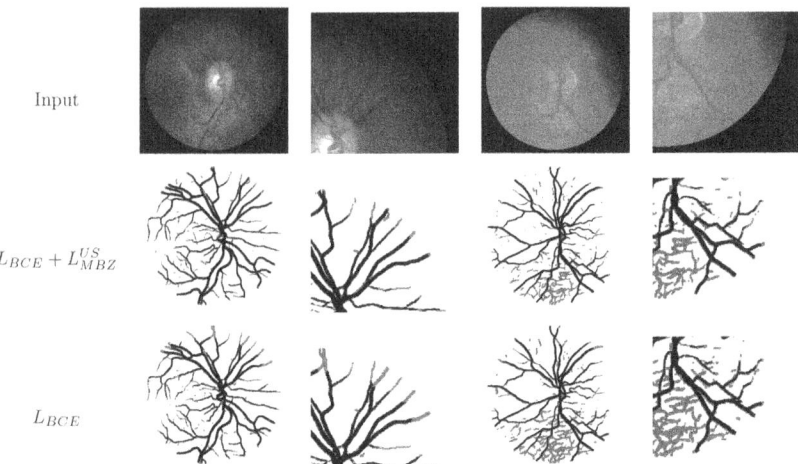

Fig. 6. Visualization of the segmentations (with zoomed parts) on testing images from CHASEDB1. Colors: black→ TP, white→ TN, red→ FP, magenta→ FN. The second column shows that the Hessian-based modular loss enables deeper segmentation of the vascular tree. The last column shows that it reduces false positives. (Color figure online)

5   Conclusion

To conclude, we proposed a novel fully-supervised modular framework requiring extremely few annotations for retinal vessel segmentation based on second-order information. It consists of a three-step process, including a modified LIOT pre-processing, a U-Net architecture trained with a new modular loss function composed of a modified Blake-Zisserman functional and the binary cross-entropy, and a U-Net architecture with a binary cross-entropy loss to enhance and clean the segmentation results. Quantitative and qualitative results show that our method outperforms state-of-the-art methods using few annotations. In future work, we will extend our framework to the 3D case and study its generalization to liver blood vessel segmentation.

References

1. Alom, M., et al.: Recurrent residual convolutional neural network for medical image segmentation. J. Med. Imaging **6**(1), 014006 (2019)
2. Ambrosio, L., et al.: Variational approximation of a second order free discontinuity problem in computer vision. SIAM J. Math. Anal. **32**(6), 1171–1197 (2001)
3. Blake, A., Zisserman, A.: Visual Reconstruction. The MIT Press, Cambridge (1987)
4. Chen, D., et al.: Semi-supervised learning method of U-Net deep learning network for blood vessel segmentation in retinal images. Symmetry **12**(7) (2020)
5. Goodfellow, I., et al.: Generative adversarial nets. In: Ghahramani, Z., et al. (eds.) NIPS 2014, vol. 27 (2014)

6. Guo, C., et al.: SA-UNet: spatial attention U-Net for retinal vessel segmentation. In: IEEE ICPR 2020, pp. 1236–1242 (2021)

7. Hou, J.M., et al.: A semi-supervised retinal vessel segmentation method via adaptive uncertainty estimation. In: IEEE EMBC 2024, pp. 1–5 (2024)

8. Hou, J., et al.: Semi-supervised semantic segmentation of vessel images using leaking perturbations. In: IEEE/CVF WACV 2022, pp. 1769–1778 (2022)

9. Huo, Q., Tang, G., Zhang, F.: Particle swarm optimization for great enhancement in semi-supervised retinal vessel segmentation with generative adversarial networks. In: Liao, H., et al. (eds.) MLMECH/CVII-STENT -2019. LNCS, vol. 11794, pp. 112–120. Springer, Cham (2019).

10. Jerman, T., Pernuš, F., Likar, B., Špiclin, Ž.: Beyond frangi: an improved multiscale vesselness filter. In: Medical Imaging 2015: Image Processing, vol. 9413, pp. 623–633. SPIE (2015)

11. Jin, Q., et al.: DUNet: a deformable network for retinal vessel segmentation. Knowl.-Based Syst. **178**, 149–162 (2019)

12. Kanski, J.J., Bowling, B.: Clinical ophthalmology: a systematic approach

13. Kingma, D.P., Ba, J.: Adam: a method for stochastic optimization. In: ICLR 2015 (2015)

14. Kuruba, C., Gopalan, N.: Robust blood vessel detection with image enhancement using relative intensity order transformation and deep learning. Biomed. Signal Process. Control **86**, 105195 (2023)

15. Lahiri, A., et al.: Retinal vessel segmentation under extreme low annotation: a GAN based semi-supervised approach. In: IEEE ICIP 2020, pp. 418–422 (2020)

16. Lee, J., et al.: Improved census transform for noise robust stereo matching. Opt. Eng. **55**(6), 063107 (2016)

17. Li, J., et al.: Multimodal image matching: a scale-invariant algorithm and an open dataset. SPRS J. Photogramm. Remote Sens. **204**, 77–88 (2023)

18. Liu, W., et al.: Full-resolution network and dual-threshold iteration for retinal vessel and coronary angiograph segmentation. IEEE J. Biomed. Health. Inf. **26**(9), 4623–4634 (2022)

19. Mumford, D., Shah, J.: Optimal approximations by piecewise smooth functions and associated variational problems. Commun. Pure Appl. Math. **42**, 577–685 (1989)

20. Owen, C.G., et al.: Measuring retinal vessel tortuosity in 10-Year-old children: validation of the computer-assisted image analysis of the retina (CAIAR) program. Invest. Ophthalmol. Vis. Sci. **50**(5), 2004–2010 (2009)

21. Peng, Y., et al.: Curvilinear object segmentation in medical images based on ODoS filter and deep learning network. Appl. Intell. **53**(20), 23470–23481 (2023)

22. Ronneberger, O., Fischer, P., Brox, T.: U-Net: convolutional networks for biomedical image segmentation. In: Navab, N., Hornegger, J., Wells, W.M., Frangi, A.F. (eds.) MICCAI 2015. LNCS, vol. 9351, pp. 234–241. Springer, Cham (2015).

23. Shen, N., et al.: SCANet: a unified semi-supervised learning framework for vessel segmentation. IEEE Trans. Med. Imaging **42**(9), 2476–2489 (2023)

24. Shi, T., et al.: Local intensity order transformation for robust curvilinear object segmentation. IEEE Trans. Image Process. **31**, 2557–2569 (2022)

25. Staal, J., et al.: Ridge-based vessel segmentation in color images of the retina. IEEE Trans. Med. Imaging **23**(4), 501–509 (2004)

26. Sule, O.O.: A survey of deep learning for retinal blood vessel segmentation methods: taxonomy, trends, challenges and future directions. IEEE Access **10**, 38202–38236 (2022)

27. Tarvainen, A., Valpola, H.: Mean teachers are better role models: weight-averaged consistency targets improve semi-supervised deep learning results. In: NIPS 2017 (2018)
28. Xu, Y., et al.: Partially-supervised learning for vessel segmentation in ocular images. In: de Bruijne, M., et al. (eds.) MICCAI 2021. LNCS, vol. 12901, pp. 271–281. Springer, Cham (2021).
29. Zabih, R., Woodfill, J.: Non-parametric local transforms for computing visual correspondence. In: Eklundh, J.-O. (ed.) ECCV 1994. LNCS, vol. 801, pp. 151–158. Springer, Heidelberg (1994).
30. Zhang, H., et al.: Mixup: beyond empirical risk minimization. In: ICLR 2018 (2018)
31. Zuiderveld, K.: VIII.5. - contrast limited adaptive histogram equalization. In: Heckbert, P.S. (ed.) Graphics Gems, pp. 474–485. Academic Press (1994)

Diffusion with Adversarial Fine-Tuning for Improving Rare Retinal Disease Diagnosis

Dominika Iwanicka$^{(\boxtimes)}$ and Ping Lu

University of Leeds, Leeds, UK
{sc20dzi,p.lu}@leeds.ac.uk

Abstract. As machine-aided disease diagnosis becomes more common, there is a rising need for high volumes of quality data, which might be unavailable for rare diseases. Generative methods offer a solution, allowing for synthesising realistic-looking data that can improve diagnosis accuracy. We investigate the applications of diffusion to a small, imbalanced dataset of Optical Coherence Tomography (OCT) images. We propose modifying the basic Denoising Diffusion Probabilistic Model with attention mechanisms, a class-aware training strategy, and the addition of adversarial fine-tuning. We demonstrate that this model is capable of synthesising realistic-looking images with class-specific features even for diseases with as little as 22 samples. We achieve values of FID at 62.58, and CLIP Similarity at 0.96. We show that the addition of generated data in the training dataset improves the overall and class-specific performance of a ResNet18 classifier on the OCT data, offering an improvement for downstream tasks such as rare retinal disease diagnosis.

Keywords: Medical imaging · Data augmentation · Deep Learning · Generative artificial intelligence · Diffusion models

1 Introduction

Retinal diseases are a becoming increasingly common, affecting over 2.5 million people in the UK alone [1]. Early and accurate diagnosis is crucial, and imaging technologies like Optical Coherence Tomography (OCT) provide high-resolution, cross-sectional images of the retina, allowing for a detailed visualisation of the pathological changes and enabling disease assessment.

In the recent years, machine learning has become prevalent in medical image analysis. Automated retinal disease classification based on OCT has shown promise in improving diagnostic accuracy, however the performance of these ML models relies on the availability of large quantities of labelled data [2]. Class imbalance is a particular challenge – in many existing datasets, certain diseases are underrepresented and lack the sufficient number of samples to enable accurate classification. This can lead to biased predictions, as the model can achieve good accuracy scores by generalising to the common conditions.

© The Author(s), under exclusive license to Springer Nature Switzerland AG 2026
S. Ali et al. (Eds.): MIUA 2025, LNCS 15918, pp. 237–250, 2026.
https://doi.org/10.1007/978-3-031-98694-9_17

Most of the existing OCT classification models focus on the retinal diseases that occur frequently and therefore have a lot of data available, however the rare diseases often get left out due to the insufficient number of samples. For example, Age-Related Macular Degeneration (AMD) is a condition that affects over 25% of people over 60 years old in Europe [3]. The dataset used in this study [4] includes images of conditions such as Retinal Artery Occlusion (RAO), which affects 0.7% of people over 55 years old in Europe [5]. AMD is included in most existing OCT classifiers and is diagnosed with a good accuracy [6–9], but RAO is not included in any of the existing models. This is the case for multiple other diseases as well. In a world where machine-aided diagnosis is on the rise, such discrepancies could lead to generalisation and misdiagnosis.

To address this problem, generative data augmentation techniques have been explored to synthesise new, high-quality medical images. A model trained on such data could become more robust and learn to classify rare conditions better. Among the existing techniques, diffusion models have emerged in the recent years as a promising technique for medical image synthesis, enabling the creation of diverse samples that could be indistinguishable from real ones. However, this task is particularly challenging due to the small volume of data for certain diseases. While diffusion has achieved promising results when trained on an unconditional dataset of 1000 images [10], we are the first ones to consider its applications for a conditional dataset with some classes having as little as 22 samples.

In this work, we investigate the use of diffusion models to augment a small, imbalanced OCT dataset. A Denoising Diffusion Probabilist Model is used as a baseline, and various techniques are implemented to improve the model's ability to focus on the overall structure and learn the fine-grained details of the retina. We evaluate the performance of a classifier model trained on the original dataset, a dataset with only basic geometric augmentation, and a dataset with generative data augmentation.

We present a diffusion model modified with attention mechanisms, adversarial fine-tuning, and and a class-aware training strategy to address the challenge of generating data based on a small, imbalanced dataset. The proposed model is capable of synthesising realistic-looking data, and the inclusion of such data in the training for a classifier improves overall and class-wise performance.

The contributions of this paper can be summarised as follows:

- We present a novel diffusion model for synthesising OCT images for a small, strongly imbalanced dataset.
- In particular, we modify a DDPM with attention mechanisms and propose a multi-step training process that modulates the class embedding weight and incorporates adversarial fine-tuning.
- We demonstrate that the proposed model can synthesise realistic-looking OCT data for classes with as little as 22 images in the original dataset.
- In addition, we show that retinal disease classification based on OCT data is significantly improved with the inclusion of synthetic data in the training dataset.

2   Related Work

Data quantity and distribution have been highlighted as significant limitations in the potential applications of deep learning in the medical field [11,12]. Augmenting the dataset is a common approach for tackling this problem. Basic augmentations, such as geometric transformations or intensity operations, are used in most studies and can improve model performance [13]. Over the past years, image synthesis has been used as a form of generative data augmentation. It has shown a lot of promise and outperformed models trained on datasets with no augmentation or basic transformations only [13,14].

Diffusion has emerged as a promising solution to medical image synthesis, allowing for generating high-quality data [15–19]. Denoising Diffusion Probabilistic Models (DDPM) were introduced in 2020 [20] as a novel approach that utilises a noise scheduler in the forward process and a UNet backbone to reverse the noise. DDPMs have since been successfully used for a variety of medical tasks, such as image segmentation [19,21], denoising [22], or classification [23], amongst multiple others [24]. DDPMs have also performed well on small and imbalanced datasets [25]. An existing study on few-shot image synthesis shows that diffusion can generate images based on an unconditional dataset of as little as 1000 images [10]. Gupta et al. [26] demonstrate the applications of diffusion to few-shot synthesis on a conditional dataset.

The performance of diffusion models can be further improved by utilising attention mechanisms in the UNet model used for denoising [27–29]. Amongst these, Multi-headed Self Attention is a prominent variant that allows the model to learn global, long-range dependencies between input and output [30]. Another promising approach to refining the model is discriminator guided training, which incorporates the predictions of a discriminator to correct the diffusion model and helps improve its generative performance [31–33].

3   Methods

3.1   Denoising Diffusion Probabilistic Models

Denoising Diffusion Probabilistic Models [20] learn to generate new data by gradually removing noise from an image.

The forward process adds noise to images from the dataset by following a pre-defined noise schedule. It is described by a Markov chain where Gaussian noise is added to an image x_0 over T timesteps according to a variance schedule β. The noisy image for a timestep t is given by:

$$x_t = \sqrt{1 - \beta_t} x_{t-1} + \sqrt{\beta_t} \epsilon_T$$

where ϵ is sampled from a standard distribution. At $t = T$, the image becomes pure random noise.

The reverse process uses a model to progressively denoise the image. Starting from pure noise at $t = T$, it predicts the noise $\epsilon_\theta(x_t, t)$ at the previous timestep.

A UNet neural network serves as the backbone of this model. The prediction is then used to remove noise from the image as follows:

$$x_{t-1} = \frac{1}{\sqrt{\alpha_t}} \left(x_t - \frac{1 - \alpha_t}{\sqrt{1 - \bar{\alpha}_t}} \epsilon_\theta(x_t, t) \right) + \sigma_t z$$

where $\alpha_t = 1 - \beta_t$ and z is random noise sample from a standard distribution. Over time, the model learns to generate entirely new images from pure random noise. Figure 1 illustrates the diffusion process.

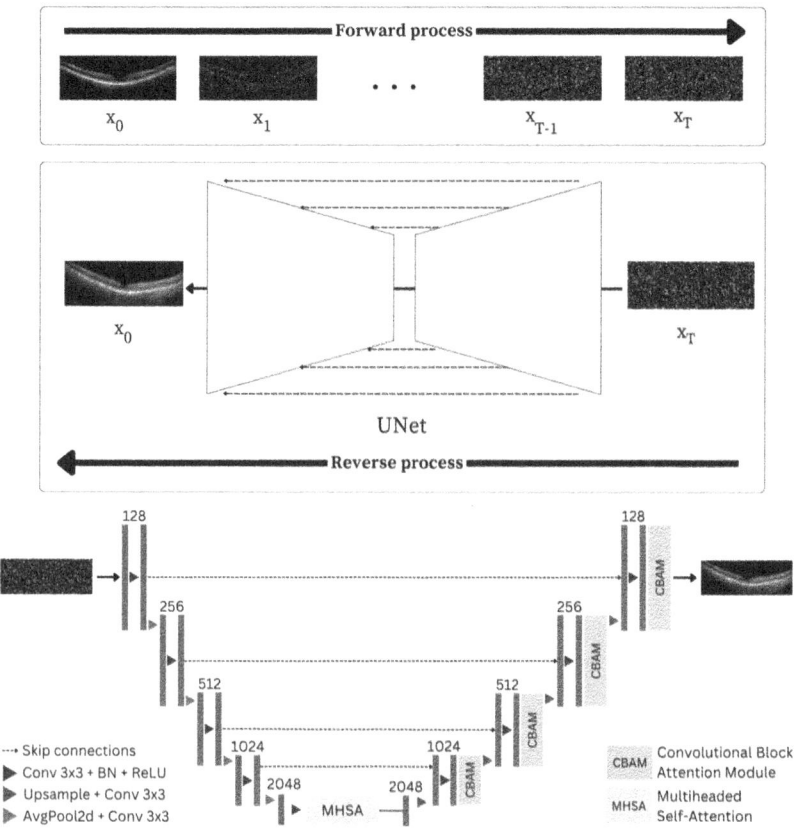

Fig. 1. An overview of the forward and reverse diffusion processes is at the top. The forward process progressively adds noise to the image, and the reverse process uses a UNet to predict the noise and remove it. The UNet architecture is further detailed at the bottom.

3.2   Attention Mechanisms

To improve the model's ability to learn fine details, attention blocks were added to the UNet. At the bottleneck between downscaling and upsampling blocks,

Multi-Headed Self Attention (MHSA) was added. Each attention module captures the complex long-range dependencies across different locations, and the multiple heads allow for learning distinct relationships [34]. This can be crucial for preserving the structural integrity of the synthesised images.

In addition, Convolutional Block Attention Module (CBAM) was added at the end of each upsampling block in the UNet [35]. CBAM combines channel and spatial attention, which enhances feature representation by allowing the model to focus on the most relevant locations in an image. This improves the model's ability to learn fine-grained details, leading to a sharper output. The UNet architecture is illustrated in Fig. 1.

3.3 Class-Aware Training

To make the model conditional, class embeddings need to be introduced and passed as input for the UNet model. This allows for generating class-specific samples of each class. The class embeddings get added to the positional embeddings. A class embedding weight was added to control how strongly the model is influenced by the class vs positional embeddings.

Due to the existing class imbalances, class weights reflecting the proportions in the dataset were included and used in a weighted loss function, to ensure the model learns to represent all classes correctly. The loss is given by:

$$L = \frac{1}{N} \sum_{i=1}^{N} w_{y_i} L_{SmoothL1}(\epsilon_i, \hat{\epsilon}_i)$$

where N is the batch size, w is the class weight for a given class label y_i, and $\epsilon, \hat{\epsilon}$ represent the true noise and predicted noise respectively.

The imbalance of the original dataset posed a particular challenge in making the model explainable and learning the class-specific features. While training the model without class embeddings results in a good generalisation and reflects the structure of the retina well, a good understanding of the class characteristics is needed to accurately represent the rare diseases. We attempt to counter the imbalance through class-aware training, by modifying the class embedding weight throughout the training process.

3.4 Adversarial Fine-Tuning

A discriminator can be used during the diffusion training process to correct and guide the diffusion model [32,33]. This has been shown to improve the results generated by the model.

Initial results showed that the proposed diffusion model was learning the important features of the retina, but struggling to capture fine details. Similar to Generative Adversarial Networks, the discriminator learns to distinguish between real and synthetic images. The discriminator was then used in a loss function for the diffusion model, enhancing its ability to learn fine-grained details.

4 Experiments

4.1 Dataset

The dataset used for this study is the Optical Coherence Tomography Dataset (OCTDL) [4], which contains 2064 images and represents 7 retinal diseases: Age-related Macular Degeneration (AMD), Diabetic Macular Edema (DME), Epiretinal Membrane (ERM), Retinal Artery Occlusion (RAO), Retinal Vein Occlusion (RVO), and Vitreomacular Interface Disease (VID). Samples of the classes are shown in Fig. 2. The dataset presents a challenge because of its severe class imbalance, as the number of class samples range from 1231 for AMD to 22 for RAO, which reflects how common or rare the diseases are.

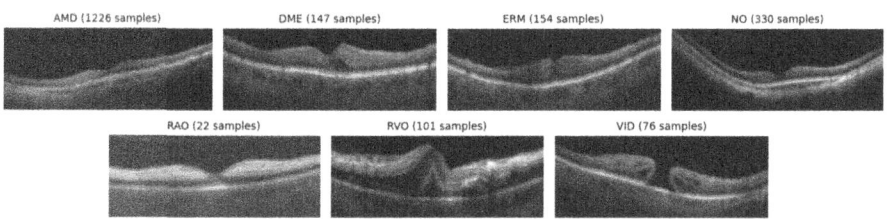

Fig. 2. Contents of the OCTDL dataset. Image captions denote class names and the number of samples.

The images in the dataset vary significantly in size. As part of the data preprocessing, 8 outliers were removed using a Z-score with a 2.5 threshold tuned experimentally. The remaining images all followed similar proportions, which were averaged to $width = 2.74 \times height$. All data points were resized according to this, using the minimum height found in the dataset, to ensure none of the images get stretched out. This resulted in a standardised dataset of 2056 images scaled to $(199, 546)$.

4.2 Implementation Details

Pre-processing. Basic data augmentation (horizontal flip) was applied to all classes except AMD to double their size. Additionally, the samples from RAO were further doubled by applying random rotation of 5–15° and decreasing their contrast. For training, the images were scaled down to $(94, 256)$ and normalised to $[-1, 1]$.

Hyperparameters. The baseline diffusion model utilises $T = 1000$ timesteps for the forward process and a 5-layer UNet as a backbone for the reverse process, with an 8-headed MHSA at the bottleneck. The UNet model was trained with a batch size of 8, Adam optimizer with a learning rate of 10^{-3}, and The Huber Loss (Smooth L1 Loss) with $\beta = 0.1$.

For adversarial fine-tuning, a simple discriminator was implemented consisting of 3 convolutional layers with batch normalisation, dropout with a 0.5 rate, and ReLU activation. The discriminator used a learning rate of 10^{-5} and a BCE loss function.

Training. The models were trained on the Aire HPC system at University of Leeds equipped with 3 NVIDIA L40S 48GB GPUs. All code was developed with Python 3.9 using Pytorch with CUDA support. The training time for the diffusion model was 7 h, followed by 20 h of fine-tuning.

The training was carried out in 3 steps:

1. The class embedding weight was set to 0 for a 100 epochs. This was done so that the model learned the overall structure of the retina without focusing on the class-specific features. Previous experiments have shown that including class embeddings from the start makes the model learn the common classes very well, but leads to poor performance for the smaller classes.
2. The class embedding weight was increased to 2 for the following 300 epochs, leading to the model learning class-specific features on top of the existing knowledge of retinal structure.
3. The diffusion model was trained alongside the discriminator for 100 epochs using an adversarial loss function, which used BCE to assess how well the discriminator distinguishes between real and fake images. This was used instead of the regular diffusion loss.

4.3 Evaluation Metrics

Quantitative Evaluation. We use Inception Score (IS), Fréchet Inception Distance (FID), Structural Similarity Index Measure (SSIM), and Peak Signal-to-Noise Ration (PSNR) for evaluation. FID calculates the difference between real and generated images by comparing the feature distribution, while IS measures the diversity of the generated images by assessing the confidence and variety of predictions made by a pre-trained classifier [36]. These are used as benchmarks in most studies on image generation. We utilise the CLIP Similarity [37] as an alternative to the inception-based metrics.

Additionally, we use SSIM and PSNR are to further assess image quality [38]. SSIM measures the perceptual similarity between the images, and PSNR expresses the ratio between the maximum power of a signal and the power of the noise. We combine the generative metrics (FID, IS, CLIP Similarity) with reconstruction metrics (SSIM and PSNR) to better assess the quality of the generated images.

Downstream Task Evaluation. We perform further evaluation by utilising a ResNet18 [39] classifier on three instances of the dataset: basic dataset, a dataset with geometric augmentations, and a dataset with generative augmentations performed by our best diffusion model. ResNet18 has been successfully used for OCT classification tasks in previous studies [9]. Previous works in this field highlight the importance of model evaluation on downstream tasks as opposed to relying only on metrics like FID or IS [40]. The classifier was trained for a 100 epochs using a batch size of 32 and the Adam optimiser with a learning rate of 10^{-3}. Prior to training, we set aside 20% of the original dataset for testing to ensure the model is evaluated only on real, unaugmented data.

5   Results

We use a DDPM model as a baseline for comparison against the proposed modifications - addition of attention modules, class-aware training, and adversarial fine-tuning. We analyse all configurations of these modifications to investigate their impact on the model's performance.

5.1   Quantitative Evaluation

Table 1 shows the quantitive evaluation for the diffusion models. The metrics were computed on 2000 images. An improvement for all metrics is visible for the final model. The lower FID value indicates a closer feature distribution between real and generated data, and the higher IS reflects the feature diversity. We noted that IS calculated for the original dataset was low, measuring 2.94 ± 0.17. While FID remains relatively high even for the best model, CLIP Similarity indicates a very good semantic similarity between the original and generated data. The increased SSIM and PSNR values show an improvement in perceptual and pixel-wise image similarity.

We can observe that in isolation, class-aware training brings the biggest improvement to the FID score, but adversarial fine-tuning influences IS, PSNR, and CLIP similarity more. SSIM only improves only with the combination of multiple additions. Including all three proposed modifications brings the best results across all metrics.

5.2   Generated Images

Table 2 showcases the synthesised images for four different classes, compared against images sampled from the original Dataset. In particular, we display AMD (1231 samples), RVO (101 samples), VID (76 samples), and RAO (22 samples) to demonstrate the performance of the different models on classes of varying sizes.

A visual inspection shows that a basic DDPM learns the general shape of the retina, but generalises too much. No class-specific features are visible, and the images for the smaller classes are more blurry and of a lower quality.

Table 1. Evaluation metrics of the proposed generative model with proposed modifications: attention modules (Atn.), class-aware training (CAT), and adversarial fine-tuning (AFT), compared to DDPM as a baseline. We measure the Inception Score (IS), Fréchet Inception Distance (FID), Structural Similarity Index Measure (SSIM), Peak Signal-to Noise Ratio (PSNR), and CLIP Similarity $\in [-1, 1]$. PSNR is given in dB.

Model configuration	IS ↑	FID ↓	SSIM ↑	PSNR ↑	CLIP Similarity ↑
DDPM	2.42 ± 0.01	160.02	0.43	7.04	0.83
DDPM + Atn.	2.72 ± 0.07	131.59	0.45	8.01	0.89
DDPM + CAT	2.36 ± 0.15	112.10	0.45	7.22	0.87
DDPM + AFT	2.85 ± 0.07	127.38	0.44	8.97	0.91
DDPM + Atn. + CAT	2.66 ± 0.09	74.26	0.47	8.04	0.93
DDPM + Atn. + AFT	2.73 ± 0.10	130.95	0.53	8.07	0.91
DDPM + CAT + AFT	2.79 ± 0.08	87.31	0.54	8.89	0.94
DDPM + Atn. + CAT + AFT	**2.91 ± 0.10**	**62.58**	**0.55**	**9.01**	**0.96**

Table 2. Images generated using the proposed model and basic DDPM, compared against the original. The images were randomly selected from the respective datasets. AMD (Age-related Macular Degeneration), RVO (Retinal Vein Occlusion), VID (Vitreomacular Interface Disease), and RAO (Retinal Artery Occlusion) represent selected classes from the OCT dataset.

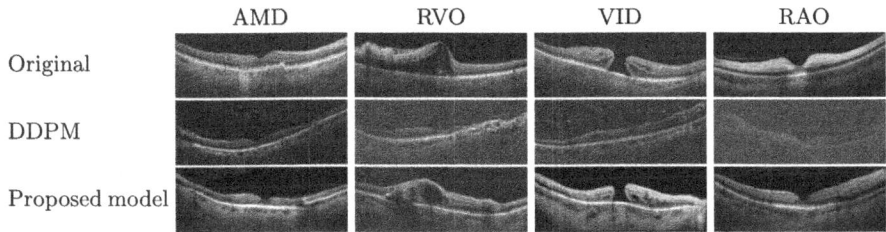

The results generated by the proposed model are closer to the original, with a similar level of detail, class-specific features, and comparable contrast. However, the model was trained on half the resolution of the original images, which leads to the generated images looking more blurry and losing some detail.

5.3   Classification Results

Table 3 demonstrates the results of the classifier trained on the OCTDL dataset using different data augmentation techniques. We compare the performance of the classifier on the unaugmented dataset, a dataset with basic geometric augmentations (horizontal flipping, 5–15° rotation), and datasets with generative augmentation done with the proposed diffusion model. We compare the overall accuracy, precision, and recall of the classifier, and the precision and recall scores for the classes.

Table 3. Classification results for datasets with different augmentation. AMD, DME, ERM, NO, RVO, RAO, and VID denote classes in the dataset and represent different retinal diseases. Results for A - Accuracy, P - Precision, and R - Recall are given in %.

Augmentation	Overall			AMD		DME		ERM		NO		RVO		RAO		VID	
	A	P	R	P	R	P	R	P	R	P	R	P	R	P	R	P	R
None	83	82	83	89	94	61	45	72	64	73	84	100	50	70	37	62	42
Geometric	83	84	83	91	86	61	64	71	66	76	89	97	93	75	68	77	97
Generative	**92**	**93**	**93**	**96**	**100**	**97**	**66**	**90**	**94**	**100**	**92**	**100**	**94**	**78**	**100**	**91**	**100**

As a baseline, we used the dataset with no augmentations trained on 1,542 data points. The classifier achieved an accuracy score of 83%. Amongst the classes, AMD achieved the best results, with the remaining classes scoring significantly lower. This showcases the expected bias of a classifier trained on an imbalanced dataset, as big disparities are visible between the class-specific results. This is also reflected in the macro average of accuracy scores, which was only 75%.

The geometric augmentation was used to increase the training dataset size to 1,917. The accuracy remained the same at 84%, but there was an improvement in the recall values for the underrepresented classes. The macro average of accuracy rose to 79%.

The generative augmentation brought the total number of images for each of the classes to 500 to ensure an even split. The final training dataset size was 3,375 images. The test dataset contained exclusively the images from the unaugmented dataset to ensure an accurate evaluation. The generative augmentations have contributed to an increase of accuracy to 92%, and an increase of precision in recall for every single class. The improvement is also reflected in the macro average of accuracy scores, which reached 93% and no longer reflected the class imbalance.

6   Discussion

The implemented additions to a basic DDPM offer significant performance improvements. From Table 2, we have observed that the inclusion of the proposed modifications have allowed the model to retain class features even for diseases with very little samples. The resulting images look realistic and resemble the original well, they retain the general shape of the retina and reflect the distinct class features, although they are of a lower resolution than the original.

Each of the modifications to the basic model has also improved the evaluation metrics, however, the FID value remained high. It is important to note that FID has recently been called into question as the predominant metric for generative models, and it has been observed to frequently contradict human judgement [41, 42]. We utilised CLIP Similarity as an alternative to the Inception-based metrics and have observed a score close to 1, indicating very good semantic similarity between real and fake images. To better assess the quality and realism of the synthetic data, a human evaluation would be necessary.

While adversarial fine-tuning has improved the results, it is important to note that this was a very time-intensive process. The base diffusion model took 8 h to train for 400 epochs, but fine-tuning it for a 100 epochs took additional 20 h. However, this had no bearing on the time it took to generate images after the training. We determine that fine-tuning is a trade-off – better visuals and metrics can be achieved, but the training time is significantly extended.

The addition of the generated data to the original dataset had a positive impact on disease classification, as shown in Table 3. We have seen a slight increase in overall accuracy, and a significant increase in the class-specific performance metrics. This is especially visible for the smaller classes, such as VID – despite only having 76 samples in the original dataset, the geometric augmentations have increased the F1 value for this class from 35% to 95%. This shows the promise of our proposed model in downstream tasks, demonstrating that training on a combination of real and synthetic data can improve classification performance on real, unseen data.

Overall, we have achieved promising results. The OCT images synthesised using the proposed diffusion model resemble the original and have a positive impact on the classification of retinal diseases.

6.1   Future Work

While our proposed modifications to DDPM offer a significant performance improvement, future work is needed to make it usable in a clinical setting. We note there is a need to train the model on full resolution images. Due to resource limitations, we used a sized-down dataset, but this could lead to critical details being masked. A possible mitigation would be fine-tuning the model on a higher image resolution. Additionally, there is a critical need for expert evaluation of the generated images to ensure the model has accurately learnt to represent the retinal pathologies. Finally, it is important to validate the performance of the proposed model on other datasets. This would demonstrate whether the model can generalise to different applications.

6.2   Ethical concerns

Outside of the existing bias towards rare diseases, it is important to consider that medical datasets often contain biases in terms of age, gender, or ethnicity. While the proposed model has successfully improved the disease imbalance, it could amplify other biases that might have existed in the data. Moreover, there could be concerns with relying heavily on synthetic data – this technically helps the classifier, but from an ethical viewpoint, it is important to consider how trustworthy that data is. If used without proper validation, it could be misleading. As a future mitigation step, we would aim to evaluate the generated images with an expert in the field to ensure proper medical representation is maintained.

7 Conclusion

In this study, we have investigated the applications of diffusion in medical image synthesis for a small, imbalanced OCT dataset. We proposed modifications to DDPM that increase the model's ability to learn details and class-specific features, even for classes containing as little as 22 samples. We have shown that this model is capable of generating images resembling the original, and that the inclusion of these images in the training dataset improves classifier performance and enhances the diagnostic accuracy for rare diseases.

Acknowledgement. This work was undertaken on the Aire HPC system at the University of Leeds, UK. The study was carried out as part of a group project comparing the performance of different generative methods. Thank you to my teammates: Kacper Roemer, Ervans Caushi, James Brierley, Jakub Kurasz, and Oleh Chernilevskyi.

References

1. Warwick, A.N., et al.: Uk biobank retinal imaging grading: methodology, baseline characteristics and findings for common ocular diseases. Eye **37**(10), 2109–2116 (2023)
2. Miladinović, A., Biscontin, A., Ajčević, M., Kresevic, S., Accardo, A., Marangoni, D., Tognetto, D., Inferrera, L.: Evaluating deep learning models for classifying oct images with limited data and noisy labels. Sci. Rep. **14**(1), 1–11 (2024)
3. Li, J.Q., Welchowski, T., Schmid, M., Mauschitz, M.M., Holz, F.G., Finger, R.P.: Prevalence and incidence of age-related macular degeneration in europe: a systematic review and meta-analysis. British J. Ophthalmol. **104**(8), 1077–1084 (2020)
4. Kulyabin, M., et al.: Octdl: optical coherence tomography dataset for image-based deep learning methods. Sci. Data **11**(1), 365 (2024)
5. Li, J.Q., et al.: Prevalence of retinal vein occlusion in europe: a systematic review and meta-analysis. Ophthalmologica **241**(4), 183–189 (2019)
6. Prabha, A.J., Venkatesan, C., Fathimal, M.S., Nithiyanantham, K.K., Kirubha, S.A.: Rd-oct net: hybrid learning system for automated diagnosis of macular diseases from oct retinal images. Biomed. Phys. Eng. Express **10**(2), 025033 (2024)
7. Subramanian, M., Shanmugavadivel, K., Naren, O. S., Premkumar, K., Rankish, K.: Classification of retinal oct images using deep learning. In: 2022 International Conference on Computer Communication and Informatics (ICCCI), pp. 1–7 (2022)
8. Rasti, R., Rabbani, H., Mehridehnavi, A., Hajizadeh, F.: Macular oct classification using a multi-scale convolutional neural network ensemble. IEEE Trans. Med. Imaging **37**(4), 1024–1034 (2018)
9. Wang, D., Wang, L.: On oct image classification via deep learning. IEEE Photonics J. **11**(5), 1–14 (2019)
10. Kim, H.K., Ryu, I.H., Choi, J.Y., Yoo, T.K.: A feasibility study on the adoption of a generative denoising diffusion model for the synthesis of fundus photographs using a small dataset. Discover Appl. Sci. **6**(4), 188 (2024)
11. Ching, T., et al.: Opportunities and obstacles for deep learning in biology and medicine. J. Royal Soc. Interface **15**(141), 20170387 (2018)
12. Piccialli, F., Di Somma, V., Giampaolo, F., Cuomo, S., Fortino, G.: A survey on deep learning in medicine: Why, how and when? Inf. Fusion **66**, 111–137 (2021)

13. Chlap, P., Min, H., Vandenberg, N., Dowling, J., Holloway, L., Haworth, A.: A review of medical image data augmentation techniques for deep learning applications. J. Med. Imaging Radiat. Oncol. **65**(5), 545–563 (2021)
14. Kebaili, A., Lapuyade-Lahorgue, J., Ruan, S.: Deep learning approaches for data augmentation in medical imaging: a review. J. Imaging **9**(4), 81 (2023)
15. Dorjsembe, Z., Odonchimed, S., Xiao, F.: Three-dimensional medical image synthesis with denoising diffusion probabilistic models. Med. Imaging Deep Learn. (2022)
16. Khader, F., et al.: Denoising diffusion probabilistic models for 3d medical image generation. Sci. Reports **13**(1), 7303 (2023)
17. Dhariwal, P., Nichol, A.: Diffusion models beat gans on image synthesis. Adv. Neural. Inf. Process. Syst. **34**, 8780–8794 (2021)
18. Müller-Franzes, G., et al.: A multimodal comparison of latent denoising diffusion probabilistic models and generative adversarial networks for medical image synthesis. Sci. Reports **13**(1), 12098 (2023)
19. Akbar, M.U., Larsson, M., Blystad, I., Eklund, A.: Brain tumor segmentation using synthetic mr images-a comparison of gans and diffusion models. Sci. Data **11**(1), 259 (2024)
20. Ho, J., Jain, A., Abbeel, P.: Denoising diffusion probabilistic models. Adv. Neural. Inf. Process. Syst. **33**, 6840–6851 (2020)
21. Junde Wu, et al.: Medsegdiff: medical image segmentation with diffusion probabilistic model. Med. Imaging Deep Learn. 1623–1639. PMLR (2024)
22. Hu, D., Tao, Y.K., Oguz, I.: Unsupervised denoising of retinal oct with diffusion probabilistic model. Medical Imaging 2022: Image Processing, vol. 12032, pp. 25–34. SPIE (2022)
23. Yang, Y., Fu, H., Aviles-Rivero, A.I., Schönlieb, C.B., Zhu, L.: Diffmic: dual-guidance diffusion network for medical image classification. In: International Conference on Medical Image Computing and Computer-Assisted Intervention, pp. 95–105. Springer (2023)
24. Kazerouni, A.,et al.: Diffusion models in medical imaging: a comprehensive survey. Med. Image Analy. 88, 102846 (2023)
25. Khazrak, I., Takhirova, S., Rezaee, M.M., Yadollahi, M., Green II, R.C., Niu, S.: Addressing small and imbalanced medical image datasets using generative models: a comparative study of ddpm and pggans with random and greedy k sampling. arXiv preprint arXiv:2412.12532 (2024)
26. Gupta, P., Hayat, M., Dhall, A., Do, T.T.: Conditional distribution modelling for few shot image synthesis with diffusion models. In: Proceedings of the Asian Conference on Computer Vision, pp. 818–834 (2024)
27. Chowdary, G.J., Yin, Z.: Diffusion transformer u-net for medical image segmentation. In: International Conference on Medical Image Computing and Computer-Assisted Intervention, pp. 622–631. Springer (2023)
28. Das, N., Das, S.: Attention-unet architectures with pretrained backbones for multiclass cardiac mr image segmentation. Curr. Probl. Cardiol. **49**(1), 102129 (2024)
29. Hejrati, B., Banerjee, S., Glide-Hurst, C., Dong, M.: Conditional diffusion model with spatial attention and latent embedding for medical image segmentation. In: International Conference on Medical Image Computing and Computer-Assisted Intervention, pp. 202–212. Springer (2024)
30. Vaswani, A., et al.:. Attention is all you need. Adv. Neural Inf. Process. Syst. 30 (2017)

31. Kelvinius, F.E., Lindsten, F.: Discriminator guidance for autoregressive diffusion models. In: International Conference on Artificial Intelligence and Statistics, pp. 3403–3411. PMLR (2024)
32. Kim, D., Kim, Y., Kwon, S.J., Kang, W., Moon, I.C.: Refining generative process with discriminator guidance in score-based diffusion models. arXiv preprint arXiv:2211.17091 (2022)
33. Yang, L., Qian, H., Zhang, Z., Liu, J., Cui, B.: Structure-guided adversarial training of diffusion models. In: Proceedings of the IEEE/CVF Conference on Computer Vision and Pattern Recognition, pp. 7256–7266 (2024)
34. Petit, O., Thome, N., Rambour, C., Themyr, L., Collins, T., Soler, L.: U-net transformer: Self and cross attention for medical image segmentation. In: Machine Learning in Medical Imaging: 12th International Workshop, MLMI 2021, Held in Conjunction with MICCAI 2021, Strasbourg, France, September 27, 2021, Proceedings 12, pp. 267–276. Springer (2021)
35. Woo, S., Park, J., Lee, J.Y., Kweon, I.S.: Cbam: Convolutional block attention module. In: Proceedings of the European Conference on Computer Vision (ECCV), pp. 3–19 (2018)
36. Betzalel, E., Penso, C., Navon, A., Fetaya, E.: A study on the evaluation of generative models. arXiv preprint arXiv:2206.10935 (2022)
37. Radford, A., et al.: Learning transferable visual models from natural language supervision. In: International Conference on Machine Learning, pp. 8748–8763. PmLR (2021)
38. Hore, A., Ziou, D.: Image quality metrics: Psnr vs. ssim. In: 2010 20th International Conference on Pattern Recognition, pp. 2366–2369. IEEE (2010)
39. He, K., Zhang, X., Ren, S., Sun, J.: Deep residual learning for image recognition. In: Proceedings of the IEEE Conference on Computer Vision and Pattern Recognition, pp. 770–778 (2016)
40. Reynaud, H., et al.: Echonet-synthetic: privacy-preserving video generation for safe medical data sharing. In: International Conference on Medical Image Computing and Computer-Assisted Intervention, pp. 285–295. Springer (2024)
41. Jayasumana, S., Ramalingam, S., Veit, A., Glasner, D., Chakrabarti, A., Kumar, S.: Rethinking fid: towards a better evaluation metric for image generation. In: Proceedings of the IEEE/CVF Conference on Computer Vision and Pattern Recognition, pp. 9307–9315 (2024)
42. Stein, G., et al.: Exposing flaws of generative model evaluation metrics and their unfair treatment of diffusion models. Adv. Neural Inf. Process. Syst. **36**, 3732–3784 (2023)

Deep Learning for Cardiovascular Risk Assessment: Proxy Features from Carotid Sonography as Predictors of Arterial Damage

Christoph Balada[1]([✉]) [iD], Aida Romano-Martinez[2,3], Vincent ten Cate[2,3],
Katharina Geschke[2], Jonas Tesarz[2], Paul Claßen[2], Alexander K. Schuster[2],
Dativa Tibyampansha[2], Karl-Patrik Kresoja[2], Philipp S. Wild[2,3],
Sheraz Ahmed[1], and Andreas Dengel[1] [iD]

[1] German Research Center for Artificial Intelligence (DFKI),
67663 Kaiserslautern, Germany
christoph.balada@dfki.de

[2] University Medical Center of the Johannes Gutenberg-University Mainz,
Mainz, Germany

[3] German Center for Cardiovascular Research (DZHK), Berlin, Germany

Abstract. This study investigates hypertension as a visual marker of individual vascular damage, which can signal an elevated risk of major cardiovascular events. By leveraging machine learning, we aim to identify such damage early and gain insight into a patient's arterial health. We adapted the VideoMAE deep learning model—originally designed for video classification—by fine-tuning it for ultrasound imaging applications. The model was trained and tested using a dataset comprising over 31,000 carotid sonography videos sourced from the Gutenberg Health Study (15,010 participants), one of the largest prospective population health studies. This adaptation facilitates the classification of individuals as hypertensive or non-hypertensive (74.6% validation accuracy), functioning as a proxy for detecting visual arterial damage. We demonstrate that our machine learning model effectively captures visual features that provide valuable insights into an individual's overall cardiovascular health.

Keywords: Cardiovascular health · Computer-aided diagnosis · Carotid sonography · Video-based Machine Learning

1 Introduction

Cardiovascular diseases (CVD) are the leading cause of death globally, accounting for 32% of all deaths in 2019 [26]. Among the numerous manifestations of CVD, thrombosis—a condition marked by the formation of blood clots within vessels—plays a pivotal role in causing myocardial infarctions (MI) and ischaemic strokes, which are major contributors to morbidity and mortality worldwide. The carotid arteries, which supply blood to the brain, are often involved in atherosclerotic disease, leading to narrowing or occlusion that heightens the risk of stroke [23]. Accurate assessment of carotid artery health is therefore critical for early detection and management of CVD and associated complications.

Carotid ultrasonography is a widely used, non-invasive imaging modality for evaluating carotid artery structure and function. By visualizing arterial plaques and measuring blood flow, carotid ultrasound plays a central role in identifying individuals at risk of stroke or other thrombotic events [18]. However, interpreting carotid ultrasound videos requires significant expertise, as it involves analysing dynamic, high-dimensional data for subtle pathological features, such as intima-media thickening and hemodynamic disturbances [1]. Furthermore, ultrasound videos contain a multitude of high-frequency textural features that are imperceptible to the human eye and even to experts with considerable expertise [16].

Recent advancements in artificial intelligence (AI) have transformed medical imaging by facilitating automated, precise, and reproducible analyses of complex datasets. AI methodologies are increasingly applied to a range of ultrasound-based tasks, including classification [11], prediction [15], and segmentation [12]. Concurrently, an increasing number of works are emerging with the objective of creating an ultrasound foundation model [14,28] or offering optimised pre-training strategies to better address domain-specific characteristics, such as those inherent to ultrasound images [6,21,24]. Despite the continued dominance of purely image-based approaches, video-based approaches [22,28] are also experiencing a marked increase in popularity.

Nevertheless, the efficacy of AI is inherently reliant upon the accessibility of substantial amounts of labelled data, which, particularly within the medical domain, can prove to be either impractical or prohibitively costly and time-consuming to obtain. This phenomenon is also evident in the domain of carotid ultrasonography, which is why artificial intelligence (AI) models that have been trained and evaluated on just a few hundred images have become the standard in many publications [11,12]. In the domain of machine learning, a range of approaches have been developed over time to address the challenge posed by the scarcity of labelled data. These include unsupervised pretraining, transfer learning and few- or zero-shot learning. In scenarios where substantial data is available, yet the necessary task labels are lacking, a potential approach involves self-supervised pre-training using soft or pseudo labels [4,19]. Another strategy, as demonstrated in this study, is to employ easily obtainable labels as a proxy task.

This study presents a novel machine learning model that analyses carotid ultrasound videos rather than images, thereby facilitating the extraction of more sophisticated features for a range of downstream tasks. The model utilises 31,019 videos from the Gutenberg Health Study (GHS) [27], a unique large-scale dataset in the domain of prospective and representative population studies. In light of our findings, we propose a novel digital biomarker that leverages hypertension as a proxy for assessing individual risk of CVDs. Furthermore, we advocate for additional research focusing on AI-driven assessment of ultrasound video data at the individual patient level.

2   Background

Video-based classification involves assigning a specific class label to sequences of frames within a video, enabling the identification of particular conditions or characteristics. In this study, we developed a machine learning pipeline designed to process video imagery obtained from medical ultrasound devices. To achieve this, we finetuned the established VideoMAE model [25], enabling the analysis of carotid artery ultrasound videos for the classification of individuals as hypertensive or non-hypertensive. VideoMAE, a video-based machine learning model, employs self-supervised pre-training to efficiently extract spatiotemporal features from video data. This capability renders it highly suitable for tasks requiring nuanced temporal analysis and aligns well with the specific requirements of our application. By focusing on the dynamic flow patterns and morphological changes captured in the ultrasound sequences, our approach aligns with the goals of advanced classification systems in medical imaging.

Transfer learning principles, integral to our model, provide substantial benefits by leveraging pre-trained models on large-scale datasets, significantly enhancing efficiency and accuracy when applied to target tasks with limited data. In our study, we utilize the GHS, one of the largest and most comprehensive ultrasound datasets available, enriched with a diverse array of clinical information. This dataset not only supports robust model training but also enables nuanced analysis of video-based medical imaging. By harnessing the temporal and spatial insights captured in these ultrasound sequences, we establish a new milestone in large-scale ultrasound analysis.

3   Method

Carotid artery ultrasound sonography is a key component of contemporary cardiovascular risk assessment. Current practices primarily focus on evaluating intima-media thickness (IMT), vascular stiffness, and the presence of plaques or stenosis to estimate an individual's statistically elevated risk relative to the expected arterial condition for their age [5]. However, the use of visual features from ultrasound imaging for individualized risk prediction is not commonly employed.

The objective of this study is to explore novel machine learning methodologies to characterize cardiovascular risk at the individual level, leveraging the actual visual features captured in ultrasound imaging. Hypertension, a principal driver of damage in the vessel and a precursor to plaque development [20], is used in this study as a proxy-indicator of individual vascular damage. Machine learning approaches enable the detection of vessel damage, even when such damage is imperceptible to the human eye in ultrasound images. These early indicators may provide valuable insights into future major cardiovascular events and the overall arterial condition of individuals. To achieve this, we set up a machine learning pipeline, to classify individuals as hypertensive or non-hypertensive. This classification serves as a proxy for identifying visible and sub-visible damage in the vessel and surrounding tissue. In order to ensure a consistently clear distinction, visual damage will be referred to in the following when the classification result of the AI model is addressed. An individual who has been classified as hypertensive by the AI model is therefore referred to as an individual with high visual damage. This serves to ensure clarity between the output of the AI model and a clinical diagnosis of hypertension.

3.1 Gutenberg Health Study

The GHS [27] is a large-scale, prospective population-based cohort study initiated in April 2007 by University Medical Center Mainz. With 15,010 participants, it is among the largest local health studies globally. The study focuses on the health status and disease progression within the Rhine-Main region (Germany), with primary emphasis on cardiovascular health. Its goal is to identify risk factors and causes of common diseases, contributing to preventive healthcare. As part of these comprehensive evaluations, each individual underwent a carotid sonography assessment, where multiple ultrasound videos from different perspectives were collected. In addition to the ultrasound assessment, individuals were screened for anthropometric characteristics, traditional risk markers, comorbidities, laboratory parameters, and also future incidents. The presence of risk factors is determined by a combination of self-reported information, in-house biomarker measurements as well as medication intake. Incidence data on cardiovascular events were assessed via structured follow-ups with subsequent validation of endpoints. All-cause death was obtained via monthly checks with German registration offices. Cardiac death was determined via quarterly review of death certificates using ICD-10 coding. Additional details regarding the study design can be found in a separate publication [27].

3.2 Training and Validation Data

In this study, we utilize ultrasound video data obtained from the GHS initial assessments, comprising 31,019 videos in total. These videos are distributed across different anatomical regions, including the left and right common carotid artery (CCA), external carotid artery (ECA), and internal carotid artery (ICA). Notably, the majority of the videos (approximately 87%) are evenly divided

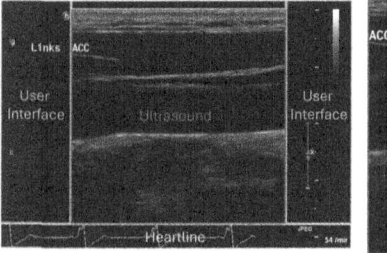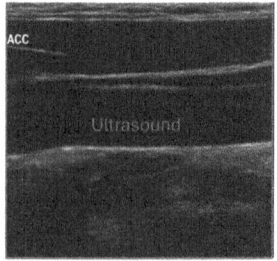

Fig. 1. Video before (left) and after (right) preprocessing. We remove the user interface and the heartline to avoid biases.

between the left CCA and right CCA. For evaluation purposes, the dataset was partitioned at the level of individuals, with 80% of the data (11,398 individuals) allocated to the training set and the remaining 20% (2,847 individuals) assigned to the validation set. This method ensures that no data leakage occurs between training and validation sets, thereby preventing the introduction of selection bias that could arise from manual splitting. Figure 2 presents the validation dataset, which was randomly sampled from the GHS baseline dataset. To address class imbalances, balanced accuracy was employed as the criterion for selecting the optimal model.

3.3   Data Preprocessing and Training

The raw videos extracted from the DICOM files initially retained elements of the ultrasound device's user interface, including the heartline displayed on-screen. To address this, the user interface and heartline were removed by applying pixel-change thresholding over time. Additionally, 45 pixels from the bottom of each frame were cropped to eliminate any remaining portions of the heartline overlay. Videos containing Doppler visualizations were excluded by filtering out those exceeding a specified threshold of red or blue pixels in the HSV colour space. These steps were implemented to avoid biases or misinterpretations potentially introduced by the presence of the heartline.

Figure 1 illustrates an example of the data before and after the removal of the user interface. From each processed video, multiple clips of 16 frames, representing a duration of 2.1 s, were uniformly sampled. The videos were normalized using the mean and standard deviation values estimated during the pre-training

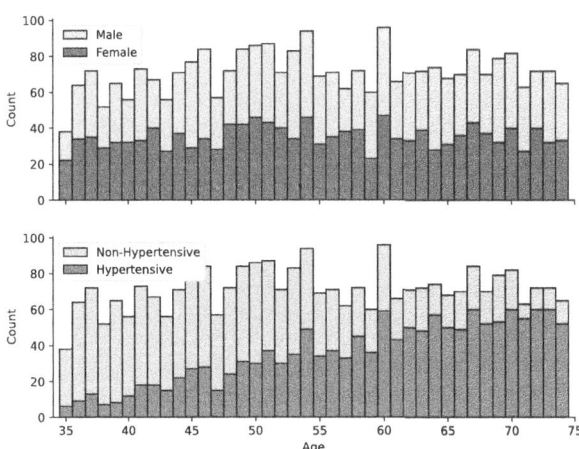

Fig. 2. Distribution of individuals' gender and hypertension diagnosis according to age. The mean age of the validation population was found to be 55.5 ± 11.2 years, with 46.9% of the female population and 55.9% of the male population diagnosed with hypertension. The validation dataset revealed a total of 49.2% women.

on the Kinetics-600 dataset. During training, data augmentation techniques were applied, including random short-side scaling, random cropping to a resolution of 224 × 224, and random horizontal flipping. Weighted random sampling was employed to address class imbalances in the dataset. Training was conducted over eight epochs, with evaluations performed five times during the training process. The final model was selected based on the best-performing evaluation results.

3.4   Statistical Analysis

To evaluate the alignment of the model's extracted features with cardiovascular risk, we conducted statistical comparisons of the clinical diagnosis of hypertension (hypertensive vs. non-hypertensive) and the degree of visual impact on the vessel (low vs. high visual damage (VD)). To assess the arterial health condition of each individual group, we analyse and compare various clinical parameters across the following categories:

Laboratory Parameters: troponin I and NT-proBNP.

Comorbidities: atrial fibrillation, congestive heart failure, past MI, past stroke, coronary artery disease, and CVD.

Traditional Risk Factors: dyslipidemia, diabetes type 2, positive family history of MI or stroke and SCORE2-Germany (applicable to individuals without prior CVD or diabetes, aged 40âĂŞ69 years).

Carotid Sonography: total plaque count.

For each parameter, the distribution of values (represented by quartiles: 25%, median, 75%) or the prevalence of specific conditions is systematically compared across groups. Additionally, GHS provides data on future cardiovascular events, including stroke (within a 5-year period), MI (over 5 years), and cardiac death (at 5- and 10-year intervals). To evaluate the model's performance, the proportions of individuals within each of the four groups experiencing these events, as recorded by the GHS, are compared.

4   Results

4.1   Performance

In addition to VideoMAE [25], we evaluated ViViT [3] and TimeSformer [7] as backbone architectures for our framework. The performance of all three models is summarized in Table 1. Due to VideoMAE's superior performance and lower hardware requirements, both alternative approaches were discarded, and Video-MAE was selected as the backbone for our experiments. The proposed model achieved a balanced accuracy of 72.2% on the validation set. This performance increased to 74.6% when multiple clips per video were aggregated using a simple majority voting approach. Figure 3 presents the confusion matrix for the validation dataset on the level of individual clips.

4.2   Comparing Classification Results

A comparison of the classification results on the validation data shows that individuals classified as high VD, regardless of their hypertension diagnosis show a drastically worse cardiovascular health condition (in terms of the presented indicators) than individuals rated as low VD. Individuals with a positive hypertension diagnosis and a detected high VD presented with the worst cardiovascular health condition, followed by individuals with high VD but no hypertension diagnosis (Fig. 4).

However, using the non-hypertensive individuals with low VD as baseline, we compare our results for (1) comorbidities, (2) traditional risk markers, (3) laboratory parameters, (4) other metrics and (5) future incidents.

Comorbidities: Individuals classified as non-hypertensive with high VD exhibit a 1.9-fold higher likelihood of dyslipidemia and a 4.9-fold higher likelihood of diabetes mellitus type 2 compared to the baseline of non-hypertensive individuals with low VD. However, the likelihood of a family history of MI or stroke is comparable among non-hypertensive individuals, regardless of whether they are classified as having high or low VD.

Table 1. Clip-level accuracy and balanced accuracy on the validation set for different backbone architectures

Model	$bACC_{val}$ ↑	$AUC_{ROC,val}$ ↑
VideoMAE	**72.2%**	**0.80**
ViViT	71.1%	0.78
TimeSformer	67.1%	0.73

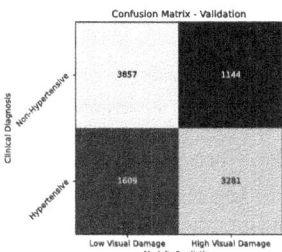

Fig. 3. Confusion matrix for the trained model on validation data. Counts are given at clip level. During an evaluation, our pipeline samples uniformly 9891 clips from 6231 unique videos from 2847 individuals in the validation dataset.

Traditional Risk-Markers: Individuals classified as non-hypertensive with high VD demonstrate a 6.4-fold higher likelihood of CVD, an 8.7-fold higher likelihood of coronary artery disease, an 8.9-fold higher likelihood of a history of MI, and a 7.7-fold higher likelihood of a history of stroke compared to the baseline group. Atrial fibrillation shows an increased likelihood of 5.8-fold, while congestive heart failure did not occur once in the baseline group, while 1.3% of all individuals in the non-hypertensive with high VD group had congestive heart failure.

Laboratory Parameters: Individuals classified as non-hypertensive with high VD exhibit a 50.0% higher Troponin I and a 26.4% higher in NT-proBNP median-measure compared to the baseline of non-hypertensive individuals with low VD.

Other: Individuals classified as non-hypertensive with high VD show a 5.1-fold increased average total plaque count and a 2.4-fold increased SCORE2 median compared to the baseline of non-hypertensive individuals with low VD.

Future Incidents: A total of 974 adverse cardiovascular events were observed within a 5-year interval and 1,229 adverse cardiovascular events within a 10-year interval in GHS. Of these, 200 incidents within a 5-year interval and 255 incidents within a 10-year interval occurred in the validation dataset.

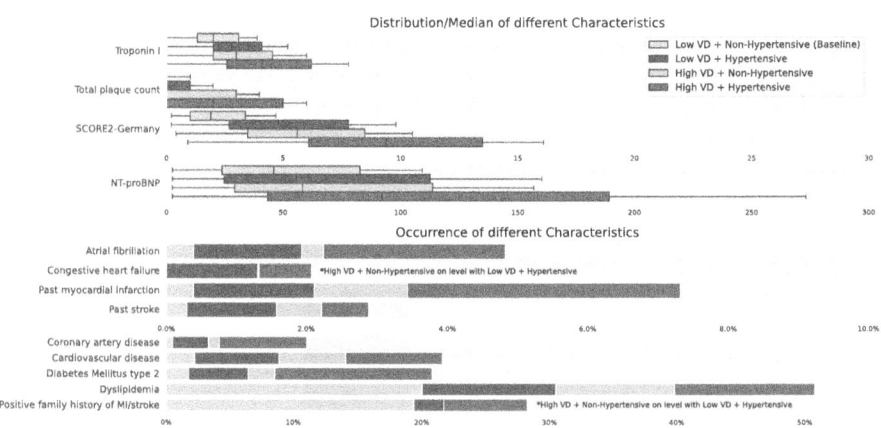

Fig. 4. Statistical comparison of the classification results on the validation data with respect to different clinical parameters. For all variables the individuals classified as "high visual arterial damage" (high VD) show a significant higher likelihood or median value than individuals with low visual damage (low VD). Individuals with high visual damage and a positive hypertension diagnosis exhibit the worst cardiovascular health condition (in terms of the presented indicators).

Figure 5 illustrates the distribution of individuals across various incident categories, with the data further stratified by the use of antihypertensive medications. Comparative analysis of the different groups indicates that individuals with high VD constitute 81.3% of all events in the absence of antihypertensive treatment and 79.8% of all events among those receiving treatment. Notably, in the absence of treatment, individuals with high VD represent the majority of incidents. Within this cohort, the subgroup of non-hypertensive individuals with high VD demonstrates a markedly elevated incidence rate compared to other groups.

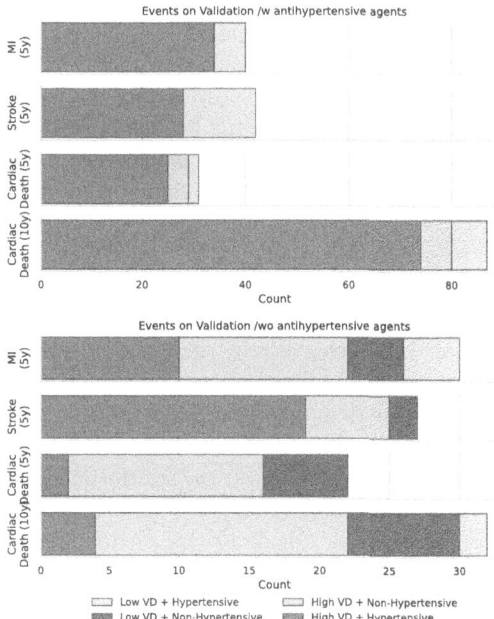

Fig. 5. The total event counts in the validation dataset with respect to the model's classifications and the use of antihypertensive agents. The upper section considers individuals taking antihypertensive agents, while the lower section focuses on those not using such medications. In both groups, the role of hypertension as a major risk factor for various cardiovascular events is emphasized by the observed incidents within the GHS cohort. Among individuals taking antihypertensive agents, the majority of events are observed in those with a positive diagnosis of hypertension and high visual arterial damage. However, in cases of untreated hypertension, individuals without hypertension but exhibiting high visual damage account for a significant proportion of all events, regardless of the type of event.

5   Discussion

5.1   Classification Performance

The model demonstrated a balanced accuracy of 74.6% on the validation set (2,847 individuals) when combining multiple sampled clips per video. It is important to emphasize that the goal is not to achieve perfect detection of the actual blood pressure condition. Given that direct measurement of hypertension, as defined by actual blood pressure, is not feasible through ultrasound without Doppler imaging, the model must rely on identifying visual features that exhibit the strongest correlation with hypertension. Among these features, arterial damage—particularly that associated with untreated hypertension [8]—provides a clear and reliable basis for the model to generate accurate predictions.

An analysis of the classifier's performance relative to the individuals' age, as illustrated in Fig. 6, reveals a performance dip among individuals aged 52 to 62. The underlying reasons for this dip warrant further investigation. However, we note that, on the one hand, the menopause in women is on the edge of this time period and, on the other hand, that pharmacological treatment for hypertension is often started during this period. It is hypothesised that both of these aspects have the capacity to affect the performance of the classifier, as they also have the capacity to affect the progression of atherosclerosis. The present findings will therefore serve as a starting point for future research.

Notably, majority voting, achieved by utilizing multiple clips per video, appears to play a critical role in enhancing model performance during this age range. This finding prompts critical questions regarding the mechanisms through which majority voting facilitates improved classification accuracy. It is plausible that the model's predictions are based on subtle nuances within the video data that may not always be discernible. These nuances may only be visible in one or even only part of a specific phase of the cardiac cycle. However, due to the uniform-random extraction of video clips, these critical features may not be consistently present across all clips.

Despite these challenges, the model behaves in a manner consistent with our expectations. Specifically, it exhibits a low rate of non-hypertensive with high VD and a higher rate of hypertensive with low VD among younger individuals. Conversely, in older individuals, hypertensive with low VD decrease while non-hypertensive with high VD increase. This pattern aligns with the anticipated progression of arterial health deterioration associated with ageing [13, 17].

5.2   Comparison with Clinical Parameters

An analysis of the presented clinical parameters reveals that individuals with high level of VD, irrespective of their hypertensive status, show the highest expression levels across all assessed parameters. Notably, non-hypertensive individuals with low VD are associated with the lowest cardiovascular risk. Furthermore, hypertensive individuals with low VD display a closer alignment in presented clinical characteristics to non-hypertensive individuals with low VD than to those with high VD. Moreover, the SCORE2 risk prognosis aligns with our predictions of VD, further supporting the reliability of our proposed approach. In particular, in combination of high VD and hypertension, the individuals show a drastically increased SCORE2 risk prediction.

In general, both non-hypertensive individuals exhibiting high VD and hypertensive individuals with low VD appear to represent edge cases. Hypertensive individuals with low VD are associated with relatively favourable arterial health, characterized by the absence of visible negative risk indicators. This suggests that VD may either not yet be present or remains below the detection threshold implicitly employed by the model to distinguish between the two classes. Conversely, non-hypertensive individuals with high VD are typically linked to poor arterial health as evidenced by the presence of significant negative visual features. This observation suggests two potential scenarios: either hypertension was undiagnosed at the time of the baseline assessment within the GHS cohort, with the VD already exceeding the model's implicit detection threshold, or these individuals are clinically non-hypertensive based on blood pressure measurements yet still display VD. Importantly, such VD may arise from factors unrelated to hypertension.

5.3   Comparison of Future Incidents

A similar pattern is evident in the future incidents reported by the GHS, mirroring the behaviour observed in clinical parameters. Hypertension, as a key co-occurring factor associated with future major cardiovascular events [2,9], is reflected in the model's performance, particularly in its ability to align hypertension with a detected high level of VD. However, a significant proportion of

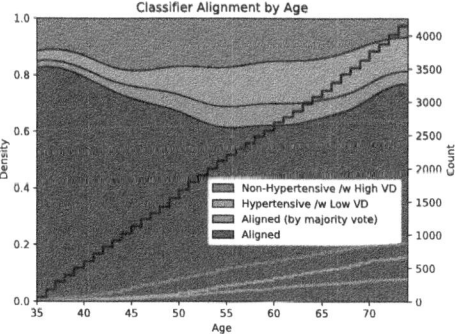

Fig. 6. The background displays a kernel density estimation which illustrates the proportion of the classification alignment on a video level in relation to the individuals' age. The term 'aligned' in this context refers to the alignment of the classifier prediction of high visual damage with the clinical diagnosis of hypertension, and conversely, the alignment of a detected low visual damage with a non-hypertensive diagnosis. The plot in the foreground shows the count of the videos with respect to the individuals' age.

major cardiovascular events within the GHS cohort without antihypertensive drug usage occur among non-hypertensive individuals who exhibit high levels of VD.

Importantly, the model appears to extract ultrasound-derived features that demonstrate a strong association with general cardiac mortality and MI. This highlights the utility of predicted VD generated by the machine learning framework and underscores its relevance to assessing general cardiovascular health at the individual patient level.

5.4   Visual Arterial Damage

As direct measurement of hypertension in terms of actual blood pressure is not feasible using ultrasound (without Doppler), it is assumed that the model relies on proxy indicators. The model is trained exclusively to classify hypertension by extracting features in an unsupervised manner, with the objective of minimizing the binary cross-entropy loss. A notable limitation of this approach is that during training, the model is solely reliant on hypertension labels. These labels may be positive even in cases where no VD is present, and may be negative despite the presence of ultrasound-detectable VD.

While it cannot be conclusively demonstrated that the features extracted by the model have a causal relationship with major cardiovascular events or represent the co-occurrence of diverse cardiovascular risks, it is evident that these features exhibit significant correlations with such phenomena. The observed discrepancies between the independent indicators of hypertension and VD suggest that the identified VD marker should not serve as a replacement for hypertension but rather as a complementary digital risk indicator. Nevertheless, it is evident that the model demonstrated the capacity to extract relevant features, despite the label noise induced by hypertension.

The VD marker reveals correlations with a broad range of clinical and laboratory parameters that are well-established and widely recognised as valuable for cardiovascular risk assessment. Importantly, it remains unaffected by phenomena such as white-coat hypertension, wherein an individual's blood pressure is elevated in clinical settings but normal in other environments, such as at home [10].

Furthermore, carotid sonography is a fast, accessible, and cost-effective diagnostic tool. Its implementation is feasible across diverse settings and does not require sophisticated medical infrastructure, making it a valuable addition to cardiovascular risk evaluation protocols.

6   Conclusion

In this study, we utilized over 31,000 carotid sonography videos from the Gutenberg Health Study to train a deep learning model for classifying individuals based on the presence of high or low visual arterial damage (VD) using hypertension as a reference. Additionally, we demonstrated that in the absence of a direct method to measure blood pressure via ultrasound, the model effectively relies on proxy features for classification.

Through an analysis of the model's predictions in conjunction with clinical parameters, we validated the relevance of the proxy features extracted. By comparing the predicted levels of VD with individuals' hypertension diagnoses, we established that the extracted features align with clinical expectations across a range of parameters, including traditional risk markers, comorbidities, and laboratory findings. These results indicate that, from a clinical perspective, cardiovascular risk is significantly elevated when our machine learning pipeline predicts high VD, even in the absence of a formal hypertension diagnosis.

Moreover, our analysis of predicted levels of VD in relation to future major cardiovascular events revealed that individuals classified as having high VD account for the majority of such events, even if they lacked a hypertension diagnosis. This pattern was particularly pronounced in hypertensive individuals with high predicted VD.

Encouraged by these findings, we advocate for the development of novel, individualized risk markers leveraging machine learning approaches. Such markers have the potential to enhance accessibility to comprehensive cardiovascular risk assessments, mitigate the confounding effects of conditions like white-coat hypertension, and improve cardiovascular prevention strategies for the broader population.

6.1   Future Research

Our hypothesis regarding the extracted features suggests that the model primarily focuses not on blood pressure directly, but on indicators of damage to the vessels, vessel walls, and surrounding tissue. Consequently, the findings demonstrate a strong correlation between the extracted features and clinical parameters, as well as future cardiovascular incidents. However, in order to refine our approach, an in-depth qualitative analysis of the extracted features is identified as a key direction for future research. The application of Explainable AI (XAI) methodologies is intended to elucidate potential medical explanations for the findings, thereby reducing the discrepancies between model predictions and clinical interpretability. XAI approaches, in the sense of feature attribution mapping and counterfactual examples, have been identified as potentially effective pathways for bridging the gap between extracted features and their biological basis.

Moreover, we aim to conduct additional analysis of other deep learning models to evaluate their performance in the field of ultrasound video classification in general, as well as to establish an additional baseline for our approach presented in this study.

Building on the promising results of this study, we aim to conduct a more detailed analysis of various clinical variables to develop an innovative, patient-centered approach to risk assessment.

Acknowledgments. This work was part of the cluster for atherothrombosis and individualized medicine (curATime), funded by the German Federal Ministry of Education and Research (03ZU1202KA).

Disclosure of Interests. The authors have no competing interests to declare that are relevant to the content of this article.

References

1. Abbott, A.L., et al.: Systematic review of guidelines for the management of asymptomatic and symptomatic carotid stenosis. Stroke **46**(11), 3288–3301 (2015)
2. Alderman, M.H., Cohen, H., Madhavan, S.: Diabetes and cardiovascular events in hypertensive patients. Hypertension **33**(5), 1130–1134 (1999)
3. Arnab, A., Dehghani, M., Heigold, G., Sun, C., Lučić, M., Schmid, C.: Vivit: a video vision transformer. In: Proceedings of the IEEE/CVF International Conference on Computer Vision, pp. 6836–6846 (2021)
4. Assran, M., et al.: Semi-supervised learning of visual features by non-parametrically predicting view assignments with support samples. In: Proceedings of the IEEE/CVF International Conference on Computer Vision, pp. 8443–8452 (2021)
5. Bao, X., Xu, B., Lind, L., Engström, G.: Carotid ultrasound and systematic coronary risk assessment 2 in the prediction of cardiovascular events. Eur. J. Prev. Cardiol. **30**(10), 1007–1014 (2023)
6. Basu, S., Gupta, M., Madan, C., Gupta, P., Arora, C.: Focusmae: gallbladder cancer detection from ultrasound videos with focused masked autoencoders. In: Proceedings of the IEEE/CVF Conference on Computer Vision and Pattern Recognition, pp. 11715–11725 (2024)
7. Bertasius, G., Wang, H., Torresani, L.: Is space-time attention all you need for video understanding? In: ICML, vol. 2, p. 4 (2021)
8. Cushman, W.C.: The burden of uncontrolled hypertension: morbidity and mortality associated with disease progression. J. Clin. Hypertens. **5**(3), 14–22 (2003)
9. Eto, M., et al.: Impact of blood pressure variability on cardiovascular events in elderly patients with hypertension. Hypertens. Res. **28**(1), 1–7 (2005)
10. Franklin, S.S., Thijs, L., Hansen, T.W., O'brien, E., Staessen, J.A.: White-coat hypertension: new insights from recent studies. Hypertension **62**(6), 982–987 (2013)
11. Gan, H., et al.: Wal-net: weakly supervised auxiliary task learning network for carotid plaques classification. arXiv preprint arXiv:2401.13998 (2024)
12. Jain, P.K., et al.: Attention-based unet deep learning model for plaque segmentation in carotid ultrasound for stroke risk stratification: an artificial intelligence paradigm. J. Cardiovasc. Dev. Disease **9**(10), 326 (2022)
13. Jani, B., Rajkumar, C.: Ageing and vascular ageing. Postgrad. Med. J. **82**(968), 357–362 (2006)
14. Jiao, J., et al.: USFM: a universal ultrasound foundation model generalized to tasks and organs towards label efficient image analysis. Med. Image Anal. **96**, 103202 (2024)
15. Lin, S.Y., et al.: Applying machine learning to carotid sonographic features for recurrent stroke in patients with acute stroke. Front. Cardiovasc. Med. **9**, 804410 (2022)

16. Loizou, C.P., Pantziaris, M., Nicolaides, A.N., Pattichis, C.S.: Atherosclerotic carotid plaque texture variability in ultrasound video. In: 6th European Conference of the International Federation for Medical and Biological Engineering: MBEC 2014, 7–11 September 2014, Dubrovnik, Croatia, pp. 176–179. Springer (2015)
17. McGrath, B.P., Liang, Y.L., Teede, H., Shiel, L.M., Cameron, J.D., Dart, A.: Age-related deterioration in arterial structure and function in postmenopausal women: impact of hormone replacement therapy. Arterioscler. Thromb. Vasc. Biol. **18**(7), 1149–1156 (1998)
18. Nezu, T., Hosomi, N.: Usefulness of carotid ultrasonography for risk stratification of cerebral and cardiovascular disease. J. Atheroscler. Thromb. **27**(10), 1023–1035 (2020)
19. Niu, S., Lin, L., Huang, J., Wang, C.: Owmatch: conditional self-labeling with consistency for open-world semi-supervised learning. Adv. Neural Inf. Process. Syst. **37**, 99836–99866 (2024)
20. Pfisterer, L.D.: Der Einfluss der Wandspannung auf die Funktion von Myokardin in glatten Gefäßmuskelzellen. Ph.D. thesis (2013)
21. Rahman, A., Patel, V.M.: Ultramae: multi-modal masked autoencoder for ultrasound pre-training. In: Medical Imaging with Deep Learning, pp. 1196–1206. PMLR (2024)
22. Shah, N.A., Bandara, C., Sikder, S., Vedula, S.S., Patel, V.M.: CSMAE: cataract surgical masked autoencoder (MAE) based pre-training. In: 2025 IEEE 22nd International Symposium on Biomedical Imaging (ISBI), pp. 1–5. IEEE (2025)
23. Stein, J.H., et al.: Use of carotid ultrasound to identify subclinical vascular disease and evaluate cardiovascular disease risk: a consensus statement from the american society of echocardiography carotid intima-media thickness task force endorsed by the society for vascular medicine. J. Am. Soc. Echocardiogr. **21**(2), 93–111 (2008)
24. Szijártó, Á., et al.: Masked autoencoders for medical ultrasound videos using roi-aware masking. In: International Workshop on Advances in Simplifying Medical Ultrasound, pp. 167–176. Springer (2024)
25. Tong, Z., Song, Y., Wang, J., Wang, L.: Videomae: masked autoencoders are data-efficient learners for self-supervised video pre-training. Adv. Neural Inf. Process. Syst. **35**, 10078–10093 (2022)
26. (WHO), W.H.O.: Cardiovascular diseases (CVD) fact sheets (2025). https://www.who.int/en/news-room/fact-sheets/detail/cardiovascular-diseases-(cvds)
27. Wild, P., et al.: The gutenberg health study. Bundesgesundheitsblatt-Gesundheitsforschung-Gesundheitsschutz **55**, 824–830 (2012)
28. Zhang, Z., Wu, Q., Ding, S., Wang, X., Ye, J.: Echo-vision-fm: a pre-training and fine-tuning framework for echocardiogram video vision foundation model. medRxiv, pp. 2024–10 (2024)

Enhanced Coronary Artery Segmentation in CTCA Using Bridging Centreline Integration

Hao Wu[1(✉)] 🆔, Sonit Singh[2] 🆔, Ramtin Gharleghi[1] 🆔, Arcot Sowmya[2] 🆔, and Susann Beier[1] 🆔

[1] School of Mechanical and Manufacturing Engineering, UNSW Sydney, Kensington, Australia
`hao.wu18@student.unsw.edu.au`
[2] School of Computer Science and Engineering, UNSW Sydney, Kensington, Australia

Abstract. Segmentation of coronary arteries is essential for subsequent diagnostic efforts. State-of-the-art segmentation methods commonly result in disconnected arterial branch prediction due to the complex nature of these segmentation tasks driven by complex anatomy and acquisition challenges. However, the coronary artery tree contains critical arterial shape information via its centrelines which offers great potential for the improvement of automated segmentations works using 3D computed tomography coronary angiograms (CTCA). In this paper, we propose a deep learning architecture using 3D CTCA from the open source dataset ASOCA that combines the centreline of the coronary artery with existing segmentation methods to improve overall segmentation performance. This architecture contains three novel modules. First, the bridging centreline extraction module searches for missing centrelines that connect two disconnected components from an initial segmentation. Second, the centreline expansion module expands the bridging centrelines into coronary artery segments. Third, the centreline fusion module further combines the centreline and the initial segmentation to remove background noise. Experiments show that the proposed architecture can consistently boost the segmentation performance of various segmentation methods.

Keywords: Medical imaging · deep learning · segmentation · coronary artery · CTCA

1 Introduction

Cardiovascular disease is the leading cause of death worldwide, causing an estimated 17.9 million deaths every year [18]. Coronary artery segmentation of standard computed tomography coronary angiogram (CTCA) imaging is essential for many subsequent diagnostic and developmental analyses [2,9,10]. However, this

S. Ali et al. (Eds.): MIUA 2025, LNCS 15918, pp. 266–278, 2026.
https://doi.org/10.1007/978-3-031-98694-9_19

still commonly requires manual annotation or at least annotation verification, which is time-consuming and labour-intensive [8,19]. Therefore, efficient and accurate algorithms to segment coronary arteries from CTCA have attracted the interest of researchers.

Most segmentation methods utilise convolutional layers to extract local features. Lately, transformer-based neural networks have been proposed [11,12] to capture long-range connections. However, both types of models rely on patch-based training and inference, and miss the topological structure of the coronary arteries and suffer from disconnected fragments. Meanwhile, centrelines of the coronary artery are usually generated from segmentation, distance map or other similar outputs after processing CTCA [4,22]. Recently, automatic methods have been proposed to extract centrelines from CTCA, such as discriminative tracker [23] and CNN tracker [20]. Although these methods preserve the general topology of coronary arteries, they commonly suffer from missing branches and ambiguous distal points.

To overcome the barrier between centreline prediction and coronary artery segmentation, we propose a novel architecture that uses the predicted centreline from CTCA to connect fragments, refine segmentation by extracting bridging centrelines and combine them with the initial segmentation. Specifically, we utilise a centreline extraction method called deep reinforced agent learning [14] to extract the predicted centreline and integrate it with deep neural networks for segmentation. We design three modules to balance both the predictions and exploit the advantages of both to improve the final segmentation accuracy. In summary, the main contributions of this work are:

- Developing a bridging centreline extraction module that extracts missing centrelines between disconnected fragments from the initial segmentation using the predicted centreline.
- Incorporating a centreline expansion module to expand the centreline into realistic coronary artery segmentation. Bridging centrelines are expanded to reconstruct the disconnected parts between two coronary artery fragments.
- Implementing a centreline fusion module to obtain the Region of Interest (ROI) to localise the coronary artery and remove background noise.
- Analysing the efficacy of the proposed architecture using multiple deep neural networks for segmentation trained on ASOCA, a publicly available CTCA dataset.

2   Related Work

For medical image segmentation, the popular U-Net [17] is capable of capturing local semantic features and reconstructing the image via skip connections. Due to its success on a range of medical segmentation tasks, different variants of deep learning (DL) architectures based on U-Net have been developed [1,5,15,24]. Attention-UNet [15] adds an attention mechanism at skip connections to emphasise salient features and suppress irrelevant features. UNet++ [24] fuses multi-scale features to fully utilise features from different levels. Recently, transformer based DL architecture have been introduced to medical image segmentation, where multi-head self-attention is employed to form multiple subspaces and focus on different aspects of information [21]. UNETR [12] replaces traditional convolutional encoders with a transformer, with the aim of extracting long-range relationships between voxels, resulting in higher boundary segmentation accuracy compared with most 2D models. Swin-UNETR [11] further improves the transformer based encoder with sliding windows and different scales, and performs well on brain tumour segmnetation. Even though these methods achieve satisfactory results on multiple medical segmentation tasks, they struggle with the narrow and curvilinear geometric properties of coronary arteries and confuse them with neighbouring tissues.

The centreline of coronary arteries plays a critical role in measuring geometric features such as tortuosity, diameter and radius and performing diagnosis. Multiple methods have been proposed to extract the centreline of coronary arteries. Discriminative coronary artery tracking [23] includes a tracker to identify the vessel orientation and radius and a discriminator to determine whether to stop tracking or not. CNN tracker [20] utilises a convolutional neural networks (CNN) based orientation classifier to estimate the artery orientation and radius, and the whole coronary artery centreline could be tracked iteratively using seed points. Deep reinforced tree-traversal agent [14] incorporates reinforcement learning to predict the direction of the vessel and a discriminator is implemented to determine bifurcation points. These methods can predict the centreline, however they are poor at determining the distal end of the coronary arteries and detecting bifurcation points, which create missing segments.

To address the issues discussed, we propose an architecture that combines a centreline extraction method and a segmentation method using three novel modules: a bridging centreline extraction module, a centreline expansion module, and a centreline fusion module. These modules can integrate the topology from the predicted centreline and combine it with various segmentation networks to improve the final prediction.

3 Methods

The architecture of the proposed centreline-segmentation combination architecture is shown in Fig. 1. Firstly, an initial segmentation is trained using any segmentation architecture. Secondly, coronary artery centrelines are predicted using deep reinforced traversal agent with given weights and the default configuration [14]. Then, the three inputs consisting the original CTCA image, predicted centreline and initial segmentation are passed through three novel modules, namely bridging centreline extraction module, centreline expansion module and centreline fusion module.

3.1 Initial Segmentation Method and Centreline Prediction

Any segmentation method that takes the CTCA image as input and generates coronary artery segmentation can be incorporated. In order to validate the

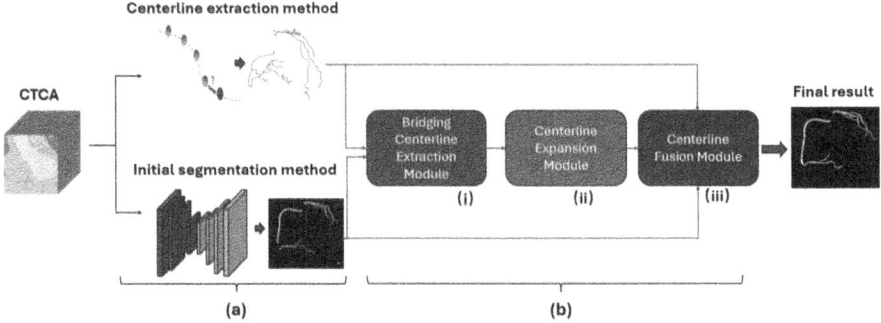

Fig. 1. Centreline-segmentation combination architecture. (a) Predicted centrelines and the initial segmentation are generated using CTCA images. (b) Predicted centerlines and the initial segmentation together with the CTCA are processed by three novel modules. (i) **Bridging centreline extraction module** generates bridging centerlines. (ii) **Centerline expansion module** takes bridging centerlines and CTCA image as input to expand bridging centerlines into segmentation. (iii) **Centerline fusion module** filters out background noise and generates the final result

---

Algorithm 1: Bridging centreline extraction

      Input   : Set of Predicted centreline voxels $\mathbf{C}$.
                Set of Initial Segmentation $\mathbf{S}$.
      Output: Set of Bridging centrelines $\mathbf{B}$.
1 Extract the contour $\mathbf{O}$ of the initial segmentation $\mathbf{S}$
2 Acquire centreline fragments $\mathbf{F} \leftarrow \mathbf{C}/\mathbf{S}$
3 $\mathbf{M} \leftarrow \mathbf{O} \cap \mathbf{C}$
4 $\mathbf{B} \leftarrow \varnothing$
5 **for** $F_i \in \mathbf{F}$ **do**
6 $\mathbf{n} \leftarrow 0$;
7 $F_i\prime \leftarrow F_i$;
8   **for** $M_j \in \mathbf{M}$ **do**
9   **if** M_j *is **adjacent** to* F_i **then**
10 $\mathbf{n} \leftarrow \mathbf{n} + 1$;
11 $F_i\prime \leftarrow F_i\prime \cup M_j$;
12   **end**
13   **end**
14   **if** $n \geq 2$ **then**
15 $\mathbf{B} \leftarrow \mathbf{B} \cup F_i\prime$;
16   **end**
17 **end**

---

generalisation ability of the proposed architecture, a wide range of initial segmentation models were trained, including U-Net variants such as 3D U-Net [3], ResUNet [5], DenseUNet [1], UNet++ [24] and nnUNet [13], and transformer-based networks such as UNETR [12] and Swin-UNETR [11].

For centreline prediction, the deep reinforced tree-traversal agent for coronary artery centreline extraction [14] is used. Two initial points of the left and right coronary artery trees are taken as input. Starting from the given point, the method will trace the coronary artery and detect bifurcations, and generate the predicted centreline. An illustration of the input and output of this method is shown in Fig. 2.

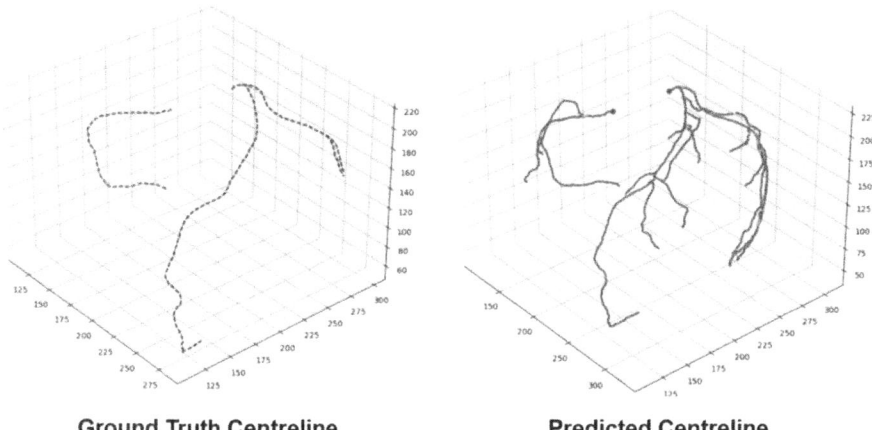

Ground Truth Centreline   **Predicted Centreline**

Fig. 2. Input and output of the deep traversal agent centreline extraction method. (a) The blue line represents the ground truth centreline. (b) The predicted centreline. Purple points are two initial points as input. Green points are predicted bifurcation points and red lines are the predicted centreline. False positive prediction is an issue with this method (Color figure online)

3.2 Bridging Centreline Extraction Module

A bridging centreline is a part of the coronary artery centreline that is not present in the initial segmentation but is predicted by the centreline extraction method with its two ends attached to the initial segmentation, which is shown in Fig. 3. The predicted centreline suffers from missing branches and ambiguous distal points, while the initial segmentation is limited by disconnected components and false positives due to background noise. Bridging centrelines are able to link between segmentation fragments by taking advantage of both predictions. The two ends of a bridging centreline are attached to the predicted coronary artery segmentation, indicating that the initial segmentation was unable to segment this specific portion due to imaging quality, artefact or stenosis, but there is an artery nearby. Therefore, bridging centrelines indicate the missing path between two disconnected components of the initial segmentation, which is essential for reconstructing connections. The algorithm for extracting bridging centrelines is shown in Algorithm 1.

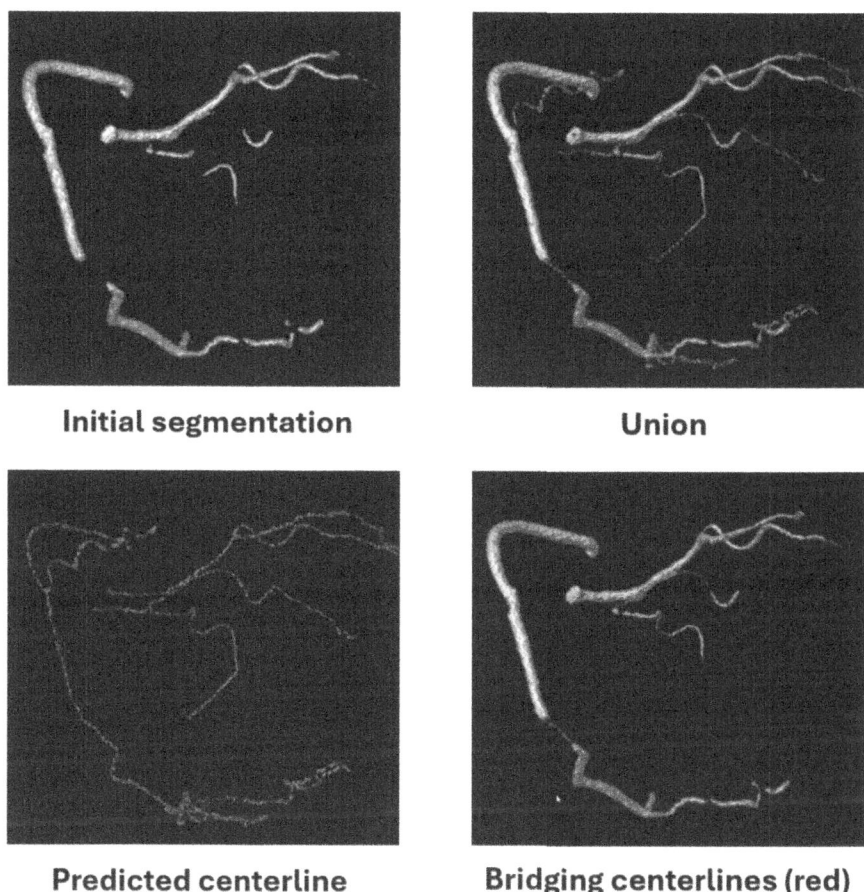

Initial segmentation   **Union**

Predicted centerline   **Bridging centerlines (red)**

Fig. 3. Illustration of bridging centreline. **White** parts are the initial segmentation, **green** parts are the predicted centreline and **red** parts are the corresponding **bridging centreline** (Color figure online)

3.3 Centreline Expansion Module

After extracting the bridging centreline, the next task is to expand the bridging centreline into coronary artery segmentation fragments. In order to fully extract the geometric information around the centreline and guarantee that only the voxels close to the centreline are predicted, a U-Net like neural network is proposed where two inputs are used: the centreline and CTCA image. The centreline input guides the network to focus on features around the centreline and suppress information outside the centreline. With the CTCA image and the U-Net architecture shown in Fig. 1, this network is able to efficiently and accurately extract the image features according to the anatomical and geometric information, with a focus on the indicated centreline. For the centreline-segmentation combination architecture, the objective is to expand the bridging centreline **B** and link it to the existing coronary artery segmentation **S**. Therefore, only the bridging centreline should be expanded and other possible coronary arteries should be excluded. To achieve this target, during training, the ground truth centreline C_{gt} and CTCA images I are used as input and the coronary artery label L is the target output. During inference, the inputs are the bridging centreline B and the CTCA images I. The training and inference strategy is shown in Fig. 4. By combining the bridging centreline extraction module and centreline expansion module, the disconnected components of the initial segmentation can be correctly connected according to the context and features of the existing prediction.

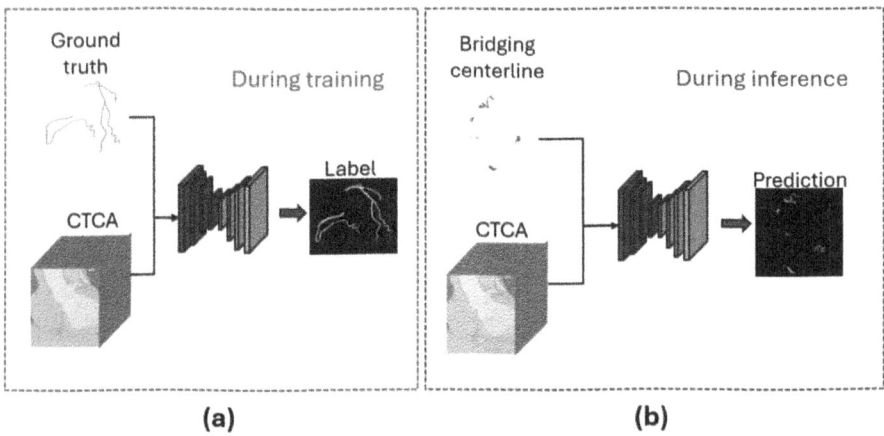

Fig. 4. Proposed centreline expansion module. (a) During training, the ground truth centreline and the CTCA image are the two inputs for the network, which generates coronary arteries following the given centreline and image features. (b) During inference, the generated bridging centreline and the CTCA image are the two inputs, and the bridging centrelines are expanded into segmented arteries according to CTCA image.

3.4   Centreline Fusion Module

Due to the background noise and similar features of other tissues and coronary arteries, patch-based inference by deep neural networks is not able to filter out background noise, resulting in a great number of false positive predictions and even completely wrong components outside the possible coronary artery region. Moreover, since the coronary artery tree contains two components, namely the left and coronary artery trees, post-processing is employed to retain the two largest components. However, in some cases where the coronary artery trees are poorly segmented and large false positive components are present, this strategy may lead to the completely missed coronary artery tree and falsely retained components, resulting in unusable segmentation. Therefore, the centreline fusion

Table 1. Architecture of the centreline expansion network

Architecture	Encoder	Decoder
Input: $2 \times 64 \times 192 \times 192$		
Layer1	$64 \times 32 \times 96 \times 96$	$1 \times 64 \times 192 \times 192$
Layer2	$128 \times 16 \times 48 \times 48$	$32 \times 32 \times 96 \times 96$
Layer3	$256 \times 8 \times 24 \times 24$	$64 \times 16 \times 48 \times 48$
Layer4	$256 \times 4 \times 12 \times 12$	$128 \times 8 \times 24 \times 24$
Bottleneck	$256 \times 4 \times 12 \times 12$	

module utilises the predicted centreline to address this issue. Figure 5 illustrates the process of this module.

Let S be the initial segmentation and C the predicted centreline. The skeleton T of S is computed via thinning. Two arbitrary voxels from the left and right coronary arteries of the predicted centreline are marked as v_1 and v_2. We expand $T \cup C$ with a radius of r as the potential coronary artery region. Since the region should contain both the left and right coronary arteries, only connected regions from $T \cup C$ with v_1 or v_2 are retained as the final region of interest (ROI). Any prediction outside this ROI will be removed. Then the final prediction is obtained by retaining two largest components.

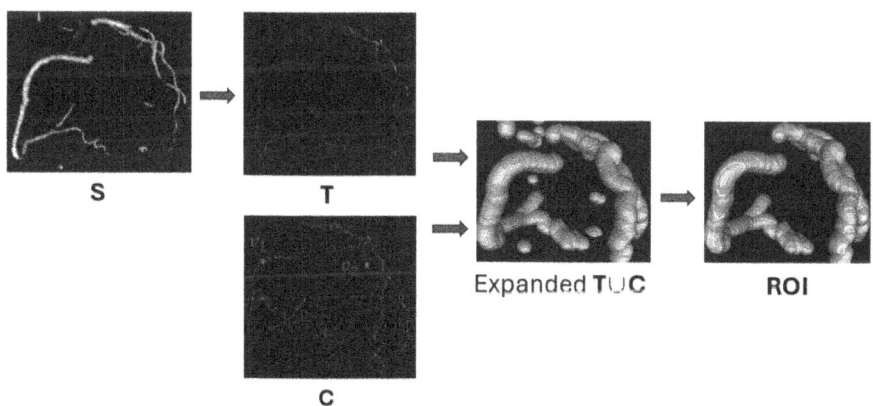

Fig. 5. Overview of centreline fusion module. Only predictions within **ROI** will be maintained before retaining the two largest components

4 Experiments and Analysis

To validate the proposed method, we conducted experiments on the ASOCA dataset [6,7], which contains 40 cases with 3D CTCA images, annotated coronary arteries and centrelines. We used five-fold cross-validation on the dataset with 32 cases for training and 8 cases for validation with the same folds used for each step to avoid data leakage. Dice score coefficient (DSC) and Hausdorf Distance (HD) are used as the evaluation metric shown below:

$$DSC = \frac{2|X \cap Y|}{|X| + |Y|} \tag{1}$$

$$HD(X, Y) = \max\{\max_{x \in X} \min_{y \in Y} d(x, y), \max_{y \in Y} \min_{x \in X} d(x, y)\} \tag{2}$$

where X and Y are the binary labels for prediction and ground truth respectively. DSC is a statistical measure that quantifies the similarity of two sets of data and HD measures how far two sets of data are from each other. In our experiments, 95% HD is employed following practical use in medical imaging.

We trained the proposed architecture using Pytorch [16] on NVIDIA TESLA V100. For training, we used the combination of dice loss and cross entropy loss as the loss function for the initial segmentation network and the centreline expansion network to adjust the learning bias and secure the whole vessel segmentation performance, defined as below:

$$L = 1 - \frac{2 \sum_{i=1}^{V} p_i y_i}{\sum_{i=1}^{V} (p_i + y_i + \epsilon)}$$
$$- \sum_{i=1}^{V} (y_i \log p_i + (1 - y_i) \log(1 - p_i)) \tag{3}$$

where p_i and y_i are the prediction and ground truth of the voxel i, V is the number of voxels in total, and ϵ represents the smoothing factor. We used SGD optimiser with the learning rate initialised to 0.01 and the decay formula $lr = lr_{init} \times (1 - k/K)^{0.9}$, where k is the current epoch and K the maximal epochs, which was set to 200. Images were randomly cropped to the size of $64 \times 192 \times 192$ during training and a sliding window of size of $64 \times 192 \times 192$ was used to predict the maps. The results of the segmentation were post-processed by retaining the two largest connected areas representing the left and right coronary artery trees.

4.1   Centreline Extraction

For centreline extraction, the deep Reinforced Tree-traversal Agent [14] was implemented with given weights and the default configuration. Given two sets of points, one as reference centreline and the other as predicted centreline. A point was covered if Euclidean distance between it and the nearest point from the other set is less than threshold $H_m = 1$ mm. Point-level overlap was evaluated, denoted as O_{both} and O_{single} representing the overlap between both centrelines and the overlap of the reference centreline. Formally, if a reference point is covered, it is marked as R_t and R_f otherwise. For the predicted point, it will be marked as T_t or T_f regarding the case. $||.||$ denotes the cardinality of the set of points, O_{both} and O_{single} are defined as:

$$O_{both} = \frac{||T_t|| + ||R_t||}{||T_t|| + ||T_f|| + ||R_t|| + ||R_f||} \tag{4}$$

$$O_{single} = \frac{||R_t||}{||R_t|| + ||R_f||} \tag{5}$$

The O_{both} and O_{single} were 0.661 and 0.900 respectively in our experiment.

Table 2. Comparison of **Dice score coefficient (DSC)** and **95%HD** with different initial segmentation methods. **Before** means the performance of the initial segmentation model, **after** means the performance of centreline-segmentation combination model.

Dataset: ASOCA
Five-fold cross-validation (32 training + 8 validation)

Initial segmentation architecture	DSC (before)	95%HD (before)	DSC (after)	95%HD (after)
nnUNet	0.8320 ± 0.1026	13.11 ± 19.64	**0.8572 ± 0.0627**	**6.14 ± 10.38**
3D-Unet	0.7752 ± 0.1358	11.13 ± 13.22	**0.7974 ± 0.1000**	**8.61 ± 10.08**
ResUNet	0.6529 ± 0.2296	30.65 ± 25.99	**0.7408 ± 0.1616**	**18.51 ± 20.16**
DenseUNet	0.4543 ± 0.3330	56.34 ± 46.81	**0.6336 ± 0.2306**	**30.63 ± 31.96**
UNet++	0.5165 ± 0.3087	45.98 ± 33.40	**0.6644 ± 0.2372**	**30.61 ± 28.98**
UNETR	0.8046 ± 0.1058	13.35 ± 17.34	**0.8364 ± 0.0583**	**5.10 ± 6.03**
Swin-UNETR	0.8154 ± 0.0813	16.77 ± 21.49	**0.8366 ± 0.0580**	**8.78 ± 14.61**

4.2   Comparison with State-of-the-Art Methods

We integrated the proposed centreline-segmentation combination architecture with several state-of-the-art segmentation models, including CNN-based models (3D-UNet, ResUNet, DenseUNet and nnUNet), and transformer-based models (UNETR and Swin-UNETR). In Table 2 the results show that the DSC increased by 2–14% and 95%HD dropped by 3–25.

4.3   Quantitative Study

The proposed centreline-segmentation combination architecture is capable of improving segmentation performance compared to the initial segmentation methods alone. When the initial segmentation cannot distinguish the coronary artery from other tissues, high false positive prediction occurs. By localising the coronary artery tree using the predicted centreline, the proposed method is able to filter out the background noise and improve the prediction to a reasonable level. When the initial segmentation is already satisfactory, extracting the bridging centreline and expanding it in the context of the surrounding features, allows disconnected components to be connected and the prediction further refined.

4.4   Qualitative Study

The proposed method is able to connect fragments based on the predicted centreline and expand bridging centrelines properly based on the surrounding geometric features, which is illustrated in Fig. 6. For nnUNet, the bottom left part is correctly connected and in the top right corner, small gaps among several components are also properly connected. For 3D-UNet, UNETR and Swin-UNETR, similar improvements may be noticed. Moreover, ResUNet, DenseUNet and Unet++ suffer significantly from false positive prediction, which shows the necessity of the centreline fusion module and post-processing.

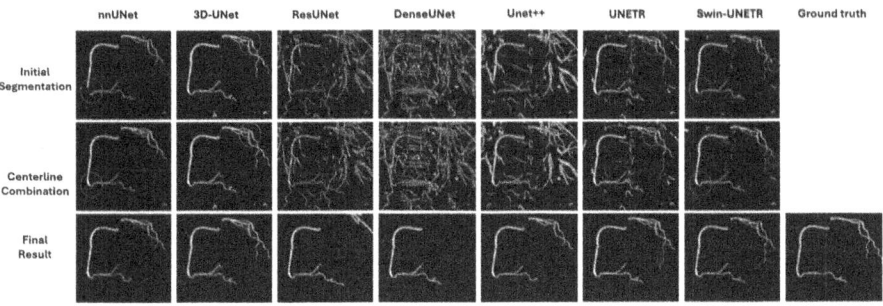

Fig. 6. Qualitative comparison between different networks. **Initial segmentation** is the segmentation result from the initial segmentation network. **Centreline combination** is the result of the union of initial segmentation and expanded bridging centrelines after adding the bridging centreline extraction module and centreline expansion module. **Final result** is the final result of postprocessing, after adding the centreline fusion module and retaining two largest components. **Red circle** shows that disconnected fragments are connected after the centreline combination. (Color figure online)

5   Conclusion

In this paper, we propose a centreline-segmentation combination architecture that incorporates centrelines to connect fragments. This novel architecture combines the advantages of both centreline extraction and segmentation methods by utilising predicted centrelines to localise potential coronary artery areas and extracting bridging centrelines to connect fragments. This architecture can be used along with various segmentation methods, and experiments show that prediction can be improved consistently. Future work will focus on improving centreline prediction accuracy and merging the bridging centreline extraction and centreline expansion module into one integrated learning architecture.

Acknowledgements. This research includes computations using the computational cluster Katana supported by Research Technology Services at UNSW Sydney. This research is supported by the University Postgraduate Award Scholarship (UIPA).

References

1. Cai, S., Tian, Y., Lui, H., Zeng, H., Wu, Y., Chen, G.: Dense-unet: a novel multi-photon in vivo cellular image segmentation model based on a convolutional neural network. Quant. Imaging Med. Surg. **10**(6), 1275 (2020). https://doi.org/10.21037/qims-19-1090
2. Chiastra, C., et al.: Computational fluid dynamics as supporting technology for coronary artery disease diagnosis and treatment: an international survey. Front. Cardiovas. Med. **10**, 1216796 (2023). https://doi.org/10.3389/fcvm.2023.1216796
3. Çiçek, Ö., Abdulkadir, A., Lienkamp, S.S., Brox, T., Ronneberger, O.: 3D U-Net: learning dense volumetric segmentation from sparse annotation. In: Ourselin, S., Joskowicz, L., Sabuncu, M.R., Unal, G., Wells, W. (eds.) MICCAI 2016. LNCS, vol. 9901, pp. 424–432. Springer, Cham (2016). https://doi.org/10.1007/978-3-319-46723-8_49
4. Cui, H., Xia, Y.: Automatic coronary centerline extraction using gradient vector flow field and fast marching method from CT images. IEEE Access **6**, 41816–41826 (2018). https://doi.org/10.1109/ACCESS.2018.2859786
5. Diakogiannis, F.I., Waldner, F., Caccetta, P., Wu, C.: Resunet-a: a deep learning framework for semantic segmentation of remotely sensed data. ISPRS J. Photogramm. Remote. Sens. **162**, 94–114 (2020). https://doi.org/10.1016/j.isprsjprs.2020.01.013
6. Gharleghi, R., et al.: Annotated computed tomography coronary angiogram images and associated data of normal and diseased arteries. Sci. Data **10**(1), 128 (2023). https://doi.org/10.1038/s41597-023-02016-2
7. Gharleghi, R., et al.: Automated segmentation of normal and diseased coronary arteries-the asoca challenge. Comput. Med. Imaging Graph. **97**, 102049 (2022). https://doi.org/10.1016/j.compmedimag.2022.102049
8. Gharleghi, R., Chen, N., Sowmya, A., Beier, S.: Towards automated coronary artery segmentation: a systematic review. Comput. Methods Programs Biomed. **225**, 107015 (2022)
9. Gharleghi, R., Samarasinghe, G., Sowmya, A., Beier, S.: Deep learning for time averaged wall shear stress prediction in left main coronary bifurcations. In: 2020 IEEE 17th International Symposium on Biomedical Imaging (ISBI), pp. 1–4 (2020). https://doi.org/10.1109/ISBI45749.2020.9098715
10. Gharleghi, R., Sowmya, A., Beier, S.: Transient wall shear stress estimation in coronary bifurcations using convolutional neural networks. Comput. Methods Programs Biomed. **225**, 107013 (2022)
11. Hatamizadeh, A., Nath, V., Tang, Y., Yang, D., Roth, H.R., Xu, D.: Swin unetr: swin transformers for semantic segmentation of brain tumors in MRI images. In: International MICCAI brainlesion Workshop, pp. 272–284. Springer, Cham (2021). https://doi.org/10.1007/978-3-031-08999-2_22
12. Hatamizadeh, A., et al.: Unetr: transformers for 3d medical image segmentation. In: Proceedings of the IEEE/CVF Winter Conference on Applications of Computer Vision, pp. 574–584 (2022)
13. Isensee, F., Jaeger, P.F., Kohl, S.A., Petersen, J., Maier-Hein, K.H.: nnu-net: a self-configuring method for deep learning-based biomedical image segmentation. Nat. Methods **18**(2), 203–211 (2021)
14. Li, Z., Xia, Q., Hu, Z., Wang, W., Xu, L., Zhang, S.: A deep reinforced tree-traversal agent for coronary artery centerline extraction. In: de Bruijne, M., et al. (eds.) MICCAI 2021. LNCS, vol. 12905, pp. 418–428. Springer, Cham (2021). https://doi.org/10.1007/978-3-030-87240-3_40

15. Oktay, O., et al.: Attention u-net: Learning where to look for the pancreas. arXiv preprint arXiv:1804.03999 (2018).https://doi.org/10.48550/arXiv.1804.03999
16. Paszke, A., et al.: Pytorch: an imperative style, high-performance deep learning library. In: Advances in Neural Information Processing Systems, vol. 32 (2019)
17. Ronneberger, O., Fischer, P., Brox, T.: U-Net: convolutional networks for biomedical image segmentation. In: Navab, N., Hornegger, J., Wells, W.M., Frangi, A.F. (eds.) MICCAI 2015. LNCS, vol. 9351, pp. 234–241. Springer, Cham (2015). https://doi.org/10.1007/978-3-319-24574-4_28
18. Roth, G.A., et al.: Global, regional, and national burden of cardiovascular diseases for 10 causes, 1990 to 2015. J. Am. Coll. Cardiol. **70**(1), 1–25 (2017). https://doi.org/10.1016/j.jacc.2017.04.052
19. Tian, F., Gao, Y., Fang, Z., Gu, J.: Automatic coronary artery segmentation algorithm based on deep learning and digital image processing. Appl. Intell. **51**(12), 8881–8895 (2021). https://doi.org/10.1007/s10489-021-02197-6
20. Wolterink, J.M., van Hamersvelt, R.W., Viergever, M.A., Leiner, T., Išgum, I.: Coronary artery centerline extraction in cardiac CT angiography using a CNN-based orientation classifier. Med. Image Anal. **51**, 46–60 (2019). https://doi.org/10.1016/j.media.2018.10.005
21. Xiao, H., Li, L., Liu, Q., Zhu, X., Zhang, Q.: Transformers in medical image segmentation: a review. Biomed. Signal Process. Control **84**, 104791 (2023). https://doi.org/10.1016/j.bspc.2023.104791
22. Yang, G., et al.: Automatic centerline extraction of coronary arteries in coronary computed tomographic angiography. Int. J. Cardiovasc. Imaging **28**, 921–933 (2012). https://doi.org/10.1007/s10554-011-9894-2
23. Yang, H., Chen, J., Chi, Y., Xie, X., Hua, X.: Discriminative coronary artery tracking via 3D CNN in cardiac CT angiography. In: Shen, D., et al. (eds.) MICCAI 2019. LNCS, vol. 11765, pp. 468–476. Springer, Cham (2019). https://doi.org/10.1007/978-3-030-32245-8_52
24. Zhou, Z., Rahman Siddiquee, M.M., Tajbakhsh, N., Liang, J.: UNet++: a nested U-net architecture for medical image segmentation. In: Stoyanov, D., et al. (eds.) DLMIA/ML-CDS -2018. LNCS, vol. 11045, pp. 3–11. Springer, Cham (2018). https://doi.org/10.1007/978-3-030-00889-5_1

QD-RetNet: Efficient Retinal Disease Classification via Quantized Knowledge Distillation

Ashutosh Kumar and Manisha Verma[✉][iD]

Indian Institute of Technology (Indian School of Mines) Dhanbad, Dhanbad, India
manisha@iitism.ac.in

Abstract. Eye diseases can lead to irreversible vision loss if not detected early, highlighting the potential of automated diagnosis systems to assist health experts in timely detection. While recent deep learning models show high diagnostic performance, they often lack efficiency and rely on costly multi-modality inputs, limiting their practical deployment. We present QD-RetNet, a Quantized Distillation Retina Network that revolutionizes retinal disease classification by delivering clinical-grade diagnosis in a low-resource setting. Unlike conventional approaches that rely on paired multi-modal imaging data for better accuracy, QD-RetNet processes OCT and fundus images independently within a shared knowledge distillation framework, removing the need for large, paired datasets. Using Quantization-Aware Training (QAT), our model achieves 4× compression while retaining diagnostic accuracy close to that of larger, high-compute models. Exhaustive evaluation on TOPCON-MM, MMC-AMD, and MultiEYE benchmark datasets confirms our model's robustness across a broad spectrum of real-world retinal disease prediction tasks. Code is available at https://github.com/ashutoshkr45/QD-RetNet.

Keywords: Retinal disease classification · Knowledge distillation · Model quantization · Computer-aided diagnosis · Quantization-aware training

1 Introduction

Retinal diseases such as age-related macular degeneration (AMD), diabetic retinopathy (DR), glaucoma, etc., are huge global health concerns and contribute significantly to a substantial percentage of visual impairment and blindness [22]. However, current diagnostic pipelines are affected by limitations such as reduced accessibility, dependency on expert knowledge, and the complexity and cost of highly advanced imaging modalities.

Computer-assisted diagnosis (CAD) systems have become revolutionary instruments in ophthalmology, providing fast, reproducible, and scalable screening options. Deep learning has revolutionized the detection of retinal disease by

© The Author(s), under exclusive license to Springer Nature Switzerland AG 2026
S. Ali et al. (Eds.): MIUA 2025, LNCS 15918, pp. 279–292, 2026.
https://doi.org/10.1007/978-3-031-98694-9_20

providing automated, high-accuracy diagnosis from fundus and Optical Coherence Tomography (OCT) images. OCT is a commonly used imaging modality that provides high-resolution cross-sectional images of the retinal layers. This functionality enables better feature learning using deep models for early disease detection with higher accuracy compared to traditional fundus photography [1]. Despite its advantages, models using only OCT as input for diagnosis face challenges due to high acquisition costs and data scarcity, as deep CNNs require huge amounts of data for training. Fundus imaging, on the other hand, provides a broader view of retinal structures, making it complementary to OCT [4,5,29]. Multimodal learning utilizing both modalities enhances diagnostic accuracy [4,29]. However, acquiring paired fundus and OCT images remains impractical, limiting the feasibility of multi-modal learning approaches for automated diagnosis. This emphasizes the need to develop a single-modality-based model, which requires an OCT or fundus image for diagnosis while getting complementary guidance of the other modality from the model and not in the input form. Knowledge distillation (KD) models have been used to transfer knowledge of one modality to another [25]. Moreover, the existing approaches in retinal disease classification rely on very large models and need a lot of computing power, making them expensive to use.

In this paper, we introduce a new framework that performs mutual learning using knowledge distillation between both modalities; the OCT model learns features of the fundus modality from the fundus model, and the fundus model gets guidance from the OCT modality. In this way, both models learn complementary features of another modality. Our method breaks the reliance on multi-model data of OCT and fundus images, allowing for strong disease prediction from a single modality. We also aim for a low-cost model by incorporating quantization-aware training in the student models, which significantly lowers the computation complexity and makes it possible to use on devices with limited resources.

Our main contributions are as follows:

- We propose a mutual distillation-based approach that supports single-modal retinal disease classification while holding high accuracy.
- The models proposed can process OCT or fundus images separately without needing expensive paired data.
- We utilize a quantization-aware training strategy to improve computational efficiency by reducing the model size and inference time with comparable diagnostic performance.

1.1 Related Work

Many existing studies have used both OCT and fundus image modalities separately and together as multi-modal learning for retinal disease prediction [5,7,10]. Multi-model typically combines features from both modalities to improve accuracy [6,15,17,20,27].

Single-Modality Learning (OCT and Fundus-Based Models). Deep learning models have been shown to perform well using CNN-based architectures as compared to conventional hand-crafted feature-based methods for single modality [2,9–11,14,19]. However, these single-modal approaches are beset by the weaknesses of their respective imaging modalities. OCT-based models are affected by high acquisition cost and limited data availability, resulting in approaches like segmentation-guided learning [3,7,16,18]. Similarly, fundus-based models, even if readily available, do not have the depth information obtained from OCT images and are less effective for some disease detections [19,30].

Multi-modal Learning. To improve classification performance, researchers have investigated multi-modal learning by combining both OCT and fundus images [6,15,17,20,27,28,30]. Such methods take advantage of the complementary nature of the two modalities, often using fusion methods at various levels—early, intermediate, or late fusion. Wang et al. [27] addressed this task in AMD classification by proposing a two-stream multi-modal CNN (MM-CNN) with spatially-invariant fusion, allowing for joint optimization of fundus and OCT features. Their end-to-end learning improves predictive performance while preserving model interpretability using an extended class activation mapping (CAM) method. Although these improvements, most multi-modal models, such as [6,27,28], need paired data, significantly reducing their clinical applicability since perfectly aligned multi-modal images are usually unavailable in real-world settings.

KD-Based Learning. Wang et al. proposed a fundus-enhanced disease-aware distillation model (FDDM) that utilizes knowledge transfer from the fundus to the OCT modality [25]. Similarly, OCT-assisted Conceptual Distillation (OCT-CoDA) [26] presents a multi-modal learning model in which OCT images facilitate disease identification from fundus data. Ju et al. use multiple teacher models to distill their knowledge into a unified model through a weighted knowledge distillation loss for long-tailed retinal disease recognition [8].

The growing demand for using artificial intelligence in actual medical situations has led to growing interest in light and practical models. Sunija et al. proposed OctNET, a lightweight model for disease classification in OCT images [24]. Quantization has been a required technique for model compression, allowing the smooth operation of deep learning models on edge devices [13]. Among the many techniques that have been investigated, Post-Training Quantization (PTQ) and QAT [12,23] are of special interest, with QAT being more successful by incorporating quantization effects right from the start of the training process, resulting in better performance in low-precision settings.

The recent literature emphasizes the advancements in single-modal and multi-modal learning methods for retinal disease classification. The QD-RetNet proposed in this work, utilizes these advancements using knowledge distillation and quantization, thus creating an efficient single-modal inference model that perfectly balances efficiency and accuracy.

2   Proposed Method

Our proposed method is inspired by [25], where knowledge distillation is used for fundus-enhanced diagnosis from OCT modality, i.e., fundus modality is used as a teacher in order to train an OCT model. Another possible but important means is to prefer the fundus model while using OCT features as supplementary guidance. In this work, we propose two models that utilize knowledge distillation through modalities, i.e., the OCT modality will help the fundus model, and the fundus modality will enhance features of the OCT model. Hence, any modality can be used for computer-aided diagnosis at inference time. Further, the enormous deep learning models utilized in most existing deep models consume significant computational resources, thus limiting their deployment on edge devices and in resource-constrained settings. We propose to use quantization-aware training for a compressed model.

We formulate the retinal disease classification as a multi-modal learning problem with the characteristic of independent modalities processing. Given a fundus $D_F = \{X_F, Y_F\}$ and a OCT $D_O = \{X_O, Y_O\}$ datasets where $X_F = \{x_i^f\}_{i=1}^{n_1}$ and $Y_F = \{y_i\}_{i=1}^{n_1}$ are fundus image and their labels, and $X_O = \{z_i^o\}_{i=1}^{n_2}$ and $Y_O = \{y_i\}_{i=1}^{n_2}$ are OCT images, and their labels, our goal is to learn generalized classification functions $f_\theta(x_i^f)$ and $f_\phi(x_i^o)$ that classify x_i^f and x_i^o images in disease classes, attempting to minimize classification error and maintain computational efficiency. During test time, only one modality is required for one model in order to make a prediction, i.e., $f_\theta(x_i^f)$ will make a prediction using fundus images and $f_\phi(x_i^o)$ will require only OCT images to make disease classification. We explain two main modules of this work in the following sections.

2.1   Quantization-Aware Training (QAT) Implementation

Quantization-aware training is a method that enables models to be trained under quantization restrictions. This approach helps models maintain accuracy when converted to reduced precision forms. We use PyTorch's quantization module [21] to approximate INT8 quantization effects during training and preserve high-precision computations for gradient updates. In contrast to PTQ, in which rounding errors have the potential to reduce model performance significantly, QAT keeps the network informed of its end quantized state during training so that it can learn accordingly.

QAT uses fake quantization, where activations and weights are rounded to simulate INT8 values during forward and backward passes. However, all the computations are still in floating-point (FP32) form. The process avoids losing learned information due to sudden quantization transitions, retaining model accuracy after quantization. However, since training computations are still in FP32, QAT does not offer memory or computational efficiency gains at this stage. The real advantages come during training when the model is entirely quantized to INT8, allowing compelling inference with much lower latency and power usage.

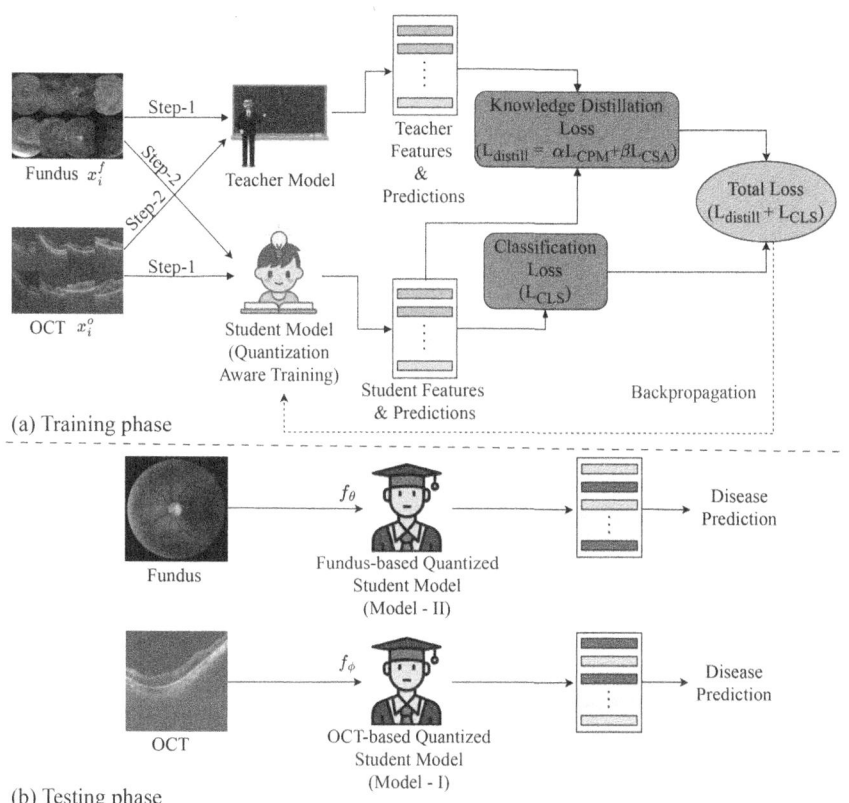

(a) Training phase

(b) Testing phase

Fig. 1. The proposed model architecture. The training phase (a) involves two steps. In step one, the fundus model serves as the teacher, while the quantized OCT model acts as the student and learns from the fundus model. In step two, the roles are reversedâĂŤthe OCT model becomes the teacher, and the quantized fundus model acts as the student. Knowledge Distillation (KD) losses are computed between the teacher and student models, while cross-entropy loss is computed using only the student model. Both losses combine into a total loss, which is minimized through backpropagation. In the testing phase (b), the quantized student model (either fundus or OCT) receives an input image (fundus or OCT) and outputs a disease prediction.

To incorporate QAT into our model, we adapt the base architecture to add quantization constraints while retaining the most important high-precision computation. We implement a quantization configuration optimized for mobile and edge device deployment to ensure that the quantization operations of parameters adhere to an efficient scheme.

After training, the model is fully INT8 quantized, enabling all forward-pass calculations to take advantage of low-bit arithmetic. The resulting deployment-ready model strikes an equilibrium between diagnostic accuracy and computational efficiency, making it an ideal choice for real-time AI-based retinal disease classification.

2.2 Knowledge Distillation Framework

Our proposed framework implements a mutual learning approach for cross-modality knowledge transfer in retinal disease classification. As illustrated in Fig. 1, the methodology adopts a symmetric training strategy involving two steps. During training, the model takes mini-batches of x_i^f (fundus) and x_i^o (OCT) as input. Using supervised learning, the teacher models are obtained by training ResNet-50 based CNNs on single-modality data (either fundus or OCT). These pre-trained models are then used to distill knowledge into the corresponding student models. In step 1, pre-trained fundus model (teacher) transfers knowledge to a student QAT OCT model, while in step 2, pre-trained OCT model acts as teacher and transfers knowledge to student QAT fundus model. Both teacher and student models utilize a ResNet backbone architecture, ensuring consistent feature extraction across modalities.

The process of knowledge transfer, adapted from [25], comprises two significant strategies: Class Prototype Matching (CPM) and Class Similarity Alignment (CSA). CPM ensures that features representing the same class are aligned across modalities by compressing individual noisy feature vectors into class-wise prototype vectors. For each class c, these prototypes e_T^c (Teacher) and e_S^c (Student) are computed as the mean of the respective modality's feature vectors over the mini-batch. These prototypes are then converted to softened distributions $E_T^c = \sigma(e_T^c/\tau)$ and $E_S^c = \sigma(e_S^c/\tau)$, where τ is the temperature scaling factor and σ denotes softmax. To align these distributions, KullbackâĂŞLeibler (KL) divergence is applied between the teacher's and student's class prototype distributions, yielding the CPM loss:

$$\mathcal{L}_{\text{CPM}} = \sum_{c=1}^{C} E_T^c \log\left(\frac{E_T^c}{E_S^c}\right) \tag{1}$$

In CSA, the model captures inter-class correlations crucial for multi-label classification. Average logits q_T and q_S from teacher and student models are used to derive similarity matrices $Q_T^c = \sigma(\text{sim}(q_T^c, q_T)/\tau)$ and $Q_S^c = \sigma(\text{sim}(q_S^c, q_S)/\tau)$ via cosine similarity. KL divergence is again employed to align the similarity matrices of the teacher and student:

$$\mathcal{L}_{\text{CSA}} = \sum_{c=1}^{C} Q_T^c \log\left(\frac{Q_T^c}{Q_S^c}\right) \tag{2}$$

These loss functions combined ensure effective cross-modal knowledge transfer. While $\mathcal{L}_{\text{CPM}}$ focuses on aligning class-wise semantic features through prototype distributions, $\mathcal{L}_{\text{CSA}}$ encourages inter-class relational structure consistency.

The model is trained in an end-to-end manner using distillation losses and cross-entropy loss as follows:

$$\mathcal{L} = \mathcal{L}_{\mathrm{CLS}} + \alpha\mathcal{L}_{\mathrm{CPM}} + \beta\mathcal{L}_{\mathrm{CSA}} \tag{3}$$

where $\mathcal{L}_{\mathrm{cls}}$ denotes binary cross-entropy classification loss from a quantized student model. Hyperparameters α and β balance each distillation term's influence. Only the lightweight student model is used during inference.

3   Experiments and Results

3.1   Dataset and Preprocessing

We evaluate our proposed approach using the TOPCON-MM dataset [25], which contains paired fundus and OCT images from 369 eyes of 203 patients. The dataset is categorized into eleven retinal disease classes: normal, dry age-related macular degeneration (dAMD), wet age-related macular degeneration (wAMD), diabetic retinopathy (DR), central serous chorioretinopathy (CSC), pigment epithelial detachment (PED), macular epiretinal membrane (MEM), fluid (FLD), exudation (EXU), choroid neovascularization (CNV), and retinal vascular occlusion (RVO).

Additionally, we evaluate our approach on the MMC-AMD dataset [27], which consists of multi-modal retinal images. This dataset contains 1,094 fundus (CFP) images from 1,093 eyes of 829 subjects, with 817 eyes having one to five associated OCT images. The OCT scans were acquired using Topcon and Heidelberg OCT cameras and manually selected by technicians. Each eye is classified into one of four categories: normal, dry AMD, polypoidal choroidal vasculopathy (PCV), or wet AMD, based on expert assessment using CFP, OCT, and additional imaging modalities when available.

We also experiment with MultiEYE [26] dataset, which is a large-scale, multi-disease dataset specifically constructed for multiple diseases, merging 13 publicly accessible fundus datasets with 4 OCT datasets and proprietary ophthalmic data. It contains nine classes of retinal diseases and has a consistent preprocessing protocol to ensure diagnostic label accuracy. It offers an extensive range of fundus and OCT images and, therefore, serves as a rich benchmark for assessing deep learning algorithms in retinal disease classification.

We employ strong data augmentation techniques like random cropping, flipping, rotation, contrast, saturation, and brightness changes to improve generalization and stability. All images are resized to 448×448 pixels before feeding to the network.

For impartial comparison, identical preprocessing, augmentation, model backbones, and numbers of training epochs are utilized in all the experiments. We implement a subject-wise 5-fold cross-validation for the TOPCON-MM dataset [25]. The database is split into five sets, and at each fold, 4 sets were used for training and one for testing. Data of one subject/patient may belong to either the train set or test set and not both. For MMC-AMD and MultiEYE datasets [26,27], we follow the original train-validation-test split for fair comparison.

3.2   Implementation Details

We implement our models in PyTorch and use the Tesla V100 GPU to support efficient training and inference. We apply stochastic gradient descent (SGD) as the optimizer with a learning rate of 1×10^{-3}, momentum of 0.9, and weight decay of 1×10^{-4}. We employ a batch size of 8. We use $\tau = 4$, $\alpha = 2$, and $\beta = 1$ following [25]. Quantization-aware training (QAT) is implemented using PyTorch's `torch.ao.quantization` module.

3.3   Baseline Methods and Experimental Setup

We assess the effectiveness of our suggested methodology by comparing it with several baseline methods.

– **Single-Fundus**: A model trained and tested only on fundus images.
– **Single-OCT**: Both training and evaluation on OCT only.
– **FDDM** [25]: A fundus teacher model enhancing an OCT student.
– **ODDM**: An adaptation of FDDM, where an OCT teacher enhances a fundus student.
– **QD-RetNet (Ours)**: Our approach integrates model quantization and knowledge distillation across input modalities. The approach is tested with two configurations:
    • Model I: Fundus teacher distilling knowledge into an OCT student.
    • Model II: OCT teacher distilling knowledge into a fundus student.

A late-fusion or two-stream CNN baseline using paired fundus and OCT data is not included in our comparisons, as the foundational work by FDDM [25], which our method builds upon, has already demonstrated superior performance over such multi-modal models, making such comparisons redundant for our study. Also, we do not include separate full-precision QD-RetNet results, as they are functionally equivalent to FDDM and ODDM models trained jointly per epoch, leading to redundancy in the results.

Table 1. Performance comparison on the TOPCON-MM dataset. All models use ResNet-50 as the backbone.

Metric	Sensitivity	Specificity	F1 Score	AUC	Accuracy	MAP	Size (MB)
Single-OCT	53.08 ±5.79	93.54 ±1.90	63.98 ±6.16	87.73 ±1.44	90.06 ±4.26	66.63 ±4.17	97.8
FDDM (I)	59.12 ±5.96	**94.96** ±3.83	**68.75** ±9.75	**91.27** ±5.12	90.86 ±2.57	**70.20** ±5.07	97.8
Ours (Model 1)	**59.32** ±4.55	94.90 ±5.74	66.21 ±7.55	90.78 ±4.60	**91.11** ±3.31	69.17 ±4.78	**24.9**
Single-Fundus	43.24 ±5.78	**91.74** ±1.64	54.91 ±7.39	79.91 ±1.78	84.48 ±4.78	50.78 ±4.18	97.8
ODDM (II)	48.96 ±6.11	90.28 ±2.46	55.16 ±5.87	83.16 ±2.01	**87.70** ±3.47	**54.82** ±5.66	97.8
Ours (Model 2)	**52.08** ±1.99	88.71 ±5.77	**56.78** ±8.71	**83.20** ±7.61	86.22 ±3.47	53.91 ±6.97	**24.9**

3.4   Evaluation Metrics

We adhere to typical test procedures, where image-level accuracy is defined as the overall performance across scans from the same eye. If any scan indicates a disease, the eye is classified as diseased. To evaluate the classification performance of our models, we report commonly used metrics in medical image classification, including sensitivity, specificity, F1-score, area under the ROC curve (AUC), accuracy, and mean average precision (MAP). These measures give a thorough analysis of how well the model can accurately indicate disease presence and distinguish between various classes.

3.5   Quantitative Results

Table 1 presents the classification performance of all methods on the TOPCON-MM dataset. Our method achieves comparative accuracy while significantly reducing model size.

From the results presented in Table 1, we can see that FDDM (I) [25] and ODDM (II) models performed better than the Single-OCT and Single-Fundus models in all the performance metrics of interest, as expected. FDDM (I) recorded the highest AUC score (91.27), specificity (94.96), and F1-score (68.75), and ODDM (II) recorded a moderate gain over Single-Fundus with an F1-score of 55.16. These results demonstrate that the use of complementary modalities enhances classification performance compared to the use of individual modalities alone.

However, after training such models within a QAT setting, we achieved a model compression of 4× (from 97.8 MB to 24.9 MB) and maintained competitive performance. Model 1, which was trained within a QAT configuration, had a sensitivity of 59.32, an F1-score of 66.21, and a MAP of 69.17, which are nearly as good as FDDM (I) despite the significant compression of the model. Similarly, Model 2, under the ODDM setting, had an F1-score of 56.78 and a MAP of 53.91, with only a slight drop in MAP from the original ODDM (II) model (54.82). This confirms that quantization-aware training (QAT) enables substantial compression without compromising model performance, thus making it a highly appropriate model for deployment to resource-constrained environments, namely for real-time retinal disease screening in remote and clinical settings.

The results presented in Table 2 of MMC-AMD dataset demonstrate that the Single-OCT and Single-Fundus models are weaker than their multi-modal versions, as anticipated. FDDM (I) yields the highest accuracy (93.40) with an F1-score of 89.55, thereby establishing the efficacy of employing complementary fundus and OCT modalities. ODDM (II) demonstrates a minor boost over Single-Fundus with an accuracy of 80.02 and an F1-score of 72.50.

However, after applying quantization-aware training (QAT), we observe a significant reduction in model size (from 97.8 MB to 24.9 MB) while maintaining a reasonable trade-off in accuracy and F1-score. Model 1 achieves an accuracy of 92.55 and an F1-score of 88.06, nearly identical to Single-OCT and close to FDDM (I). Model 2, following the ODDM setting, attains an accuracy of 76.52

Table 2. Performance comparison on the MMC-AMD dataset. All models use ResNet-50 as the backbone.

Metric	Sensitivity	Specificity	Accuracy	F1 Score	Size (MB)
Single-OCT	89.60	95.87	92.51	88.06	97.8
FDDM (I)	**90.76**	**96.38**	**93.40**	**89.55**	97.8
Ours (Model 1)	89.85	95.89	92.55	88.06	**24.9**
Single-Fundus	71.25	90.42	77.29	71.25	97.8
ODDM (II)	**72.55**	**90.83**	**80.02**	**72.50**	97.8
Ours (Model 2)	67.50	89.17	76.52	67.50	**24.9**

and an F1-score of 67.50, showing a moderate drop compared to the original ODDM (II) model.

The performance degradation is notable primarily in Model 2, where the fundus modality is dominant. Since fundus images hold weaker discriminative information than OCT for retinal disease classification, this degradation is expected. However, Model 1 demonstrates that our quantized approach can remain competitive with Single-OCT and even outperform ODDM (II) under some circumstances. This demonstrates the real-world potential of applying our method in resource-constrained situations with a significant model size reduction without compromising competitive classification performance.

Table 3. Performance comparison on the MultiEYE dataset. All models use ResNet-50 as the backbone. We select the best-performing model on the validation set and report the results on the test set.

Metric	MAP	Accuracy	AUC	$F1_{PR}$	$F1_{SS}$	Kappa	Size (MB)
Single-OCT	98.44	**98.13**	99.89	**96.35**	**98.11**	**96.51**	103
FDDM (I)	98.73	97.62	99.90	96.06	97.65	95.54	103
Ours (Model 1)	**99.10**	97.05	**99.93**	95.57	97.80	94.55	**26.1**
Single-Fundus	59.22	76.48	93.62	55.62	68.21	54.12	103
ODDM (II)	**61.11**	**76.86**	**93.81**	**56.58**	**73.93**	**55.31**	103
Ours (Model 2)	55.51	74.46	93.53	52.03	73.34	51.46	**26.1**

Table 3 shows the performance of our model and other baselines on the MultiEYE dataset. The results reflect a curious performance trend across modalities. The widespread availability of OCT data in the MultiEYE dataset has allowed the Single-OCT model to achieve near-saturation performance, with nearly no scope for improvement for the FDDM (I) model. This happens because of huge amount of data available for training OCT model. Similarly, Model 1 (our quantized version) achieves nearly comparable accuracy and MAP figures to FDDM (I), which suggests that in situations where adequate OCT data are available, single-modal models can achieve optimal performance as compared to the distilled model. This finding then begs the very relevant question of whether or not knowledge distillation is still necessary in such a scenario.

On the other hand, the performance of ODDM (II) is better than the Single-Fundus model, while there is a slight drop in its quantized counterpart (Model 2) for some measures. This is more proof of the observed preference of clinicians between fundus imaging and OCT imaging for the diagnosis of retinal disease. The comparatively poor performance for fundus-based models indicates the reduced discriminative ability of fundus images in some disease conditions, which may constrain the effectiveness of multi-modal learning when fundus data predominates.

Table 4. Inference time of different models

Method	Modality Used (Training | Inference)	Paired	Quantized	Time Taken (s)
Single-Modal (OCT)	OCT | OCT	–	✗	23.705
Single-Modal (Fundus)	Fundus | Fundus	–	✗	23.828
Multi-Modal (Two-Stream CNN)	Both | Both	✓	✗	31.325
FDDM [25]	Both | OCT	✗	✗	23.788
ODDM	Both | Fundus	✗	✗	23.985
QD-RetNet (Model-I)	Both | OCT	✗	✓	**10.444**
QD-RetNet (Model-II)	Both | Fundus	✗	✓	**10.630**

Despite the trends revealed, our quantized models obtain comparable performance and significantly reduce in size (from 103 MB to 26.1 MB), thus making them particularly well-suited for deployment within resource-constrained environments. Such a trade-off between accuracy and efficiency is particularly relevant to real-world applications, where efficient models are critical to enable fast and scalable screening of diseases. Results derived from the MultiEYE dataset provide meaningful insight into the use of multi-modal learning for the classification of retinal disease and provide a foundation for subsequent studies on the optimal point and manner in which distillation methods should be implemented.

We also present inference time for disease prediction in Table 4. Reported times are the average of 10 test samples from the TOPCON-MM dataset. The inference time includes the entire test pipeline, including model forward pass and final prediction. All models use ResNet-50 as the backbone and are evaluated on an Intel i5 10th Gen CPU laptop. It shows that quantized QD-RetNet models have significantly reduced inference time compared to all the baseline methods. While single-modal, multi-modal, and other distillation-based models take over 23 s to process an image in most cases, QD-RetNet reduces the time to around 10 s. This substantial reduction reflects the gains in efficiency that come with quantization, making our models especially well-suited to real-time deployment in low-resource environments or clinical settings, all without sacrificing predictive accuracy.

Table 5. Ablation study of CPM and CSA loss for quantized model

Method		Ours (Model-I)				Ours (Model-II)			
CPM	CSA	MAP	AUC	F1 Score	Accuracy	MAP	AUC	F1 Score	Accuracy
✗	✗	67.61	88.01	75.59	87.63	49.02	77.02	**55.06**	83.51
✓	✗	69.72	88.82	76.99	**88.87**	50.90	80.28	52.42	83.40
✗	✓	68.32	89.08	**78.41**	86.79	50.16	77.19	54.41	81.82
✓	✓	**71.23**	**91.05**	74.21	88.48	**53.77**	**82.63**	54.32	**83.92**

3.6 Ablation Study

Table 5 shows the ablation study conducted to test the separate and combined impact of Class Prototype Matching (CPM) and Class Similarity Alignment (CSA) [25] on the quantized models. CPM instructs the student to learn class-specific attributes for the disease from the teacher without any need for paired data, thereby enhancing intra-class consistency. CSA captures inter-class relations by learning co-occurrence patterns of labels, enhancing the student's understanding of class dependencies. While each enhances performance separately, their combined use leads to consistently enhanced performance, proving their complementary role in distillation.

4 Conclusion

In this work, we propose the QD-RetNet framework, which combines knowledge distillation and quantization-aware training for retinal disease prediction. We achieved a stunning 4× model size compression from 97.8 MB to 24.9 MB while retaining comparable diagnostic performance on TOPCON-MM, MMC-AMD, and MultiEYE. At training time, KD transfers knowledge from fundus to OCT and OCT to fundus using two different models. During inference, our quantized models can take either of the two modalities and give a disease diagnosis. Our solution demonstrates that computational efficiency does not have to come at the expense of clinical accuracy. Future work directions include extending the framework to other imaging modalities, extending the methodology to other medical imaging tasks, and exploring more advanced quantization techniques.

Acknowledgements. This work is supported by IIT (ISM) Dhanbad under the project FRS(220)/2024-2025/M&C.

References

1. Bernardes, R., Serranho, P., Lobo, C.: Digital ocular fundus imaging: a review. Ophthalmologica **226**(4), 161–181 (2011)
2. Cen, L.P., et al.: Automatic detection of 39 fundus diseases and conditions in retinal photographs using deep neural networks. Nat. Commun. **12**(1), 4828 (2021)
3. Fang, L., Wang, C., Li, S., Rabbani, H., Chen, X., Liu, Z.: Attention to lesion: lesion-aware convolutional neural network for retinal optical coherence tomography image classification. IEEE Trans. Med. Imaging **38**(8), 1959–1970 (2019)
4. Hao, Y., Liu, S., Yu, Z.: Value of combining optical coherence tomography with fundus photography in screening retinopathy in patients with high myopia. J. Healthc. Eng. **2022**(1), 6556867 (2022)
5. Hassan, T., Akram, M.U., Hassan, B., Nasim, A., Bazaz, S.A.: Review of OCT and fundus images for detection of macular edema. In: 2015 IEEE International Conference on Imaging Systems and Techniques (IST), pp. 1–4. IEEE (2015)
6. He, X., Deng, Y., Fang, L., Peng, Q.: Multi-modal retinal image classification with modality-specific attention network. IEEE Trans. Med. Imaging **40**(6), 1591–1602 (2021)
7. Huang, L., He, X., Fang, L., Rabbani, H., Chen, X.: Automatic classification of retinal optical coherence tomography images with layer guided convolutional neural network. IEEE Signal Process. Lett. **26**(7), 1026–1030 (2019)
8. Ju, L., et al.: Relational subsets knowledge distillation for long-tailed retinal diseases recognition. In: Medical Image Computing and Computer Assisted Intervention (MICCAI), pp. 3–12. Springer (2021)
9. Karri, S., Chakraborty, D., Chatterjee, J.: Transfer learning based classification of optical coherence tomography images with diabetic macular edema and dry age-related macular degeneration. Biomed. Opt. Express **8**(2), 579–592 (2017)
10. Kermany, D.S., et al.: Identifying medical diagnoses and treatable diseases by image-based deep learning. Cell **172**(5), 1122–1131 (2018)
11. Lee, C.S., Baughman, D.M., Lee, A.Y.: Deep learning is effective for classifying normal versus age-related macular degeneration OCT images. Ophthalmol. Retina **1**(4), 322–327 (2017)
12. Lee, H., Lee, N., Lee, S.: A method of deep learning model optimization for image classification on edge device. Sensors **22**(19), 7344 (2022)
13. Lee, N., Ajanthan, T., Torr, P.H.: SNIP: single-shot network pruning based on connection sensitivity. arXiv preprint arXiv:1810.02340 (2018)
14. Li, L., Verma, M., Wang, B., Nakashima, Y., Nagahara, H., Kawasaki, R.: Automated grading system of retinal arterio-venous crossing patterns: a deep learning approach replicating ophthalmologist's diagnostic process of arteriolosclerosis. PLOS Digital Health **2**(1), e0000174 (2023)
15. Li, X., et al.: Multi-modal multi-instance learning for retinal disease recognition. In: Proceedings of the 29th ACM International Conference on Multimedia, pp. 2474–2482 (2021)
16. Li, X., Shen, L., Shen, M., Tan, F., Qiu, C.S.: Deep learning based early stage diabetic retinopathy detection using optical coherence tomography. Neurocomputing **369**, 134–144 (2019)
17. Li, Y., et al.: Multimodal information fusion for glaucoma and diabetic retinopathy classification. In: International Workshop on Ophthalmic Medical Image Analysis, pp. 53–62. Springer (2022)

18. Liu, X., Bai, Y., Jiang, M.: One-stage attention-based network for image classification and segmentation on optical coherence tomography image. In: 2021 IEEE International Conference on Systems, Man, and Cybernetics (SMC), pp. 3025–3029. IEEE (2021)

19. Orlando, J.I., et al.: Refuge challenge: a unified framework for evaluating automated methods for glaucoma assessment from fundus photographs. Med. Image Anal. **59**, 101570 (2020)

20. Ou, Z., et al.: M 2 LC-Net: a multi-modal multi-disease long-tailed classification network for real clinical scenes. China Commun. **18**(9), 210–220 (2021)

21. PyTorch Team: Quantization aware training — pytorch documentation (2024). https://pytorch.org/docs/stable/quantization.html#quantization-aware-training-for-static-quantization. Accessed 06 Apr 2025

22. Resnikoff, S., et al.: Global data on visual impairment in the year 2002. Bull. World Health Organ. **82**(11), 844–851 (2004)

23. Sinha, P., Gichoya, J.W., Purkayastha, S.: Leapfrogging medical AI in low-resource contexts using edge tensor processing unit. In: 2022 IEEE Healthcare Innovations and Point of Care Technologies (HI-POCT), pp. 67–70. IEEE (2022)

24. Sunija, A., Kar, S., Gayathri, S., Gopi, V.P., Palanisamy, P.: OctNET: a lightweight CNN for retinal disease classification from optical coherence tomography images. Comput. Methods Programs Biomed. **200**, 105877 (2021)

25. Wang, L., Dai, W., Jin, M., Ou, C., Li, X.: Fundus-enhanced disease-aware distillation model for retinal disease classification from OCT images. In: International Conference on Medical Image Computing and Computer-Assisted Intervention, pp. 639–648. Springer (2023)

26. Wang, L., et al.: MultiEYE: dataset and benchmark for OCT-enhanced retinal disease recognition from fundus images. IEEE Trans. Med. Imaging (2024)

27. Wang, W., et al.: Learning two-stream CNN for multi-modal age-related macular degeneration categorization. IEEE J. Biomed. Health Inform. **26**(8), 4111–4122 (2022)

28. Wang, W., et al.: Two-stream CNN with loose pair training for multi-modal AMD categorization. In: Medical Image Computing and Computer Assisted Intervention (MICCAI), pp. 156–164. Springer (2019)

29. Watanabe, T., et al.: Combining optical coherence tomography and fundus photography to improve glaucoma screening. Diagnostics **12**(5), 1100 (2022)

30. Yoo, T.K., Choi, J.Y., Seo, J.G., Ramasubramanian, B., Selvaperumal, S., Kim, D.W.: The possibility of the combination of OCT and fundus images for improving the diagnostic accuracy of deep learning for age-related macular degeneration: a preliminary experiment. Med. Biol. Eng. Comput. **57**, 677–687 (2019)

Exploring the Effectiveness of Deep Features from Domain-Specific Foundation Models in Retinal Image Synthesis

Zuzanna Skórniewska$^{(\boxtimes)}$ (ID) and Bartłomiej W. Papież (ID)

Nuffield Department of Population Health, University of Oxford, Oxford, England
`zuzanna.skorniewska@ndph.ox.ac.uk`

Abstract. The adoption of neural network models in medical imaging has been constrained by strict privacy regulations, limited data availability, high acquisition costs, and demographic biases. Deep generative models offer a promising solution by generating synthetic data that bypasses privacy concerns and addresses fairness by producing samples for under-represented groups. However, unlike natural images, medical imaging requires validation not only for fidelity (e.g., Fréchet Inception Score) but also for morphological and clinical accuracy. This is particularly true for colour fundus retinal imaging, which requires precise replication of the retinal vascular network, including vessel topology, continuity, and thickness. In this study, we investigated whether a distance-based loss function based on deep activation layers of a large foundational model trained on large corpus of domain data, colour fundus imaging, offers advantages over a perceptual loss and edge-detection based loss functions. Our extensive validation pipeline, based on both domain-free and domain specific tasks, suggests that domain-specific deep features do not improve autoencoder image generation. Conversely, our findings highlight the effectiveness of conventional edge detection filters in improving the sharpness of vascular structures in synthetic samples.

Keywords: Colour fundus imaging · VQ-GAN · Generative Modelling

1 Introduction

Colour fundus imaging is a non-invasive, affordable imaging technique routinely used in ophthalmologic clinics for retinal diagnostics. However, this imaging shows promise beside clinical practice - in biomarker discovery, with discoverable features associated with cardiovascular [1, 2] neural [3, 4] and ophthalmic [3, 5] conditions. While the use of deep learning for biomarker extraction would remove the need for manually crafted features, there have only been a few works demonstrating a fully automated deep learning approach [1, 3, 6]. The main barrier to further progress is the limited availability of large-scale datasets, as most retinal datasets, such as DRIVE [7] and STARE [8], are small fully labelled sets primarily used for segmentation tasks.

The scarcity of data can potentially be addressed by generating synthetic samples using generative neural networks. This approach may also help mitigate privacy concerns

S. Ali et al. (Eds.): MIUA 2025, LNCS 15918, pp. 293–305, 2026.
https://doi.org/10.1007/978-3-031-98694-9_21

and reduce sampling biases stemming from a lack of diversity in existing clinical studies [9]. While generative neural networks, such as VQ-GAN [10] or more recently diffusion models [11, 12, 13], have proven capable of producing high resolution realistic and diverse natural images, as validated by e.g., Fréchet Inception Score, there is currently no standardized method for assessing the morphological accuracy of medical images, including synthetic colour fundus images. This includes validating aspects such as vessel continuity, differentiation between arteries and veins, and clinically relevant vascular thickness and topology.

To date, the use of generative models for medical imaging have been predominantly synthetic brain [14, 15, 16] and breast MRI [17], tissue [18], cell [19], and PET/CT [20, 21] imaging data. The image generation is controlled and validated for its semantic correctness associated with the domain in question via incorporation of domain-specific supervision losses [16], meta-data conditioning [16, 17, 19], self-supervision strategies [15, 18] and downstream validation on external clinical data or extracted biomarkers, [14, 17]. However, colour fundus image synthesis has to date been proportionally unaddressed, with a few notable exceptions [22, 23, 24].

This paper explores colour fundus generation using an encoder-decoder model, inspired by VQ-GAN architecture [10] capable of generating high-quality synthetic colour fundus images and trained with a range of auxiliary loss functions, which enforce either perceptual fidelity, vessel continuity or domain-specific morphological & clinical feature preservation. We extend the standard validation beyond fidelity metrics to a range of relevant downstream clinical prediction tasks, as well as a direct comparison of retinal morphological features relating to vascular networks and the optic disc.

Specifically, inspired by the success of training guidance based on deep features from networks trained on large natural image datasets to enforce perceptual similarity – what was coined as perceptual loss [25] – this paper introduces a novel loss term, conceptually similar to perceptual loss. The novel loss term leverages a RETFound [3] backbone, a large vision transformer trained via self-supervised learning on a dataset of 1.6 million unlabelled colour fundus images. We refer to this as *RETFound loss*, which directly optimizes the imaging latent space. By minimizing the distance between synthetic images and real counterparts in the latent space, we hypothesise that the generated images retain deep features associated with domain-specific imaging fidelity – relating to retinal morphology and clinical information contained within the image. Our hypothesis is based on the strong performance of the backbone model – RETFound in various downstream classification tasks on external clinical metadata, supporting its effectiveness in this context.

2 Background

2.1 VQ-GAN

Our model follows the architecture of VQ-GAN encoder-decoder model [10] with latent space quantization and supervision by a CNN-based patched discriminator, trained concurrently as the autoencoder in an adversarial way. The encoder and decoder are convolutional, featuring down-sampling and up-sampling layers respectively, followed by ResNet [26] blocks. Additionally, an attention block is applied after down-sampling in the encoder and before up-sampling in the decoder. Specifically, the model com-prises of an encoder, which projects an input image, $x \in R^{H \times W \times 3}$, to a compressed la-tent space, $z \in R^{h \times w \times nz}$, where nz is the dimensionality of the embedding space and $h = \frac{H}{c}$ and $w = \frac{W}{c}$, where H, W are an image height and width, and c is the compression magnitude based on encoder's depth and the input image resolution. This latent representation contains $h \times w$ vectors $z_{i,j} \in R^{n_z}$. In the quantization stage, each of zi,j is mapped to its nearest neighbour, $\hat{Z}_j \in R^{n\hat{z}}$, based on the Euclidean distance, where $\hat{z}_j$ is chosen from the set of K codebook entries. The codebook $Z = \{e_k \in R^{n_z}\}_{k=1}^{K}$ is a dis-crete set of learnable embedding vectors used to quantize the continuous latent representations; it is optimized jointly with the encoder and decoder by minimizing a loss encouraging quantized vectors to stay close to the encoder output. Upon the quantization stage, the parametrised embedding space is fed through a decoder, which recon-struct the information in the compressed latent space back to pixel space (Fig. 1).

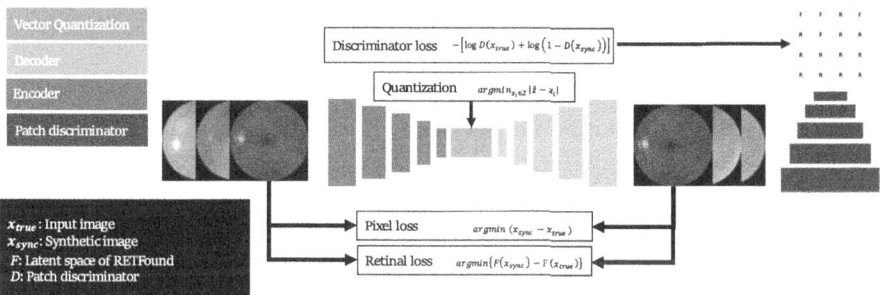

Fig. 1. The model is a standard VQ-GAN with an autoencoder-decoder architecture, incorporating quantization reparameterization in the latent space and a CNN-based patch-based discriminator supervision. The proposed training strategy introduces a loss function defined in the latent space of RETFound [3] trained on 1.6 million retinal images.

This encoder-decoder model, referred to as the *generator*, is trained using GAN loss equilibrium, with a CNN patch-based discriminator enforcing the generation of realistic-looking samples. The generator's training process is driven by gradient updates from three sources: the pixel loss (Hinge loss), the GAN penalty term, and the novel RETFound loss term. The RETFound loss minimizes the distance between embedding vectors of synthetic and real samples in the RETFound latent space, ensuring that both images capture similar semantic information related to the retina. In parallel with training the generator and discriminator, the set of codebook entries is optimized on the training data via *commitment loss* [27].

2.2 RETFound

The RETFound model, similar to VQ-GAN, follows an encoder-decoder architecture. The encoder is a large vision transformer [28] (ViT-large) with 24 transformer blocks, which partitions the input image into 16×16 patches and encodes it into a 1024-dimensional embedding vector. The decoder is a small vision transformer (ViT-small) with 8 transformer blocks. The model was trained on a curated dataset of 1.6 million unlabelled colour fundus retinal images with a resolution of 224. The authors compare the model performance with models trained using a range of self-supervised strategies, concluding the mask autoencoder as the one yielding the best performance.

2.3 Perceptual Loss

Perceptual loss was introduced as a stronger alternative to model-free perceptual distance metrics, such as the Structural Similarity Index (SSIM), which struggle to accurately capture certain types of image degradation, like blurring [25]. Instead of relying on traditional similarity measures, perceptual loss quantifies perceptual similarity between image pairs using the L1 distance between deep feature activations from large CNN models trained on natural images. This approach is based on the idea that deep network layers, having learned to recognize meaningful patterns in images, are inherently sensitive to degradations that align with human perception.

3 Methods

3.1 VQ-GAN Implementation Details

Our model was trained on 90,344 left and right colour fundus images at a resolution of 256×256 from the UK Biobank. The encoder compresses the 3-channel input images using scaling factors of [1, 2, 4], with each down sampling followed by one ResNet block, progressively reducing image's spatial dimensions to 32×32. This results in a latent representation consisting of 1,024 embedding vectors, each with 256 channels. During the quantization stage, the embedding channels are reduced from 256 to 128, and each of the 1,024 vectors is mapped to one of 512 learned codebook entries. This represents a mild compression, which retains essential information while eliminating redundancy present in the highly correlated pixel space, ensuring that the latent representation captures the most meaningful features of the image.

3.2 Retinal Feature Extraction

Assessment of morphological correctness and clinical usefulness of synthetic colour fundus imaging is based on retinal features extracted by an external end-to-end model, AutoMorph [6], which extracts a set of 45 interpretable features, relating to geometric properties of the optic disc and cup (height and width) and the retinal vascular network (e.g., vascular thickness or fractal dimension).

3.3 RETFound Loss

Our *RETFound* loss is based on the RETFound model trained on Moorfields Hospital data using masking training strategy. The loss is computed as the L1 distance in the 1024-dimensional embedding space – the activation layer of the encoder's last transformer block. Since the RETFound model was trained on images with a resolution of 224, our images are resized accordingly.

3.4 Edge Loss

Most handcrafted retinal biomarkers are linked to retinal vascular networks, as evidenced by tools like AutoMorph, where the majority of features are vascular-related. Inspired by this, we implemented an L2-distance loss function between the "vesselness maps" of an image pair. Specifically, the vesselness response is computed on the green channel using the Meijering filter [29]— an intensity-based filter based on the eigenvalues of the Hessian matrix of the image gradient. This filter response effectively highlights tube-like structures, such as blood vessels (Fig. 2).

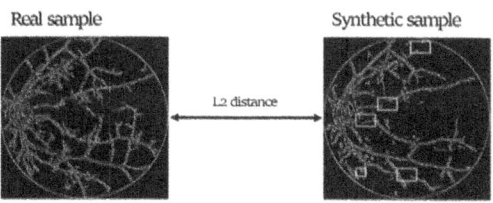

Fig. 2. Meijering filter-based edge loss: Computes the L2 distance between vesselness scores to enforce topological correctness and vessel continuity. Note that the visualization shows a thresholded signal, while the loss operates on the continuous vesselness response.

3.5 Perceptual Loss

Perceptual loss is computed using a VGG-16 [30] backbone trained on ImageNet for classification. The loss is calculated as the sum of L2 distances between feature maps extracted from the 4th, 9th, 16th, 23rd, and 30th activation layers of the network.

4 Experiments

We performed a comprehensive validation of the generated samples, beginning with standard validation methods using commonly used fidelity metrics, followed by evaluation on downstream classification tasks incorporating additional clinical metadata, and finally, direct comparison of extracted biomarkers related to retinal vasculature and optic disc properties.

4.1 Image Fidelity Evaluation

To validate the quality of synthetic images, we used several metrics: Fréchet Inception Distance (FID), Maximum Mean Discrepancy (MMD), and Multi-scale Structural Similarity Index Measure (MS-SSIM). These metrics respectively evaluate the fidelity of synthetic samples, their coverage relative to real samples, and their structural similarity. Each metric is based on 20,000 synthetic and real samples. FID is based on the latent space of InceptionV3 [31] trained on natural images (ImageNet), while MMD is based on Gaussian kernel operating in pixel space (Fig. 3).

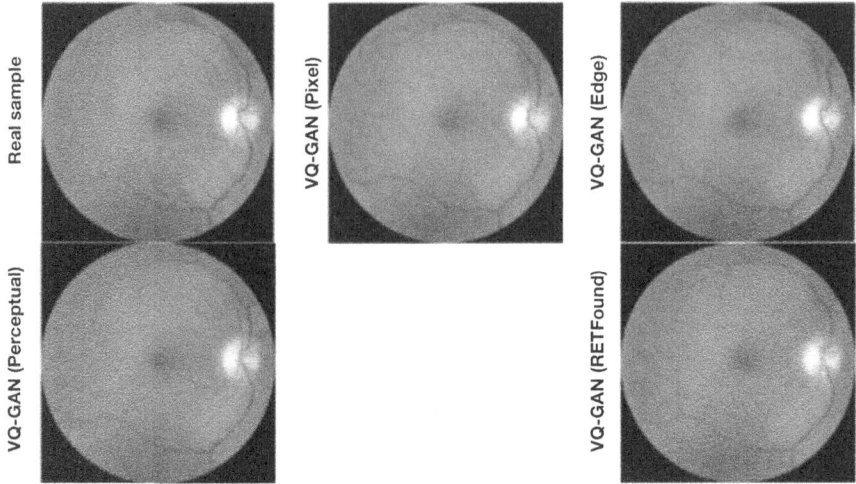

Fig. 3. Qualitative comparison of tested VQ-GAN models on a single sample. All models achieve good reconstruction, but VQ-GAN (Edge) and VQ-GAN (Perceptual) exhibit slightly sharper contrast, enhancing vessel detection, whilst VQ-GAN (RETFound) struggles to replicate the optic cup.

As shown in Table 1, VQ-GAN trained with perceptual loss achieves the FID closest to that of real samples, followed closely by VQ-GAN trained with edge loss. Interestingly, incorporating deep features from the RETFound model led to only a slight improvement in the fidelity of synthetic samples compared to the pixel-only loss baseline. Unlike the FID score, both MMD and MS-SSIM offered limited insight, as they produced similar values across all four models. Specifically, MMD remained consistently low (below 0.05), indicating satisfactory sample coverage, while MS-SSIM values were higher than those of real samples. This increase in structural similarity may be attributed to the filtering effect of autoencoders, which generate synthetic images that are free of imaging artifacts found in real data.

Table 1. Commonly used metrics to assess synthetic samples fidelity and diversity. VQGAN (RETFound) - model trained with RETFound loss; VQGAN (Perceptual) - trained with perceptual loss; VQ-GAN (Pixel) - trained only with pixel-based losses; VQ-GAN (Edge) - trained with edge loss. MS-SSIM is reported as mean [standard deviation].

Model	FID ↓	MMD ↓	MS-SSIM ↑
Real	0.64	0.022	0.706 [0.065]
VQ-GAN (RETFound)	11.43	0.020	0.968 [0.010]
VQ-GAN (Perceptual)	**2.45**	0.019	0.975 [0.007]
VQ-GAN (Pixel)	19.95	0.020	**0.980 [0.006]**
VQ-GAN (Edge)	5.47	**0.018**	0.975 [0.007]

4.2   Evaluation on Downstream Tasks

Beyond assessing visual fidelity, synthetic medical images must also preserve clinical relevance and morphological accuracy. To validate this, we quantified the predictive power of retinal features extracted using AutoMorph on various cardiovascular risk factors, specifically age, sex, BMI, blood pressure, and blood glucose levels, which were previously shown to be directly predictable from colour fundus images [1]. The evaluation follows the standard *Train-Synthetic, Test-Real* framework [32]. As shown in Table 2, all models except VQ-GAN (RETFound) achieved the lowest error in two variables each. VQ-GAN (Perceptual) had the best results for age and BMI, VQ-GAN (Edge) for systolic blood pressure and HbA1c, and the baseline VQ-GAN (Pixel) for diastolic blood pressure and glucose levels. Notably, VQ-GAN trained with RETFound deep features underperformed, yielding worse results than even the baseline VQ-GAN (Pixel). However, none of the synthetic models achieved error rates as low as those based on real data, highlighting a persistent and yet unresolved generative inconsistency.

Table 2. Validation of synthetic samples on prediction tasks on external data, reported as (MAE - mean (standard deviation) for age, BMI, diastolic/systolic blood pressure, HbA1c and glucose, and F1-score for sex.

Validation variable	Real	VQ-GAN (RETFound)	VQ-GAN (Perceptual)	VQ-GAN (Pixel)	VQ-GAN (Edge)
Sex	0.52 (0.01)	0.53 (0.01)	0.51 (0.02)	0.51 (0.01)	0.51 (0.012)
Age	7.72 (0.13)	9.32 (1.68)	**7.60 (0.27)**	8.00 (0.43)	7.94 (0.18)
BMI	4.01 (0.06)	5.21 (0.68)	**4.29 (0.27)**	4.31 (0.24)	4.30 (0.33)
Diastolic BP	9.12 (0.18)	11.84 (0.80)	10.17 (0.47)	**9.60 (0.29)**	10.58 (0.93)
Systolic BP	16.98 (0.22)	20.88 (4.26)	18.52 (0.71)	18.01 (0.83)	**17.55 (1.71)**
HbA1c	4.27 (0.09)	6.93 (1.34)	5.28 (0.57)	4.98 (0.77)	**4.59 (0.25)**
Glucose	0.63 (0.06)	1.48 (0.79)	0.77 (0.16)	**0.74 (0.09)**	0.78 (0.12)

4.3   Morphological Evaluation

In addition to evaluating extracted retinal features for predicting external clinical variables, we also directly assessed the similarity of sample distributions. Specifically, for a set of 45 AutoMorph features, we computed the mean and standard deviation for each sample. For non-real samples, we further assessed the probability of belonging to the same distribution as real data using a permutation test, where a high p-value indicates a faithful recreation of the real sample distribution. This analysis was conducted on a set of 5,000 randomly selected images. Figures 4, 5 and 6 present the results for all variables, with features categorized as follows: optic disc and cup features (Fig. 4; Table S1), vascular width (Fig. 5; Table S2), vessel density (measured as the proportion of vessel to non-vessel pixels; Fig. 6 – right top panel; Table S3), fractal dimension (expressing vascular complexity; Fig. 6 – left top panel; Table S4), and vascular calibre metrics, including CRAE (central retinal arteriolar equivalent), CRVE (central retinal venular equivalent), and AVR (arteriolar–venular ratio) (Fig. 6 – bottom panel; Table S5). Figures 4, 5 and 6 show the distribution of synthetic features relative to the real sample distribution (z-score normalized). Coloured distributions indicate substantial overlap with the real data, as determined by a permutation test (p-value > 0.05). Exact summary statistics are provided in the Supplement.

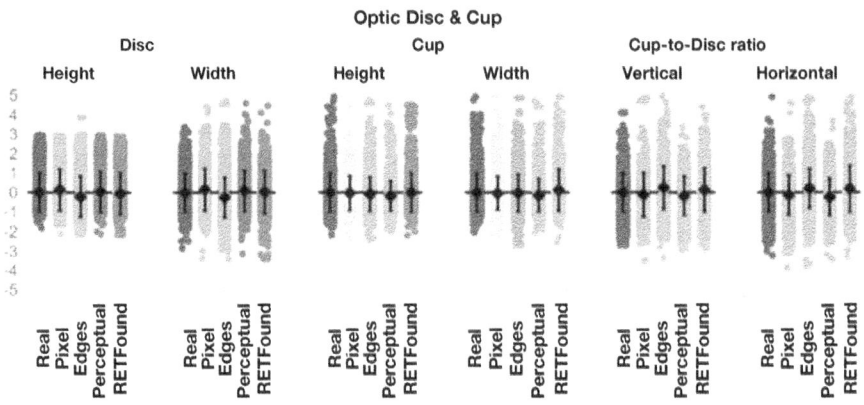

Fig. 4. Comparison of retinal features related to the optic disc and cup. Each boxplot shows the mean and standard deviation for each model. Non-grey distributions indicate samples' overlap with the real data distribution, as supported by a permutation test (p-value > 0.05). All features are z-score normalized relative to the real sample.

As indicated by Figs. 4, 5 and 6, VQ-GAN trained with perceptual loss demonstrated the highest consistency, yielding 5 high p-values, matching only a fraction of all 45 features. This was followed by VQ-GAN (Edge) with 4 high p-values, VQ-GAN (Pixel) with 3, and VQ-GAN (RETFound) with 3. These findings align with the models' performance in downstream prediction tasks and further highlight the underperformance of fundus image generation when leveraging deep features from a foundational model trained on target domain data.

Notably, VQ-GAN (Edge) achieved a relatively high number of matches compared to VQ-GAN (Perceptual), while requiring significantly lower computational resources and being more data-efficient. Since edge detection is a weight-free process that does not require extensive training on large datasets, it offers a practical alternative to perceptual loss.

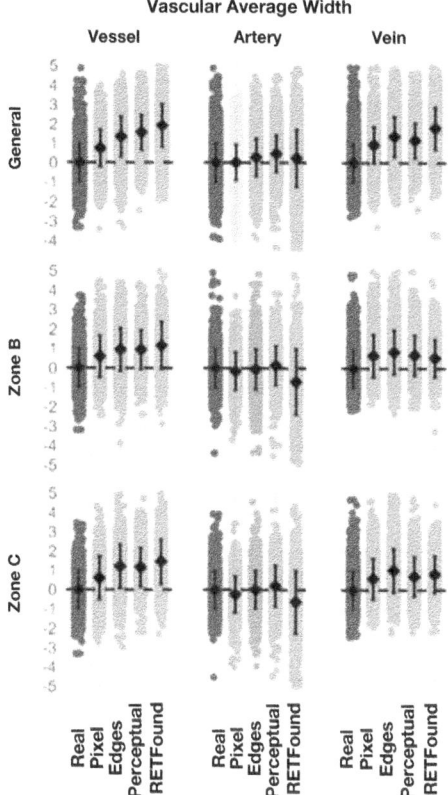

Fig. 5. Comparison of retinal features related to vascular average width. Each boxplot shows the mean and standard deviation for each model. Non-grey distributions indicate samples' overlap with the real data distribution, as supported by a permutation test (p-value > 0.05). All features are z-score normalized relative to the real sample.

Interestingly, synthetic data performance varied considerably across different retinal features. Features related to the optic disc and cup were well represented, whereas those linked to average vascular width and fractal dimension were consistently less accurate. Specifically, synthetic models tended to generate vasculature that appeared thicker than in real samples, as shown in Fig. 5. While VQ-GAN (Edge) performed best in this category, it still only matched two out of nine features. Conversely, synthetic samples consistently produced lower values for fractal dimension features, suggesting a tendency to simplify vascular complexity compared to real data, as shown in Fig. 6, with VQ-GAN (RETFound) having the largest deviation from the real sample distribution.

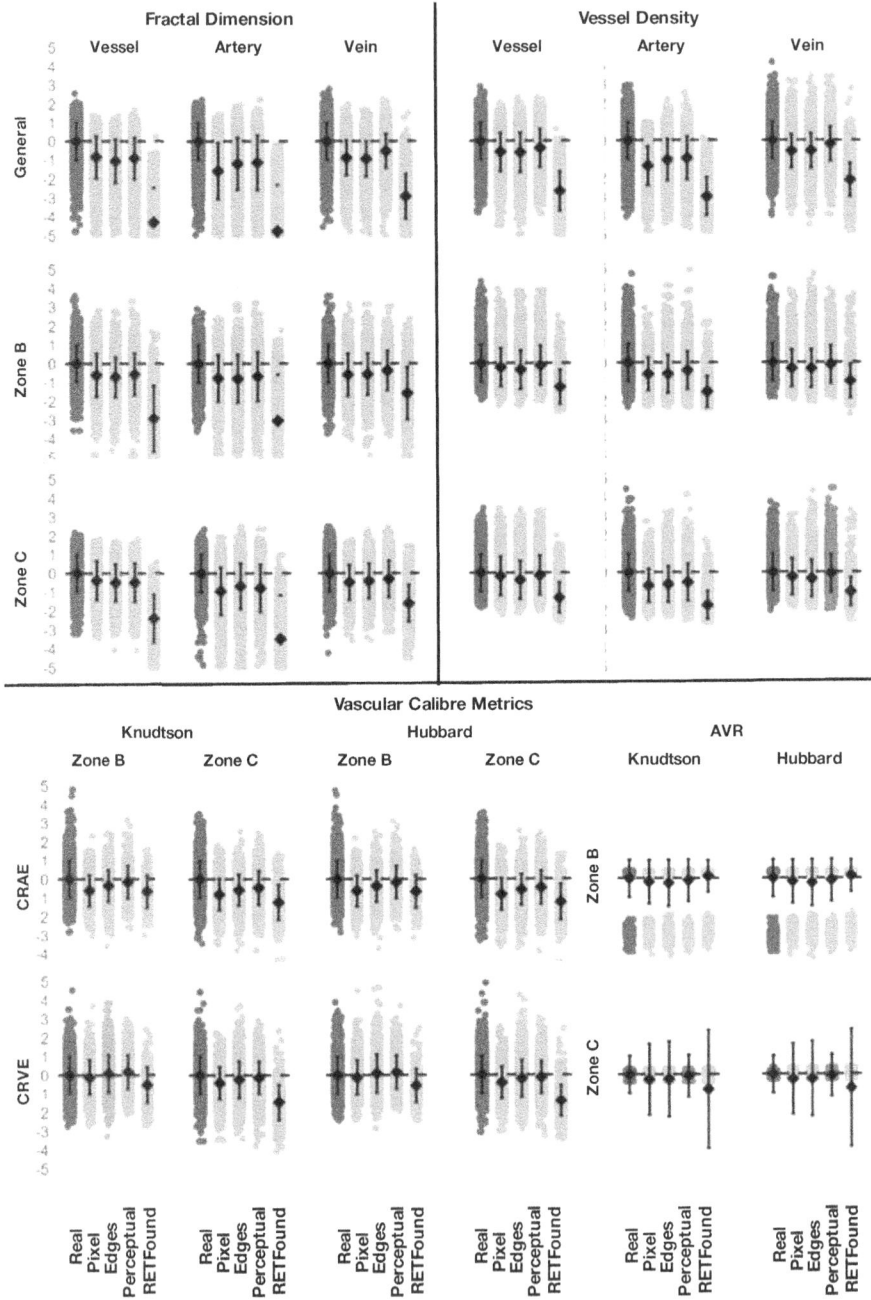

Fig. 6. Comparison of retinal features related to fractal dimension, vessel density and vascular calibre metrics. Each boxplot shows the mean and standard deviation for each model. Non-grey distributions indicate samples' overlap with the real data distribution, as supported by a permutation test (p-value > 0.05). All features are z-score normalized relative to the real sample.

5 Discussion

This paper compares different colour fundus image generation strategies enforcing either perceptual similarity (Perceptual loss), vessel continuity (Edge loss) or domain specific information (RETFound loss). We tested the proposed models on a range of validation tasks, starting from the domain-invariant validation on fidelity metrics, and finishing by direct comparison of extracted retinal features. Our work suggests that leveraging deep features of foundational models trained on domain data **does not** yield samples, which are more realistic or better preserve morphological and clinical information within colour fundus images. Conversely, models which are supervised by a perceptual loss, i.e., by models trained on natural imaging data, better learn to generate images that are both more realistic and morphologically and clinically correct. This is a surprising result, given the demonstrated use of RETFound encoder features for risk prediction of various cardiovascular events, e.g., myocardial infarction or ischaemic stroke [3]. Whilst the RETFound loss consistently underperformed, the autoencoder supervised by a simple edge detection filter achieved results comparable to the autoencoder supervised by deep features from the VGG-16 network - which serves as the backbone for the perceptual loss and was trained on over a million images from ImageNet. This outcome suggests that large pretrained networks, extensive datasets, or high computational resources may not always be required to achieve competitive performance.

Nevertheless, even the best-performing autoencoder in the study, VQ-GAN with perceptual loss, produced samples that underperformed relative to real samples in downstream tasks based on extracted retinal features. This issue may stem from the low-resolution regime used in our study. Typically, colour fundus imaging is performed at high resolution, and estimating vascular thickness from lower resolution data can inherently lead to inaccuracies. The underperformance of RETFound compared to VGG-16 may also stem from differences in model architecture, with RETFound being a vision transformer and VGG-16 a CNN. Notably, however, perceptual losses based on vision transformers have been shown to outperform their pixel-based loss counterparts [33] Another possible reason for the relative drop in RETFound loss performance compared to perceptual loss is the difference in the number of activation layers used, with RETFound loss relying only on the final activation layer. Nevertheless, future research should explore alternative strategies for colour fundus synthetic sample generation that better preserve topological structures and retinal biomarkers than perceptual-based loss functions, such as those based on VGG-16 or RETFound. Furthermore, it would be beneficial to explore further whether CNN-based models are inherently more effective at preserving deep imaging features, which could be leveraged as imaging biomarkers in downstream tasks or serve as a backbone for a perceptual-style loss function.

Acknowledgments. This research has been conducted using data from UK Biobank with access provided through application 80521.

References

1. Poplin, R., et al.: Prediction of cardiovascular risk factors from retinal fundus photographs via deep learning. Nat. Biomed. Eng. **2**(3), 158–164 (2018). https://doi.org/10.1038/s41551-018-0195-0
2. Cheung, C.Y., et al.: A deep-learning system for the assessment of cardiovascular disease risk via the measurement of retinal-vessel calibre. Nat Biomed Eng. **5**(6), 498–508 (2021). https://doi.org/10.1038/s41551-020-00626-4
3. Zhou, Y., et al.: A foundation model for generalizable disease detection from retinal images. Nature **622**(7981), 156–163 (2023). https://doi.org/10.1038/s41586-023-06555-x
4. Cheung, C.Y., et al.: A deep learning model for detection of Alzheimer's disease based on retinal photographs: a retrospective, multicentre case-control study. Lancet. Digit. Health **4**(11), e806–e815 (2022). https://doi.org/10.1016/S2589-7500(22)00169-8
5. An, G., et al.: Glaucoma diagnosis with machine learning based on optical coherence tomography and color fundus images. J. Healthc. Eng. **2019**(1), 4061313 (2019). https://doi.org/10.1155/2019/4061313
6. Zhou, Y., et al.: AutoMorph: automated retinal vascular morphology quantification via a deep learning pipeline. Transl. Vision Sci. Technol. **11**(7), 12 (2022). https://doi.org/10.1167/tvst.11.7.12
7. Staal, J., Abràmoff, M.D., Niemeijer, M., Viergever, M.A., Van Ginneken, B.: Ridge-based vessel segmentation in color images of the retina. IEEE Trans. Med. Imaging **23**(4), 501–509 (2004). https://doi.org/10.1109/TMI.2004.825627
8. Hoover, A.: Locating blood vessels in retinal images by piecewise threshold probing of a matched filter response. IEEE Trans. Med. Imaging **19**(3), 203–210 (2000). https://doi.org/10.1109/42.845178
9. Alloula, A., Mustafa, R., McGowan, D.R., Papież, B.W.: On Biases in a UK Biobank-based Retinal Image Classification Model (2024). https://arxiv.org/abs/2408.02676
10. Esser, P., Rombach, R., Ommer, B.: Taming Transformers for High-Resolution Image Synthesis (2021). https://arxiv.org/abs/2012.09841
11. Rombach, R., Blattmann, A., Lorenz, D., Esser, P., Ommer, B.: High-resolution image synthesis with latent diffusion models. Proc. IEEE Comput. Soci. Conf. Comput. Vision Pattern Recognit. (2022). https://doi.org/10.1109/CVPR52688.2022.01042
12. Ho, J., Jain, A., Abbeel, P.: Denoising diffusion probabilistic models. Adv. Neural Inf. Proc. Syst. **33**, 6840–6851 (2020)
13. Song, J., Meng, C., Ermon, S.: Denoising diffusion implicit models. In: ICLR 2021 - 9th International Conference on Learning Representations (2021)
14. Tudosiu, P.-D., et al.: Morphology-preserving Autoregressive 3D Generative Modelling of the Brain (2022). https://doi.org/10.48550/ARXIV.2209.03177
15. Zhu, X., Zhang, W., Li, Y., O'Donnell, L.J., Zhang, F.: When Diffusion MRI Meets Diffusion Model: A Novel Deep Generative Model for Diffusion MRI Generation (2024). https://doi.org/10.48550/ARXIV.2408.12897
16. Litrico, M., Guarnera, F., Giuffrida, M.V., Ravì, D., Battiato, S.: TADM: Temporally-aware diffusion model for neurodegenerative progression on brain MRI. In: proceedings of Medical Image Computing and Computer Assisted Intervention – MICCAI 2024. Springer, Switzerland (2024)
17. Konz, N., Chen, Y., Dong, H., Mazurowski, M.A.: Anatomically-controllable medical image generation with segmentation-guided diffusion models. In: proceedings of Medical Image Computing and Computer Assisted Intervention – MICCAI 2024. Springer Nature, Switzerland (2024)

18. Doerrich, S., Di Salvo, F., Ledig, C.: Self-supervised vision transformer are scalable generative models for domain generalization. In: Proceedings of Medical Image Computing and Computer Assisted Intervention – MICCAI 2024. Springer Nature, Switzerland (2024)
19. Sturm, M., Cerrone, L., Hamprecht, F.A.: SynCellFactory: generative data augmentation for cell tracking. In: Proceedings of Medical Image Computing and Computer Assisted Intervention – MICCAI 2024. Springer Nature, Switzerland (2024)
20. Zhang, H., et al.: LeFusion: Controllable Pathology Synthesis via Lesion-Focused Diffusion Models (2024). https://doi.org/10.48550/ARXIV.2403.14066
21. Bradbury, R., Vallis, K.A., Papiez, B.W.: Paired diffusion: generation of related, synthetic PET-CT-segmentation scans using linked denoising diffusion probabilistic models. In: Proceedings - International Symposium on Biomedical Imaging (2024). https://doi.org/10.1109/ISBI56570.2024.10635593
22. Zhang, L., Wu, F., Bronik, K., Papiez, B.W.: DiffuSeg: domain-driven diffusion for medical image segmentation. IEEE J. Biomed. Health Inform. (2025). https://doi.org/10.1109/JBHI.2025.3526806
23. Hou, Q., et al.: FundusGAN: a Hierarchical Feature-Aware Generative Framework for High-Fidelity Fundus Image Generation (2025). Accessed 05 Apr 2025. https://arxiv.org/abs/2503.17831v1
24. Ahn, S., Song, S.J., Shin, J.: FundusGAN: fundus image synthesis based on semi-supervised learning. Biomed. Signal Process. Control **86**, 105289 (2023). https://doi.org/10.1016/J.BSPC.2023.105289
25. Zhang, R., Isola, P., Efros, A.A., Shechtman, E., Wang, O.: The unreasonable effectiveness of deep features as a perceptual metric. In: 2018 IEEE/CVF Conference on Computer Vision and Pattern Recognition, pp. 586–595 (2018). https://doi.org/10.1109/CVPR.2018.00068
26. He, K., Zhang, X., Ren, S., Sun, J.: Deep residual learning for image recognition. In: Proceedings of the IEEE Computer Society Conference on Computer Vision and Pattern Recognition, pp. 770–778 (2015). https://doi.org/10.1109/CVPR.2016.90
27. van den Oord, A., Vinyals, O., Kavukcuoglu, K.: Neural Discrete Representation Learning (2018). https://arxiv.org/abs/1711.00937
28. Dosovitskiy, A., et al.: An image is worth 16x16 words: transformers for image recognition at scale (2021). https://arxiv.org/abs/2010.11929
29. Meijering, E., Jacob, M., Sarria, J.C.F., Steiner, P., Hirling, H., Unser, M.: Design and validation of a tool for neurite tracing and analysis in fluorescence microscopy images. Cytometry A **58**(2), 167–176 (2004). https://doi.org/10.1002/cyto.a.20022
30. Simonyan, K., Zisserman, A.: Very deep convolutional networks for large-scale image recognition. In: 3rd International Conference on Learning Representations, ICLR 2015 - Conference Track Proceedings (2014). Accessed 06 Apr. 2025. https://arxiv.org/abs/1409.1556v6
31. Szegedy, C., Vanhoucke, V., Ioffe, S., Shlens, J., Wojna, Z.: Rethinking the inception architecture for computer vision. In: Proceedings of the IEEE Computer Society Conference on Computer Vision and Pattern Recognition (2016). https://doi.org/10.1109/CVPR.2016.308
32. Jordon, J., et al.: Synthetic Data -- what, why and how?` (2022)
33. Dong, X., et al.: PeCo: Perceptual codebook for BERT pre-training of vision transformers. In: Proceedings of the AAAI Conference on Artificial Intelligence, vol. 37, no. 1, pp. 552–560 (2023). https://doi.org/10.1609/AAAI.V37I1.25130

GenVOG: A Diffusion Probabilistic Framework for Patient-Independent Pose-Guided Nystagmus Video-Oculography (VOG) Generation

Aimon Rahman[1], Kemar E. Green[2], and Vishal M. Patel[1(✉)]

[1] Department of Electrical and Computer Engineering, Johns Hopkins University, Baltimore, USA
{arahma30,vpatel36}@jhu.edu
[2] Department of Neurology, Johns Hopkins University School of Medicine, Baltimore, USA
kgreen66@jhmi.edu

Abstract. Nystagmus, a condition characterized by involuntary, repetitive eye movements that significantly impair visual acuity and are indicative of various neurological disorders. Creating deep learning models for nystagmus research has been hindered by a lack of publicly available data, largely due to concerns regarding patient privacy, as eye movement patterns can potentially identify individuals. To overcome this, the research generates synthetic nystagmus videos based on different types of nystagmus waveforms, without using real patient data (*GenVOG*). This is achieved by utilizing publicly accessible datasets to create long, clinically relevant videos that realistically simulate nystagmus. The effectiveness of the generated videos is evaluated through their application to downstream tasks using real patient datasets.

Keywords: Video Generation · Diffusion Model · Nystagmus · Synthetic Data · Eye Movements · Video-Oculography (VOG)

1 Introduction

Nystagmus is an eye movement disorder characterized by involuntary, repetitive ocular oscillations, significantly affecting visual acuity and balance [1,13]. For clear vision, images must remain relatively still on the central fovea of the retina [2,4,6]. Nystagmus develops from failure of neural mechanisms responsible for retinal image stability; as a result, the eye drifts from the visual target (slow phase) followed by corrective (fast or slow phase) in the opposite direction [13]. Nystagmus can occur in the x, y or z plane as uniplanar or biplanar. It can be further categorized into two waveform morphologies: jerk (with a slow phase followed by a fast phase) and pendular (with two slow phases). The specific waveform and velocity profile of the slow-phase response in jerk nystagmus

S. Ali et al. (Eds.): MIUA 2025, LNCS 15918, pp. 306–316, 2026.
https://doi.org/10.1007/978-3-031-98694-9_22

(constant, decreasing, or increasing velocity) are indicative of underlying neural dysfunctions (Fig. 1) . Nystagmus can be congenital or acquired due to various medical conditions like strokes, neuro-inflammatory disorders, brain tumors, and neurodegenerative diseases [7].

Recent research leveraging machine learning algorithms has attempted to detect and analyze nystagmus from video-oculography (VOG) data (video and waveform) [19–24, 28, 33]. However, these studies often use small, limited datasets with few nystagmus variations and are generally not publicly available due to privacy concerns[17, 18, 34], hindering further research. The prediction of nystagmus dynamics, considering variations in eye, head, and body position, is a complex process rooted in ocular motor physiology and biomechanics [14–16, 19–24, 28, 33]. A common approach to address the scarcity of public datasets in the medical field is the generation of synthetic datasets using real patient data [9, 10, 29], a method that has proven effective in various downstream tasks. However, generating synthetic data from real-world datasets poses its own challenges. For instance, generative models sometimes replicate training data too closely, undermining the purpose of creating synthetic datasets [26]. Lastly, for nystagmus, creating a clinically relevant dataset involves generating long-form videos that accurately incorporate nystagmus oculographs (pupil-position waveforms) with physiologic eye movements, adding to the complexity of the task.

In this paper, we address the challenge of creating long-form nystagmus videos without compromising patient data by developing *GenVOG*. Our key contributions are as follows:

– We successfully generate synthetic nystagmus videos encompassing a range of nystagmus types, overcoming the limitation of being restricted to a single or specific type.
– Our method avoids the use of real patient data, thereby preserving patient privacy. This approach is especially valuable in scenarios where data availability is limited. We validate our dataset using real patient data for comparison and engage experts for further validation.
– We will make the synthetic dataset publicly available, aiming to enhance research and understanding of nystagmus in the broader scientific community.

2   Method

2.1   Preliminaries

Nystagmus Waveforms. In the following section, we present equations representing pupil location over time for different types of nystagmus, as illustrated in the plots in Fig. 1. The variables in these equations are consistent across all types: A represents the amplitude, indicating the maximum extent of eye movement; ω is the angular frequency, determining the speed of oscillation; ϕ is the phase, accounting for any initial positional offset; and t denotes time.

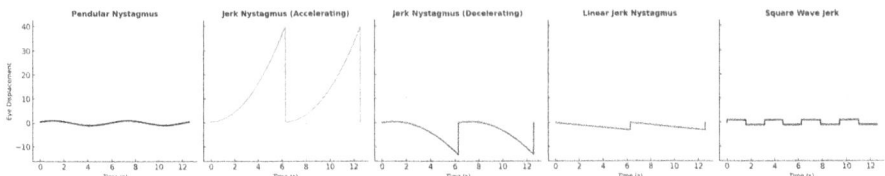

Fig. 1. Waveform morphologies of various nystagmus types and nystagmoid eye movements. Nystagmus can be categorized into two main types based on the pattern of eye movements: jerk nystagmus, which consists of a slow phase followed by a quick phase, and pendular nystagmus, characterized by movements that are slow in both directions. These patterns reflect the underlying issues with the neural pathways responsible for eye stability. Additionally, jerk nystagmus can be subdivided into three categories based on the speed of the slow phase: constant or linear velocity, decelerating velocity, and accelerating velocity.

1. *Pendular Nystagmus*: Characterized by rhythmic, oscillatory eye movements, similar to the motion of a pendulum. It is described by the equation: $P(t) = A \times \sin(\omega t + \phi)$.
2. *Jerk Nystagmus with Accelerating Slow Phase*: This type involves eye movements that slowly accelerate in one direction and then quickly jerk back. The equation representing this motion is: $J_a(t) = A \times (t^2 + \phi)$.
3. *Jerk Nystagmus with Decelerating Slow Phase*: In this variation, the eye slowly moves in one direction with a gradually decreasing speed before jerking back. This is characterized by the equation: $J_d(t) = A \times (t - 0.5 \times t^2)$.
4. *Linear Jerk Nystagmus*: This type features linear, steady eye movements in one direction followed by a rapid jerk in the opposite direction. It is described by: $J_l(t) = A \times (-0.5 \times t)$.
5. *Square Wave Jerk*: This type of nystagmoid movement (nystagmus mimic) consists of sudden, small, saccadic eye movements that shift the gaze away from the target, followed by a quick corrective movement back. It is characterized by a step-like function:

$$S_w(t) = \begin{cases} A, & \text{for } 0 \leq t < T/2 \\ -A, & \text{for } T/2 \leq t < T \end{cases}$$

where A represents the amplitude of the eye movement and T is the period of the square wave oscillation.

Nystagmus Characteristics. Nystagmus movements can occur in both horizontal and vertical directions. The criteria for waveform generation are based on Kocak et al. [12]: For normal cases, the slow phase velocity decrement should range between 0% and 24%. Within this range, the initial slow phase velocity should be between 5 and 25 °C per second, increasing in increments of 0.5 °C per second.

2.2   Patient-Independent Ocular Edge Map

In the process of modeling videos with the pupil kinetic patterns of nystagmus, the initial step involves choosing a specific nystagmus waveform equation, symbolized as $f(t; \theta)$. Here, t signifies time, and θ encompasses parameters such as amplitude, frequency, phase, among others, which are essential for shaping the waveform. Upon selecting the waveform equation, a binary mask video $V(t, x, y)$ is crafted to depict the pupil's trajectory over time. This is accomplished by calculating the pupil's coordinates $(x(t), y(t))$ for each time instance t, based on the waveform equation. Subsequently, the binary mask video is updated to indicate the pupil's position, with $V(t, x(t), y(t)) = 1$ marking the pupil's location, and $V(t, x \neq x(t), y \neq y(t)) = 0$ for all other points, effectively distinguishing the pupil from the remainder of the video frame. If we were to represent this as a continuous process, the creation of the binary mask video could be expressed as:

$$V(t, x, y) = \begin{cases} 1, & \text{if } x = x(t) \text{ and } y = y(t) \\ 0, & \text{otherwise.} \end{cases}$$

This method outlines a systematic approach to dynamically map the pupil's movements across time, utilizing the nystagmus waveform equation to precisely replicate this ocular phenomenon. Due to the absence of publicly available nystagmus datasets and our objective of generating a synthetic dataset independent of patient data, we utilize publicly available gaze datasets as an initial framework. Specifically, to establish a conditioning mechanism for the diffusion model, we first extract the Canny edge maps [3] from the eye region in the gaze videos. The edge map extraction process is represented as:

$$C = \mathcal{C}(I; \sigma, T_l, T_h),$$

where C is the extracted Canny edge map [3], $\mathcal{C}(\cdot)$ denotes the Canny edge detection operator, I is the grayscale eye region image, σ is the standard deviation for Gaussian smoothing, and T_l and T_h are the lower and upper threshold values for edge detection.

Next, the pupil is removed from these extracted eye videos to eliminate any inherent motion bias. The synthetic nystagmus waveform is then superimposed onto the Canny edge map [3] of the eye socket, effectively encoding the motion prior necessary for video generation. This approach ensures the generation of realistic yet synthetic ocular motion patterns that mimic nystagmus without relying on real patient data.

2.3   Eye Movement Video Generation

Network Architecture. Fig. 2 gives an overview of the proposed network architectue for video synthesis. The core of this model is the latent diffusion mechanism, essential for the conversion of noise to visual representations [25,30]. This process is orchestrated by a U-Net structure, labeled as ε_θ. A key element in this architecture is the VQGAN, which serves to bridge the visual and latent domains. Given a training video v^{gt} in the RGB format, it first undergoes encoding by the VQGAN encoder, $\mathcal{E}$, represented mathematically as

$$Z^{gt} = [\mathcal{E}(f_1), ..., \mathcal{E}(f_F)],$$

where $v^{gt} = [f_1, ... f_F]$ symbolizes the frames of the training video. The U-Net, denoted as ε_θ, operates in the latent space, iteratively refining the video's representation through a fixed number of T steps. During inference, the model's primary goal is to predict noise as

$$\varepsilon_t^{pred} = \varepsilon_\theta(Z_t^{pred}), \tag{1}$$

with Z_t^{pred} being the latent variable at the t-th step. The predicted denoised latent Z^{pred} is eventually decoded through the VQGAN decoder $\mathcal{D}$ and projected back into the pixel domain. The efficacy of the denoising UNet is evaluated using the loss function

$$\mathcal{L} = \mathbb{E}_{Z^{gt}, \varepsilon^{gt} \sim N(0,1)} \left[\| \varepsilon^{gt} - \varepsilon^{pred} \|^2 \right], \tag{2}$$

where ε^{pred} and ε^{gt} signify the predicted and ground-truth noise, respectively. The U-Net architecture encompasses various segments, including initial, down-sampling, spatio-temporal, and upsampling blocks. The spatio-temporal block, crucial for video generation, captures spatial and temporal dynamics in eye movement videos [30]. It processes individual frames, employing spatiotemporal attention within a transformer architecture [8], to discern spatial details and their sequential progression. In the spatial attention block of the multi-head attention layer, we utilize the text embedding of the prompt as both the key and the value. We leverage the capabilities of large-scale pre-trained generative models, which have been trained on extensive datasets and can effectively reconstruct the eye region. Since our objective is not to generate motion directly but rather to synthesize the eye region on top of the provided motion prior, we utilize a pre-trained video diffusion model for this purpose. The model is based on Latent Diffusion Models (LDMs) [11] and extends ControlNet [32] for video generation by incorporating additional trainable temporal layers into both the UNet and ControlNet [32] components to model temporal dynamics. The framework follows a two-stage approach that integrates both content and motion priors to enhance video quality and temporal consistency. Initially, the model is trained using a first-frame conditioning scheme [5], where video generation is guided by a single reference frame. This strategy facilitates the disentanglement of content and motion modeling, ensuring structural consistency of objects across frames. To further improve motion coherence, the training process incorporates two types of noise initialization: residual-based and optical flow-based noise priors, which help align frame transitions with realistic motion patterns.

2.4   Nystagmus Video Generation Process

The inference process for Nystagmus video generation follows a Text-to-Image-to-Video (T2I-I2V) pipeline [5], where a first frame is generated and used as a content prior representing the ocular region for denoising subsequent frames. The first frame F_0 is synthesized from Gaussian noise, conditioned on a text prompt P and a first-frame canny edge map C_0:

$$F_0 = \mathcal{G}_{T2I}(\mathbf{z}_0, P, C_0),$$

where $\mathcal{G}_{T2I}$ is the pre-trained diffusion model, $\mathbf{z}_0 \sim \mathcal{N}(0, I)$ is the Gaussian noise sample for the first frame of the ocular region, P is the text prompt providing semantic guidance for ocular region generation, and C_0 is the modified canny edge map [3] for structural guidance. The latent representation of the first frame is then extracted:

$$\mathbf{h}_0 = \mathcal{E}(F_0),$$

where $\mathcal{E}$ is the encoder projecting the first frame into the model's latent space, and $\mathbf{h}_0$ is the latent embedding of the first frame. Subsequent frames F_t ($t = 1, \ldots, T$) are iteratively denoised using the pre-trained text-to-video model $\mathcal{G}_{T2V}$, conditioned on the text prompt, modified nystagmus edge maps, and the first-frame embedding:

$$F_t = \mathcal{G}_{T2V}(\mathbf{z}_t, P, C_t, \mathbf{h}_0),$$

where $\mathbf{z}_t \sim \mathcal{N}(0, I)$ is the Gaussian noise sample for frame t, C_t is the modified nystagmus edge map for frame t, providing motion structure guidance, and $\mathbf{h}_0$ ensures content consistency across frames.

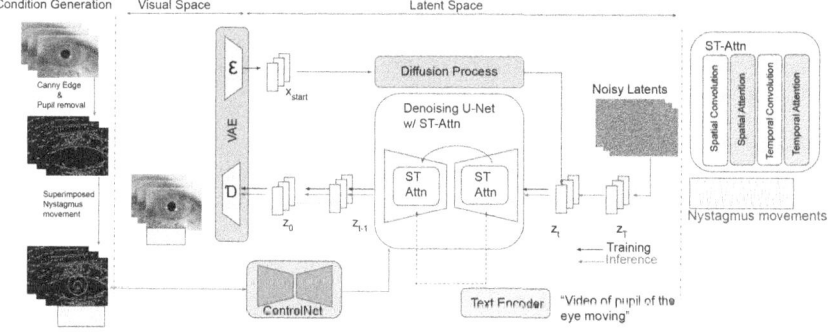

Fig. 2. The figure depicts the architecture and workflow of the proposed method. An edge map is extracted from real videos, with pupils removed, and nystagmus movements are superimposed onto the edge map video. This processed edge map then serves as a control signal for generating nystagmus data.

3   Experiments and Results

3.1   Quantitative and Qualitative Analysis

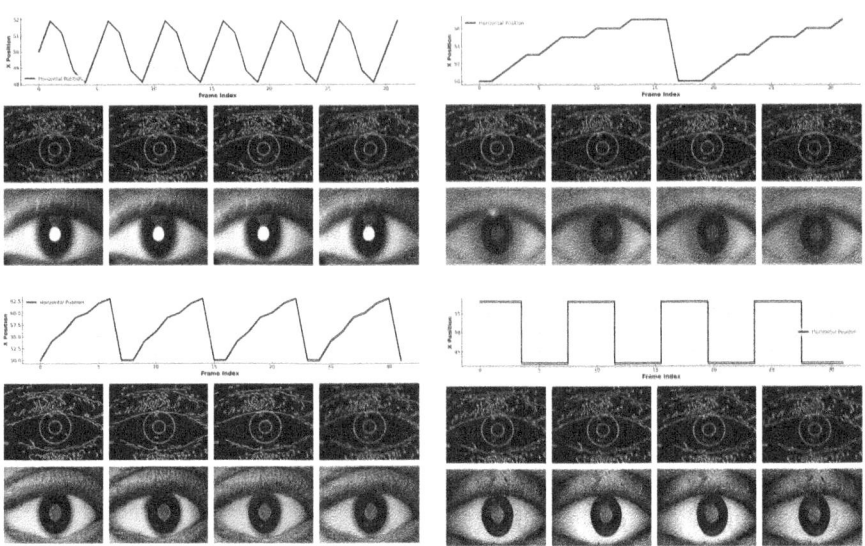

Fig. 3. Input nystagmus waveform, its corresponding Canny edge map, and sample frames extracted from the synthesized nystagmus video. The example illustrates the same base ocular region eye edge maps.

Quantitative Results. For quantitative evaluation, we used Fréchet Video Distance (FVD) as our primary assessment metric, achieving a score of 536. To further validate the quality of our generated videos, we trained a classifier on the synthetic dataset produced using our approach. Since there is no direct baseline for comparison, we evaluate our method against two alternative settings: **Supervised Model** and **DDIM Inversion of Generated Masks**. In the Supervised Model setting, we fine-tune the ModelScope [30] Text-to-Video (T2V) model on the private Nystagmus dataset, using text prompts corresponding to video labels. This model then generates Nystagmus videos based on these prompts. However, due to the limited size of the dataset, the supervised approach can only produce a restricted variety of Nystagmus patterns seen during training. Additionally, supervised models require sufficient labeled data, which is scarce, limiting their effectiveness. Furthermore, privacy concerns prevent the release of synthetic data. For DDIM Inversion, we adapt the approach from [31] for controllable video generation. Starting with a pre-trained T2V model [30], we fine-tune only the temporal layers on eye videos. We then generate Nystagmus mask videos as described in Sect. 2.2, which serve as conditioning inputs. By introducing noise and denoising iteratively, we guide the generation process using the masks as priors. However, this approach has limitations: DDIM Inversion does not always adhere strictly to the provided masks since the conditioning is implicit. Moreover, assigning excessive weight to the initial video results in noisy outputs. In contrast, our method does not require Nystagmus dataset while ensuring faithful adherence to input conditions. A comparative analysis of all methods is presented in Table 1. As an upper bound, we also report classifier performance when trained exclusively on real data, along with downstream performance on the full dataset.

Qualitative Analysis. Fig. 3 displays frames extracted from the generated videos, showcasing the network's ability to create videos of high quality.

Table 1. Quantitative results of the generated videos in terms of FVD and their impact on downstream performance. Upper bound indicates a classifier trained on the full dataset and tested on the independent test set.

Data	Supervised Model		DDIM Inversion		Ours	
	FVD ($\downarrow$)	Accuracy ($\uparrow$)	FVD ($\downarrow$)	Accuracy ($\uparrow$)	FVD ($\downarrow$)	Accuracy ($\uparrow$)
Upper Bound: Accuracy = 87.14						
Real + Synthetic	–	88.34	–	87.35	–	**88.76**
Synthetic Only	678	54.87	759	51.45	**536**	**65.41**

3.2   Datasets

Our method does not rely on any dataset for training the model. For the Canny edge maps [3] of the ocular region, we utilize videos from the Labelled Pupils in the Wild (LPW) dataset [27]. This dataset comprises 66 high-quality, high-speed videos focused on the eye region, designed to support the development and evaluation of pupil detection algorithms. To train the supervised generative model, we use a private Nystagmus dataset described in [12]. A separate validation set was created, consisting of videos from 5 normal and 5 nystagmus patients. The final training and test sets contain 1000 and 200 short video clips, respectively.

3.3   Limitation and Ethical Impact

A notable limitation of the model is its occasional production of videos with unrealistic features. Given the stochastic nature of the sampling process, it's also prone to introducing artifacts. Moreover, video generation technologies, particularly sophisticated video diffusion models, pose ethical and social challenges. These challenges encompass the potential for generating misleading content, which could contribute to misinformation and infringe on privacy rights; the risk of biases in AI-generated content, which could result in discriminatory or unfair outcomes; and concerns regarding the impact on intellectual property rights. It is imperative for both developers and users of these technologies to recognize these risks and commit to their responsible utilization.

4   Conclusion and Future Work

In this research, we introduce *GenVOG*, a novel approach for generating nystagmus video-oculography (VOG) data without requiring patient-specific datasets. Our method leverages the physics of nystagmus movement as a conditioning mechanism for pupil motion. We have developed a model capable of synthesizing various types of nystagmus using video diffusion models, integrating both waveform and prompt-based conditioning to generate realistic nystagmus videos. By eliminating the need for patient data, our approach safeguards patient privacy and mitigates data duplication issues through the use of a pre-trained model. We plan to release the synthetically generated videos and their corresponding waveforms to the research community for further validation. Future work could focus on more extensive validation of the generated data and the inclusion of additional nystagmus variants with real-world noise. We believe this contribution will significantly enhance deep learning-based eye movement detection for neurological and ophthalmological disorders.

Acknowledgments. This research was supported by the Johns Hopkins Discovery Award and the Institute for Data Intensive Engineering and Science (IDIES) at Johns Hopkins University.

Disclosure of Interests. The authors have no competing interests to declare that are relevant to the content of this article.

References

1. Anastasio, T.J., et al.: David A. Robinson's Modeling the Oculomotor Control System. Elsevier (2022)
2. Barnes, G., Smith, R.: The effects of visual discrimination of image movement across the stationary retina. Aviat. Space Environ. Med. **52**(8), 466–472 (1981)
3. Canny, J.: A computational approach to edge detection. IEEE Trans. Pattern Anal. Mach. Intell. **6**, 679–698 (1986)
4. Carpenter, R.H., Cronly-Dillon, J.R.: Vision and Visual Dysfunction: Eye Movements. Macmillan (1991)
5. Chen, W., et al.: Control-a-video: Controllable text-to-video generation with diffusion models. arXiv preprint arXiv:2305.13840 (2023)
6. Demer, J.L., Honrubia, V., Baloh, R.W.: Dynamic visual acuity: a test for oscillopsia and vestibulo-ocular reflex function. Am. J. Otol. **15**(3), 340–347 (1994)
7. Derwenskus, J., Rucker, J.C., Serra, A., Stahl, J.S., Downey, D.L., Adams, N.L., Leigh, R.J.: Abnormal eye movements predict disability in MS: two-year follow-up. Ann. N. Y. Acad. Sci. **1039**(1), 521–523 (2005)
8. Dosovitskiy, A., et al.: An image is worth 16x16 words: transformers for image recognition at scale. arXiv preprint arXiv:2010.11929 (2020)
9. Garcea, F., Serra, A., Lamberti, F., Morra, L.: Data augmentation for medical imaging: a systematic literature review. Comput. Biol. Med. **152**, 106391 (2023)
10. Guibas, J.T., Virdi, T.S., Li, P.S.: Synthetic medical images from dual generative adversarial networks. arXiv preprint arXiv:1709.01872 (2017)

11. He, Y., Yang, T., Zhang, Y., Shan, Y., Chen, Q.: Latent video diffusion models for high-fidelity video generation with arbitrary lengths. arXiv preprint arXiv:2211.13221 (2022)
12. Kocak, G.S., et al.: A novel diagnostic method for myasthenia gravis. Muscle Nerve **64**(3), 328–335 (2021)
13. Leigh, R.J., Zee, D.S.: The neurology of eye movements. Oxford University Press (2015)
14. Li, H., Yang, Z.: Torsional nystagmus recognition based on deep learning for vertigo diagnosis. Front. Neurosci. **17**, 1160904 (2023)
15. Li, H., Yang, Z.: Vertical nystagmus recognition based on deep learning. Sensors **23**(3), 1592 (2023)
16. Lim, E.C., et al.: Developing a diagnostic decision support system for benign paroxysmal positional vertigo using a deep-learning model. J. Clin. Med. **8**(5), 633 (2019)
17. Lohr, D., Komogortsev, O.V.: Eye know you too: toward viable end-to-end eye movement biometrics for user authentication. IEEE Trans. Inf. Forensics Secur. **17**, 3151–3164 (2022)
18. Lohr, D.J., Aziz, S., Komogortsev, O.: Eye movement biometrics using a new dataset collected in virtual reality. In: ACM Symposium on Eye Tracking Research and Applications, pp. 1–3 (2020)
19. Lu, W., et al.: A deep learning model for three-dimensional nystagmus detection and its preliminary application. Front. Neurosci. **16**, 930028 (2022)
20. Newman, J.L., Phillips, J.S., Cox, S.J.: 1D convolutional neural networks for detecting nystagmus. IEEE J. Biomed. Health Inform. **25**(5), 1814–1823 (2021)
21. Newman, J.L., Phillips, J.S., Cox, S.J.: Detecting positional vertigo using an ensemble of 2D convolutional neural networks. Biomed. Signal Process. Control **68**, 102708 (2021)
22. Phillips, J.S., Newman, J.L., Cox, S.J.: An investigation into the diagnostic accuracy, reliability, acceptability and safety of a novel device for Continuous Ambulatory Vestibular Assessment (CAVA). Sci. Rep. **9**(1), 10452 (2019)
23. Punuganti, S.A., Tian, J., Otero-Millan, J.: Automatic quick-phase detection in bedside recordings from patients with acute dizziness and nystagmus. In: Proc. 11th ACM Symposium on Eye Tracking Research & Applications, pp. 1–3 (2019)
24. Reinhardt, S., Schmidt, J., Leuschel, M., Schüle, C., Schipper, J.: VertiGo–a pilot project in nystagmus detection via webcam. In: Current Directions in Biomedical Engineering, vol. 6, p. 20200043. De Gruyter (2020)
25. Rombach, R., Blattmann, A., Lorenz, D., Esser, P., Ommer, B.: High-resolution image synthesis with latent diffusion models. In: Proceedings of the IEEE/CVF conference on computer vision and pattern recognition, pp. 10684–10695 (2022)
26. Somepalli, G., Singla, V., Goldblum, M., Geiping, J., Goldstein, T.: Diffusion art or digital forgery? investigating data replication in diffusion models. In: Proceedings of the IEEE/CVF Conference on Computer Vision and Pattern Recognition, pp. 6048–6058 (2023)
27. Tonsen, M., Zhang, X., Sugano, Y., Bulling, A.: Labelled pupils in the wild: a dataset for studying pupil detection in unconstrained environments. In: Proceedings of the Ninth Biennial ACM Symposium on Eye Tracking Research & Applications, pp. 139–142 (2016)
28. Wagle, N., et al.: aEYE: a deep learning system for video nystagmus detection. Front. Neurol. **13**, 963968 (2022)
29. Wang, C., et al.: Deep learning model for static ocular torsion detection using synthetically generated fundus images. Transl. Vision Sci. Technol. **12**(1), 17–17 (2023)

30. Wang, J., Yuan, H., Chen, D., Zhang, Y., Wang, X., Zhang, S.: Modelscope text-to-video technical report. arXiv preprint arXiv:2308.06571 (2023)
31. Wu, J.Z., et al.: Tune-a-video: One-shot tuning of image diffusion models for text-to-video generation. In: Proceedings of the IEEE/CVF International Conference on Computer Vision, pp. 7623–7633 (2023)
32. Zhang, L., Rao, A., Agrawala, M.: Adding conditional control to text-to-image diffusion models. In: Proceedings of the IEEE/CVF International Conference on Computer Vision, pp. 3836–3847 (2023)
33. Zhang, W., et al.: Deep learning based torsional nystagmus detection for dizziness and vertigo diagnosis. Biomed. Signal Process. Control **68**, 102616 (2021)
34. Zola Matuvanga, T., et al.: Use of iris scanning for biometric recognition of healthy adults participating in an ebola vaccine trial in the democratic republic of the congo: mixed methods study. J. Med. Internet Res. **23**(8), e28573 (2021)

Structurally Different Neural Network Blocks for the Segmentation of Atrial and Aortic Perivascular Adipose Tissue in Multi-centre CT Angiography Scans

Ikboljon Sobirov[1,2]([⊠]), Cheng Xie[2]([⊠]), Muhammad Siddique[2,4],
Parijat Patel[2,4], Kenneth Chan[2], Thomas Halborg[2], Christos P. Kotanidis[2],
Zarqaish Fatima[3], Henry West[2], Sheena Thomas[2], Maria Lyasheva[2],
Donna Alexander[5], David Adlam[5], Praveen Rao[5], Das Indrajeet[5],
Aparna Deshpande[5], Amrita Bajaj[5], Jonathan C. L. Rodrigues[6],
Benjamin J. Hudson[6], Vivek Srivastava[7], George Krasopoulos[7], Rana Sayeed[7],
Qiang Zhang[7], Pete Tomlins[4], Cheerag Shirodaria[4], Keith M. Channon[2],
Stefan Neubauer[2], Charalambos Antoniades[2], and Mohammad Yaqub[1]

[1] Department of Computer Vision, Mohamed Bin Zayed University of Artificial
Intelligence, Abu Dhabi, UAE
[2] Acute Multidisciplinary Imaging & Interventional Centre, Division of
Cardiovascular Medicine, Radcliffe Department of Medicine, University of Oxford,
Oxford, UK
ikboljon.sobirov@cardiov.ox.ac.uk
[3] Oxford University Hospitals NHS Foundation Trust, Oxford, UK
[4] Caristo Diagnostics LTD, Oxford, UK
[5] Department of Cardiovascular Sciences and NIHR Leicester Biomedical Research
Centre, University of Leicester, Leicester, UK
[6] Department of Radiology, Royal United Hospitals Bath NHS Foundation Trust,
Bath, UK
[7] Department of Cardiothoracic Surgery, Oxford, UK

Abstract. Since the emergence of convolutional neural networks
(CNNs) and, later, vision transformers (ViTs), deep learning architectures have predominantly relied on identical block types with varying hyperparameters. We propose a novel block alternation strategy to
leverage the complementary strengths of different architectural designs,
assembling structurally distinct components similar to Lego blocks. We
introduce *LegoNet*, a deep learning framework that alternates CNN-based
and SwinViT-based blocks to enhance feature learning for medical image
segmentation. We investigate three variations of *LegoNet* and apply this
concept to a previously unexplored clinical problem: the segmentation
of the internal mammary artery (IMA), aorta, and perivascular adipose
tissue (PVAT) from computed tomography angiography (CTA) scans.
These PVAT regions have been shown to possess prognostic value in

Supplementary Information The online version contains supplementary material
available at https://doi.org/10.1007/978-3-031-98694-9_23.

assessing cardiovascular risk and primary clinical outcomes. We evaluate *LegoNet* on large datasets, achieving superior performance to other leading architectures. Furthermore, we assess the model's generalizability on external testing cohorts, where an expert clinician corrects the model's segmentations, achieving DSC > 0.90 across various external, international, and public cohorts. To further validate the model's clinical reliability, we perform intra- and inter-observer variability analysis, demonstrating strong agreement with human annotations. The proposed methodology has significant implications for diagnostic cardiovascular management and early prognosis, offering a robust, automated solution for vascular and perivascular segmentation and risk assessment in clinical practice, paving the way for personalised medicine.

Keywords: Alternating Blocks · Arterial Segmentation · Internal Mammary Artery Segmentation · LegoNet · Medical Imaging Segmentation

1 Introduction

From the early convolutional neural network (CNN)-based U-Net [4] to the most recent vision transformer (ViT) models [7,8], deep learning (DL) segmentation architectures follow the typical style of an encoder and decoder network, where the encoder is typically consists of a series of identical blocks with varying hyperparameters. This design is not limited to segmentation but extends to other tasks, such as classification and detection. While such architectures have demonstrated strong performance across various applications, little attention has been given to exploring alternative encoder designs that move beyond identical block structures. This raises a fundamental question: *Does a deep learning encoder learn better representations when built with identical or non-identical blocks?*

We study the impact of harmonizing internally nonidentical blocks for segmenting the internal mammary artery (IMA), aorta, and perivascular adipose tissue (PVAT) from multi-centre computed tomography angiography (CTA) scans. While previous works have explored hybrid architectures that integrate ViT and CNN encoders [3,20], either side-by-side or sequentially, to the best of our knowledge, no study has examined the block-level integration of different deep learning architectures. We propose an approach where structurally distinct yet compatible blocks are alternated within a deep learning model. This perspective introduces new possibilities in model design and block selection, which we evaluate using three types of blocks: CNN-based and SwinViT-based, resulting in three architectural variations. Conceptually, this approach resembles assembling a model using compatible Lego pieces, inspiring the name *LegoNet*. We hypothesize that incorporating structurally diverse blocks can lead to richer feature representations, particularly in complex tasks like medical image segmentation. To validate this, we assess *LegoNet* in the challenging task of vessel-level segmentation in 3D scans.

The internal mammary artery (IMA), aorta, and their surrounding perivascular adipose tissue (PVAT) have been recognized as clinically valuable in sev-

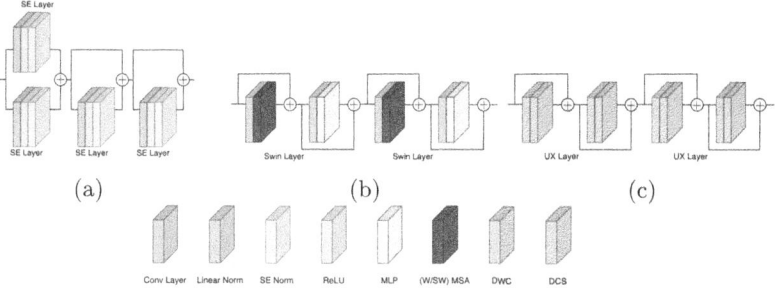

Fig. 1. The figure shows the inner structure of each block type used for our model construction. (a) is the squeeze-and-excitation block; (b) is the Swin block; and (c) is the UX block.

eral studies as they have been shown to reflect inflammatory processes influencing cardiovascular health [1,11,16]. The vascular wall secretes inflammatory molecules that diffuse into PVAT, triggering adipocyte changes at the perivascular level [1,11,15]. In a recent study, Kotanidis et al. [11] manually segmented these regions to assess the vascular inflammatory signature of COVID-19 (C19RS inflammatory signature) using CTA scans from 435 patients in the long-running Oxford Risk Factors and Non-Invasive Imaging (ORFAN) study. This novel non-invasive imaging biomarker, derived from the IMA, aorta, and PVAT, has demonstrated strong predictive power for acute vascular inflammation and in-hospital mortality. Additionally, it enables the extraction of reliable radiomic features from perivascular regions.

However, manual segmentation is highly time-consuming and labor-intensive, particularly as larger patient cohorts are required for improved generalizability. For instance, extending segmentation to new cohorts within the ORFAN study, which includes over 250,000 patient datasets, would make an automatic segmentation approach indispensable. Localizing the PVAT region is particularly challenging due to its small, suppressed appearance in axial views and its elongated, vertical structure in the chest. Therefore, this study focuses on developing an automated method for segmenting the IMA, aorta, and PVAT from CTA scans.

The key contributions of this work are as follows:

- We introduce a novel deep learning paradigm that alternates different block types within a single architecture, demonstrating how the aggregation of diverse structural components enhances representation learning. The proposed *LegoNet* achieves superior performance compared to state-of-the-art CNN and ViT-based models while maintaining lower complexity than ViT models.
- We address a previously unexplored problem in medical image analysis—the IMA and aorta PVAT space segmentation—which holds significant potential for cardiovascular disease prognosis and targeted therapeutic interventions.
- We conduct an extensive evaluation using external datasets, including intra-observer variability, inter-observer variability, model-versus-clinician perfor-

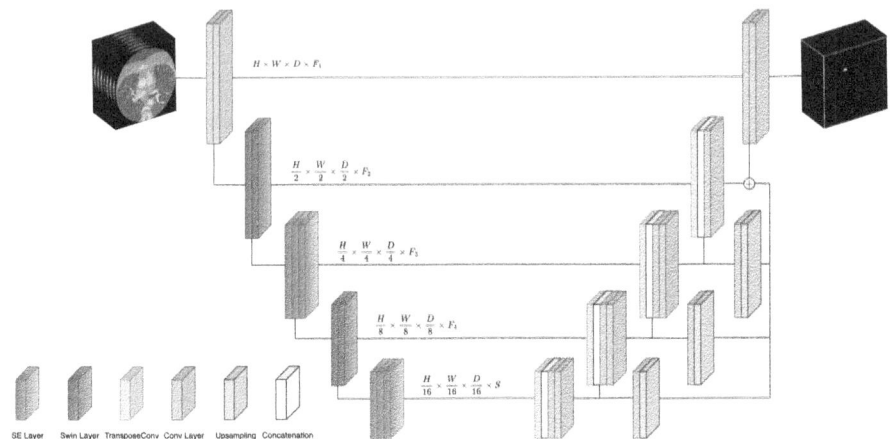

Fig. 2. The figure shows the *LegoNet* (specifically, *LegoNet-2*) architecture. F_{1-4} indicate the feature size, which is set to $\{24, 48, 96, 192\}$, and S is the hidden size, set to 768. This typical U-shaped architecture utilizes the block alternation concept, switching between Swin and SE blocks in the encoder in this example. The decoder is kept the same for all the variations of the model.

mance analysis, and post-segmentation refinement studies with expert clinicians.

2   Methodology

We propose a simple yet effective alternating block method for constructing a DL architecture. Inspired by the modular nature of Lego blocks, this approach enables the integration of structurally diverse components to form a unified model, leveraging their complementary strengths to enhance feature representation and segmentation performance. Specifically, we explore three different types of blocks—CNN-based and SwinViT-based-and construct architectures that alternate between two of these blocks in various configurations.

2.1   Building Blocks

SE Block. The squeeze-and-excitation (SE) block consists of stacks of a $3 \times 3 \times 3$ convolutional block with residuals, a ReLU activation function, and a SE normalization (norm) module [9] within the layers, as shown in Fig. 1(a). SE norm operates similarly to instance norm (IN) [17] but differs in the parameters γ_i and β_i in Eq. 1. While IN treats these parameters as fixed during inference, SE norm dynamically models them as functions of the input, allowing for adaptive normalization based on feature responses [9]

$$y_i = \gamma_i x_i' + \beta_i, \tag{1}$$

where x_i' is the normalized value of a batch of input data X, and γ_i and β_i are the scale and shift normalization values.

Swin Block. Swin transformer [13] with shifted windows has boosted the performance of ViT-based models due to its ability to capture global and local information. We employ the Swin block to see its compatibility with other CNN-based blocks and how well it performs in conjunction. The block consists of a linear normalization, regular and window partitioning multi-head attention (W-MSA and SW-MSA, respectively), and MLP, with skip connections as shown in Fig. 1(b) and Eq. 2.

The outputs of the Swin block are computed in the sequential layers of l and $l + 1$ as:

$$\hat{z}^l = \text{W-MSA}(\text{LN}(z^{l-1})) + z^{l-1},$$
$$z^l = \text{MLP}(\text{LN}(\hat{z}^l)) + \hat{z}^l,$$
$$\hat{z}^{l+1} = \text{SW-MSA}(\text{LN}(z^l)) + z^l,$$
$$z^{l+1} = \text{MLP}(\text{LN}(\hat{z}^{l+1})) + \hat{z}^{l+1}, \tag{2}$$

where $\hat{z}^l$ and z^l are the outputs of the modules, W-MSA and SW-MSA denote regular and window partitioning multi-head self-attention modules, respectively, MLP is multi-layer perceptrons, and LN is a layer normalization.

UX Block. The UX block, introduced in [12], is a convolution-based network block designed around large kernel sizes and depth-wise convolutions (DWC). Structurally, it mirrors the Swin block but replaces self-attention with depth-wise convolution using $7 \times 7 \times 7$ kernels, along with depth-wise convolutional scaling (DCS) and linear normalization as illustrated in Fig. 1(c) and formulated in Eq. 3.

The outputs of the UX block are computed in the sequential layers of l and $l + 1$ as:

$$\hat{z}^l = \text{DWC}(\text{LN}(z^{l-1})) + z^{l-1},$$
$$z^l = \text{DCS}(\text{LN}(\hat{z}^l)) + \hat{z}^l,$$
$$\hat{z}^{l+1} = \text{DWC}(\text{LN}(z^l)) + z^l,$$
$$z^{l+1} = \text{DCS}(\text{LN}(\hat{z}^{l+1})) + \hat{z}^{l+1}, \tag{3}$$

where $\hat{z}^l$ and z^l are the outputs of the modules, DWC and DCS denote depthwise convolution (with kernel size starting from $7 \times 7 \times 7$) and depthwise convolution scaling modules, respectively, and LN is a layer normalization.

2.2   LegoNet Architecture

The proposed network uses combinations of the blocks mentioned above. The input in the size of $X \in \mathbb{R}^{H \times W \times D \times C}$ (where H, W, D and C correspond to dimensions and the number of channels, respectively) passes through a stem block, as shown in Fig. 2. This stem consists of two $3D$ convolutional blocks with $7 \times 7 \times 7$ and $3 \times 3 \times 3$ kernel sizes, respectively, rearranging the input to the size of $H \times W \times D \times 24$.

The alternating block mechanism is introduced at this stage, where two sets of blocks are applied in rotation. We propose three variations of this architecture, detailed in Sect. 2.3. Depicted in Fig. 2 is the second version of *LegoNet* with Swin and SE blocks. The first block (i.e., Swin) downsamples the data to $\frac{H}{2} \times \frac{W}{2} \times \frac{D}{2} \times 48$. The next block (i.e., SE) reshapes the output to $\frac{H}{4} \times \frac{W}{4} \times \frac{D}{4} \times 96$. The same two blocks will repeat the procedure to generate the representations with the sizes $\frac{H}{8} \times \frac{W}{8} \times \frac{D}{8} \times 192$ and $\frac{H}{16} \times \frac{W}{16} \times \frac{D}{16} \times S$, respectively, where S is the hidden size of the final block and is set to 768.

2.3 Alternating Composition of LegoNet

Although we believe that *LegoNet* as a concept is agnostic to the block type, we demonstrate the idea in three distinct versions, each differing in the block types used for model construction, as listed in Table 1. Figure 2 illustrates the second version, alternating between Swin and SE blocks. The other versions follow the same structural framework, with SE and UX blocks in the first version and Swin and UX blocks in the third.

Table 1. The table shows the different configurations for the network. These configurations can easily be changed in the code.

Network	Used blocks	Hidden size	Feature size
LegoNet-1	SE→UX→SE→UX	768	(24, 48, 96, 192)
LegoNet-2	Swin→SE→Swin→SE	768	(24, 48, 96, 192)
LegoNet-3	Swin→UX→Swin→UX	768	(24, 48, 96, 192)

2.4 Decoder

The decoder of *LegoNet* is designed to effectively integrate features from both the encoder output and the skip connections between the encoder and decoder. At each stage, encoder features are upsampled and concatenated with corresponding skip connection features, followed by two 3D convolutional blocks. The process repeats at each stage, with each block comprising upsampling, concatenation, and two convolutional blocks. At the same time, the outputs at each stage are carried over on which additional convolutional and upsampling are applied (See Fig. 2 right-most part). We perform this additional skip connection in the decoder to leverage a better flow of features during reconstruction. The final segmentation head constitutes two 3D convolutional blocks to generate the segmentation masks.

2.5 Model Refinement via Iterative Learning

Given the high cost of manual vascular segmentation, we employ a cost-effective approach called model refinement via iterative learning, which enables model

Fig. 3. Model Refinement via Iterative Learning. This approach improves the segmentation model to maturity before deploying it in large cohort data. The model is initially trained with a small, feasible cohort and is internally validated. Several cohorts of data are then used to improve the model by adding more value to the learning process iteratively.

development with a limited dataset while progressively improving performance until maturity. Before applying the deep learning model to large cohorts like ORFAN, we ensure it reaches maturity, which we quantify through two key factors: (i) model refinement through iterative learning, ensuring high segmentation performance and (ii) inter- and intra-observer variability analysis, validating consistency against expert clinicians.

Guided by clinical feedback, we implement model refinement via iterative learning, as illustrated in Fig. 3. The process begins by training the model on a small, ground-truth-labeled dataset, followed by internal validation using k-fold cross-validation. Next, we run inference on a new batch of data, and clinicians correct the model's predictions, significantly reducing the manual effort compared to annotating from scratch. The corrected masks are then compared against the model's predictions and incorporated into the training pool to refine the model further. This iterative process continues until a highly acceptable performance is reached (e.g., DSC > 0.90).

Additionally, we conduct a second set of experiments to assess the model's reliability against inter- and intra-observer variability. In this study, a separate small dataset is blindly annotated by one clinician at two different time points and by another clinician once. The model's performance is then evaluated against the agreement between clinicians, serving as an external benchmark for segmentation accuracy and robustness.

3   Dataset and Preprocessing

The proposed concept was trained and validated using a multi-cohort, multi-scanner subset of ORFAN and the publicly available ASOCA [5,6] dataset. Our dataset comprises 155 patients from three different centres for initial model training and validation, followed by 49 patients designated for inter- and intra-observer variability analysis. We used three additional cohorts comprising 54, 41, and 39 patients, all sourced from different UK sites for "model refinement via iterative learning" process. Furthermore, we incorporate an additional subset from the U.S., comprising 712 scans. All of these cohorts are sourced from ORFAN, and detailed information on data acquisition and study protocols can be found in [2,11]. Finally, we used the publicly available ASOCA dataset [5,6] for external validation, which includes 30 healthy subjects and 30 patients diagnosed with coronary artery disease, to test the model's performance in a different study protocol.

Manual segmentation is performed around the IMA, which extends from the level of the aortic arch to 120mm caudally. One diameter of the IMA defines the perivascular space. In contrast, the aorta is segmented from the bifurcation point, extending 67.5mm caudally. Its perivascular adipose tissue (PVAT) is similarly measured as one diameter of the aorta.

Since the datasets originate from multiple centres, variations exist in scanning parameters, scanner types, and image characteristics, leading to differences in scan dimensions, spacing, orientation, and direction. We apply a standardised preprocessing pipeline to ensure consistency, aligning all scans to a uniform direction and orientation with isotropic spacing of $1 \times 1 \times 1\text{mm}^3$. Additionally, we clip CT intensity values to the range $[-1024, 1024]$ and normalize them to $[-1, 1]$ for improved numerical stability and model robustness.

4   Experimental Setup

We evaluate our proposed method against a range of state-of-the-art deep learning networks, including U-Net [10], SegResNet [14], UNETR [8], Swin UNETR [7], UX-Net [12], and UNesT [19]. These models are first rigorously tested on the IMA+PVAT segmentation task, followed by an extended evaluation on the aorta+PVAT task for further comparison. All models are trained for 100 epochs, starting from random initialization.

For training, we use the AdamW optimizer with a learning rate of $1e-3$, weight decay of $1e-5$, and cosine annealing scheduler with minimum η of $1e-5$ and T_0 at 25. The batch size is set to 1, and the loss function is computed as the sum of Dice and Focal losses (Eq. 4 and Eq. 5) for segmentation. All experiments are conducted on a single NVIDIA Tesla V100 GPU.

$$\mathcal{L}_{Dice} = \frac{2\sum_i^N \hat{y}_i y_i}{\sum_i^N \hat{y_i}^2 + \sum_i^N y_i^2}, \tag{4}$$

Table 2. The table reports the mean and standard deviation of DSC, precision, recall, and HD95 for 5-fold cross-validation and the number of parameters and FLOPs of different models. All the experiments in this table are trained with random initialization.

Models	DSC↑	Precision↑	Recall↑	HD95↓	Params (M)	FLOPs (G)
UNet [4,10]	0.686 ± 0.03	0.72 ± 0.04	0.69 ± 0.03	2.70	3.99	27.64
SegResNet [14]	0.732 ± 0.01	0.75 ± 0.02	0.74 ± 0.03	2.50	4.7	61.71
UX-Net [12]	0.695 ± 0.03	0.73 ± 0.06	0.70 ± 0.01	3.17	27.98	164.17
UNETR [8]	0.690 ± 0.02	0.72 ± 0.03	0.69 ± 0.03	3.00	92.78	82.48
SwinUNETR [7]	0.713 ± 0.02	0.74 ± 0.02	0.71 ± 0.04	2.46	62.83	384.20
UNesT [19]	0.555 ± 0.04	0.59 ± 0.06	0.55 ± 0.05	4.35	87.20	257.91
LegoNet-1	0.747 ± 0.02	0.75 ± 0.02	**0.77** ± 0.03	2.34	50.58	175.77
LegoNet-2	**0.749** ± 0.02	**0.77** ± 0.01	0.76 ± 0.04	**2.11**	50.71	188.02
LegoNet-3	0.741 ± 0.02	0.76 ± 0.02	0.75 ± 0.03	2.34	11.14	173.41

$$\mathcal{L}_{Focal} = -\sum_{i}^{N} \epsilon y_i (1 - \hat{y}_i)^{\psi} log(\hat{y}_i) - (1 - y_i)\hat{y}_i^{\psi} log(1 - \hat{y}_i), \tag{5}$$

$$\mathcal{L}_{Segmentation} = \mathcal{L}_{Dice} + \mathcal{L}_{Focal} \tag{6}$$

where $\hat{y}$ is the prediction of the model, y is the ground truth, ϵ is the weightage for the trade-off between precision and recall in the focal loss (empirically set to 1), ψ is focusing parameter (set to 2), and N is the sample size.

The primary performance metric for evaluation is the Dice Similarity Coefficient (DSC). Additionally, we report precision, recall, and the 95% Hausdorff Distance to provide a more comprehensive comparison. The results are presented as the mean and standard deviation from 5-fold cross-validation on the training and validation data. We compare the number of learnable parameters and floating-point operations (FLOPs) for each model to assess model complexity. DSC and volume-based comparisons are further analysed in the clinical evaluation section to assess segmentation performance in a real-world clinical setting.

5   Results

5.1   Initial Model Training

For efficiency purposes, we investigated the performance of different architectures on the initial dataset of 155 scans in the IMA+PVAT task. Table 2 presents the segmentation performance and model complexities.

Among the baseline models, U-Net (CNN-based) and UNETR (ViT-based) exhibit similar performance, with mean DSC scores of 0.686 and 0.690, respectively. UX-Net achieves a slightly higher DSC of 0.695, while UNesT significantly underperforms with a DSC of 0.555. SwinUNETR shows a notable improvement, yielding a DSC of 0.713, whereas SegResNet demonstrates the highest performance among existing models.

All three variations of LegoNet surpass the baseline models across DSC, precision, recall, and HD95 metrics. LegoNet-2 (Swin and SE alternation) achieves the highest DSC of 0.749, followed closely by the other two versions with DSC scores of 0.747 and 0.741, respectively. A similar trend is observed across precision, recall, and HD95, with LegoNet consistently outperforming existing architectures.

5.2   Statistical Analysis

To further assess the model's performance, we performed a statistical significance analysis comparing *LegoNet* with SegResNet and SwinUNETR, the two strongest baseline models. This analysis is based on the results of the initial data set presented in Table 2.

We apply the Wilcoxon signed rank test [18] to determine whether *LegoNet* exhibits statistically significant improvements over competing models. The null hypothesis H_0 assumes that the segmentation performance of *LegoNet* is statistically indistinguishable from the other models, while the alternative hypothesis H_1 posits that *LegoNet* outperforms SwinUNETR and SegResNet.

The results of the Wilcoxon signed rank test reveal a p value of 1.59e-4 for the *LegoNet* vs. SegResNet comparison and a p value of 2.13e-10 for *LegoNet* vs. SwinUNETR, both indicating highly significant differences. These findings confirm that *LegoNet* is not only the best-performing model in terms of DSC but also statistically superior to the strongest baselines.

5.3   Clinical Evaluation Setting

Once LegoNet was cross-validated, we evaluated its performance in a clinical setting through two key analyses: (i) inter-/intra-observer variability analysis and (ii) post-model agreement analysis.

Inter and Intra-observer Variability Analysis. We conducted a comparative segmentation study on a new cohort of 49 scans to evaluate the model's agreement with human experts. Two expert clinicians performed manual segmentation and we compared their annotations with the automatic segmentations generated by LegoNet. For intraobserver variability, an expert radiologist with six years of experience manually segmented the same cohort twice, with a 12-month interval between annotations. DSC between these two instances was 0.804, reflecting intra-rater consistency. For interobserver variability, a less senior radiologist with three years of experience independently segmented the same cohort. The inter-clinician variability, calculated as the DSC between the two manual segmentations from different clinicians, reached 0.761.

We computed the mean DSC between the model's segmentations and the three manual annotations (two from the first clinician and one from the second) to assess model vs. human agreement. The model vs. human agreement resulted in a DSC of 0.733, demonstrating strong alignment with expert annotations.

Table 3. DSC, recall, precision metrics for a random split in the aorta segmentation. The same models were validated with the same settings as IMA+PVAT. The proposed model variations performed consistently with a different but relatively easier task of aorta segmentation.

Models	DSC↑	Precision↑	Recall↑
UNet	0.895	0.907	0.891
SegResNet	0.885	0.875	0.900
UX-Net	0.919	0.918	0.925
UNETR	0.817	0.827	0.831
SwinUNETR	0.906	0.887	0.931
UNesT	0.838	0.853	0.847
LegoNet-1	**0.939**	**0.919**	**0.961**
LegoNet-2	0.898	0.850	0.957
LegoNet-3	0.903	0.912	0.891

Post-model Agreement Analysis via Iterative Refinement. We conducted a post-model agreement analysis (see Fig. 3) using an iterative learning strategy to improve model performance and assess its adaptability to new cohorts. We generated segmentation masks for three completely unseen cohorts ($n = 54$, $n = 41$, and $n = 39$) (distinct from training, validation, and inter/intra-observer datasets), and a clinician corrected the model predictions. These refined segmentations were added to the training set, increasing dataset diversity and improving model performance. This process was repeated three times, progressively expanding the dataset.

Volume-Based Analysis and Model Refinement Impact. In Fig. 4, we present a volume-based comparison of segmentation performance in different refinement stages. We computed the segmentation volume for each patient using the clinician's manual annotations and LegoNet's automatic predictions. In the first cohort (Fig. 4(a)), the model over-segmented the IMA & perivascular space for many patients, with a Mean Absolute Error (MAE) of 0.982, Spearman's ρ of 0.874 ($p < 0.0001$), and DSC of 0.935. With iterative refinement, the segmentation accuracy progressively improved. By the third cohort (Fig. 4(c)), the model's predictions closely matched the clinician's annotations, with an MAE of 0.491, Spearman's ρ of 0.959 ($p < 0.0001$), and DSC of 0.947, demonstrating effective learning from corrections. These findings underscore the progressive enhancement of model performance through iterative refinement.

5.4   Evaluation on a Large External U.S. Cohort

To further assess the generalizability of LegoNet, we retrained the model on the entire dataset. We examined its performance on a completely new US cohort

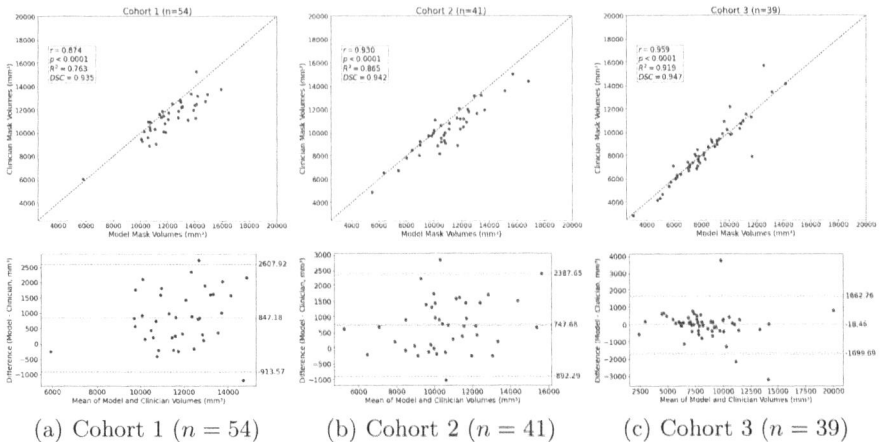

(a) Cohort 1 ($n = 54$)   (b) Cohort 2 ($n = 41$)   (c) Cohort 3 ($n = 39$)

Fig. 4. The figure shows the correlation and Bland-Altman plots for three external cohorts, comparing the model's prediction and clinician's segmentation masks.

consisting of 712 scans (part of the ORFAN study). Each predicted segmentation mask was reviewed by an expert clinician for the sole purpose of quality assurance. 32 cases were rejected due to a limited field of view (FOV), where either the IMA or aorta (or both) were partially or entirely outside the scan range. The remaining 680 scans were deemed clinically acceptable and were subsequently used for downstream tasks.

5.5   External Public Data

The primary objective of evaluating LegoNet in the public ASOCA cohort is to demonstrate its generalisability in (i) different acquisition techniques, (ii) different imaging machines and centres, and (iii) different medical protocols. Unlike internal data sets, the ASOCA cohort was collected under different medical protocols, providing a challenging validation scenario for the model.

For this evaluation, we again used the model, which had been trained with all in-house CTA data, including the training/validation set and external in-house cohorts, totalling 338 patient cases. The expert clinician manually corrected the model's segmentation masks, and we computed the DSC agreement. Remarkably, the model maintains high consistency with the three previously tested model refinement cohorts, achieving a DSC of 0.961, a precision of 0.961, and a recall of 0.938. To support further research and validation, the segmentation masks for this cohort will be made publicly available upon request.

5.6   Evaluation on Aorta

All the experiments discussed above were conducted on the IMA+PVAT segmentation task. To further assess the generalizability of the proposed approach, we extended the study to evaluate the same models on the aorta+PVAT segmentation task. LegoNet consistently outperformed other leading architectures across DSC, precision, and recall, maintaining superior performance across different segmentation tasks (see Table 3). In the aorta segmentation task, the UX-Net and SwinUNETR achieve better performance compared to other CNN and ViT models, with 0.919 and 0.906 DSC, respectively. Version one of LegoNet reaches the highest performance with 0.939 DSC, 0.919 precision, and 0.961 recall values. While the other two versions are slightly lower, they are on par with other leading architectures. These findings suggest that LegoNet is robust and generalizable, effectively adapting to similar vascular segmentation problems.

6   Discussion

This study addresses a novel medical imaging challenge - the automatic segmentation of the IMA, aorta, and PVAT from CTA images. This segmentation is a critical precursor to predictive prognostic modelling, facilitating risk assessment and patient outcome prediction in subsequent studies. The clinical value of these segmented regions has already been demonstrated in predicting acute vascular inflammation and in-hospital mortality [11]. The PVAT analysis is not limited to acute inflammation and can and will be extended to capture other molecular changes in the region, such as fibrosis, adipogenesis, lipolysis, etc. This investigation can eventually lead to a better understanding of the molecular mechanisms driving these medical disorders, unlocking avenues to new therapeutic targets.

To tackle this problem, we introduce a new deep learning paradigm based on block alternation, where structurally distinct yet complementary blocks are interleaved to enhance feature learning. We propose three variations of LegoNet, all of which outperform leading CNN- and ViT-based models on multi-centre datasets. Additionally, we examined the models' complexities to ensure the balance of performance and cost. Finally, the proposed model is exhaustively tested in multiple settings and cohorts.

We observe a discrepancy between the cross-validation results ($\approx$0.750 DSC) and post-model agreement on external cohorts ($\approx$0.900 DSC). This difference is primarily attributed to variability in segmentation interpretation. In clinical practice, expert clinicians accept model-generated masks as valid representations of the IMA and perivascular space, provided they are sufficiently accurate for diagnostic purposes [11]. Our inter- and intra-observer variability and model vs. human agreement analyses further confirm that these results align with expected variability in manual segmentation.

We attribute the superior performance of *LegoNet* to (i) structurally different blocks that are assumed to learn more discriminative features and (ii) the complexity of the model. Compared to CNN models, the complexity in the number of parameters and GFLOPs is much higher. However, that is on par with ViT models, such as UNETR, SwinUNETR, and UNesT. The best-performing *LegoNet-2*, for example, stands at 50.71M parameters and 188.02G FLOPs, which is smaller than the three ViT-driven models. In the future, the model's behaviour with more recent models, such as Mamba-based blocks, could be studied. The use of more than two repetitive blocks could be another avenue to investigate.

7   Conclusion

This work introduces a new deep learning paradigm that alternates structurally distinct blocks, leveraging their complementary strengths to construct a more effective architecture. Moving beyond the conventional approach of using identical blocks, we demonstrate that integrating dissimilar blocks enhances model learning. LegoNet consistently outperforms leading CNN and ViT-based models on two CTA datasets, with further validation on external, international, and public cohorts, where clinician-model agreement in DSC remains high. Additionally, intra- and inter-observer variability studies further confirm the reliability of our approach. We propose three variations of LegoNet, applying this concept to segment the IMA, aorta, and their perivascular space—a clinically valuable but previously unstudied region. Given its proven significance in vascular inflammation and cardiovascular disease prognosis, accurate segmentation of PVAT regions holds potential for advancing risk assessment and therapeutic planning.

References

1. Akoumianakis, I., et al.: Adipose tissue–derived wnt5a regulates vascular redox signaling in obesity via usp17/rac1-mediated activation of nadph oxidases. Science translational medicine **11**(510), eaav5055 (2019)
2. Chan, K., et al.: Inflammatory risk and cardiovascular events in patients without obstructive coronary artery disease: the orfan multicentre, longitudinal cohort study. Lancet **403**(10444), 2606–2618 (2024)
3. Chen, J., et al.: Transunet: Transformers make strong encoders for medical image segmentation. arXiv preprint arXiv:2102.04306 (2021)
4. Çiçek, Ö., Abdulkadir, A., Lienkamp, S.S., Brox, T., Ronneberger, O.: 3D U-Net: Learning Dense Volumetric Segmentation from Sparse Annotation. In: Ourselin, S., Joskowicz, L., Sabuncu, M.R., Unal, G., Wells, W. (eds.) MICCAI 2016. LNCS, vol. 9901, pp. 424–432. Springer, Cham (2016). https://doi.org/10.1007/978-3-319-46723-8_49
5. Gharleghi, R., Adikari, D., Ellenberger, K., Webster, M., Ellis, C., Sowmya, A., Ooi, S., Beier, S.: Annotated computed tomography coronary angiogram images and associated data of normal and diseased arteries. Sci. Data **10**(1), 128 (2023)
6. Gharleghi, R., Adikari, D., Ellenberger, K., Ooi, S.Y., Ellis, C., Chen, C.M., Gao, R., He, Y., Hussain, R., Lee, C.Y., et al.: Automated segmentation of normal and diseased coronary arteries-the asoca challenge. Comput. Med. Imaging Graph. **97**, 102049 (2022)
7. Hatamizadeh, A., et al.: Swin unetr: swin transformers for semantic segmentation of brain tumors in mri images. In: Brainlesion: Glioma, Multiple Sclerosis, Stroke and Traumatic Brain Injuries: 7th International Workshop, BrainLes 2021, Held in Conjunction with MICCAI 2021, Virtual Event, pp. 272–284. Springer (2022)
8. Hatamizadeh, A., et al.: Unetr: transformers for 3d medical image segmentation. In: Proceedings of the IEEE/CVF winter conference on applications of computer vision, pp. 574–584 (2022)

9. Iantsen, A., Jaouen, V., Visvikis, D., Hatt, M.: Squeeze-and-excitation normalization for brain tumor segmentation. In: Brainlesion: Glioma, Multiple Sclerosis, Stroke and Traumatic Brain Injuries: 6th International Workshop, BrainLes 2020, Held in Conjunction with MICCAI 2020, Lima, Part II 6, pp. 366–373. Springer (2021)

10. Kerfoot, E., Clough, J., Oksuz, I., Lee, J., King, A.P., Schnabel, J.A.: Left-ventricle quantification using residual u-net. In: Statistical Atlases and Computational Models of the Heart. Atrial Segmentation and LV Quantification Challenges: 9th International Workshop, STACOM 2018, Held in Conjunction with MICCAI 2018, Granada, pp. 371–380. Springer (2019)

11. Kotanidis, C.P., et al.: Constructing custom-made radiotranscriptomic signatures of vascular inflammation from routine ct angiograms: a prospective outcomes validation study in covid-19. Lancet Digital Health 4(10), e705–e716 (2022)

12. Lee, H.H., et al.: 3d ux-net: A large kernel volumetric convnet modernizing hierarchical transformer for medical image segmentation. arXiv preprint arXiv:2209.15076 (2022)

13. Liu, Z., et al.: Swin transformer: Hierarchical vision transformer using shifted windows. In: Proceedings of the IEEE/CVF international conference on computer vision, pp. 10012–10022 (2021)

14. Myronenko, A.: 3d mri brain tumor segmentation using autoencoder regularization. In: Brainlesion: Glioma, Multiple Sclerosis, Stroke and Traumatic Brain Injuries: 4th International Workshop, BrainLes 2018, Held in Conjunction with MICCAI 2018, Granada, Part II 4. pp. 311–320. Springer (2019)

15. Oikonomou, E.K., et al.: A novel machine learning-derived radiotranscriptomic signature of perivascular fat improves cardiac risk prediction using coronary ct angiography. Eur. Heart J. 40(43), 3529–3543 (2019)

16. Otsuka, F., Yahagi, K., Sakakura, K., Virmani, R.: Why is the mammary artery so special and what protects it from atherosclerosis? Ann. Cardiothoracic Surg. 2(4), 519 (2013)

17. Ulyanov, D., Vedaldi, A., Lempitsky, V.: Instance normalization: The missing ingredient for fast stylization. arXiv preprint arXiv:1607.08022 (2016)

18. Wilcoxon, F.: Individual comparisons by ranking methods. In: Breakthroughs in Statistics: Methodology and Distribution, pp. 196–202. Springer (1992)

19. Yu, X., et al.: Unest: Local spatial representation learning with hierarchical transformer for efficient medical segmentation. arXiv preprint arXiv:2209.14378 (2022)

20. Zhang, Y., Liu, H., Hu, Q.: TransFuse: Fusing Transformers and CNNs for Medical Image Segmentation. In: de Bruijne, M., Cattin, P.C., Cotin, S., Padoy, N., Speidel, S., Zheng, Y., Essert, C. (eds.) MICCAI 2021. LNCS, vol. 12901, pp. 14–24. Springer, Cham (2021). https://doi.org/10.1007/978-3-030-87193-2_2

Author Index

The manufacturer's authorised representative in the EU is Springer
Nature Customer Service Centre GmbH, Europaplatz 3, 69115 Heidelberg,
Germany. If you have any concerns regarding our products, please
contact ProductSafety@springernature.com

Printed and bound by CPI Group (UK) Ltd, Croydon, CR0 4YY
28/04/2026
02098521-0005